TOM STOPPARD
a reference guide

*A
Reference
Guide
to
Literature*

Jackson Bryer
Editor

TOM STOPPARD
a reference guide

DAVID BRATT

G.K. HALL & CO.
70 LINCOLN STREET, BOSTON, MASS.

Copyright © 1982 by David Bratt

Library of Congress Cataloging in Publication Data

Bratt, David.
  Tom Stoppard.

  Bibliography:
  Includes index.
  1. Stoppard, Tom—Bibliography. I. Title.
Z8848.8.B7   1982   016.822914   82-11739
[PR6069.T6]
ISBN 0-8161-8576-X

This publication is printed on permanent/durable acid-free paper
MANUFACTURED IN THE UNITED STATES OF AMERICA

Contents

The Author vi

Preface. vii

Acknowledgments. ix

Introduction xi

Addenda. xxvii

Writings by Tom Stoppard xxxi

Writings about Tom Stoppard. 1

Index. 215

The Author

David Bratt took his M.A. in Dramatic Art from the University of Iowa and his Ph.D. from the University of California, Santa Barbara. He is currently an associate professor of Communication and Theater Arts at Winona State University, where he teaches, directs plays, and does research into contemporary British theatre, irony, and audience-oriented dramatic theory.

Preface

An eclectic playwright such as Tom Stoppard may attract students from a wide range of disciplines. Moreover--as he is fond of demonstrating in his plays--it would be naïve to try to predict what uses others will and will not wish to make of something. For these reasons, I have decided that this bibliography should be as exhaustive as possible rather than selective. (Readers should note, however, that, owing to a late decision to include 1978-1980 in the work, this period is covered less extensively than earlier years.) In the name of completeness, for instance, I have included reviews published in university newspapers against the time when, after one of their authors has been hired as the New York Times's drama critic, someone somewhere will wonder what he wrote about Stoppard as an undergraduate.

Accordingly, readers interested in a particular topic would do well to turn first to the Index in order to reduce the number of items to be examined. There they will find an alphabetically interfiled list of headings which include (1) names of authors of items, (2) names of the periodicals and books in which items appeared, and (3) titles of Stoppard's works discussed in them. This last heading is divided into the categories of analyses, news items, and reviews; reviews, in turn, are arranged alphabetically according to the city and producing organization. Other headings include (4) biographical data, (5) items in a foreign language, (6) interviews, (7) feature articles and profiles, (8) news items, (9) pedagogical items (intended for use by teachers), (10) radio items, and (11) television items. Entries are identified by item numbers, which consist of the year of publication, an "A" (if a book) or a "B" (if a shorter writing), and an arabic numeral (indicating the entry's place in an alphabetical list of the items published about Stoppard during that year).

Entries identified by the prefix "Incomplete" are ones about which I could not find complete bibliographical data. They are located following the entries for 1980. Nearly all are reviews sent to me from scrapbooks compiled by the Press and Publicity Departments of various producing organizations. Most are missing only the

Preface

number of the page on which they were published. Items I have not seen have been identified by asterisks.

I have annotated each item descriptively: very briefly when its contents are identical to those of many other items, at greater length when it contains rare material, advances unusual claims, or makes common points uncommonly well. Whenever possible, I have used authors' own words to give some indication of the flavor of their pieces. My parenthetical comments within these quotations have been enclosed in brackets.

Items written by unknown authors have been labelled "Anon." Names learned from other sources and pseudonyms have been supplied in brackets. Titles of items not set off within quotation marks are ones I have supplied for untitled articles. Cities of publication have been added to the names of newspapers.

When no page numbers appear, the reason is usually that I could not locate the information, but occasionally it is because the publication was not paginated. The only other abbreviations I have used are BBC (British Broadcasting Corporation), ACT (American Conservatory Theatre, a production organization in San Francisco), BARC (British-American Repertory Company), and ERIC (Educational Resources Information Center).

I have underlined the names of Stoppard's stage plays, screenplays, and his novel but enclosed in quotation marks the titles of his short stories and radio and television plays. In addition, I have adopted the British use of "transmission" for radio productions and "broadcast" for television.

Bibliography involves the reading of so many mundane items that the compiler is extraordinarily grateful for the occasional anomaly. My thanks, therefore, to Christopher Nichols and Stanley Kauffmann for reviews (1967.B98 and 1974.B96) which set new standards for critics aspiring to virulence; to Stanley Eichelbaum of the _San Francisco Examiner_, who claimed that no fewer than three West Coast productions of Stoppard's plays were superior to the Broadway versions; and to Richard Watts, who in a single review managed not only to follow one of _After Magritte_'s characters in misattributing the play's title to Simenon's Inspector Maigret but also to express his feelings about an actress in _The Real Inspector Hound_ in terms remarkably similar to those of one of the critics being parodied in the play.

Acknowledgments

This work is indebted to Fraser & Dunlop (Scripts) Ltd., to the librarians and clerks at the British Newspaper Library and the New York Public Library, and to the dozens of people at newspaper offices, theatrical production organizations, and libraries throughout the world who sent me items and answered my inquiries.

I also owe a great deal to Jacqueline Kavanagh of the BBC Written Archives Centre; to Susan Bratt, who spent hours paging through twenty-year-old Bristol newspapers; to Bernard Levy, who sent me items I had not located elsewhere; to Jane Burke, for arranging late-arriving entries and working on the indexes; and to my translators, Jordon Hodgson, Jane Ochrymowycz, Yoshiko Ohkura, Barbara Rusterholz, and especially Ronald Mazur.

Finally, I gratefully acknowledge financial assistance from the University of California and Minnesota State University systems.

Introduction

In January of 1973, <u>Plays and Players</u> announced the results of its annual poll of London's theatre critics, taken to determine the best work of the past season. Accompanying that article was one by the magazine's editor, who, outraged by their choice of Best Play, proposed that the winner also be given an "award" as "Most Overrated Play of the Year" and that its leading actor be commended "For Rising above His Material."

The object of this dichotomous critical opinion was <u>Jumpers</u>, written by Tom Stoppard. I have chosen to compile this bibliography of his work only partly in light of the fact that none of the others even remotely approaches completeness. More significant is the fact that widely divergent reactions such as those in <u>Plays and Players</u> have characterized criticism of Stoppard's work since the beginning of his career.

Therein lies his importance to students of contemporary dramatic theory and criticism. As Kenneth Tynan, the British critic, noted (1977.B125), even within the rather narrow field of serious contemporary British theatre, other writers are more widely respected (Harold Pinter, for instance) or more commercially successful (Peter Shaffer) than he. Still others, such as John Osborne, are more prolific. But of no other major contemporary playwright, certainly in Britain and perhaps in this country as well, can it be said that so many critics find it nearly impossible to react in a lukewarm manner to his work. Tom Stoppard's plays are extraordinarily reliable litmus tests: a critic exposed to them nearly always reveals his fundamental aesthetic convictions.

Tom Stoppard came to playwriting by way of journalism--a circuitous route, perhaps, but no more so than the oblique path his life had followed to that point. Born Tomas Straussler in Zlin, Czechoslovakia, on 3 July 1937, he fled from the Germans with his parents and older brother to Singapore. From there they moved to India to escape the Japanese. Widowed by the war, his mother married Kenneth Stoppard, a British army officer, who took his new

Introduction

family back to England in 1946. Tom, who had learned English at a multiracial American school in India, attended "public" (i.e., private) prep and grammar institutions until he was seventeen, when he became a reporter for the Western Daily Press in Bristol in 1954. By 1960, having moved to the rival Evening World and then returned to the Western Daily Press, he had begun to specialize in film and theatre criticism. He had also begun writing plays, inspired by the early successes of John Osborne and other "Angry Young Men."

From 1960 through 1966, he divided his time between criticism and fiction, gradually concentrating on plays. Two years of freelance journalism in Bristol were followed by seven months as theatre critic and interviewer for Scene in London, during which time he saw more than 130 productions for the magazine. Following its demise, he wrote freelance reviews and radio serials to make a living while trying to take advantage of the favorable climate then existing in London for writers of television and radio plays. (See 1974.B122 for a discussion of this subject.)

Stoppard's more serious work during these years, however, brought him virtually no critical attention. "A Walk on the Water" was broadcast only days after the assassination of President Kennedy, and neither the subsequent German stage production (1964) nor the BBC radio version (1965) received any notice--except, says Stoppard (1974.B1), from the German audience, which booed. The Gamblers, the first play he wrote, is reported (1976.B21) to have received a production at the University of Bristol, but has left no trace. Receiving equally scant notice during these years were three brief scripts for radio, two for television, three short stories, and a novel. His work on episodes for a BBC radio serial aroused no critical interest, of course, although it did pay the rent.

In fact, between 1960 and 1966, only two of his pieces brought him any significant attention--and one of them was not original (his adaptation of Mrozek's play, Tango, produced by the Royal Shakespeare Company in 1966). The second began inauspiciously enough late in 1964, when, at a fringe theatre in London, Stoppard himself staged a twenty-minute segment of Guildenstern and Rosencrantz, which he had written while attending a colloquium in West Berlin for five months earlier in the year. However, twenty-two months later, revised and expanded almost beyond recognition, it was produced as a fringe event at the Edinburgh Festival of 1966. There, amidst a flurry of negative and tepid notices, it received a rave from Ronald Bryden of the Observer, who called the play "the most brilliant debut . . . since John Arden's" (1966.B13). Those words caught the attention of Kenneth Tynan at the National Theatre, and Rosencrantz & Guildenstern Are Dead opened there in 1967 to an almost unanimously favorable reception. Three weeks later, Stoppard delivered his last radio serial script to the BBC.

Since the success of Rosencrantz & Guildenstern Are Dead--it re-

Introduction

ceived at least eight professional productions in 1967 alone—Stoppard's production record reveals two interesting facts. The first is that, although nearly all of his full-length works are stage plays, he has continued to write radio and television dramas, screenplays, adaptations, and documentaries. Similarly, as a glance at his personal bibliography reveals, while he has certainly written less for newspapers since 1967 than before, he has not given it up entirely: indeed, his output in this area has increased since 1977. He has expressed admiration (in 1977.A1) for the kind of journalist "who does a bit of everything"—much as he himself had to do in Bristol—and seems determined to avoid becoming too specialized, lest he find himself unable to adapt to changing circumstances.

In my own study of Stoppard's work (1976.A3), I have suggested that his production record reveals a distinctly cyclical pattern of activity. It usually begins with a series of minor works exploring certain subject matter or techniques, followed by one or more major plays which integrate and display the fruits of the earlier trial runs. Then comes a hiatus, during which, having exhausted one thematic area or pushed certain techniques as far as he can, Stoppard looks around for new material to present itself. When a likely candidate appears, he begins a new series of brief forays into it. Moreover, as the cycle repeats itself, Stoppard has revealed an increasing awareness of the value of irony, both as a technique of style and as a way of coping with life. (His oft-confessed habit of procrastination and his comments to interviewers about works in progress over the years make it quite clear that, since 1967, chronological lists of the plays he has written and of those he has had performed would be vitually identical: the time between his completion of a script and its production is nearly always only a matter of months or even weeks.)

This cycle began in the early 1960s with two extremely derivative stage plays (The Gamblers and "A Walk on the Water"), three somewhat less imitative short stories, and two more original minor radio plays. These were followed by a hiatus between October 1964 and the end of 1965. (He had three plays produced in that time, but all were revisions of earlier works.) The cycle began anew with short experimental plays in 1966 and early 1967 and an extremely prolific period of integration through mid-1968, the high points of which were his novel (Lord Malquist & Mr Moon, 1966) and the productions of the greatly expanded Rosencrantz & Guildenstern Are Dead (1966 and 1967) and The Real Inspector Hound (1968). Then followed another pause: from mid-1968 through the end of 1969, he produced only a television play, "Neutral Ground." In 1970 and 1971, he wrote more short works, which were followed by the major accomplishments of "Artist Descending a Staircase" and Jumpers in 1972. Although 1973 brought no new plays, he spent much of the year tinkering with Jumpers while watching over some of its productions and working on its successor, Travesties (1974), the culmination of nearly fourteen years spent exploring ironic things and ways of

Introduction

being ironical about them.

Following the premiere of Travesties, Stoppard paused again (he had only three works produced between mid-1974 and April 1976, two of them adaptations and the other co-authored). It is quite clear that he was using this time once more to look for new areas to deal with: see, for instance, his claim in 1976.B50 that he wanted to abandon the "circus" atmosphere of Jumpers and Travesties to write a simple, quiet play about "a man and his dog." And it is equally clear that he found a fruitful area to explore, for the months between mid-1976 and the end of 1979 have seen as many new works by Stoppard as any similar period since the early 1960s: an award-winning television play ("Professional Foul," 1977), two screenplays (Despair and The Human Factor, 1978 and 1979), a stage adaptation (Undiscovered Country, 1979), and three one-act and two full-length stage plays.

Like his earlier periods of activity, this cycle began with brief and tentative essays of new materials and stylistic techniques. But these trial runs are not like their predecessors, for the areas of experience which Stoppard is exploring this time are substantively different from those with which he had been engaged during the previous fifteen years.

The results have been quite unexpected. Prior to this latest cycle, many of his plays had been generated from visual (i.e., essentially theatrical) images; most of their subjects had been drawn from anecdotes, history, or literature; and almost invariably their materials had been filtered through an imaginative (some have said fanciful) lens. His latest works, on the other hand, deal with contemporary social and political events, the stuff of headlines. Indeed, the role of the press is one of the recurring subjects of this period; others include parliamentary investigations, international conferences, and political dissidents. Stylistically, too, there is a clear difference between the ebullience of his works through Travesties and the less fanciful tone of these more recent pieces, particularly as we move past Dirty Linen and New-Found-Land (1975), where Stoppard's ironic techniques create an atmosphere of bedroom farce in a British parliamentary committee room, and approach "Professional Foul" and Every Good Boy Deserves Favour (1977), where the ironies underscore the brutality of totalitarianism and the moral dilemmas it creates for those who must either oppose or accommodate themselves to it. Even more striking is Night and Day (1978), in which, apparently determined to deal with "the real world" as unambiguously as possible, Stoppard adopts a style more realistic than that of any of his works since "Neutral Ground" (1968).

In this regard, his most recent play, Dogg's Hamlet, Cahoot's Macbeth (1979), seems an attempt to marry the ebullient style with which he is most comfortable to the socially conscious material he

Introduction

has lately been exploring: it uses a fanciful language (in which words sound like--but are not--English) to depict the repression of artists in contemporary Czechoslovakia. Since the premiere of this work, Stoppard has entered another hiatus: the months between mid-1979 and the end of 1980, when this bibliography ends, have brought only productions of two adaptations and an appearance in a documentary drama.

(Among the best articles analyzing Stoppard's corpus, written at various stages in its development, are 1968.B115, 1971.B17 and 20, 1973.B21, 1975.B64, 1977.B107, and 1979.B26; good longer studies of his works are 1976.A2, 1977.A1, and 1979.A1. Stoppard himself often comments about his works and intentions in interviews. A good chronological sampling of the most accessible would include 1967.B61, 65, and 123, 1968.B51, 1972.B57, 1973.B85, 1974.B90, 1975.B40, 1976.B50, 1977.A1, 1978.B72, 1979.B22 and 47, and 1980.B11. Few profiles of Stoppard have been published, but two good ones are 1974.B1 and Kenneth Tynan's superb piece, 1977.B125.)

No less striking than the difference between <u>Travesties</u> and <u>Night and Day</u> is that between Stoppard's journalistic output during this most recent period and his pieces of earlier years. Formerly, he had written reviews of books, films, television programs, and plays, revealing a decided preference for ironic juxtaposition and careful construction; explanations of his aims as a playwright, making clear that thematic considerations were less on his mind than theatricality; and feature articles about various subjects, more than occasionally displaying himself at the expense of his subject (a failing to which he has confessed in many interviews). After <u>Travesties</u>, however, he wrote very little journalism until 1977, which saw the beginning of a small but steady stream of articles and letters to editors about social and political issues: the use of psychiatry as a punitive tool in the Soviet Union, the treatment of artists and political dissidents in his native Czechoslovakia, the feasibility of holding to Western liberal democratic ideals in the face of totalitarian ideologies, the illogicality of a spokesman for a journalists' union calling the newspaper owners a "closed shop," and the legitimacy of a boycott of the Olympics in Moscow.

The conclusion is unmistakable: this "quondam apostle of detachment," as Tynan called him (1977.B125), has begun to bear public witness to his political and ethical convictions. In his journalism, he has done so unambiguously, in a style often quite unleavened by the wit of his earlier pieces. In his plays, however, he has seemed less certain of the balance between involvement and detachment which his new subject matter seems to require of him--a point to which we will find ourselves returning at the conclusion of a survey of critics' reactions to his works.

At first glance, the amount and variety of those reactions may seen overwhelming, even random and unfocused. But as I have already

Introduction

noted, his critics may quite accurately be divided into two camps, supporters and detractors: few if any are caught in no-man's land between the lines, and even fewer defect from one side to the other. Moreover, as his career has progressed, his detractors have tended to focus their attack on a few specific issues--usually the very ones which some of his admirers had long before identified as particularly praiseworthy. Most of these issues are raised in easily accessible articles by Stoppard's long-time admirers--among them Clive Barnes, Harold Hobson, David Wade, and Irving Wardle--and his most consistent (and virulent) detractors, Harold Clurman and Martin Gottfried. Among the few who have changed sides are J. C. Trewin, who surprisingly recommended Travesties after a rather consistent pattern of disapproval, and Walter Kerr, who has become increasingly disenchanted with Stoppard as his career has progressed. Jack Richardson, John Simon, and John Weightman, however, have been the most consistently thought-provoking observers of his plays.

It is hardly necessary to read all of these critics' articles in order to become acquainted with these central issues: as few as six items will do. In addition, because they arrange themselves into three pairs in terms of chronology and length, these six items provide a convenient way of measuring the rate at which criticism of Stoppard's work has grown in length and in scope.

Among the first to appear, of course, were reviews of the London and New York productions of Rosencrantz & Guildenstern Are Dead in 1967. One of the most thoughtful of these was Charles Marowitz's (1967.B94). Beginning by acknowledging that the play's "craft" was more original than its "thought," Marowitz nevertheless insisted that the skill with which Stoppard had manipulated what he had borrowed from Shakespeare and Absurdist writers transformed their material into something new. The opposite reaction is best illustrated by Robert Brustein (1967.B37), who also noticed that Stoppard's play depended heavily upon existentialist and Absurdist thought. Unlike Marowitz, however, Brustein charged Stoppard with failing to appreciate what he had borrowed, saying that his characters philosophized in a purely "cerebral" manner and did not (because Stoppard did not) feel the truth of what they were saying. In short, said Brustein in a justly celebrated passage, Stoppard was living like a parasite upon "a Zeitgeist created by authors whose works nobody wants to see, and [was] achieving his success by offering a form of Beckett without tears."

Such are the deadlines of scholarly journals, even in the relatively uncrowded field of theatre, that months or even years may separate the composition of an article from its publication. It is therefore surprising that the first true pieces of criticism or analysis--i.e., articles concerned primarily with qualities of a text rather than of a specific production, published in a scholarly journal--appeared as early as they did, scarcely a year after the London and New York productions had opened. These were followed in

Introduction

1969 by a handful of others devoted entirely or in part to a variety of Stoppard's works, including his novel. Since then, the number has grown annually, averaging more than a dozen per year over the past five years.

One of these early analytical pieces was R. H. Lee's "The Circle and Its Tangent" (1969.B37), which suggested that <u>Rosencrantz & Guildenstern Are Dead</u> constitutes a comparison of the assumptions and implications of seventeenth- and twentieth-century views of the world, the former illustrated by <u>Hamlet</u>, the latter by <u>Waiting for Godot</u>. Lee drew some distinctions between the two points of view and illustrated each by explicating Stoppard's use of conventions derived from Shakespeare's and Beckett's plays. Seven months later there appeared an instructive response to Lee's analysis. **Rather** than question any particular parts of the article, C. O. Gardner (1970.B24) attacked the play's origins, asserting that no "serious critical attention" ought to be given it, because "the thing is in fact a swill, composed of second-hand Beckett, third-hand Kafka, and the goon show, with casual sprinklings of Chaplinesque pathos, logical-positivist shadow-boxing, Pinterian 'grimness', and so on."

After reviews come critical articles, and after articles, books: so to 1976 and the third pair of items. Thirteen years after "A Walk on the Water" had been broadcast on British television and scarcely a decade since <u>Rosencrantz & Guildenstern Are Dead</u> had caught Kenneth Tynan's attention, there appeared a handbook which examined Stoppard's entire corpus and two doctoral dissertations, the first book-length studies devoted entirely to his work.

The point of view of one of these dissertations is indicated by its title: "Beyond Absurdity: The Plays of Tom Stoppard" (1976.A4). In it, Victor L. Cahn traced a three-part movement in Stoppard's career, from its "semi-realistic beginnings," through an Absurdist phase, and into its latest period, in which he "combines both traditions in an original theatrical form," marked by the appearance of characters who "are aware of absurdity, yet unwilling to resign themselves to it." Somewhat different is the assessment found in my own "The Ironic Muse of Tom Stoppard" (1976.A3), in which, rather than identify specific characters who personify his approach to life's problems, I tried to define a consistent set of values which infuses all the elements of his works. As my title indicates, Stoppard's career seems to me most comprehensible when seen as his attempt to apply a consistently ironic point of view to a series of widely varied subjects.

Even in this brief sampling of six items, one can distinguish not only the rival camps of detractors and defenders of Stoppard but also the disagreement among the latter about the proper grounds and the most effective means of defending him. (Incidentally, although "camps" and "defenders" and "attacks" have about them more of the redolence of the battlefield than might seem appropriate in an

Introduction

aesthetic discussion, they do remind us that critics and theorists do not write in an intellectual vacuum. Instead, as one of Stoppard's characters says in Dirty Linen and New-Found-Land, "They're writing it for the writers writing it on the other papers." Even the least pretentious reviewer has read the thoughts of his colleagues on earlier occasions and is aware that his own will be read by them on this one. Thus, he writes--at least in part--to respond to their claims and to clarify his own position. In so doing, he stakes out an intellectual or aesthetic post, identifies potential allies, and aligns himself against possible antagonists.)

The three pairs of items we have examined lay down the general boundaries of the battlefield. On the one hand, there are those who join Gardner in accusing Stoppard of lacking a voice of his own and borrowing more or less irresponsibly from his betters. Brustein and others agree with these charges, adding that Stoppard's characters express too little emotion (or express it in an inadequately evocative manner). Ranged against these groups are Stoppard's supporters, who seem undecided how best to proceed. Some, with Cahn, would join the battle on grounds chosen by the attackers. These defenders try to demonstrate the existence of admirable characters who are capable of expressing emotion effectively. They also argue that only in the early stages of his development did Stoppard use others' material uncritically: his more mature works, they say, use Absurdism but go beyond it. The other band of Stoppard's supporters, such as Marowitz and myself, would prefer not to let his detractors define the terms of the conflict. They would rather insist that a playwright's decision to bare his soul to an audience is not in and of itself praiseworthy and that aggressive borrowing is no less valid as an aesthetic modus vivendi than thoroughgoing self-sufficiency.

Of the two issues, the charge that Stoppard lacks a voice of his own is the more crucial; the other--that he does not depict or arouse emotions effectively--follows as a consequence. From the first proceed three major lines of criticism. Of these, the band most sympathetic to Stoppard accepts that his failure to develop a unique voice is linked to his genuine lack of commitment to any philosophical or social position; nevertheless, these critics insist that a playwright cannot afford such a luxury because his ambivalence gives birth to artificial, manipulative plays populated by characters who strain an audience's credibility. In an otherwise favorable review of Rosencrantz & Guildenstern Are Dead, for instance, Kerr (1967. B80) charged that when the title characters expressed their frustration, they sounded as if they were "lost in [their author's] ways, not their own." Roberts (1972.B107) said much the same of Jumpers, in which Stoppard displayed considerable "ingenuity in manipulating characters in which we do not believe." Wetzsteon (1975.B123) summarized the position of this group of critics when he criticized Stoppard's habit of treating ideas as "hard, impersonal artifacts, a kind of coinage of the mind," rather than as "the living, mutable

Introduction

gropings of human minds." The problem, he added, was that when Stoppard's characters expressed ideas, the playwright himself "never . . . really . . . believe[d] any of them." (Interestingly enough, the only play Wetzsteon exempted from this charge was Travesties, which most observers regard as Stoppard's most thoroughly artificial construct to date.)

This group of critics, the smallest among Stoppard's detractors, do not doubt that his lack of commitment to any school of thought is sincere--they simply insist that it is an overwhelming handicap. Less sympathetic and more numerous are those who attribute to him a desperate insecurity which tempts him to value the approval of an audience above anything else. (Stoppard himself supplies ammunition to such attacks whenever he speak to interviewers of his personal "insecurity" [in 1972.B99, for instance] or discusses his attempts to hold his viewers' attention by laying "ambushes for the audience" [1974.B90].)

Thus, as early as 1967, Duchene (1967.B52) called him an "over anxious entertainer," a judgment still in circulation nine years later, when Simon (1976.B97) found in most of his plays evidence of the "desperate strategies" authors employ in their attempts to hold their audiences' attention. Similarly, Lambert charged that Stoppard has chosen "unlikely" characters as his spokesmen in Travesties so that he could not be "accused of being . . . square" (1974.B104). This group of detractors is particularly critical of his language, finding "Albert's Bridge" "remorselessly articulate" (1967.B132), the style of Lord Malquist & Mr Moon "immensely pleased with anything it can come up with" (1968.B90), the "poetry" in Rosencrantz & Guildenstern Are Dead "spurious" because Stoppard did not wholeheartedly commit himself to it (1967.B137), and the style of Jumpers typical of "a dramatist who has more wish than need to write and who takes the offensive stylistically in order to cow us" (1974.B96). The position of this group is summarized by Weightman, who, after noting that Stoppard has always been uniquely immoderate in his "cannibalising" of others' works, wondered whether the reason was that he was "in love with art and . . . not quite sure that he himself [was] a true artist" (1974.B182; see also 1979.B61 for a similar assessment of Stoppard's parody).

Linking this band of Stoppard's detractors to the third and largest group is their mutual disapproval of the parody and mixture of styles which is typical of his works. Those discussed above tend to regard the parody as his way of trying to get his audience's approval, and they generally limit their criticism of it to the comment that it confuses the purpose of his plays. The third group of critics, however, is less sympathetic: to them, Stoppard is a chameleon who, at the promise of commercial success (and to hide the poverty of his imagination), will change his color to whichever hue is popular at the moment.

Introduction

When feeling particularly sanguine, this group regards Stoppard as a "clever popularizer" who plays "over-elaborate games" (1975. B76); in their more critical moods, they call him an affected show off who writes smart-ass, pretentious, trendy plays, filled with undergraduate chatter (see the reviews of Clurman and Gottfried). The ferocity of this group's abuse is remarkable, but their criticism does not stop there. Stoppard's two major weaknesses, in their eyes, are laziness and insensitive derivativeness. The first implies that he needs a good editor: his form is sloppy, his satire too easy, his jokes without serious purpose and unconnected to character—altogether, he is "too quick to give us what is on the very tip of his tongue" (1975.B70). The second criticism, which touches on an area less responsive to editorial ministrations, was clearly voiced by Brustein, who, as we have already noted, accused Stoppard of profiting by using the inventions of more original writers and of cynically offering "a form of Beckett without tears" (1967.B37; see also his 1980.B7).

Few of his other detractors in this group are as harsh as Brustein, but they, too, focus upon his failure to deal effectively with emotion. Taylor (1971.B20) called him clever but "bloodless" and said his ideas were the product of "fancy" rather than "imagination." Duchene (1967.B52) said his "activity seems almost entirely cerebral and verbal," unlike that of Beckett, whose "every word issues from the tripes before being proved upon the pulses." Berlin (1973.B20) identified Rosencrantz & Guildenstern Are Dead as "Theatre of criticism," in that, while giving rise to insights about theatre, it lacks integration of thought and emotion. Many others have dismissed his plays as nothing more than unoriginal and undistinguished Absurdism (see, for instance, 1967.B76 and 98, 1968.B95, 1969.B17, 1974.B183, and 1977.B39). Occasionally, they contradict one another: Smith (1967.B119) advised him not to try "to push [Rosencrantz & Guildenstern Are Dead] to deep significance," while Kriegsman (1974.B102) complained that Stoppard was too inclined to play with ideas rather than explore them in Jumpers.

In the face of attacks of such variety (and often virulence), it is hardly surprising that the tone of many pieces written by his admirers should be apologetic and their strategy exclusively defensive. Already in 1968, for instance, Dawson (1968.B45) predicted that Stoppard would undoubtedly face the charge that he could not be said to have proven himself until he had tackled "more angst-ridden territory" than he had in The Real Inspector Hound. Similarly, Trewin (1968.B107) anticipated that this same play would not be welcomed by those who liked their satire "astringent." Others have confronted the charge that he fails to resolve his plays' conflicts by arguing, with Chekhov, that the task of the artist is to raise issues, not necessarily to settle them. Similarly, to the claim that Stoppard's ambivalence is fatal to a dramatist, James (1975. B62) replied that a playwright need not "believe" or take sides with either party in a dispute—it is enough that he believe in the pain

Introduction

which the clash between them must inevitably bring.

In general, the play which Stoppard's defenders have felt needed their attention most is Jumpers, which they have described as "moral" as well as "madcap," "weighty" in addition to farcical, or "witty, funny, and benevolent" (see, for instance, 1972.B30, 72, and 135)--well aware that his detractors would find it incoherent and frivolous (as did 1974.B137). The charge which his admirers have devoted most of their energy to meeting is the claim that his plays are merely pale imitations of Absurdists' works, particularly Beckett's. Callen (1969.B13) and Levenson (1971.B17), for instance, enumerated the many ways in which Stoppard's plots and characters mirror Beckett's, as if to suggest that, because he is a very close, rather than distant, relation to the master, he is more to be praised for his good taste than criticized for his mimicry. However, others admirers contradict these claims, insisting that Stoppard is not in any significant sense an Absurdist. This approach has a long and unbroken pedigree, stretching from Gianakaris (1968.B49), who claimed that Stoppard "altered Absurdism" by reconciling "the disparities between drama anchored to personal/social responsibility" and drama of the Absurdists; through Cahn (1976.A4), who traced Stoppard's movement from a period of imitation to one in which he combined the Realist and Absurdist traditions in a form which goes "beyond absurdity"; to Egan (1979.B36) and Salmon (1979.B88), who argued that it was "seriously misleading and quite untenable" to consider Jumpers an Absurdist play or Rosencrantz & Guildenstern Are Dead a "recasting" of Waiting for Godot.

It is worth noting that all the critics examined to this point, attackers and defenders alike, have centered their discussion around three issues: whether Stoppard lacks a voice of his own; whether, as a consequence, he fails to express emotion effectively (or fails to evoke it in his viewers); and whether he borrows indiscriminately from his betters. The legitimacy of these issues rests in turn upon the assumptions that (1) certain authorial strategies--among them eclecticism, systematic parody, and aggressive borrowing--do not constitute valid approaches to experience but are more or less desperate attempts to substitute for the absence of a legitimate "voice"; (2) the playwright's job consists, in part, of displaying his thoughts and feelings, in order that others may be moved; (3) to do so, the playwright must develop sincerity and individuality of expression; and (4) in the final analysis, ideas are to be believed in, not played with.

Those who accept these assumptions belong to what has been called the Traditionalist school of criticism. According to Leonard B. Meyer (in his excellent book, Music, the Arts, and Ideas [Chicago: University of Chicago Press, 1967]), Traditionalists are characterized by their stands on four issues. The most important of these is that (1) ends (content, theme, subject matter) are to be served by means (style, form, processes). Accordingly, (2) Traditionalists

Introduction

evaluate a work in terms of the accuracy with which it imitates reality (objects, actions, and passions), expresses feelings or represents ideas, and contributes to an understanding of social issues. This content- and socially-oriented basis of valuation invites (3) an interpretative mode of criticism, one which sets forth "what the play 'really' means," and it implies that (4) the role of art is essentially moral and the task of the playwright didactic.

Given these standards, it is easy to see why Stoppard's detractors take so seriously his failure to develop a voice of his own, to resolve the issues his plays raise, to depict "real" emotions, or to construct his characters according to the blueprints of Realism. To the Traditionalist, success in these enterprises is absolutely crucial, and Stoppard's ineptness at them (or worse, his indifference to them) is more than enough to merit his dismissal.

However, Meyer also identifies a second school of criticism, the Formalist, whose adherents make up Stoppard's largest group of admirers. The Formalist position may be distinguished from the Traditionalist on all four counts: means and ends, criteria of value, mode of criticism, and function of art and role of the artist.

First, in contrast to the Traditionalist's emphasis upon the importance of a work's content and the primacy of ends over means, the Formalist holds that art is an experiment or exercise in problem-solving and that a work's content is less important than are the processes by which it is manipulated and arranged into a satisfying form. As Bert O. States, in his "Pinter's <u>Homecoming</u>: The Shock of Nonrecognition" (<u>Hudson Review</u> 21 [August 1968]), has said of Britain's best-known Formalist playwright, "There is about [Pinter's] remarks on himself a very refreshing sense of the craftsman in his shop (or rather, <u>out</u> of it, and wanting to get back) and none of the displaced philosopher taking his chance to talk (art being mute). All questions, if possible, are converted to matters of technique--'writing the bloody play!'"

Second, because the Formalist denegrates the importance of ends (content) vis-à-vis means (form), it is not surprising that he should refuse to attach special value to art that features any particular kind of content--e.g., the kind that "imitates reality" or "contributes to an understanding of social issues." That is to say, whereas the Traditionalist bases his evaluation of a work's worth upon its content, the Formalist emphasizes the skill and elegance with which the artist manipulates whatever subject he happens to have chosen. Of all the differences between the two positions, this one has the most far-reaching consequences, for it underlies the Formalists' rejection of any evaluative criteria which permit moving beyond the work itself into the external world. Traditionalist art "represents reality"; Formalist art "constructs <u>a</u> reality" (Meyer, p. 222).

Introduction

Nor do Formalist artists feel any compunction to place their feelings on public display by embodying them in their work. Stoppard put their case forcefully when, in answer to the charge that his plays "failed to convey genuine emotion," he said, "That criticism is always being presented to me as if it were a membrane that I must somehow break through in order to grow up. Well, I don't see any special virtue in making my private emotions the quarry for the statue I'm carving. . . . That sort of truth-telling writing is . . . based on the fallacy of naturalism. There's a direct line of descent from the naturalistic theatre[,] which leads you straight down to the dregs of bad theatre, bad thinking, and bad feeling" (1977.B125).

Accordingly, the third distinction between the two schools is that, whereas the Traditionalist favors an interpretative kind of criticism, which explicates what the work really means, the Formalist prefers the analytic or formal mode--one which describes how it can mean by demonstrating the way its pieces fit together. And, finally, whereas the Traditionalist considers art a moral activity and assigns to the artist the role of teacher, the Formalist regards it as an amoral, aesthetic object and looks upon the artist as a "maker" or fabricator. As Meyer says (p. 232), the Formalist is typically less concerned with what is accomplished in life than he is with how life is led.

Given this survey of the two schools of thought, we may more accurately describe the divisions among Stoppard's critics as follows: nearly all of his detractors are Traditionalists who see serious flaws in his work; some of his defenders are Traditionalists who, calling their colleagues' eyesight into question, see much in Stoppard's work that is praiseworthy; and a second group of his defenders are Formalists who posit entirely different standards of evaluation than either of the Traditionalist camps.

So complete is the difference between Traditionalists' and Formalists' standards that in their criticism of Stoppard's plays a single word may describe two very different reactions. Some of the most common of these are "eclectic" (or "pastiche"), "juggler," and "nonsense." Traditionalists use these words to criticize Stoppard for borrowing from others or for playing with ideas instead of saying what he really means; Formalists employ them to describe his ability to put old styles and material together in a new way. Other oft-repeated words are "amusing," "brilliant" (or "dazzling"), "clever," and, perhaps the most common of all, "witty." Formalists use them in the context of praising Stoppard for "refusing to believe that weight and wit are incompatible" (1972.B72) or for radiating "sheer intellectual joie de vivre" (1974.B35); Traditionalists, on the other hand, typically add that these qualities too often degenerate into trickiness, frivolousness, or tiresome, bewildering self-indulgence (see, for instance, 1967.B62 and 1974.B178).

Introduction

Besides using similar words in different ways, Formalists and Traditionalists respectively admire and criticize identical features in Stoppard's works. One of these is language (dialogue which a Formalist may regard as "literate" Traditionalists will call "literary"), but, predictably enough, the major areas of contention are his sources and his organization of material. As we have seen, Stoppard's refusal to resolve the issues he raises is a serious fault from the Traditionalist point of view because that school considers it the task of art to contribute to an understanding of extra-aesthetic issues. But this same characteristic is praised by Formalists, who reject the claim that art must serve social issues, holding instead that it may devote itself to the creation of "an intricate and beautiful construction" (1967.B87) or "a series of beautifully contrived theatrical patterns" (1972.B48). Similarly, other Formalists suggest that a play may find its unity by balancing alternatives rather than by resolving issues (1972.B108). All of these criteria are consistent with what Meyer (p. 233) describes as the Formalists' attempt to evaluate art in terms of "elegance of design and ingenuity of process" rather than "accuracy of representation . . . or righteousness of moral doctrine."

The Formalists are no less aggressive in countering the criticism of Stoppard's use of others' material. As we have seen, to the Traditionalist, Stoppard's relationship to other playwrights is that of a thief burgling a homeowner or, at best, a callow scribbler sketching an Old Master. Formalists, however, recalling Oscar Wilde's words--"In a very ugly and sensible age, the arts borrow, not from life, but from each other"--see the relationship as that of a collage artist to his materials. Thus, they are less disturbed by the fact that Rosencrantz & Guildenstern Are Dead depends upon the prior existence of Hamlet than they are interested in understanding how Stoppard used his audience's knowledge of Shakespeare's play in order to affect their reactions to his own (see, for instance, 1980.B12 and 31). Similarly, Rogers pointed out that, when an author engages in parody as systematically as Stoppard did in Lord Malquist & Mr Moon, the results may be greater than the sum of the parts: in this case, the parody suggests "a way of looking with exuberant high spirits at a potentially dismaying reality" (1968.B96).

Formalist critics, then, evaluate an artist in terms of the quality (not the source) of his material and his deployment of it. Through 1974, they have generally admired Stoppard's work on these terms, aside from his readiness to use logic "with more single-mindedness than dramatic effect" (1973.B21) and to let parody distract him from his serious themes (1974.B80).

Related to this is a more far-reaching--albeit seldom voiced--reservation having to do with Stoppard's avoidance of the most unpleasant stuff of life: the traditional materials of tragedy. It is all very well to practice turning the tables on characters who

Introduction

are (largely, if not wholly) comic stereotypes, especially when the reversals they suffer are (in large part, if not entirely) comic turns. It is no mean accomplishment to do this as well and as consistently as any other English-speaking playwright today. Even so, nagging questions remain. One of Stoppard's Formalist admirers has said that a play such as The Real Inspector Hound "delights . . . by the intentional relaxation of moral awareness [and, by so doing,] . . . tells us as much about life's possibilities as moral intensity" (1968.B38, quoting Lionel Trilling). Very well: could Stoppard "tell us as much about life's possibilities" were his plays to deal with betrayals more serious than sexual infidelity? Could he give to his admirers a sense of his (and, by extension, our) mastery of intractable reality were he to confront immediate conflicts, not merely those buried in history, and to allow death to become an active power and not simply an "absence"? In short, how well would he deal--and help us deal--with evil?

It may be that these questions have been or will soon be answered, for, as I noted in my sketch of Stoppard's career, his most recent journalism and plays have seemed to be moving obliquely into territories which, if not obviously "more angst-ridden" (1968.B45), certainly have more immediate social and political pertinence to his audience. However, as his gaze has shifted toward these new thematic areas, he has apparently felt it appropriate to return to something like the style of Enter a Free Man and "Neutral Ground" (both 1968)--a mode at once more realistic and more constricting than the dense, imaginative, ironic one he had developed over more than a decade.

This stylistic shift is most obvious in Night and Day (1978), although some observers noticed it in Every Good Boy Deserves Favour, "Professional Foul" (both 1977), and Dogg's Hamlet, Cahoot's Macbeth (1979) as well. Their reactions to its appearance are instructive. The Traditionalists among them found nothing to criticize in the plays' interest in political repression, journalism, and individual responsibility. Indeed, those Traditionalists who are also political activists--and a good many of the critical community are, particularly in Britain--noted the shift with some satisfaction (see 1974.B90 and 1978.B67 for examples of this group's reactions to Stoppard's earlier works).

At the same time, however, the Traditionalists criticized the plays for not carrying out that school's program well enough. For example, Kerr found Night and Day's argument "fragmented, . . . circuitous, . . . [and] inconclusive" and its plot divided into "three separate compartments [with] no connecting doors" (1979.B62). Similarly, Simon (1979.B99) noted that in the "contrivedly interlocked" Dogg's Hamlet, Cahoot's Macbeth Stoppard was "rapidly becoming the Twitgenstein of our theatre," and he again raised the familiar charge that Stoppard cannot deal effectively with emotion, finding in Night and Day a "great emptiness where the play's depth ought to

Introduction

be--where the poetic, emotional, moral universe should take over."
(1979.B100; for a dissenting opinion from another Traditionalist,
however, see 1978.B84, who found evidence of a "strong sense of
humanity tempering [Stoppard's] wit" in Every Good Boy Deserves
Favour and "Professional Foul.")

Stoppard's Formalist admirers must also have some qualms about
his recent work: not, of course, because it fails to carry out the
Traditionalists' program adequately, but because it indicates that
he may be paying too little attention to some of his best qualities.
One of these is formal sophistication: Wardle (1978.B82) and Levin
(1978.B54) both expressed concern with the attitudinizing characters
and the "awkwardly woven and implausible" plot of Night and Day, and
Nightingale (1979.B81) found Dogg's Hamlet, Cahoot's Macbeth "fragmented" in its attempt to force a synthesis between comedy and political commitment. By now it should be clear that Formalists are not
prejudiced against socially pertinent material per se; it is simply
that they mistrust art which is unduly influenced by a commitment to
some extra-aesthetic "truth," which seems to know from the beginning
what it wants to say, and which takes the shortest, most direct
route to its goal (see, for instance, 1978.B54, in which Levin complains that Night and Day is "suspiciously unambiguous for so subtle
an artist" and that Stoppard "put his viewpoint before his drama").
Formalists recall Voltaire's assertion that "doubt is not a very
agreeable state, but certainty is a ridiculous one." They prefer
artists whose works sustain them in their uncertainty.

For many playgoers--more of them Formalists than Traditionalists--
Tom Stoppard has been such an artist. Whether he will continue to
be may depend on whether the work of his most recent cycle (such as
Night and Day, "a play Stoppard had to write") represents "the final
synthesis of his gifts" (1978.B51). Certainly his admirers can hope
it does not. They can hope, too, that he will remember his own
words, spoken to Ronald Hayman (1977.A1) only two days after the
premiere of Travesties, at the beginning of this latest cycle of
activity: "What's wrong with bad art is that the artist knows exactly what he's doing."

Addenda

Charles A. Carpenter, "Bond, Shaffer, Stoppard, Storey: An International Checklist of Commentary," Modern Drama 24 (December 1981): 546-56, appeared too late for me to incorporate the following twenty items into my text or index.

1971

GRIFFITHS, GARETH. "New Lines: English Theatre in the Sixties and After." Kansas Quarterly 3 (Spring):77-88.

NERI, NICOLETTE. "Il 'dramma nel dramma' nel teatro inglese contemporaneo." In Aspetti e figure del teatro inglese contemporaneo. Turin: Giappichelli, pp. 3-24.
   "Stresses Stoppard."

RYAN, PAT M. "Tom Stoppard's Cryptic R & G." Albany Theatre Journal 10 (Fall):3-9.

1975

BASSNETT-McGUIRE, SUSAN. "Textual Understructures in Jean-Louis Barrault's Rabelais and Tom Stoppard's Rosencrantz and Guildenstern Are Dead." Comparison 1:102-40.

CARDENAS DE BECU, ISABEL. "Lo trágico en el teatro tradicional y de vanguardia." Teatro de vanguardia: polémica y vida. Buenos Aires: Búsqueda, pp. 29-44.
   "Hamlet vs. Rosencrantz."

KRUSE, AXEL. "Tragicomedy and Tragic Burlesque: Waiting for Godot and Rosencrantz and Guildenstern Are Dead." Sydney Studies in English 1:76-96.

Addenda

1976

COHN, RUBY. <u>Modern Shakespeare Offshoots</u>. Princeton: Princeton University Press, pp. 211-18.

1977

BURTON, DEIRDRE. "Dialogue and Discourse in Tom Stoppard." <u>Nottingham Linguistic Circular</u> 4, no. 2:28-49.
   "Not verified."

WEBER, HANS. "Tom Stoppard: 'Where Are They Now?' (1970)." In <u>Das englische Hörspiel</u>. Edited by Horst Priessnitz. Düsseldorf: Bagel, pp. 319-31.

WEISE, WOLF D. "Tom Stoppard: 'Albert's Bridge' (1967)." In <u>Das englische Hörspiel</u>. Edited by Horst Priessnitz. Düsseldorf: Bagel, pp. 291-305.

1979

BOUFFARD, JEAN C. "<u>Rosenkrantz et Guildenstern pas morts</u>: à propos de <u>Rosenkrantz</u> [sic] <u>and Guildenstern Are Dead</u> de Tom Stoppard." <u>Acta Universitatis Wratislaviensis</u> 462:167-77.

DJORDJEVIC, JELENA. "Tri drame Toma Stoparda: nacelo ironije." <u>Savremenik</u> 25:529-41.
   "<u>Rosencrantz</u>, <u>Jumpers</u>, <u>Travesties</u>."

ZIMMERMAN, HEINZ, "T. Stoppards Publikumsverwirrung: zu Rezeption und Sinn von <u>Rosencrantz and Guildenstern Are Dead</u>." <u>Deutsche Shakespeare-Gesellschaft West: Jahrbuch 1978-1979</u>, pp. 184-200.

1980

BILLMAN, CAROL. "The Art of History in Tom Stoppard's <u>Travesties</u>." <u>Kansas Quarterly</u> 12:47-52.

BROICH, ULRICH. "Das englische historische Drama der Gegenwart." <u>Anglia</u> 98:357-82.
   "374-78 on <u>Travesties</u>."

KUURMAN, JOOST. "An Interview with Tom Stoppard." <u>Dutch Quarterly Review</u> 10:41-57.

MINER, MICHAEL D. "Grotesque Drama in the '70s." <u>Kansas Quarterly</u> 12:99-109.
   "Part on <u>Dirty Linen</u>."

Addenda

NITZSCHE, J. C. "McLuhan's Message and Stoppard's Medium in <u>Rosencrantz and Guildenstern Are Dead</u>." <u>Dutch Quarterly Review</u> 10:32-40.

ROTHSTEIN, BOBBI. "The Reappearance of Public Man: Stoppard's <u>Jumpers</u> and 'Professional Foul.'" <u>Kansas Quarterly</u> 12:35-44.

VAREY, SIMON. "Nobody Special: On <u>Rosencrantz and Guildenstern Are Dead</u>." <u>Dutch Quarterly Review</u> 10:20-31.

Writings by Tom Stoppard

1963

"A Walk on the Water" (television play, 25 November, London; also transmitted in radio version, 8 November 1965, London)

1964

"Life, Times: Fragments"; "Reunion"; and "The Story" (short stories published by Faber & Faber in <u>Introduction 2</u>)

"The Dales" (five episodes of radio serial, reported in 1971.A1 but unverified by BBC)

"The Dissolution of Dominic Boot" (radio play, 20 February, London)

"'M' Is for 'Moon,' among Other Things" (radio play, 6 April, London)

<u>Old Riley geht über'n Ozean</u> (German stage version of "A Walk on the Water," 30 June, Hamburg)

1965

<u>The Gamblers</u> (stage play, June, Bristol, according to 1976.B21 [but <u>see also</u> 1977.B125]; the former account is the more circumstantial, but neither has been verified)

"A Paragraph for Mr Blake" (television play, 23 October, Boreham Wood; based on short story, "The Story")

1966

<u>Lord Malquist & Mr Moon</u> (novel, published by Anthony Blond)

"If You're Glad I'll Be Frank" (radio play, 8 February, London)

Writings by Tom Stoppard

"A Student's Diary: An Arab in London" (radio serial, London; Stoppard's biweekly contributions began 3 April, ended 18 June 1967)

Tango (adaptation of stage play by Slawomir Mrozek, 25 May, London)

"A Separate Peace" (television play, 22 August, London; reportedly accompanied by a documentary by Stoppard about chess players, but unverified)

1967

"Teeth" (television play, 8 February, London)

Rosencrantz & Guildenstern Are Dead (stage play, 11 April, London; earlier amateur version, 24 August 1966, Edinburgh)

"Another Moon Called Earth" (television play, 28 June, London)

"Albert's Bridge" (radio play, 13 July, London)

1968

Enter a Free Man (revised stage version of "A Walk on the Water," 28 March, London, following 19 February tryout, Oxford)

The Real Inspector Hound (stage play, 17 June, London)

"Neutral Ground" (television play, 2 December, Manchester)

1970

"Where Are They Now?" (radio play, 18 December, London, following Schools Broadcasting production on 28 January)

"The Engagement" (screenplay based on "The Dissolution of Dominic Boot," television broadcast on 8 March, New York; released to cinemas in May)

After Magritte (stage play, 9 April, London)

1971

Dogg's Our Pet (stage play, 8 December, London)

Writings by Tom Stoppard

1972

Jumpers (stage play, 2 February, London)

"One Pair of Eyes: Tom Stoppard Doesn't Know" (television documentary, 7 July, London)

"Artist Descending a Staircase" (radio play, 14 November, London)

1973

The House of Bernarda Alba (adaptation of stage play by Federico Lorca, 22 March, London)

Born Yesterday (direction of stage play by Garson Kanin, 18 April, London)

1974

Travesties (stage play, 10 June, London)

1975

"The Boundary" (television play co-authored by Clive Exton, 19 July, London)

"The Romantic Englishwoman" (screenplay of the novel by Thomas Wiseman, released to cinemas in November, London)

"Three Men in a Boat" (adaptation for television of the novel by Jerome K. Jerome, 31 December, London)

1976

Dirty Linen and New-Found-Land (stage play, 6 April, London)

The (15 Minute) Dogg's Troupe "Hamlet" (stage abridgment, 24 August, London)

1977

Every Good Boy Deserves Favour (stage play, 1 July, London)

"Professional Foul" (television play, 21 September, London)

Writings by Tom Stoppard

1978

"Despair" (screenplay of the novel by Vladimir Nabokov, released to cinemas February 1979, London)

Night and Day (stage play, 8 November, London)

1979

Dogg's "Hamlet," Cahoot's "Macbeth" (stage play, 21 May, Coventry)

Undiscovered Country (adaptation of stage play by Arthur Schnitzler, 20 June, London)

"The Human Factor" (screenplay of the novel by Graham Greene, released to cinemas in December, Los Angeles)

1980

Acting (untitled stage documentary, 9 February, Munich)

Writings about Tom Stoppard

1964

A BOOKS--NONE

B SHORTER WRITINGS

   1   ANON. "Biographical Notes: Tom Stoppard." In <u>Introduction 2: Stories by New Writers</u>. London: Faber & Faber, pp. 11-12.
      Brief summary of Stoppard's journalistic career in a collection containing three of his short stories.

   2   ANON. "Tom Stoppard." In <u>Thalia Theater: "Old Riley geht über'n Ozean.</u>" Production program, 30 June, Hamburg, p. 3.
      Biographical data (in German) in the program of the stage premiere of the earliest version of <u>Enter a Free Man</u>.

   3   ANON. "Helping Playwrights Get Ideas." <u>Times</u> (London), 11 September, p. 16.
      News story with brief review. Describes the Literarisches Colloquium that Stoppard and five other British and American writers attended in West Berlin for five months; discusses its organizer, Walter Hasenclever; calls <u>Guildenstern and Rosencrantz</u> a "rhythmic jamboree" and the "strangest" of the pieces performed at a showing of the participants' works.

   4   ANON. "About the Authors: Tom Stoppard." In <u>The Questor's Theatre's "Five Plays from Berlin</u>." Production program, 4 October, London, n.p. Photocopied.
      Brief biographical notes in the program of a production consisting of brief excerpts from plays, including <u>Guildenstern and Rosencrantz</u>, written during British authors' participation in a colloquium in West Berlin.

Writings about Tom Stoppard

1965

1965

A   BOOKS--NONE

B   SHORTER WRITINGS

1   ANON. 23 October: "A Paragraph for Mr Blake." TV Times, no. 521 (21 October):29.
    Plot summary, cast list, and transmission information about Stoppard's first play intended for television.

2   DAVIS, ANTHONY. "Publish--and Be Ruined." TV Times, no. 521 (21 October):14.
    Brief interview with Stoppard about the origin of "A Paragraph for Mr Blake."

3   HUGHES, PENNETHORNE. "Radio Drama." Listener 74 (18 November):820.
    Review of "A Walk on the Water" (London, BBC Radio).

1966

A   BOOKS--NONE

B   SHORTER WRITINGS

1   ANON. "Notes on Broadcasting: With It, within It, and without It." Times (London), 5 March, p. 12.
    Review of "If You're Glad I'll Be Frank" (London, BBC Radio).

2   ANON. "Tango." Times (London), 21 May, p. 15.
    Photograph of cast and setting of the London, Royal Shakespeare Company production.

3   ANON. "The Arts: Polish Writer's Target in Doubt." Times (London), 26 May, p. 19.
    Review of Tango (London, Royal Shakespeare Company); suggests that "the task of placing jokes in a schematic framework and working to a length beyond his previous range seems to have dulled [Mrozek's] invention."

4   ANON. "Shows Abroad: Tango." Variety, 15 June, p. 68.
    Review of the London, Royal Shakespeare Company production: "a mildly comical but superficial and unsatisfying

Writings about Tom Stoppard

1966

philosophical allegory."

5 ANON. "Arts Chronicle: A Scathing Likeness." Atlas 12 (July):57.
 Review of Tango (London, Royal Shakespeare Company).

6 ANON. "Another Corner of Elsinore." Times (London), 3 September, p. 6.
 Review of Rosencrantz & Guildenstern Are Dead (Edinburgh, Oxford Theatre Group); one of two favorable notices (see also 1966.B13).

7 ANON. "Losses on Fringe Total at Least £4000." Scotsman (Edinburgh), 12 September, p. 8.
 News item reporting full houses at Rosencrantz & Guildenstern Are Dead at Edinburgh and a profit for the Oxford Theatre Group.

8 ANON. "Other New Novels." Times Literary Supplement (London), 15 September, p. 864.
 Review of Lord Malquist & Mr Moon, which begins with "pleasant, surrealist stuff" but soon "loses its glitter."

9 ANON. "National Theatre's 'Fringe' Play." Times (London), 14 December, p. 6.
 News item reporting the British National Theatre's plans to produce Rosencrantz & Guildenstern Are Dead in 1967.

10 BAKER, ROGER. "Theatre." London Life (11 June):44.
 Brief review of Tango (London, Royal Shakespeare Company).

11 BARKER, FELIX. "One to Please Billy Graham." Evening News (London), 26 May, p. 7.
 Review of Tango (London, Royal Shakespeare Company).

12 BLAKE, DOUGLAS F. "Rosencrantz and Guildenstern." Stage and Television Today (London), 1 September, p. 14.
 Unfavorable review of the Edinburgh, Oxford Theatre Group production.

13 BRYDEN, RONALD. "Theatre: Wyndy Excitement." Observer (London), 28 August, p. 15.
 Review of Rosencrantz & Guildenstern Are Dead (Edinburgh, Oxford Theatre Group): "the most brilliant debut . . . since John Arden's."

14 COX, FRANK. "Two Cheers for Mr Diamand." Plays and Players

3

1966

     14 (November):51.
          Brief review of Rosencrantz & Guildenstern Are Dead
     (Edinburgh, Oxford Theatre Group); a play "too clearly in
     love with its own intellectuality."

15   CROZIER, MARY. "Double Image on BBC 2." Guardian (London),
     24 August, p. 6.
          Review of "A Separate Peace" (London, BBC Television):
     despite the "many psychological implications," the play's
     effect was "more amusing than moralistic."

16   DARLINGTON, W. A. "The Theatre of the Absurder-Than-Ever."
     Daily Telegraph (London), 26 May, p. 21.
          Review of Tango (London, Royal Shakespeare Company).

17   DIBB, FRANK W. "Theatre Group's World Premiere." Oxford
     Times, 26 August, p. 24.
          Unfavorable review of Rosencrantz & Guildenstern Are
     Dead (Edinburgh, Oxford Theatre Group).

18   DUFFY, MAUREEN. "First Novels." Books and Bookmen 13 (November):91.
          Review of Lord Malquist & Mr Moon.

19   FRICK, N. ALICE. "Two-in-One Is Well Worth Watching." Stage
     and Television Today (London), 25 August, p. 12.
          Review of "A Separate Peace" (London, BBC Television).

20   HOBSON, HAROLD. "Honour Your Partners." Sunday Times
     (London), 3 July, p. 46.
          Review of Tango (London, Royal Shakespeare Company):
     "a work of considerable intellectual stature," although
     its "extravagances . . . are less than inspired. . . . Its
     interest is in its dialectics."

21   _____. "Edinburgh Festival Theatre: Educating Edinburgh."
     Sunday Times (London), 4 September, p. 24.
          Review of Rosencrantz & Guildenstern Are Dead (Edinburgh, Oxford Theatre Group): "a mindful sport" which
     "applies to Shakespeare the methods of Robbe-Grillet."

22   _____. "Full Theater at Edinburgh." Christian Science
     Monitor, 12 September, p. 6.
          Review of the "ambiguous and tentative" Rosencrantz &
     Guildenstern Are Dead (Edinburgh, Oxford Theatre Group)
     for American readers. Continued in 1966.B23.

23   _____. "Theater Can Be a Matter of Taste." Christian

Writings about Tom Stoppard

1966

Science Monitor, 16 September, p. 4.
Continuation of 1966.B22: discusses critical reactions to Rosencrantz & Guildenstern Are Dead as examples of the differences between London's and the provinces' critics.

24 HOLLAND, MARY. "Theatre." Queen 426 (8 June):15.
Review of Tango (London, Royal Shakespeare Company), in which "everything is aggressively symbolic and none the better for that."

25 HOLMSTROM, JOHN. "Danse Macabre." Plays and Players 13 (July):15.
Review of Tango (London, Royal Shakespeare Company): a "wretchedly unsatisfying" play which "contrives to be both unfunny and tedious."

26 JONES, D. A. N. "Theatre: What about the Workers?" New Statesman 71 (3 June):819-20.
Review of Tango (London, Royal Shakespeare Company), expressing bewilderment at the play's shifts from the political to the familial and the lack of specificity in its allegorical references.

27 KINGSTON, JEREMY. "Theatre." Punch 250 (8 June):853-54.
Review of Tango (London, Royal Shakespeare Company).

28 KNIGHT, JOHN. "Saturday Night Sunday Morning." Sunday Mirror (London), 18 December, p. 13.
Brief interview with Stoppard following the National Theatre's announcement that it would produce Rosencrantz & Guildenstern Are Dead in 1967.

29 LAMBERT, J. W. "Trivial and Terrific." Sunday Times (London), 29 May, p. 29.
Review of Tango (London, Royal Shakespeare Company): the play is "too thin in comic invention," and Mrozek's characters are "either too much or too little like symbolic puppets."

30 LARNER, GERALD. "Disasters on the Fringe." Guardian (London), 2 September, p. 9.
Includes a review of Rosencrantz & Guildenstern Are Dead (Edinburgh, Oxford Theatre Group): a "fascinating essay" which moves "with no ultimate effect, but with thoughtfulness and brightness of dialogue."

31 LEWIS, ANTHONY. "Edinburgh Festival Enlivened by California Student Actors." New York Times, 2 September, p. 35.

1966

   Includes a brief review of Rosencrantz & Guildenstern Are Dead (Oxford Theatre Group): an "unnerving but also witty and provocative" play.

32 PURSER, PHILIP. "Television: Mockers Go Home." Sunday Telegraph (London), 28 August, p. 9.
   Brief review of "A Separate Peace" (London, BBC Television).

33 S., C. "Inexplicable, but Good." Scottish Daily Mail (Edinburgh), 25 August, p. 5.
   Mixed review of Rosencrantz & Guildenstern Are Dead (Edinburgh, Oxford Theatre Group).

34 TREWIN, J. C. "Theatre: Hammering It Out." Illustrated London News 249 (4 June):36.
   Review of the "laborious" Tango (London, Royal Shakespeare Company).

35 _____. "Rosencrantz & Guildenstern Are Dead." Birmingham Post, 27 August, p. 7.
   Mixed review of the Edinburgh, Oxford Theatre Group production.

36 _____. "The Glories of Greece." Illustrated London News 249 (10 September):30.
   Brief review of Rosencrantz & Guildenstern Are Dead (Edinburgh, Oxford Theatre Group): an "amorphous and uneasy, . . . too consciously clever" play.

37 WADE, DAVID. "Radio Drama." Listener 75 (17 February):258.
   Review of "If You're Glad I'll Be Frank" (London, BBC Radio).

38 WARDLE, IRVING. "Arts in Society: Shakespeare as Folklore." New Society 8 (29 September):495-96.
   Includes a brief review of Rosencrantz & Guildenstern Are Dead (Edinburgh, Oxford Theatre Group) in a discussion of British dramatists' reluctance to use Shakespeare's plays as sources for their own. Abridged in 1967.B130.

39 WEIGHTMAN, JOHN. "Theatre: Ideas and the Drama." Encounter 27 (September):46-48.
   Review of Tango (London, Royal Shakespeare Company) with analytical comments about the text. Asserts that a "play of ideas" cannot "solve the problem it poses; it can merely present it as an . . . experience, and such resolution as occurs cannot be more than aesthetic." Criticizes Mrozek

for failing to hold "the problem firmly in focus and devising a satisfactory dramatic expression for it."

40 WRIGHT, ALLEN. "Enigma Variations on Hamlet." Scotsman (Edinburgh), 25 August, p. 6.
    Unfavorable review of Rosencrantz & Guildenstern Are Dead (Edinburgh, Oxford Theatre Group).

41 YOUNG, B. A. "First Novels." Punch 251 (14 September):416.
    Review of Lord Malquist & Mr Moon: criticizes Stoppard for "keeping the thing going" only by "the exercise of all his . . . determination."

1967

A BOOKS--NONE

B SHORTER WRITINGS

1 ADAMS, BERNARD. "Tom Stoppard on 'Teeth.'" Radio Times (24 August):19.
   Brief interview: Stoppard claims that, under pressure of a deadline, he wrote half the play in one day and finished it within two weeks.

2 ALBRECHT, ERNEST. "R & G Are Dead a Rare Feast." New Brunswick (N.J.) Daily Home News, 18 October, p. 32.
   Review of the Broadway production.

3 ANON. "Dexter Dispute over As You Like It." Times (London), 23 March, p. 10.
   News item reporting that the British National Theatre's decision to produce Rosencrantz & Guildenstern Are Dead instead of As You Like It influenced John Dexter's decision to resign his position as one of the company's directors.

4 ANON. "Londoner's Diary: Worried Author." Evening Standard (London), 8 April, p. 6.
   Interview and biographical data: discusses the commercial failure of Lord Malquist & Mr Moon and Stoppard's preference for concentrating on dialogue rather than plot when writing plays.

5 ANON. "Footnote to the Bard." Observer (London), 9 April, p. 23.

1967

Interview: Stoppard discusses his early work; his preference for writing comedy rather than serious drama; and the influence of Runyon, Capote, and Hemingway on his short stories.

6   ANON. "Note on the Author." In The National Theatre: "Rosencrantz and Guildenstern Are Dead." Production program, 11 April, London, n.p.
    Biographical data.

7   ANON. "Rosencrantz and Guildenstern Are Dead." Variety, 19 April, p. 102.
    Favorable review of the London, National Theatre production.

8   ANON. "Merrick Is Bringing London Hit Here." New York Times, 15 May, p. 53.
    News item reporting David Merrick's agreement to give all profits to the British National Theatre in exchange for the Broadway rights to Rosencrantz & Guildenstern Are Dead.

9   ANON. "Stoppard Play for Broadway." Times (London), 17 May, p. 6.
    News item reporting that Rosencrantz & Guildenstern Are Dead would be produced on Broadway by David Merrick.

10 ANON. "The Times Diary: Tom Stoppard." Times (London), 12 June, p. 8.
    News item announcing Stoppard's forthcoming play about "the critics" (eventually produced as The Real Inspector Hound).

11 ANON. "Anything but Dead." Times (London), 19 June, p. 6.
    News item reporting David Merrick's plans to transfer the London, National Theatre production of Rosencrantz & Guildenstern Are Dead to Washington, D.C., and New York in toto.

12 ANON. "Big Demand for Rosencrantz." Stage and Television Today (London), 22 June, p. 13.
    News item listing opening dates of forthcoming foreign productions of Rosencrantz & Guildenstern Are Dead.

13 ANON. "Two Playwrights Win £500." Times (London), 3 July, p. 6.
    News item reporting that Stoppard and Wole Soyinka of Nigeria would share the John Whiting Award for the year's

best new play.

14 ANON. "Sound: Thursday 13 July." Observer (London), 9 July, p. 18.
Preview description of "Albert's Bridge" (London, BBC Radio).

15 ANON. "London Critics' Poll Results: 1966-67 Season." Variety, 2 August, p. 56.
News item reporting that Rosencrantz & Guildenstern Are Dead had been selected as the Best New British Play by London's theatre critics.

16 ANON. "What's All This About?" Newsweek 70 (7 August):72.
Interview with some biographical data. Stoppard discusses the modern mistrust of heroes and his fears that Rosencrantz & Guildenstern Are Dead would prove "too much of an in-joke" or the product of a purely private neurosis.

17 ANON. "Theater Notes: R & G Are Dead Due Oct. 11." New York Post, 17 August, p. 55.
News item announcing the play's opening on Broadway.

18 ANON. "Alec Guinness in New Play." Times (London), 1 September, p. 6.
News item includes announcement of Michael Codron's plans to produce The Real Inspector Hound in London.

19 ANON. "Paris, Sept. 25." Times (London), 26 September, p. 11.
News item reporting the "mixed reception" given Rosencrantz & Guildenstern Are Dead by critics of the production in Paris.

20 ANON. "Tom Stoppard." In Burgtheater im Akademietheater: "Rosenkranz und Güldenstern." Production program, 14 October, Vienna, p. 15.
Biographical information (in German).

21 ANON. "B'way Better: Soup $34,234 for 7, R & G $54,900, I Do $66,700 for 7." Variety (25 October):54.
News item summarizing the first-night reviews of Rosencrantz & Guildenstern Are Dead (Broadway) as unanimously "enthusiastic."

22 ANON. "The Talk of the Town: R. and G., G. and R." New Yorker 43 (4 November):52.
Interview with Brian Murray and John Wood, Rosencrantz and Guildenstern in the Broadway production.

Writings about Tom Stoppard

1967

23 ANON. "A Rough Time for the Paris Theatre." <u>Times</u> (London), 6 November, p. 6.
    News item mentioning that critics had "pilloried" <u>Rosencrantz & Guildenstern Are Dead</u> in Paris.

24 ANON. "Forecasts: Non-Fiction." <u>Publishers' Weekly</u> 192 (13 November):82.
    Review of the text of <u>Rosencrantz & Guildenstern Are Dead</u>.

25 ANON. "The Times Diary: A Trio of Stoppard." <u>Times</u> (London), 5 December, p. 8.
    News items announcing the coming production of <u>Enter a Free Man</u> (then known as <u>The Preservation of George Riley</u>).

26 ANON. "Drama Mailbag." <u>New York Times</u>, 17 December, sec. D, pp. 4, 13.
    Letter to the editor from "William Shakespeare, President of the Association of Dead Playwrights," protesting violations of dead authors' intentions in recent productions. One of these, <u>Rosencrantz & Guildenstern Are Dead</u> (Broadway), "finds me beyond anger or sorrow." See also 1967.B113.

27 BALL, IAN G. "Radio: Pure Sound Technique in <u>Bridge</u>." <u>Scotsman</u> (Edinburgh), 24 July, p. 4.
    Favorable review of "Albert's Bridge" (London, BBC Radio).

28 BARKER, FELIX. "Critic's View: A Witty Web of Ideas." <u>Evening News</u> (London), 12 April, p. 3.
    Favorable review of <u>Rosencrantz & Guildenstern Are Dead</u> (London, National Theatre).

29 BARNES, CLIVE. "Theater: <u>Rosenkrantz</u> [sic] <u>and Guildenstern Are Dead</u>. <u>New York Times</u>, 17 October, p. 53.
    Review of the Broadway production, which reveals that Stoppard is already "among the finest English-speaking writers of our stage." Reprinted in 1967.B92.

30 BARRETT, LESLIE. "Drama Mailbag: Return to Sender." <u>New York Times</u>, 26 November, sec. D, p. 14.
    Letter to the editor, asking that "we relegate these two nonentities [Rosencrantz and Guildenstern], with their puerile wit, back to the place where Shakespeare so knowingly placed them."

31 BENEDICT, STEWART H. "<u>Rosencrantz and Guildenstern Are Dead</u>

1967

Fine Play." Jersey City (N.J.) <u>Jersey Journal</u>, 17 October, p. 29.
    Favorable review of the Broadway production.

32 BILLINGTON, MICHAEL. "Confessions of Nicol Williamson." <u>Times</u> (London), 13 March, p. 8.
    Interview with the actor, containing an incidental mention of the opening of <u>Rosencrantz & Guildenstern Are Dead</u> (London, National Theatre) on 11 April.

33 BLAHA, PAUL. "Kultur: Warten auf Hamlet." <u>Kurier</u> (Vienna), 16 October, p. 12.
    Review (in German) of <u>Rosencrantz & Guildenstern Are Dead</u> (Vienna, Akademietheater).

34 BOLTON, WHITNEY. "An Enchanting Rewrite Job on <u>Hamlet</u>." <u>New York Morning Telegraph</u>, 18 October, p. 3.
    Favorable review of <u>Rosencrantz & Guildenstern Are Dead</u> (Broadway).

35 BOWEN, JOHN. "The Lively Arts." BBC Radio Third Programme (6 April).
    Unedited transcript of radio interview recorded prior to the opening of <u>Rosencrantz & Guildenstern Are Dead</u> (London, National Theatre). Stoppard discusses the earlier production in Edinburgh, answers charges that the play is overwritten and wanders from the point, and describes cuts made for the National Theatre's production. Notably less fluent than in later interviews. Repeated: 1968.B35. Transcript housed, London: BBC Written Archives Centre.

36 BRIEN, ALAN. "Theatre: Reluctant Heroes." <u>Sunday Telegraph</u> (London), 16 April, p. 10.
    Review of <u>Rosencrantz & Guildenstern Are Dead</u> (London, National Theatre).

37 BRUSTEIN, ROBERT. "Waiting for Hamlet." <u>New Republic</u> 157 (4 November):25-26.
    Review of <u>Rosencrantz & Guildenstern Are Dead</u> (Broadway). Admires the "noble conception" but criticizes the lack of "any real weight or texture": Stoppard's "air of pessimism seems affected and his philosophical meditations . . . never obtain the thickness of <u>felt</u> knowledge." He lives parasitically upon "a <u>Zeitgeist</u> created by authors whose works nobody wants to see, and is achieving his success by offering a form of Beckett without tears." Reprinted in 1968.B36 and 1969.B12. Abridged in 1975.B96 and 1975.B117.

1967

38 BRYDEN, RONALD. "Theatre: Out of Their World." Observer (London), 16 April, p. 24.
    Review of Rosencrantz & Guildenstern Are Dead (London, National Theatre): "an undergraduate joke carried to poetry" which brings to British theatre "the Continental genre of modernised myth." Reprinted in 1968.B84.

39 BUNCE, ALAN N. "Rosencrantz and Guildenstern on Broadway." Christian Science Monitor, 23 October, p. 6.
    Review of the Broadway production.

40 BUSH, MIRIAM. "Macabre Spoof Stars Two Hamlet 'Friends.'" Asbury Park (N.J.) Press, 17 October, p. 14.
    Favorable review of Rosencrantz & Guildenstern Are Dead (Broadway).

41 CHAPMAN, JOHN. "Rosencrantz & Guildenstern Are Dead Is a Most Delightful Prank." New York Daily News, 17 October, p. 53.
    Review of the Broadway production which "drags now and then . . . but in the main . . . is fine theater." Reprinted in 1967.B92.

42 _____. "Britons Invade Broadway: And It's a Good Thing; Without English Plays We'd Be Sunk." New York Sunday News, 19 October, sec. S, p. 3.
    Largely concerned with Rosencrantz & Guildenstern Are Dead (Broadway), "a happy, literate . . . jest."

43 CLURMAN, HAROLD. "Theatre." Nation 205 (6 November):476-77.
    Review of Rosencrantz & Guildenstern Are Dead (Broadway): "a scintillating debut. . . . But we need not take the play's 'deeper significance' too seriously; it is not thought but student chatter on a brightly dignified level." Abridged in 1973.B68 and 1975.B117.

44 COE, RICHARD. "One on the Aisle: Witty, Literate and Haunting." Washington Post, 22 September, sec. D, p. 13.
    Favorable review of Rosencrantz & Guildenstern Are Dead (Washington, D.C. tryout of Broadway production).

45 COOKE, RICHARD P. "Lively Ghosts." Wall Street Journal, 18 October, p. 16.
    Review of Rosencrantz & Guildenstern Are Dead (Broadway): "easily the best production so far [in the season]--and, for a wonder, the most theatrical." Reprinted in 1967.B92.

1967

46 COOPER, R. W. "Trite Reflections of Life." Times (London), 9 February, p. 4.
   Includes a review of "Teeth" (title refers to another work, not to Stoppard's "ingenious little piece").

47 DARLINGTON, W. A. "First Night: Two Characters in a Dreadful Limbo." Daily Telegraph (London), 12 April, p. 19.
   Unfavorable review of Rosencrantz & Guildenstern Are Dead (London, National Theatre). Reprinted in 1968.B84.

48 DAVIES, HUNTER. "Stoppard Goes." Sunday Times (London), 23 April, p. 13.
   Interview, largely devoted to non-theatrical matters: Stoppard's dislike of driving, pubs, and beer; his wish to own a house in the country; his failure as a journalist; and the effect of financial pressures on his work prior to Rosencrantz & Guildenstern Are Dead.

49 DAVIS, MALCOLM McTEAR. "Pick of the Pack: Rosencrantz and Guildenstern Are Dead." Travel 128 (December):22.
   Favorable review of the Broadway production.

50 DAY-LEWIS, SEAN. "Plays and Players: Shakespeare Plus." Daily Telegraph (London), 8 April, p. 13.
   Interview prior to the opening of Rosencrantz & Guildenstern Are Dead (London, National Theatre). Covers biographical data and the source and history of the play; includes a brief discussion of what later became The Real Inspector Hound.

51 DREW, BERNARD. "Brilliant British Export Brightens Up Broadway." Hartford (Conn.) Times, 24 October, p. 5.
   Favorable review of Rosencrantz & Guildenstern Are Dead (Broadway).

52 DUCHENE, ANNE. "'Albert's Bridge.'" Guardian (London), 17 July, p. 5.
   Review of the London, BBC Radio production of the play, which exhibits "more ease in the writing, and less anxiety to entertain" than had "If You're Glad I'll Be Frank"; nevertheless, "Stoppard's almost staunchless eloquence . . . was very repetitive in places." Unlike Beckett, whose "every word issues from the tripes before being proved upon the pulses, . . . Stoppard's activity seems almost entirely cerebral and verbal."

53 ESSLIN, MARTIN. "Theater in London: Again, a Storm over Hochhuth." New York Times, 28 May, sec. 2, pp. 3, 18.

Writings about Tom Stoppard

1967

       Reviews and news items, including a section about Rosencrantz & Guildenstern Are Dead (London, National Theatre): "undoubtedly the most significant dramatic discovery of this year's London season."

54 FERRIS, PAUL. "Sound: Views from the Bridge." Observer (London), 23 July, p. 19.
    Favorable review of "Albert's Bridge" (London, BBC Radio).

55 FUNKE, PHYLLIS. "Hamlet Gets a Brilliant New Offshoot." Suffolk (N.J.) Sun, 17 October, p. 8.
    Favorable review of Rosencrantz & Guildenstern Are Dead (Broadway).

56 GALE, JOHN. "Writing's My 43rd Priority, Says Tom Stoppard." Observer (London), 17 December, p. 4.
    Brief interview. Discusses Stoppard's writing habits and contains a short self-description.

57 GAVER, JACK. Review of Rosencrantz & Guildenstern Are Dead. UPI Wireservice. London: National Theatre.
    Review of the Broadway production, which "only occasionally . . . achieve[s] the plane of high comedy" because Stoppard "too often settles for a vaudeville style of patter . . . that has little point." Abridged in 1967.B58.

58 _____. "Hamlet Characters Live Again." Cleveland Press, 18 October, sec. G, p. 7.
    Abridgement of 1967.B57.

59 GERSTINGER, HEINZ. "Rosenkranz und Güldenstern." In Burgtheater im Akademietheater: "Rosenkranz und Güldenstern." Production program, 14 October, Vienna, pp. 2-6.
    Criticism (in German); states that the title characters represent the modern Everyman who, in fear or for convenience, has given up all initiative. Unlike Beckett's characters in Waiting for Godot, who "are waiting for something indefinite" and who "fear non-sense," Stoppard's "know that something powerful is taking place" and "are afraid of acting sensibly."

60 GLOVER, WILLIAM. "Hamlet's Chums Romp in Bright, Provocative New Play." Chicago Sun Times, 18 October, p. 57.
    Favorable review of Rosencrantz & Guildenstern Are Dead (Broadway).

61 _____. "Enter Playwright, Successfully." AP Wireservice.

Writings about Tom Stoppard

1967

New York: Public Library, Lincoln Center Drama Collection.
Interview and biographical data. Stoppard discusses his reactions to the success of Rosencrantz & Guildenstern Are Dead and his appreciation of Samuel Beckett. Revised: 1969.B38.

62 GOTTFRIED, MARTIN. "Rosencrantz and Guildenstern Are Dead." Women's Wear Daily, 17 October, p. 40.
Review of the Broadway production. Generally favorable, but says the play "is not profound . . . so much as it is a theatrical flamboyance." It is "generally but not always effective as a stage piece, . . . comic, . . . terribly bright, . . . very literate, occasionally moving and very eclectic." It is also "confused at times because of the excessive trickiness of its concept." Reprinted in 1967.B92.

63 GOW, GORDON. "Woman's Hour: Showpiece." BBC Radio Light Programme (13 April).
Brief statements by Stoppard about Rosencrantz & Guildenstern Are Dead. Transcript housed, London: BBC Written Archives Centre.

64 HALTON, KATHLEEN. "Tom Stoppard." Vogue 150 (15 October): 112.
Brief interview and feature article. Summarizes the success of Rosencrantz & Guildenstern Are Dead; also contains Stoppard's description of his "personal neuroses," his opinion of Lord Malquist & Mr Moon, and his preoccupation with landings on the moon (which figures later in "Another Moon Called Earth" and Jumpers).

65 HARPER, KEITH. "The Devious Route to Waterloo Road." Guardian (London), 12 April, p. 7.
Interview and feature article. Contains biographical data (particularly about Stoppard's journalistic ambitions and early career as a playwright); touches on his habit of procrastinating, his good opinion of Lord Malquist & Mr Moon, and his hopes for Rosencrantz & Guildenstern Are Dead, soon to open in the London, National Theatre, production.

66 HAYMAN, RONALD. "Theatre." Queen 428 (26 April):11.
Favorable review of Rosencrantz & Guildenstern Are Dead (London, National Theatre).

67 HEDGEPETH, WILLIAM. "Playwright Tom Stoppard: Go Home British Boy Genius!" Look 31 (26 December):92-96.

1967

   Interview and feature article. Stoppard describes
   Rosencrantz & Guildenstern Are Dead as his conscious attempt to write about a comic situation and as a "subcon-
   scious expression of my private neuroses."

68 HEWES, HENRY. "The Indifferent Children of the Earth."
   Saturday Review 50 (4 November):28.
      Review of Rosencrantz & Guildenstern Are Dead, "the
   freest exercise of theatrical imagination and intelligence
   to reach Broadway in the last two seasons."

69 HIPP, EDWARD SOTHERN. "Two Hamlet Spies Get Drama of Own."
   Newark (N.J.) Evening News, 17 October, p. 54.
      Favorable review of Rosencrantz & Guildenstern Are Dead
   (Broadway).

70 _____. "Stage: Closeup of Two Timeservers." Newark (N.J.)
   Evening News, 29 October, sec. G, p. E1.
      Favorable review of Rosencrantz & Guildenstern Are Dead
   (Broadway).

71 HOBE. "Shows on Broadway: Rosencrantz & Guildenstern Are
   Dead." Variety, 18 October, p. 56.
      Review of the New York production.

72 HOBSON, HAROLD. "A Fearful Summons." Sunday Times (London),
   16 April, p. 49.
      Review of Rosencrantz & Guildenstern Are Dead (London,
   National Theatre): "the most important event in the
   British professional theatre of the last nine years." Reprinted in 1968.B84.

73 _____. "Rosencrantz, Guildenstern Heard from in Fine New
   Play." Christian Science Monitor, 21 April, p. 10.
      Favorable review of Rosencrantz & Guildenstern Are Dead
   (London, National Theatre) for American readers.

74 HOPE-WALLACE, PHILIP. "Rosencrantz & Guildenstern Are Dead
   at the National Theatre." Guardian (London), 12 April,
   p. 7.
      Mixed review of the London production. Reprinted in
   1968.B84.

75 JONES, D. A. N. "Arts: Spear-Carriers." New Statesman 73
   (21 April):553-54.
      Theatrical reviews; includes the comment that he would
   rather report on the text of Rosencrantz & Guildenstern
   Are Dead (see 1967.B76) than on the London, National

1967

Theatre production.

76 ———. "Safe Play." New Statesman 73 (5 May):620, 622.
Review of the text of Rosencrantz & Guildenstern Are Dead (see 1967.B75). Considers Stoppard's characters "facile imitations of Beckett's hard work" and his "wordplay . . . neither serious nor funny."

77 JÜRG, DR. "Die Kleinen Räder der 'Schicksalsuhr.'" Kleine Volksblatt (Vienna), 17 October, p. 6.
Review (in German) of Rosencrantz & Guildenstern Are Dead (Vienna, Akademietheater): declares that the play, although blessed with poetic moments, wit, irony, and explicit statement, lacks action.

78 KALEM, T. E. "Skull beneath the Skin." Time 90 (27 October): 84.
Review of Rosencrantz & Guildenstern Are Dead (Broadway); also includes biographical data and Stoppard's comment that he, like his protagonists, feels he is "a nobody. A cipher, not even a cog."

79 KAUER, EDMUND. "Ein Grosser Abend im Akademietheater." Kleine Volksstimme (Vienna), 17 October, p. 7.
Review of Rosencrantz & Guildenstern Are Dead (Vienna, Akademietheater); characterizes Stoppard's humor as "a primordial, old fashioned [kind]. . . . But it is never black humor, never a fashionable end in itself, . . . but rather the other aspect of a deep, mysterious seriousness." In German.

80 KERR, WALTER. "Taking Revenge on Life." New York Times, 29 October, sec. 2, p. 1.
Review of Rosencrantz & Guildenstern Are Dead (Broadway). Generally favorable, but notes that "Mr. Stoppard himself is watching too closely": the title characters "are not baffled and lost in their own ways [but] . . . in his, speaking his words for him, placarding his thoughts." Reprinted in 1967.B93 and 1969.B34.

81 KINGSTON, JEREMY. "Theatre." Punch 252 (19 April):577.
Review of Rosencrantz & Guildenstern Are Dead (London, National Theatre): a "witty, constantly enjoyable and visually delightful" production.

82 KNOX, COLLIE. "Letter from London." New York Morning Telegraph, 22 April, p. 3.
Favorable review of Rosencrantz & Guildenstern Are Dead

Writings about Tom Stoppard

1967

(London, National Theatre).

83 KRAFT, DAPHNE. "Guildenstern Alive, Rosencrantz, Too." Newark (N.J.) Sunday News, 17 December, sec. 6, p. 2.
    Interview with Brian Murray and John Wood, Rosencrantz and Guildenstern in the Broadway production. Covers various subjects, including the actors' conception of their characters' situation, British theatre since 1956, matinee performances, and the running time of the French production of the play.

84 KRETZMER, HERBERT. "The Play's Quite a Thing, Mr. Stoppard." Daily Express (London), 12 April, p. 5.
    Review of Rosencrantz & Guildenstern Are Dead (London, National Theatre): "a formidable work, . . . funny and profound and immensely skilful."

85 KROLL, JACK. "Rosencrantz and Guildenstern." Newsweek 70 (30 October):90, 92.
    Favorable review of the Broadway production.

86 LAWRENCE, ANN. "Televiews: Making the Convent Part of Small-Screen 'Show-Biz.'" Morning Star (London), 1 July, p. 2.
    Unfavorable review of "Another Moon Called Earth" (London, BBC Television).

87 LEWIS, PETER. "Faces in the Crowd Are Lords at Last." Daily Mail (London), 12 April, p. 12.
    Review of Rosencrantz & Guildenstern Are Dead (London, National Theatre): "an intricate and beautiful construction."

88 _____. "How Tom Went to Work on an Absent Mind and Picked up £20,000." Daily Mail (London), 24 May, p. 6.
    Interview following the opening of Rosencrantz & Guildenstern Are Dead (London, National Theatre): discusses changes in his life brought about by the play's success, his career as a reporter, and his procrastination while writing Lord Malquist & Mr Moon.

89 M., A. "Kurt Meisel: Ich Bin Kein Diktator." Illustrierte Kronenzeitung (Vienna), 15 October, p. 10.
    Interview (in German) with the director of Rosencrantz & Guildenstern Are Dead (Vienna, Akademietheater).

90 McCARTEN, JOHN. "The Theatre: The Outsiders." New Yorker 43 (28 October):105.
    Review of Rosencrantz & Guildenstern Are Dead (Broadway).

1967

91 MacLOUGHLIN, SHAUN. "'Another Moon Called Earth.'" Radio Times 175 (22 June):33.
 Brief interview: Stoppard speaks more explicitly than anywhere else about the play's theme.

92 MARLOWE, JOAN, and BLAKE, BETTY, eds. "Rosencrantz & Guildenstern Are Dead." New York Theatre Critics' Review 28 (23 October):254-57.
 Reprints of 1967.B29, 41, 45, 62, 134.

93 _____. "Rosencrantz & Guildenstern Are Dead." New York Theatre Critics' Review 28 (30 October):250.
 Reprint of 1967.B80.

94 MAROWITZ, CHARLES. "Writer in Our Midst." Village Voice, 4 May, p. 22.
 Review of Rosencrantz & Guildenstern Are Dead (London, National Theatre): although its "craft" is more original than its "thought," Stoppard "displays a remarkable skill in juggling the données of existential philosophy." The play "bounces off Shakespeare's play the way Hamlet bounces off The Spanish Tragedy." Reprinted, with an introduction, in 1973.B57; abridged in 1973.B68.

95 MELLY, GEORGE. "Rounding up the Global Platitudes." Observer (London), 2 July, p. 19.
 Brief review of "Another Moon Called Earth" (London, BBC Television): "an improbable fable" which "had something of the fussy dated quality of Christopher Fry."

96 MICK. "Shows out of Town: Rosencrantz & Guildenstern Are Dead." Variety, 27 September, p. 62.
 Review of the Washington, D.C. tryout of the Broadway production: although "funny, sometimes uproariously so," the play "demands a good deal of [its] audience."

97 NADEL, NORMAN. "London Theater: Rosencrantz and Guildenstern Are Dead." New York World Journal Tribune, 25 April, p. 20.
 Review of the London, National Theatre production of the "robustly funny play."

98 NICHOLS, CHRISTOPHER. "Theater: R & G: A Minority Report." National Review 19 (12 December):1393-95.
 Review of the Broadway production: excoriates the play as an Absurdist tract.

99 NORTON, ELLIOT. "Rosencrantz and Guildenstern." Boston Herald American, 29 October, p. A13.

1967

>   Review of the Broadway production: "a most extraordinarily original drama" in which "tragedy and farce are . . . shrewdly and truly integrated."

100 OPPENHEIMER, GEORGE. "On Stage: Rosencrantz, Guildenstern Alive and Well." Long Island City (N.Y.) Newsday, 17 October, p. 3A.
>   Review of Rosencrantz & Guildenstern Are Dead (Broadway): an "original, . . . wise and witty, and . . . compelling" play.

101 P., L. "Theater-Konzert: Total Verrückt Normal." Illustrierte Kronenzeitung (Vienna), 16 October, p. 14.
>   Review of Rosencrantz & Guildenstern Are Dead (Vienna, Akademietheater): finds the production's treatment of Stoppard's humor too heavy and the absurdity too philosophical. In German.

102 PALMER, RAYMOND. "Play by an Unknown Stuns British Theatre." Winnipeg Tribune, 15 July, Showcase section, p. 12.
>   Feature article with biographical data following the success of the London, National Theatre production of Rosencrantz & Guildenstern Are Dead. Based on more accessible articles; distributed by Associated Press. Reprinted in 1967.B103-4.

103 _____. "The London Scene." Philadelphia Inquirer, 16 July, p. 10.
>   Reprint of 1967.B102.

104 _____. "Unheralded Author Hit of London." Canton (Ohio) Repository, 16 July, p. 37.
>   Reprint of 1967.B102.

105 PANTER-DOWNES, MOLLIE. "Letter from London." New Yorker 43 (6 May):179-80.
>   Includes a brief review of Rosencrantz & Guildenstern Are Dead (London, National Theatre).

106 RAIDY, WILLIAM A. "Play on Bard's Buffoons Superb." Long Island Star Journal, 17 October, p. 4.
>   Favorable review of Rosencrantz & Guildenstern Are Dead (Broadway).

107 REYNOLDS, STANLEY. "Television." Guardian (London), 29 June, p. 6.
>   Review of "Another Moon Called Earth" (London, BBC Television): "a morality play" in which Stoppard's

1967

"stance wasn't argued with enough . . . logic."

108 _____. "Television: Brian Rix and Tom Stoppard." <u>Guardian</u> (London), 29 August, p. 5.
Review of "Teeth" (London, BBC Television): recalling Stoppard's former association with a radio serial about an Arab boy, notes that this play could be "a hasty retranslation from the Arabic."

109 RICHARDSON, BOYCE. "Rosencrantz and . . . What Did You Say His Name Was?" <u>Montreal Star</u>, 12 August, p. 30.
Review of <u>Rosencrantz & Guildenstern Are Dead</u> (London, National Theatre).

110 RICHARDSON, JACK. "Two New Plays." <u>Commentary</u> 44 (December): 82-84.
Includes a review of <u>Rosencrantz & Guildenstern Are Dead</u> (Broadway): notes that the title characters "really have no play for themselves, merely an ironic counterpoint to the drama we know is happening about them. Stoppard has discovered no action for them once they are on their own."

111 RISCHBIETER, HENNING. "Der Ersatz-<u>Hamlet</u>." <u>Theater Heute</u> 12 (December):34-38.
Review (in German) of three productions of <u>Rosencrantz & Guildenstern Are Dead</u>: Bochum, Schauspielhaus; Berlin, Schiller-Theater (the most vital and emphatic of the three); and Vienna, Akademietheater ("pompous"). Says the play is part of the British music-hall tradition which takes pleasure in "empty-minded chatter"; accordingly, the characters lack depth.

112 RUNDALL, JEREMY. "Radio: Destruction on the Bridge." <u>Sunday Times</u> (London), 16 July, p. 42.
Favorable review of "Albert's Bridge" (London, BBC Radio).

113 SHAKESPEARE, WILLIAM [pseud.]. "Drama Mailbag." <u>New York Times</u>, 17 December, sec. D, pp. 4, 13.
See 1967.B26.

114 SHEPARD, RICHARD F. "Hamlet's Chums Develop a Certain Affinity." <u>New York Times</u>, 23 October, p. 55.
Interview with Brian Murray and John Wood, Rosencrantz and Guildenstern in the Broadway production, who believe that "the two roles represent the two halves of the same person."

Writings about Tom Stoppard

1967

115 SHULMAN, MILTON. "Denmark's Dynamic Duo. . . ." Evening Standard (London), 12 April, p. 22.
 Review of Rosencrantz & Guildenstern Are Dead (London, National Theatre).

116 SIMON, JOHN. "Who's on First?" Commonweal 87 (10 November): 171-72.
 Review of Rosencrantz & Guildenstern Are Dead (Broadway): Stoppard's idea is "brilliant" and his "gift for words will last you one act, maybe two," but "for the full distance you need people and story as motor and vehicle."

117 _____. "Theatre Chronicle." Hudson Review 20 (Winter):664-65.
 Review of Rosencrantz & Guildenstern Are Dead (Broadway): a "literate and, for the first half, entertaining play." Unfortunately, "its idea is a conception of genius, which requires genius to develop it, whereas, in the event, it gets only cleverness and charm." Abridged in 1975.B96.

118 S[MITH], L[ISA] G[ORDON]. "Hamlet from the Inside." Stage and Television Today (London), 13 April, p. 19.
 Review of Rosencrantz & Guildenstern Are Dead (London, National Theatre).

119 SMITH, MICHAEL. "Theatre Journal." Village Voice, 26 October, pp. 27-28.
 Review of Rosencrantz & Guildenstern Are Dead (Broadway): an "immensely witty and charming play. . . . The drawback is Stoppard's attempt to push it to deep significance." Abridged in 1973.B68.

120 SPURLING, HILARY. "Arts: Prints of the Japanese Buskin." Spectator 218 (21 April):465.
 Includes a review of Rosencrantz & Guildenstern Are Dead (London, National Theatre), in which "a pair of green undergraduates" give vent to "all the clichés of the last ten years, . . . viewed without irony by their author."

121 STILES, PATRICIA. "The Book Review: Theater." Library Journal 92 (1 December):4432.
 Review of the text of Rosencrantz & Guildenstern Are Dead.

122 SULLIVAN, DAN. "Young British Playwright Here for Rehearsal of Rosencrantz." New York Times, 29 August, p. 27.
 Interview; Stoppard discusses the "pure farce" draft of the play written at his agent's suggestion after seeing

1967

Hamlet at the British National Theatre in 1964.

123 TALLMER, JERRY. "Closeup: Rosencrantz' Friend." New York Post, 8 December, p. 55.
Interview: Stoppard discusses his early life and career, Lord Malquist & Mr Moon, and Rosencrantz & Guildenstern Are Dead.

124 TAYLOR, JOHN RUSSELL. "The Road to Dusty Death." Plays and Players 14 (June):12-13, 15.
Mixed review of Rosencrantz & Guildenstern Are Dead (London, National Theatre), much of it incorporated into 1969.B54 and 1971.B20.

125 THIRKELL, ARTHUR. "Theatre." Daily Mirror (London), 12 April, p. 14.
Review of Rosencrantz & Guildenstern Are Dead (London, National Theatre).

126 TREWIN, J. C. "Theatre: The Proud Man Volumnia Bred." Illustrated London News 250 (22 April):33.
Includes a review of Rosencrantz & Guildenstern Are Dead (London, National Theatre), in which Stoppard's "agreeable notion . . . quiver[s] on the edge of the pretentious" because he "teased [it] out . . . to twice its natural length."

127 _____. "The New Plays." Lady (27 April):740.
Includes a review of Rosencrantz & Guildenstern Are Dead (London, National Theatre): a "tenuous and faint" play.

128 WADE, DAVID. "Radio Drama." Listener 78 (20 July):94.
Favorable review of "Albert's Bridge" (London, BBC Radio).

129 WAHLS, ROBERT. "Footlight: The Bard's Smothers Brothers." New York Sunday News, 26 November, sec. 2, p. 2.
Interview with Brian Murray and John Wood, Rosencrantz and Guildenstern in the Broadway production.

130 WARDLE, IRVING. "Shakespeare as Folklore." In The National Theatre: "Rosencrantz and Guildenstern Are Dead." Production program, 11 April, London, n.p.
Abridgement of 1966.B38.

131 _____. "Drama Unearthed from Elsinore's Depths." Times (London), 12 April, p. 8.

1967

>Review of <u>Rosencrantz & Guildenstern Are Dead</u> (London, National Theatre); particularly appreciates Stoppard's ability to relate the courtiers' "preoccupation with free will to the players, whose profession insists on fixed destiny." Reprinted in 1968.B84.

132 _____. "Don't Miss Stoppard's Radio Play." <u>Times</u> (London), 13 July, p. 8.

>Advance review of "Albert's Bridge" (London, BBC Radio). Praises the "cunningly plotted" action but not the "remorselessly articulate dialogue"; notes that, as in <u>Rosencrantz & Guildenstern Are Dead</u>, Stoppard balances "riddlesome metaphysical speculation against abrupt descents to the commonplace."

133 WATT, DOUGLAS. "Show Business: <u>R.&G.</u> Author Busy on Play for Next Season." <u>New York Daily News</u>, 21 October, p. 25.

>News item reporting Stoppard's work on <u>The Real Inspector Hound</u> and negotiations about the film rights to <u>Rosencrantz & Guildenstern Are Dead</u>.

134 WATTS, RICHARD, Jr. "A Drama of High Distinction." <u>New York Post</u>, 17 October, p. 62.

>Review of <u>Rosencrantz & Guildenstern Are Dead</u> (Broadway): "a superb play, . . . oddly moving as well as stimulating." Reprinted in 1967.B92.

135 _____. "Two on the Aisle: But Which One Is Guildenstern?" <u>New York Post</u>, 28 October, p. 22.

>Repeats the evaluation found in 1967.B134.

136 WEALES, GERALD. "To Be and Not to Be." <u>Reporter</u> 37 (16 November):39-40.

>Review of <u>Rosencrantz & Guildenstern Are Dead</u> (Broadway): calls Stoppard "the most interesting English playwright . . . since Harold Pinter." Abridged in 1973.B68.

137 WEIGHTMAN, JOHN. "Theatre: Mini-Hamlets in Limbo." <u>Encounter</u> 29 (July):38-40.

>Review of <u>Rosencrantz & Guildenstern Are Dead</u> (London, National Theatre): the play's "brilliant" idea is not "worked out with complete success"; moreover, "now and again, one suspects that Mr. Stoppard is trying to be genuinely poetic, [but] . . . the poetry is spurious."

138 WEST, ANTHONY. "Vogue's Notebook: Theatre." <u>Vogue</u> 150 (15 November):72.

>Review of <u>Rosencrantz & Guildenstern Are Dead</u> (Broad-

way): a "lighthearted display of intellectual vitality." Warns that American audiences may not share the British "national appetite for intricate word games [with] . . . private and parochial" references.

139 WHITMAN, DENNIS. Review of <u>Rosencrantz & Guildenstern Are Dead</u>. <u>London Life</u> (29 April):40.
Review of the "brilliant" London, National Theatre production.

140 WOODFORDE, JOHN. "The Rock Radio Rests On." <u>Sunday Telegraph</u> (London), 16 July, p. 11.
Includes a review of "Albert's Bridge" (London, BBC Radio).

141 YOUNG, B. A. "<u>Rosencrantz & Guildenstern Are Dead</u>." <u>Financial Times</u> (London), 12 April, p. 30.
Review of the London, National Theatre production: finds a "deeper question that dignifies the laughter with a serious purpose." Reprinted in 1968.B84.

1968

A BOOKS--NONE

B SHORTER WRITINGS

1 ADAMS, PHOEBE. "Potpourri." <u>Atlantic</u> 221 (May):114.
Favorable review of <u>Lord Malquist & Mr Moon</u>.

2 ANON. Photograph of Stoppard. <u>Times</u> (London), 1 January, p. 12.
Speaking at the National Student Drama Festival at Bradford.

3 ANON. "What to Look Out For." <u>Times</u> (London), 13 January, p. 19.
Announces the London opening of <u>Enter a Free Man</u> in March.

4 ANON. "<u>Plays and Players</u> 1967 Awards." <u>Plays and Players</u> 15 (February):37-43.
Reports the award of Best New Play to <u>Rosencrantz & Guildenstern Are Dead</u> in an article containing thirteen critics' brief comments about the 1967 London theatre season.

Writings about Tom Stoppard

1968

5   ANON. Review of <u>Lord Malquist & Mr Moon</u>. <u>Kirkus Service</u> 36 (1 February):142.
    Appreciates the novel's "wise nonsense" and "witty and often hilarious" style.

6   ANON. "Forecasts: Fiction." <u>Publishers' Weekly</u> 193 (5 February):64.
    Review of <u>Lord Malquist & Mr Moon</u>.

7   ANON. "Female Rosencrantz in Stoppard Play." <u>Times</u> (London), 22 February, p. 13.
    Review of <u>Rosencrantz & Guildenstern Are Dead</u> (Milan, Compagnia del Quattro): praises the director for realizing that the play's "strength . . . is not so much its content as its form," and notes that in this production "one feels less tempted than one did in London to talk of Pirandello and Beckett."

8   ANON. "Hochhuth's Next Play." <u>Times</u> (London), 9 March, p. 19.
    News item, including a notice of the London opening of <u>Enter a Free Man</u>.

9   ANON. "Polonaise." <u>Times Literary Supplement</u> (London), 21 March, p. 285.
    Review of the text of <u>Tango</u>: finds Stoppard's adaptation "more modern, nearer to English speech patterns" than the earlier translation.

10 ANON. Photograph. <u>Times</u> (London), 25 March, p. 6.
    The set for <u>Enter a Free Man</u> (London, West End).

11 ANON. "Stoppard Play Is Top of the Tonys." <u>Evening Standard</u> (London), 22 April, p. 1.
    News item, reporting that <u>Rosencrantz & Guildenstern Are Dead</u> had been named Best Play of the 1967-68 Broadway season in New York.

12 ANON. "Tom Stoppard's Tony Award." <u>Times</u> (London), 24 April, p. 8.
    News item, printed only in the Early (or Four Star) Edition, reporting that <u>Rosencrantz & Guildenstern Are Dead</u> had been named Best Play of the 1967-68 Broadway season in New York.

13 ANON. "The Talk of the Town: Playwright-Novelist." <u>New Yorker</u> 44 (4 May):40-41.
    Interview: Stoppard discusses the Hamburg, Germany,

1968

production of Enter a Free Man, his satisfaction with Lord Malquist & Mr Moon, and his early life and journalistic career.

14 ANON. "London Shows." Variety, 8 May, p. 255.
    News item, including the report of the closing of Enter a Free Man (London, West End).

15 ANON. "The Times Diary: The One That Got Away." Times (London), 8 May, p. 10.
    News item, reporting that the Pulitzer Prize committee would have nominated Rosencrantz & Guildenstern Are Dead or Peter Nichols' Joe Egg for the award had either been written by an American.

16 ANON. "What to Look Out For." Times (London), 18 May, p. 23.
    News item, announcing the opening of The Real Inspector Hound (London, West End).

17 ANON. "Briefly Noted: Fiction." New Yorker 44 (25 May):159.
    Review of Lord Malquist & Mr Moon.

18 ANON. "Czech Prize for Stoppard Play." Times (London), 28 May, p. 7.
    News item, reporting that "Albert's Bridge" had been named Best Radio Play in a Czechoslovakian international drama contest and that Stoppard had been offered a two-week vacation in Czechoslovakia as a prize.

19 ANON. "Anticipating the Drama Critics." Times (London), 29 May, p. 9.
    News item, reporting that The Real Inspector Hound would be the first new play in a West End theatre to have a week of paid preview performances instead of tryouts out of town.

20 ANON. "Fiction." Booklist 64 (15 June):1175.
    Review of Lord Malquist & Mr Moon.

21 ANON. "Rosencrantz Will Play Ahmanson, L. A., in March." Variety, 31 July, p. 58.
    News item reporting the play's opening in Los Angeles as part of the Center Theatre Group's season for 1969.

22 ANON. "Paperbacks: Lord Malquist & Mr Moon." Times (London), 10 August, p. 20.
    Review of the novel.

Writings about Tom Stoppard

1968

23 ANON. "Pick of the Paperbacks: Theater." Saturday Review 51 (31 August):27.
    Brief review of the text of Rosencrantz & Guildenstern Are Dead.

24 ANON. "Albert's Bridge." Washington Star Sunday Magazine, 1 September, pp. 6-7.
    Brief plot summary accompanying photographs of film and stage design elements used in the Washington, D.C., St. Albans School production.

25 ANON. "Hat-Trick for BBC." Times (London), 25 September, p. 6.
    News item reporting that three BBC productions, including "Albert's Bridge" (London, BBC Radio), had won Prix Italia awards.

26 ANON. News item about "Albert's Bridge." Times (London), 28 September, p. 19.
    Announces the London, BBC Radio production's receipt of the Prix Italia for radio drama.

27 ANON. "Broadway Perks Again." Variety, 23 October, p. 56.
    News items, including the closing date of Rosencrantz & Guildenstern Are Dead (Broadway). Reports a "nominal profit" for the Merrick Foundation.

28 ANON. "Language and Literature." Choice 5 (November):1134.
    Review of Lord Malquist & Mr Moon.

29 ANON. News item about "Neutral Ground." TV Times (30 November):49.
    Cast list and broadcast information about the Manchester, Granada Television Centre production.

30 BALL, IAN G. "Radio: Focus on Students." Scotsman (Edinburgh), 1 April, p. 4.
    Review of "Tango" (London, BBC Radio).

31 BARKER, FELIX. "Hordern Makes the Most of So Little." Evening News (London), 29 March, p. 3.
    Review of Enter a Free Man (London, West End), in which Michael Hordern's acting is so good that "we only just notice that Mr. Stoppard has done everything but provide him with a play."

32 _____. "Wishful Thinking by Another Mr. Barker." Evening News (London), 18 June, p. 3.

1968

Review of The Real Inspector Hound (London, West End).

33 BARNES, CLIVE. "The Theater: Playwrights and Critics." New York Times, 8 July, p. 45.
Review of The Real Inspector Hound (London, West End): "the humor is great, the fun is furious, but Stoppard's more serious portent . . . is never made apparent." Abridged in 1973.B68.

34 BILLINGTON, MICHAEL. "Television: Sophoclean Spy Tale." Times (London), 3 December, p. 12.
Review of "Neutral Ground" (Manchester, Granada Television Centre), praising Stoppard for exploiting "an effective, Le Carré-like situation . . . both for its moral content and its human values."

35 BOWEN, JOHN. "The Lively Arts." BBC Radio Third Programme (12 April).
Rebroadcast of 1967.B35. Transcript housed, London: BBC Written Archives Centre.

36 BRUSTEIN, ROBERT. "Waiting for Hamlet: Robert Brustein Reports from New York." Plays and Players 15 (January):51-52.
Includes a reprint of 1967.B37.

37 BRYDEN, RONALD. "Follow-Up Debut." Observer (London), 31 March, p. 31.
Review of Enter a Free Man (London, West End): the play "confirms that [Stoppard will] never be wholly serious."

38 _____. "A Critics' Nightmare." Observer (London), 23 June, p. 26.
Review of The Real Inspector Hound (London, West End): "an object of pure, virtuoso craft and display, luxurious and self-sufficient as a netsuke or Fabergé Easter egg." The play exemplifies Lionel Trilling's claim that art which "'delights . . . by the intentional relaxation of moral awareness . . . tells us as much about life's possibilities as moral intensity.'"

39 CASHIN, FERGUS. "Stoppard Takes a Step Backwards." Daily Sketch (London), 29 March, p. 23.
Review of Enter a Free Man (London, West End): "very slight and slightly sad and slightly comic and mainly boring."

1968

40 CASSIDY, CLAUDIA. "On the Aisle." Chicago Tribune, 18 March, p. 11.
    Favorable review of Rosencrantz & Guildenstern Are Dead (American touring production).

41 CAVANAUGH, ARTHUR. "Stage: Play Reviews." Sign 47 (January): 48-49.
    Review of Rosencrantz & Guildenstern Are Dead (Broadway): "for brilliance of idea and execution, theatrical excitement, gleaming language and flashing intellect, no other play in a decade is its equal."

42 CLAYTON, SYLVIA. "Spy Who Was Necessary Once More." Daily Telegraph (London), 3 December, p. 19.
    Mixed review of "Neutral Ground" (Manchester, Granada Television Centre).

43 CORODIMAS, PETER. Review of Lord Malquist & Mr Moon. Best Sellers 28 (1 May):61.
    Finds that, "although flecked with brilliant observations and witty aphorisms, the action . . . seems to form no meaningful pattern."

44 DARLINGTON, W. A. "Burlesque of Critics Involved on Stage." Daily Telegraph (London), 18 June, p. 19.
    Review of The Real Inspector Hound (London, West End): a "burlesque" of the way Rosencrantz & Guildenstern Are Dead had yanked "two men . . . out of their normal lives and . . . involved [them] in . . . a play."

45 DAWSON, HELEN. "Critics at Play." Plays and Players 15 (August):12, 14.
    Review of The Real Inspector Hound (London, West End). Stoppard "is a polisher and a parer . . . and makes his points cumulatively and with self-deceptive ease. And the fact that he also manages to be very funny . . . has . . . brought the response that before he can be said to have proved himself, he must tackle more angst-ridden territory."

46 DOWNER, ALAN S. "Old, New, Borrowed, and (a Trifle) Blue: Notes on the New York Theatre, 1967-1968." Quarterly Journal of Speech 54 (October):207-8.
    Includes a review of the "very nearly flawless" production of Rosencrantz & Guildenstern Are Dead (Broadway); compares the play to Waiting for Godot.

47 ESSLIN, MARTIN. "Two Trifles and a Failure." New York Times, 14 July, sec. 2, p. 4.

1968

Review of The Real Inspector Hound (London, West End), one of the "trifles."

48 EVSLIN, BERNARD. "A Cinder-Block Elsinore." Dimensions in American Judaism 2 (Spring):48-50.
   Review of Rosencrantz & Guildenstern Are Dead (Broadway), with analyses of the two protagonists' "marriage" and of the play's "stark confrontation" between "common" and "uncommon" man and between "modern drama" and "a more honorable species." Also explicates the theme of evil caused by blind obedience.
   Notes that all of these elements are united in the figure of the homosexual, whose fear makes him "obscenely adaptable." As the modern Utilitarian, obsessed with survival, he stand opposed to Hamlet, the Romantic obsessed with honor: the juxtaposition of the two figures shows "how very much we have lost." A response to this identification of Stoppard's courtiers with a homosexual couple is found in 1968.B67.

49 GIANAKARIS, C. J. "Absurdism Altered: Rosencrantz & Guildenstern Are Dead." Drama Survey 7 (Winter):52-58.
   Analysis: argues that the play "reconciles the disparities between drama anchored to personal/social responsibility" and drama written by Absurdist authors, who are "pledged to the stripping of hackneyed illusions." Stoppard's "jerringless laughter" indicates his sympathy with "men in their earthly dilemmas."

50 GORDON, DAVID J. "Some Recent Novels: Styles of Martyrdom." Yale Review 58 (October):121, 123-25.
   Includes a review of Lord Malquist & Mr Moon: claims that the title characters personify two responses to chaos in a novel in which "individual ideals . . . are seen as reflective purely of real social forces or of a given human condition." Abridged in 1973.B68 and 1975.B117.

51 GORDON, GILES. "Tom Stoppard." Transatlantic Review, no. 29 (Summer):17-25.
   Interview. Stoppard discusses the evolution of Rosencrantz & Guildenstern Are Dead, Enter a Free Man, and his short stories; his "distrust" of self-revelatory or autobiographical fiction; his reasons for preferring writing plays to novels; and literary and dramatic influences upon him, with emphasis on Samuel Beckett. Reprinted in 1971.B12.

52 GRANT, LOUIS T. "Of Cowboys, Animals, and a Coach and Six."

Writings about Tom Stoppard

1968

> Saturday Review 51 (29 June):25.
> Review of Lord Malquist & Mr Moon: "an arch, over-anxious comedy."

53 GREEN, JAMES. "Show News." Evening News (London), 23 March, p. 4.
    News item announcing the opening of Enter a Free Man (London, West End).

54 GUERNSEY, OTIS L., Jr., ed. "The New York Season." In The Best Plays of 1967-68. The Burns Mantle Yearbook. New York: Dodd, Mead & Company, p. 13.
    Analytical comments about Rosencrantz & Guildenstern Are Dead, in which "stand-ins for Everyman" are "interrupted in a happy-go-lucky course by overwhelming events."

55 HASTINGS, RONALD. "Rosencrantz Was Not the First." Daily Telegraph (London), 17 February, p. 13.
    Interview dealing with The Real Inspector Hound and the checkered history of Enter a Free Man (known in earlier incarnations as A Walk on the Water, The Preservation of George Riley, and Home and Dry).

56 HEWES, HENRY. "The Bests of the 1967-68 Theater Season." Saturday Review 51 (1 June):12-16.
    Summary review of the Broadway season, including Rosencrantz & Guildenstern Are Dead.

57 HOAGLAND, JOAN M. "Fiction." Library Journal 93 (1 April):1504.
    Review of Lord Malquist & Mr Moon.

58 HOBSON, HAROLD. "Critic through the Looking-Glass." Sunday Times (London), 23 June, p. 49.
    Review of The Real Inspector Hound (London, West End).

59 HOLLAND, MARY. "Plays." Queen 430 (24 April):25-26.
    Review of Enter a Free Man (London, West End): "a slight, and interesting, sketch for" Rosencrantz & Guildenstern Are Dead.

60 _____. "Cards of Identity." Plays and Players 15 (June):23.
    Review of Enter a Free Man (London, West End); notes the themes it shares with Rosencrantz & Guildenstern Are Dead.

61 _____. "Plays." Queen 431 (3 July):21.
    Review of The Real Inspector Hound (London, West End).

1968

62 HOPE-WALLACE, PHILIP. "Enter a Free Man." Guardian (London), 29 March, p. 8.
    Review of the London, West End production.

63 _____. "The Real Inspector Hound." Guardian (London), 18 June, p. 6.
    Review of the London, West End production.

64 HUMM. "Legit Followup: Rosencrantz and Guildenstern Are Dead." Variety, 7 August, p. 54.
    Favorable re-review of the Broadway production some months into its run.

65 IRONSIDE, VIRGINIA. "TV." Daily Mail (London), 3 December, p. 3.
    Favorable review of "Neutral Gound" (Manchester, Granada Television Centre).

66 JOEL, YALE. "'Who Are We?' 'I Don't Know.'" Life 64 (9 February):72-73.
    Two-page photograph of Brian Murray and John Wood, Rosencrantz and Guildenstern in the Broadway production. Accompanied by 1968.B89.

67 KAHN, ROBERT I. "Speaking Out: Homosexual Overtones." Dimensions in American Judaism 3 (Fall):63.
    Letter to the editor protesting the identification of Rosencrantz and Guildenstern as a homosexual couple in 1968.B48.

68 KINGSTON, JEREMY. "Theatre." Punch 254 (10 April):545.
    Review of Enter a Free Man (London, West End): notes that in Rosencrantz & Guildenstern Are Dead Stoppard had investigated the "limbo" in which his characters found themselves, while in Enter a Free Man he "is content to present just the situation."

69 _____. "Theatre." Punch 254 (26 June):933.
    Review of The Real Inspector Hound (London, West End).

70 KRETZMER, HERBERT. "Mini-Joke (Where the Critic Ends Up a Corpse) But No New Rosencrantz." Daily Express (London), 18 June, p. 5.
    Review of The Real Inspector Hound (London, West End): "an intermittently amusing sketch about the nature of identity."

71 LAMBERT, J. W. "The Life of Riley." Sunday Times (London),

1968

    31 March, p. 53.
    Favorable review of Enter a Free Man (London, West End).

72 LASK, THOMAS. "Books of The Times: Two on the Lighter Side." New York Times, 8 May, p. 45.
    Review of Lord Malquist & Mr Moon.

73 LEWIS, PETER. "A Free Man Suffering from Cramp." Daily Mail (London), 29 March, p. 14.
    Review of Enter a Free Man (London, West End), which Stoppard "would have been better advised to leave . . . in the junior league."

74 _____. "Critics Beware! This Is a Murder Warning." Daily Mail (London), 18 June, p. 10.
    Review of The Real Inspector Hound (London, West End).

75 LONEY, GLENN. "Broadway in Review." Educational Theatre Journal 20 (March):103.
    Includes a review of Rosencrantz & Guildenstern Are Dead (Broadway).

76 LOUIS, PATRICIA. "See the Father. See the Baby. See the Father Playing with the Baby. Doesn't the Father Look Happy? Yes, He Does." New York Times, 24 March, p. D3.
    Interview following the two-hundredth performance of Rosencrantz & Guildenstern Are Dead (Broadway). Focuses on Stoppard's lack of a consistent "philosophy" and his denial that any of his characters are spokesmen for his beliefs.

77 MADDOCKS, MELVIN. "Stoppard's Black-Froth Comedy." Christian Science Monitor, 11 April, p. 13.
    Review of Lord Malquist & Mr Moon, pointing out its similarity to Rosencrantz & Guildenstern Are Dead: both have a tone of "slightly romantic pessimism" and both are determined to "deal with the most serious questions in the most witty way."

78 MALONE, MARY. "The Spy Who Came Back to the Fold." Daily Mirror (London), 3 December, p. 18.
    Favorable review of "Neutral Ground" (Manchester, Granada Television Centre).

79 MARCUS, FRANK. "Theatre: Midsummer Madness." Sunday Telegraph (London), 23 June, p. 14.
    Review of The Real Inspector Hound (London, West End).

80 MAROWITZ, CHARLES. "Theater in London: From Rosencrantz to

1968

Our Time." New York Times, 7 April, sec. 2, p. 8.
Review of Enter a Free Man (London, West End): "a great steaming chestnut . . . warmed up from the murkiest naturalistic days of the last decade. . . . The work is played for comedy, invites pathos, is disposed to serious implications, but takes refuge in bursts of facile wit."

81 MARRIOTT, R. B. "A Successful Failure Doing What He Always Wanted to Do." Stage and Television Today (London), 4 April, p. 17.
Review of Enter a Free Man (London, West End).

82 _____. "From Wilde to Stoppard." Stage and Television Today (London), 20 June, p. 6.
Interview with Robert Chetwyn, director of The Real Inspector Hound (London, West End), who compares Stoppard to Wilde, mentions some of the play's technical problems, and explains how he tried to achieve a "nightmare feeling" at its climax.

83 _____. "Tom Stoppard on Plays and Critics and the Problem of Who's Who." Stage and Television Today (London), 20 June, p. 7.
Review of The Real Inspector Hound (London, West End).

84 MORGAN, GEOFFREY, ed. "Rosencrantz and Guildenstern Are Dead by Tom Stoppard." In Contemporary Theatre: A Selection of Reviews, 1966-67. London: London Magazine Editions, pp. 97-103.
Reprints of 1967.B38, 47, 72, 74, 131, and 141 (reviews of the London, National Theatre production).

85 NATHAN, DAVID. "Critics as Part of the Play." Sun (London), 18 June, p. 3.
Review of The Real Inspector Hound (London, West End): "a good joke gone to partial waste" because the parody of murder mysteries was poorly written.

86 OTTAWAY, ROBERT. "Too Bitter, to Be True. . . ." Daily Sketch (London), 3 December, p. 23.
Mixed review of "Neutral Ground" (Manchester, Granada Television Centre).

87 OVERMYER, JANET. "Feature Review: Lord Malquist and Mr. Moon." Ave Maria 109 (22 June):19-20.
Says the novel may "be read as either a brilliant, original farce or a warning polemic"; notes the similarity between Stoppard's themes and Kafka's, although "Stoppard's

1968

tone is considerably lighter."

88 PHILLIPS, JOHN L. "Surprisingly, Just an Ordinary Play." Stage and Television Today (London), 5 December, p. 12.
Mixed review of "Neutral Ground" (Manchester, Granada Television Centre).

89 PRIDEAUX, TOM. "Uncertainty Makes the Bigtime." Life 64 (9 February):75-76.
Feature article. Examines the success of Rosencrantz & Guildenstern Are Dead; notes Stoppard's comments about moral relativism, "progress," and social splintering in contemporary culture, and his insistence, nevertheless, that "it would be fatal . . . to set out to write primarily on an intellectual level. Instead, one writes about human beings under stress." Accompanied by 1968.B66.

90 PRITCHARD, WILLIAM H. "Fiction Chronicle." Hudson Review 21 (Summer):366.
Brief review of Lord Malquist & Mr Moon noting that "Stoppard's prose is immensely pleased with anything it can come up with."

91 PURSER, PHILIP. "Television: Singing Scots." Sunday Telegraph (London), 8 December, p. 15.
Brief review of "Neutral Ground" (Manchester, Granada Television Centre).

92 REYNOLDS, STANLEY. "Television: Tom Stoppard's 'Neutral Ground.'" Guardian (London), 3 December, p. 6.
Review of the Manchester, Granada Television Centre production: complains that Stoppard "once again shows a startling lack of originality in a television play."

93 RICH. "Shows Abroad: Enter a Free Man." Variety, 10 April, p. 66.
Review of the London, West End production: says the play seemed better suited to television than to the stage.

94 _____. "Shows Abroad: The Real Inspector Hound and The Audition." Variety, 10 July, p. 46.
Review of the London, West End production: calls the play an "elongated revue sketch idea."

95 RICHLER, MORDECAI. "The Bomb Misfired." New York Times Book Review, 25 August, p. 32.
Review of Lord Malquist & Mr Moon: "a sequence of clever, funny first acts" rather than "a developing, in-

Writings about Tom Stoppard

1968

evitable satire." Says Stoppard's tone is "too charming, too gentle" for the Absurdist material.

96 ROGERS, THOMAS. "Funny, Sad and British." New Republic 158 (15 June):37-38.
 Review of Lord Malquist & Mr Moon: it uses parody as "a way of looking with exuberant high spirits at a potentially dismaying reality. This gives the book its importance." Abridged in 1973.B68.

97 SAY, ROSEMARY. "Theatre: Despair with a Dying Fall." Sunday Telegraph (London), 31 March, p. 14.
 Review of Enter a Free Man (London, West End): "a neat, efficient, touching comedy that would have fitted more happily into . . . television."

98 SHORTER, ERIC. "Dreamy Inventor Is Undeveloped Theme." Daily Telegraph (London), 29 March, p. 19.
 Review of Enter a Free Man (London, West End).

99 SHULMAN, MILTON. "The Limelight Is Too Strong for These Dreams." Evening Standard (London), 29 March, p. 4.
 Review of Enter a Free Man (London, West End): the play is "disappointingly arch and obvious."

100 _____. "At the Theatre: But Why Hound the Critics?" Evening Standard (London), 18 June, p. 4.
 Review of The Real Inspector Hound (London, West End).

101 SIMMONS, CHARLES. "Rompings and Squeakings." New York 1 (6 May):58-59.
 Review of Lord Malquist & Mr Moon: it uses parody as the styles being parodied. Notes that he "couldn't really take Mr. Stoppard's nonsense seriously."

102 THIRKELL, ARTHUR. "Theatre." Daily Mirror (London), 29 March, p. 20.
 Review of Enter a Free Man (London, West End).

103 _____. "A First Rate Double Laugh." Daily Mirror (London), 18 June, p. 16.
 Review of The Real Inspector Hound (London, West End).

104 THORPE, MICHAEL. "Current Literature 1967." English Studies 49 (June):274-75.
 Review of the text of Rosencrantz & Guildenstern Are Dead.

1968

105 TREWIN, J. C. "Theatre: Enter a Free Man." Illustrated London News 252 (6 April):30.
    Review of the London, West End production.

106 _____. "The New Plays." Lady (18 April):720.
    Review of Enter a Free Man (London, West End).

107 _____. "Theatre: A Swipe at the Critics." Illustrated London News 252 (29 June):28.
    Review of The Real Inspector Hound (London, West End). Predicts that "it will annoy those in search of modern 'satire' at its most astringent" because Stoppard "seems to be doing most of it with mirrors [which] . . . reflect an eccentric world."

108 _____. "The New Plays." Lady (4 July):4.
    Brief favorable review of The Real Inspector Hound (London, West End).

109 TR[ILLING], O[SSIA]. "Biography: Stoppard, Tom." In Britannica Book of the Year: 1968. Chicago: Encyclopaedia Britannica, p. 163.
    Biographical information and summary of the production history of Rosencrantz & Guildenstern Are Dead.

110 WADE, DAVID. "Radio: Delights of Mzorek [sic] Play." Times (London), 27 March, p. 14.
    Review of Tango (London, BBC Radio): "a very powerful case for the proposition that if nothing is forbidden the end is barbarism."

111 _____. "Radio: Real Pleasure." Times (London), 5 October, p. 19.
    Comments that "Albert's Bridge" (London, BBC Radio) did not deserve the Prix Italia it won for radio drama.

112 WARDLE, IRVING. "Stoppard's Efficient Laughter Machine." Times (London), 29 March, p. 13.
    Review of Enter a Free Man (London, West End), which "proves . . . the power of theatrical convention to take over from the playright [sic]." Nor does the play "give . . . much of a chance" to Stoppard's "most conspicuous gifts," which are "for creating drama from a molecular interplay of ideas, and translating abstract speculation into fantastic events."

113 _____. "Evening of Actuality Games." Times (London), 18 June, p. 12.

Writings about Tom Stoppard

1968

Review of The Real Inspector Hound (London, West End), continued in 1968.B115. Claims that, because the two critics in the play "are as much creatures of fantasy" as the other characters, their entrance into the thriller gives "no sense of their breaking the barrier of illusion."

114 _____. "New Light Comedy by Tom Stoppard Playing in London." New York Times, 19 June, p. 38.
Review of The Real Inspector Hound (London, West End) for American readers. Repeats the criticism of 1968.B113.

115 _____. "Theatre: A Grin without a Cat." Times (London), 22 June, p. 19.
Continuing thoughts first expressed in 1968.B113: analyzes The Real Inspector Hound, Rosencrantz & Guildenstern Are Dead, Enter a Free Man, and "Albert's Bridge," in each of which Stoppard establishes "different planes of action" and subsequently negates all of them "by showing up every plane as equally unreal." While Pirandello always reveals "a face under the mask" and Beckett's "vacant world" is "charged with the sense of terminal anguish," Stoppard shows "no anguish, only the vacancy." Moreover, it is only when Stoppard's characters "set life at a distance [that they] get into a stride of confident eloquence. . . . They come to life by withdrawing from it."

116 WATTS, RICHARD, Jr. "Two on the Aisle: Drama Critics and Homicide." New York Post, 25 July, p. 29.
Favorable review of The Real Inspector Hound (London, West End).

117 WEILER, A. H. "They Only Die Twice." New York Times, 25 February, sec. D, p. 17.
News item reporting that M-G-M had purchased the film rights to Rosencrantz & Guildenstern Are Dead for $350,000 plus ten percent of the profits and that Bob Chartoff and Irwin Winkler would produce, John Boorman direct, and Stoppard write the screenplay for the film (but see 1970.B3).

118 _____. "Jazz Up Your Shakespeare." New York Times, 7 April, sec. D, p. 13.
News items, including a brief summary of 1968.B117.

119 WOLFF, GEOFFREY. "A Good, Funny Novel." Washington Post, 16 April, sec. A, p. 18.
Review of Lord Malquist & Mr Moon: "a remarkable entertainment."

1968

120 YOUNG, B. A. "Enter a Free Man." Financial Times (London), 29 March, p. 32.
   Review of the London, West End production.

121 _____. "The Real Inspector Hound." Financial Times (London), 19 June, p. 34.
   Review of the London, West End production, noting that the play uses the device of involving onlookers in a play as in Rosencrantz & Guildenstern Are Dead, but employs different materials to a different end.

122 ZOLOTOW, SAM. "Critics Pick Rosencrantz and Your Own Thing." New York Times, 26 April, p. 33.
   News item reporting that Stoppard's play had been named best play of the year by the New York Drama Critics' Circle.

1969

A BOOKS--NONE

B SHORTER WRITINGS

1 ALLDREDGE, DON. "Rosencrantz & Guildenstern Are Dead." In Masterplots: 1968 Annual. Edited by Frank N. Magill. New York: Salem Press, pp. 275-79.
   Analysis. Regards the play's circular structure and depiction of purposelessness and lack of control as evidence of its Absurdist orientation. Praises its theatricality, "sparkling and playful rhetoric, burlesque routines, and sly wit." Reprinted in 1971.B1.

2 ANON. "Rosencrantz and Guildenstern: Alive and Well at ACT." Sacramento Union, 27 April, sec. D, p. 14.
   Favorable review of the San Francisco, ACT production.

3 ANON. "Stoppard's R&G in South African Bow." Variety, 7 May, p. 253.
   News item reporting the opening of Rosencrantz & Guildenstern Are Dead in Capetown, South Africa.

4 ANON. "Two Plays by Stoppard." Times (London), 5 August, p. 13.
   News item announcing the Oxford Theatre Group's plans to adapt "Albert's Bridge" and "If You're Glad I'll Be Frank" to the stage for the Edinburgh Festival.

Writings about Tom Stoppard

1969

5   ANON. "Familiar Targets." <u>Times Literary Supplement</u> (London), 9 October, p. 1153.
    Brief favorable review of the texts of "Albert's Bridge" and "If You're Glad I'll Be Frank."

6   BARKER, CLIVE. "Contemporary Shakespearean Parody in British Theatre." <u>Shakespeare Jahrbuch</u> 105:109-14.
    Examines <u>Rosencrantz & Guildenstern Are Dead</u>, among other plays: declares that it has "a complete lack of cohesion or intellectual integrity."

7   BARRON, KARL. "<u>Rosencrantz</u> . . . in a Brilliant Staging." <u>San Rafael</u> (Calif.) <u>Independent Journal</u>, 25 April, p. 15.
    Favorable review of the San Francisco, ACT production.

8   BATDORFF, EMERSON. "<u>Rosencrantz</u> Not Dead but Alive and Ailing." <u>Cleveland Plain Dealer</u>, 4 June, sec. C, p. 6.
    Review of the American touring production, which "seems to have . . . much portent" but "actually says little."

8a BATES, MERETE. "The Students Play to the Whistle." <u>Guardian</u> (London), 8 September, p. 6.
    Includes reviews of stage adaptations of "Albert's Bridge" and "If You're Glad I'll Be Frank" (Edinburgh, Oxford Theatre Group): "sure, delicate elucidations of nightmares, . . . poetical rather than dramatic."

9   BLADEN, BARBARA. "Theatre Marquee." <u>San Mateo</u> (Calif.) <u>Times</u>, 25 April, p. 17.
    Review of <u>Rosencrantz & Guildenstern Are Dead</u> (San Francisco, ACT).

10 BLEVINNS, WINIFRED. "Civil War, All War, on Canvas." <u>Los Angeles Herald Examiner</u>, 8 June, sec. E, p. 4.
    Includes a review of <u>Rosencrantz & Guildenstern Are Dead</u> (San Francisco, ACT): the production reveals "that the script can seem less extraordinary when not handled by deft and fully expert comic actors."

11 BRADBROOK, M[URIEL] C. "Old Things Made New." In <u>Shakespeare the Craftsman: The Clark Lectures 1968</u>. London: Chatto & Windus, pp. 122-43.
    Briefly discusses <u>Rosencrantz & Guildenstern Are Dead</u> as an "absurd" parody of <u>Hamlet</u> in which "the anguish of Hamlet is transferred to the two little men caught up into his drama."

12 BRUSTEIN, ROBERT. "Waiting for Hamlet." In <u>The Third</u>

1969

   Theatre. New York: Alfred A. Knopf, pp. 149-53.
   Reprint of 1967.B37; abridged in 1975.B96.

13 CALLEN, ANTHONY. "Stoppard's Godot: Some French Influences on Post-War English Drama." New Theatre Magazine 10 (Winter):22-30.
   Briefly discusses the influence of Ionesco upon N. F. Simpson and of Beckett upon Pinter; primarily devoted to similarities between Waiting for Godot and Rosencrantz & Guildenstern Are Dead, particularly in plot, language, and qualities of their protagonists.
   Also notes, however, that Stoppard "seems to doubt" the existentialists' vision, despite the fact that his use of Hamlet is similar to Sartre's use of Greek myth in The Flies. Claims that Stoppard's failure to write as economically as Beckett reduces the impact of his play.

14 CLALIP, ALICE GRACE. "ACT Joke Falls Flat." Alameda (Calif.) Times-Star, 9 July, p. 21.
   Unfavorable review of Rosencrantz & Guildenstern Are Dead (San Francisco, ACT).

15 COHEN, NATHAN. "Rosencrantz and Friend beyond Heart Transplant." Daily Star (Toronto), 7 January, p. 18.
   Review of Rosencrantz & Guildenstern Are Dead (American touring production): "Tom Stoppard has taken a clever idea and harried it into the ground" with his "third-rate pseudoserious cerebration."

16 ____. "Hamlet: After Being Performed for 367 Years It's Here Again." Daily Star (Toronto), 18 October, p. 49.
   News item announcing the openings of Rosencrantz & Guildenstern Are Dead and Hamlet (Toronto, Royal Alexandria Theatre).

17 ____. "This Rosencrantz Is a Very Dull One." Daily Star (Toronto), 21 October, p. 26.
   Review of the Toronto, Royal Alexandria Theatre production: the play applies "a thick patina of commercial varnish to some outmoded experimental techniques and viewpoints."

18 COMPTON, RUSS, and NICKOLSON, LEONARD. "Two Critics View Rosencrantz and Guildenstern." Mill Valley (Calif.) Pacific Sun, 7 May, p. N7.
   Reviews expressing opposite opinions of the San Francisco, ACT production.

Writings about Tom Stoppard

1969

19 CURCIO, CHRIS. "ACT's Architect an Excuse for Vulgarity." California State University (Hayward) Pioneer (15 April), p. 5.
   Includes a brief review of Rosencrantz & Guildenstern Are Dead (San Francisco, ACT).

20 DAY-LEWIS, SEAN. "Radio Drama." Drama: The Quarterly Theatre Review, no. 94 (Autumn):58-59.
   Review of the texts of "Albert's Bridge" and "If You're Glad I'll Be Frank": two "clever ideas" made pleasurable by "the verbal skill with which Stoppard pursues" them.

21 DETTMER, ROGER. "Drama: Rosencrantz, Guildenstern." Chicago Today, 29 April, sec. 2, p. 14.
   Favorable review of the American touring production.

22 DURBAND, ALAN, ed. Introduction to Playbill Two. London: Hutchinson Educational, pp. 8-11.
   Includes brief biographical notes and a summary of "A Separate Peace."

23 EICHELBAUM, STANLEY. "A Scintillating Offshoot of Hamlet." San Francisco Examiner, 23 April, p. 29.
   Review of Rosencrantz & Guildenstern Are Dead (San Francisco, ACT): the production was "in many ways better than the one . . . in New York."

24 F., R. "Stoppard." Stage and Television Today (London), 4 September, p. 14.
   Review of stage adaptations of "Albert's Bridge" and "If You're Glad I'll Be Frank" (Edinburgh, Oxford Theatre Group).

25 FANNING, GARTH. "The Bard Yields a Modern Nugget." Sacramento (Calif.) Bee, 27 April, Leisure section, p. 16.
   Favorable review of Rosencrantz & Guildenstern Are Dead (San Francisco, ACT).

26 FLAHERTY, PAT. "This Spoof on Hamlet Rip-Roaring, Slam-Bang." San Jose (Calif.) Mercury-News, 4 May, p. 7E.
   Favorable review of Rosencrantz & Guildenstern Are Dead (San Francisco, ACT).

27 GOLDMAN, WILLIAM. The Season: A Candid Look at Broadway. New York: Harcourt, Brace & World, pp. 113-14.
   Characterizes Rosencrantz & Guildenstern Are Dead as a "Snob Hit," i.e., a play which encourages elitism because, being British and "at least a little unintelligible," it

1969

allows the viewer to believe that most other people would not like it."

28 HARRIS, SYDNEY J. "Rosencrantz--Caviar in the Theater." Chicago Daily News, 29 April, p. 32.
    Favorable review of the American touring production.

29 HEWES, HENRY. "The Theater: Re: ACT." Saturday Review 52 (5 July):20.
    Review of Rosencrantz & Guildenstern Are Dead (San Francisco, ACT): unlike the "elegiac" Broadway production, this one "unabashedly exploits the use of farcical device and tour de force."

30 HINCHLIFFE, ARNOLD P. The Absurd. Critical Idiom series. London: Methuen & Co., pp. 85, 87.
    Brief analytical comments suggesting that Rosencrantz & Guildenstern Are Dead has "anthologized absurd features." Found it "at once funny and not even mildly disturbing--and hence its popularity."

31 HOBSON, HAROLD. "Edinburgh Theatre: Fringe Benefits." Sunday Times (London), 7 September, p. 52.
    Review of the stage adaptations of "Albert's Bridge" and "If You're Glad I'll Be Frank" (Edinburgh, Oxford Theatre Group), the former "a very impressive study of subjective reality."

32 _____. "At Edinburgh: Stage's Morality under Fire." Christian Science Monitor, 13 September, p. 6.
    Reviews the Festival for American readers: calls the stage adaptations of "Albert's Bridge" and "If You're Glad I'll Be Frank" (Edinburgh, Oxford Theatre Group) "the very best thing on the Fringe."

33 KENNEDY, ANDREW K. "Old and New in London Now." Modern Drama 11 (February):437-42.
    Reviews and analyses, including Rosencrantz & Guildenstern Are Dead (London, National Theatre) and The Real Inspector Hound (London, West End). The "real pressure" of the former derives from "thought about the theatre rather than from any more personal experience"; the latter is "a comedy of juxtaposition, where . . . one false world merges into another . . . to engender a brilliant piece." In both, Stoppard uses parody to reflect his moral relativism: it is "as if [he] surveyed the world of action with something like a neutrally ironic god's eye-view." Abridged in 1975.B117.

Writings about Tom Stoppard

1969

34 KERR, WALTER. "The Comedy that Kills." In Thirty Plays Hath November: Pain and Pleasure in the Contemporary Theater. New York: Simon & Schuster, pp. 50-53.
    Reprint of 1967.B80.

35 KNICKERBOCKER, PAINE. "A Comedy at Elsinore." San Francisco Chronicle, 24 April, p. 50.
    Favorable review of Rosencrantz & Guildenstern Are Dead (San Francisco, ACT).

36 KUEHL, BROOKS. "Hamlet in Bizarre Setting." Concord (Calif.) Transcript, 30 April, p. 10.
    Review of Rosencrantz & Guildenstern Are Dead (San Francisco, ACT).

37 LEE, R. H. "The Circle and Its Tangent." Theoria: A Journal of Studies in the Arts, Humanities and Social Sciences 33 (October):37-43.
    Analysis of Rosencrantz & Guildenstern Are Dead. Suggests that the play juxtaposes seventeenth- and twentieth-century views of the world, represented by Hamlet and Waiting for Godot: whereas the former believed in tragedy (requiring acceptance of causality, of the purposefulness of events, and of the explicability of that purpose), the latter does not (one dies before one understands). For a reaction against this analysis, see 1970.B24.

38 LEONARD, WILLIAM. "R&G Are Dead Brings Life to Hamlet Legend." Chicago Tribune, 27 April, sec. 5, pp. 7-8.
    Feature story, posing as an interview, based on 1967.B61.

39 _____. "Stoppard's Rosencrantz an Entertaining Enigma." Chicago Tribune, 29 April, sec. 2, p. 5.
    Favorable review of the American touring production.

40 MACCOUN, WENDY. "Modern Hamlet Reviewed." Vallejo (Calif.) Times-Herald, 3 May, p. TV11.
    Review of Rosencrantz & Guildenstern Are Dead (San Francisco, ACT).

41 MASTROIANNI, TONY. "R & G Are Dead Sparks with Life." Cleveland Press, 3 June, p. D2.
    Favorable review of the American touring production.

42 MATTER, SAM. "Rosencrantz and Guildenstern: A Play to Stand for All Time." Miami Beach Sun Reporter, 27 February, p. 12.

Writings about Tom Stoppard

1969

    Favorable review of the Miami, Coconut Grove Playhouse production.

43 MICK. "Repertory-Stock Reviews: Albert's Bridge." Variety, 16 July, p. 68.
    Review of the Washington, D.C., St. Albans Repertory Theatre staging of the radio play.

44 NACHMAN, GERALD. "Stage and Screen." Oakland (Calif.) Tribune, 24 April, p. 47.
    Review of Rosencrantz & Guildenstern Are Dead (San Francisco, ACT).

45 NICHOLS, DOROTHY. "New Play Given Brilliant Staging." Palo Alto (Calif.) Times, 23 April, p. 29.
    Review of Rosencrantz & Guildenstern Are Dead (San Francisco, ACT).

46 PETERSON, ROLFE. "Can a Naked Behind Express a Beautiful Thought?" San Francisco Bay Guardian, 22 May, p. 12.
    Includes a review of Rosencrantz & Guildenstern Are Dead (San Francisco, ACT).

47 PLOTTEL, ESTHER. "A Comical Tragedy." Hillsborough (Calif.) Boutique, 29 April, p. 2.
    Review of Rosencrantz & Guildenstern Are Dead (San Francisco, ACT).

48 QUINN, JAMES E. "Rosencrantz and Guildenstern Are Alive in the Classroom." Missouri English Bulletin 26 (15 October): 16-19.
    Contains plot summary, biographical information about Stoppard, and topics for classroom discussion or compositions. Also published by ERIC, number ED 035 649.

49 REID, WALTER. "Around the Fringe." Scotsman (Edinburgh), 30 August, p. 7.
    Review of the stage adaptations of "Albert's Bridge" and "If You're Glad I'll Be Frank" (Edinburgh, Oxford Theatre Group), two "jeus d'esprit. Within each full-blown play there is a revue sketch struggling to get out."

50 SCHLÖSSER, ANSELM. "Zur Bedeutung der Anachronismen bei Shakespeare." Shakespeare Jahrbuch 105:18.
    Brief analytical comments (in German) about Rosencrantz & Guildenstern Are Dead, which "represents the modern capitalistic economic wonderland with its crises, automation and unemployment, electronic brains and criminality, hyper-

1969

sensibility and naked barbarism."

51 STUTZIN, LEO. "Rosencrantz, Guildenstern Are Alive and Funny in S F." Modesto (Calif.) Bee, 27 April, p. A8.
    Favorable review of Rosencrantz & Guildenstern Are Dead (San Francisco, ACT).

52 SWAEBLY, FRANCES. "Drama Review: R & G Great, but Production Uneven." Miami Herald, 27 February, p. 5D.
    Mixed review of the Miami, Coconut Grove Playhouse production.

53 SYSE, GLENNA. "At the Back Door of Elsinore: A Clever Conceit on Hamlet." Chicago Sun-Times, 29 April, p. 57.
    Review of Rosencrantz & Guildenstern Are Dead (American touring production). Finds its reputation for "distinction and significance" unwarranted: it is "sometimes a very clever conceit, sometimes merely a childish one."

54 TAYLOR, JOHN RUSSELL. The Angry Theater: New British Drama. Revised and expanded edition. New York: Hill & Wang, pp. 314, 318-20.
    Contains brief analyses of Rosencrantz & Guildenstern Are Dead, Enter a Free Man, and "Albert's Bridge" which did not appear in the book's first edition (published in Great Britain as Anger and After).
    For the most part, repeats his evaluation of Stoppard found in 1967.B124: finds him "clever but rather bloodless." Biographical data marred by errors. Expanded and brought up to date in 1971.B20.

55 TURAN, KENNY. "Actors Don't Live Up to Parts." Fremont (Calif.) News Register, 26 April, Entertainment section, p. 7.
    Review of Rosencrantz & Guildenstern Are Dead (San Francisco, ACT).

56 YEOMANS, JEANNINE. "A Drama for Those of Us with 'Bit Parts' in Life." Contra Costa (Calif.) Times, 11 May, p. 4B.
    Review of Rosencrantz & Guildenstern Are Dead (San Francisco, ACT).

1970

A BOOKS

1 ROGERS, F. W., ed. Oregon Shakespearean Festival Teacher's

1970

<u>Manual for Tom Stoppard's "Rosencrantz & Guildenstern Are Dead."</u> [Ashland, Oreg.]: Oregon Shakespearean Festival Association, 34 pp.
    Handbook containing an analysis of the play, biographical data about Stoppard, suggested questions for discussion, and sample student essays.

B   SHORTER WRITINGS

1 A., E. "Opening Night Play Called Sort of Parable of Life." <u>Medford</u> (Oreg.) <u>Mail Tribune</u>, 23 March, p. 9.
    Review of <u>Rosencrantz & Guildenstern Are Dead</u> (Ashland, Oregon Shakespearean Festival): may have challenged the audience more than they had expected.

2 ANON. "Eating People Is Metaphorical." <u>Times Literary Supplement</u> (London), 15 January, p. 54.
    Includes a review of the text of <u>Enter a Free Man</u>.

3 ANON. "The Times Diary: Non Stop." <u>Times</u> (London), 11 April, p. 8.
    Interview: Stoppard discusses <u>After Magritte</u>, the failure of <u>Rosencrantz & Guildenstern Are Dead</u> to be filmed, plans to film "Albert's Bridge" and <u>Lord Malquist & Mr Moon</u>, and his hopes to have a full-length play (<u>Jumpers</u>) completed by September.

4 ANON. "Troupe at Olney, Md., Sets Foreign Plays." <u>Variety</u>, 20 May, p. 57.
    News item listing the summer's season at the Olney Playhouse, including <u>Enter a Free Man</u>.

5 ANON. "<u>Albert's Bridge</u>." <u>Stage and Television Today</u> (London), 24 September, p. 1.
    News item announcing an extension of the run of the play, adapted for the stage in a London lunch-time theatre production (Lamb and Flag).

6 ANON. "Speech, Theater and Dance." <u>Choice</u> 7 (October):1066-67.
    Review of the text of <u>The Real Inspector Hound</u>.

7 ASMUS, WALTER D. "<u>Rosencrantz and Guildenstern Are Dead</u>." <u>Jahrbuch der Deutschen Shakespeare-Gesellschaft West</u> 106: 118-31.
    Criticism of Stoppard's "literary-aesthetic frivolity." Finds its "alleged depths" to be "shallows" and its meta-

1970

phoric values out of touch with reality. Comments upon the splinter-like, associative nature of the dialogue, from which deeper resonances arise almost accidentally; notes that the "pseudoreflection" in which the characters engage "seems . . . forced, in fact parodistic," since it does not influence their actions.

8   B., D. F. "Albert's Bridge." Stage and Television Today (London), 17 September, p. 15.
    Review of the stage adaptation (London, Lamb and Flag): "practically nothing is gained" by transferring the play from radio to the stage.

9   B., P. W. "Surrealism Takes Over." Stage and Television Today (London), 16 April, p. 13.
    Review of After Magritte (London, Ambiance Lunch-Hour Theatre).

10 BARNES, CLIVE. "Stage: Rosencrantz & Guildenstern." New York Times, 19 November, p. 39.
    Favorable review of the New York, Classic Stage Company production.

11 BEAUCHAMP, EMERSON. "The Passing Show: Enter a Warm and Human Comedy." Washington Evening Star, 5 August, p. C12.
    Review of Enter a Free Man (Olney, Maryland; Olney Theatre). "Structurally [the play] leaves a good deal to be desired, but it contains ample evidence of Stoppard's gift for dialogue and eye for humanity."

12 BERLINER, MILTON. "Olney Theater Scores with Stoppard Comedy." Washington Daily News, 6 August, p. 41.
    Review of Enter a Free Man (Olney, Maryland; Olney Theatre): finds that Stoppard's "sensitive" depiction of the characters' relationships is undercut by the "limitations of the [play's] situation."

13 BISHOFF, DON. "Stage II Opening Spectacular." Eugene (Oreg.) Register-Guard, 23 March, sec. A, p. 11.
    Review of Rosencrantz & Guildenstern Are Dead (Ashland, Oregon Shakespearean Festival): a "wildly funny . . . sense-making venture into the nonsensical world of theater of the absurd."

14 BLADEN, BARBARA. "Theatre Marquee." San Mateo (Calif.) Times, 16 April, p. 12.
    Review of Rosencrantz & Guildenstern Are Dead (San Francisco, ACT revival).

*15 BONDY, FRANCOIS. "Tendenzen des 'neuen Theaters,' I: Rede auf einer Dramaturgentagung." Merkur: Deutsche Zeitschrift für europäisches Denken 24 (October):963-71.
    Analysis (in German); claims that the unity of the

1970

theatre of the 1950's, centered in Paris, is being shaken by playwrights' recent interest in ritual, elitist theatre, and the revival of classic plots and themes (e.g., Rosencrantz & Guildenstern Are Dead). (Annotation summarizes account of article in Abstracts of English Studies: 1974.)

16 BOYD, JUDITH. "The Critics: A Double Act--and Destiny." Bath & Wilts Evening Chronicle (Bristol), 28 August, p. 13.
Favorable review of Rosencrantz & Guildenstern Are Dead (Bristol, Bristol Old Vic Company).

17 BRIEN, JEREMY. "Comedy Is Ideal Choice for Bristol Old Vic." Evening Post (Bristol), 27 August, p. 27.
Review of the Bristol company's production of Rosencrantz & Guildenstern Are Dead: appreciates the text but expresses mixed feelings about the production.

18 COE, RICHARD L. "Enter a Free Man." Washington Post, 6 August, sec. B, p. 10.
Favorable review of the Olney, Maryland, Olney Theatre production.

19 CURCIO, CHRIS. "A.C.T. Brings Back Rosencrantz." California State University (Hayward) Pioneer, 17 April, p. 3.
Review of the San Francisco company's revival.

20 _____. "What Went Wrong at ACT This Year?" California State University (Hayward) Pioneer, 22 July, p. 7.
Includes a brief review of the revival of Rosencrantz & Guildenstern Are Dead by the San Francisco company.

21 D., T. "R & G Are Alive!" Ashland (Oreg.) Siskiyou, 17 April, p. 5.
Favorable review of Rosencrantz & Guildenstern Are Dead (Ashland, Oregon Shakespearean Festival).

22 de JONGH, NICHOLAS. "After Magritte at the Green Banana." Guardian (London), 10 April, p. 8.
Favorable review of the London, Ambiance Lunch-Hour Theatre production.

23 FILICHIA, PETER. "Stoppard's Hound." Boston after Dark, 21 January, pp. 4, 5.
Review of The Real Inspector Hound (Boston, Emerson College): "the best play to appear in Boston this season."

24 GARDNER, C. O. "Correspondence: Rosencrantz and Guildenstern Are Dead." Theoria: A Journal of Studies in the Arts, Humanities and Social Sciences 34 (May):83-84.

Writings about Tom Stoppard

1970

Letter to the editor in reaction against 1969.B37. Claims that the play "does not merit serious critical attention" because it is a potpourri of styles and themes received at second and third hand.

25 GLOVER, WILLIAM. "A Top Start for Ashland." Salem (Oreg.) Capital Journal, 23 March, sec. 1, p. 6.
    Favorable review of Rosencrantz & Guildenstern Are Dead (Ashland, Oregon Shakespearean Festival).

26 HAMLIN, MILTON. "Four Plays at Bowmer Theatre." Seattle North Central Outlook, 2 April, p. 12.
    Includes a brief favorable review of Rosencrantz & Guildenstern Are Dead (Ashland, Oregon Shakespearean Festival).

27 HEARN, LAWRENCE. "R. & G. Are Dead Comedy Dazzles." Berkeley (Calif.) Gazette, 15 April, p. 28.
    Favorable review of the revival by the ACT in San Francisco.

28 HEWES, HENRY. "The Theater: Oregon Expands." Saturday Review 53 (11 April):20.
    Includes a mixed review of Rosencrantz & Guildenstern Are Dead (Ashland, Oregon Shakespearean Festival).

29 HINXMAN, MARGARET. "The Uses of Telly." Sunday Telegraph (London), 23 August, p. 10.
    Review of The Engagement (London, Memorial Enterprises).

30 JOHNSON, WAYNE. "Ashland Has Good Production." Seattle Times, 1 April, p. C8.
    Includes a favorable review of Rosencrantz & Guildenstern Are Dead (Ashland, Oregon Shakespearean Festival).

31 KNICKERBOCKER, PAINE. "Shorter and Funnier Now." San Francisco Chronicle, 15 April, p. 47.
    Favorable review of Rosencrantz & Guildenstern Are Dead (San Francisco, ACT revival).

32 LANDMANN, DAVID. "Pomp and Two Competent Productions: Ashland's Stage II Dedicated." Grants Pass (Oreg.) Daily Courier, 23 March, p. 6.
    Includes a mixed review of Rosencrantz & Guildenstern Are Dead (Ashland, Oregon Shakespearean Festival).

33 LOCKHART, FREDA BRUCE. "Films: Short but Highly Professional." Catholic Herald (London), 28 August, p. 6.

Writings about Tom Stoppard

1970

    Favorable review of The Engagement (London, Memorial Enterprises).

34 McNAY, MICHAEL. "Adalen 70." Guardian (London), 20 August, p. 8.
    Review of The Engagement (London, Memorial Enterprises).

35 MAHAR, TED. "Pan on Shakespeare Appropriately Opens Ashland's New Indoor Theatre." Portland Oregonian, 23 March, sec. 1, p. 15.
    Favorable review of Rosencrantz & Guildenstern Are Dead (Ashland, Oregon Shakespearean Festival).

36 MALLETT, RICHARD. "Cinema." Punch 259 (26 August):314.
    Favorable review of The Engagement (London, Memorial Enterprises).

37 MANSAT, A. "Rosencrantz et Guildenstern Sont Morts." Les Langues Modernes 64 (September-October):396-400.
    Analysis (in French). Claims that "literature offers few examples where the will to depersonalize has been pushed so far": not even Swift, whose "morbid taste for the game of massacre" Stoppard shares, "pushed pessimism to absolute negation."
    Argues that Stoppard's characterization, treatment of the "spatial and temporal dimensions," and language deny his characters a sense of self and thereby refuse them existence; that the pervasive influence of Death in the play "makes the reading of it . . . almost unbearable" for the French public (while the British are more comfortable with "this type of tragicomic 'burlesque,'" which achieves "'grotesque, . . . often atrocious" effects by depicting man's "most wretched infirmities"); and that Stoppard's thought is dominated by despair.

38 MARKS, ARNOLD. "Entertainment." Portland Oregon Journal, 25 March, sec. 2, p. 7.
    Favorable review of Rosencrantz & Guildenstern Are Dead (Ashland, Oregon Shakespearean Festival).

39 MEHL, DIETER, ed. "Tom Stoppard: Rosencrantz and Guildenstern Are Dead." In Das englische Drama: Von Mittelalter bis zur Gegenwart. Vol. 2. Düsseldorf: August Bagel, pp. 336-46.
    Criticism (in German): analyzes the play's relationship to Absurdism and its "entirely new illumination of" Hamlet. Claims that, while using Absurdist techniques and motifs, its "brilliance of wit," playfully facile jokes,

1970

and use of montage prevent the appearance of that "icy lack of contact or hopelessness" present in Beckett's plays, and its inclusion of scenes from Hamlet leads to "repeatedly surprising constellations" which simultaneously alienate the classic and "bring it into a stimulating proximity."

40 MICK. "Stock Review: Enter a Free Man." Variety, 19 August, p. 59.
   Review of the Olney, Maryland, Olney Theatre production: finds that the play's "daffy comedy" is successful, but its "serious family drama . . . seems sour by comparison."

41 MILLER, JEANNE. "Hamlet's Spies Are Still Alive." San Francisco Examiner, 14 April, p. 27.
   Review of Rosencrantz & Guildenstern Are Dead (San Francisco, ACT revival).

42 PETER, JOHN. "Theatre: Gruesome Threesome." Sunday Times (London), 12 April, p. 28.
   Includes a brief review of After Magritte (London, Ambiance Lunch-Hour Theatre).

43 PHILLIPS, PEARSON. "Have a Laugh for Lunch." Daily Mail (London), 10 April, p. 14.
   Favorable review of After Magritte (London, Ambiance Lunch-Hour Theatre).

44 POWELL, DILYS. "Films: As Long as They're Happy." Sunday Times (London), 23 August, p. 24.
   Review of The Engagement (London, Memorial Enterprises).

45 ROBINSON, DAVID. "Edinburgh Preview." Financial Times (London), 21 August, p. 3.
   Review of The Engagement (London, Memorial Enterprises).

46 ROSENBERG, ARTHUR. "Rosencrantz, Guildenstern Are Dead." University of Pittsburgh Pitt News, 10 March, pp. 7-8.
   Favorable review of the university's production.

47 RUNDALL, JEREMY. "Radio: Old School Ties." Sunday Times (London), 20 December, p. 24.
   Review of "Where Are They Now?" (London, BBC Radio): "a near flawless miniature by a craftsman utterly at home with his tools."

48 S., R. "R and G ACT Production a Memorable Experience." Sacramento Union, 19 April, sec. B, p. 4.

Writings about Tom Stoppard

1970

      Review of the San Francisco company's revival.

49 SALT, GARY. "ACT Resurrects Smash Hit Rosencrantz and Guildenstern." Stanford (Calif.) Daily, 17 April, p. 4.
      Review of the San Francisco company's revival.

50 SHORTER, ERIC. "His Own Man." Daily Telegraph (London), 21 August, p. 9.
      Review of The Engagement (London, Memorial Enterprises).

51 SIMON, JOHN. "Piddling Profundities." New York 3 (4 October): 54.
      Review of Rosencrantz & Guildenstern Are Dead (New York, Classic Stage Company): Stoppard's "ingenious, stimulating play" did not receive the "visually suggestive and brilliantly staged and acted production" it requires.

52 SMELTZER, VENE. "Ashland Series a Success for Local Theatre-Goer." Livermore (Calif.) Independent, 26 April, p. 7B.
      Includes a review of the "disappointing" Rosencrantz & Guildenstern Are Dead (Ashland, Oregon Shakespearean Festival).

53 SOKOLOV, RAYMOND A. "Snake Oil." Newsweek 76 (31 August): 77.
      Favorable review of Enter a Free Man (Olney, Maryland, Olney Theatre).

54 S[TARK], L[ARRY]. "Hamlet's Sidekicks at Tufts." Boston after Dark, 20 October, p. 27.
      Review of Rosencrantz & Guildenstern Are Dead (Boston, Tufts University).

55 S[TASIO], M[ARILYN]. "Rosencrantz and Guildenstern Are Dead." Cue 39 (1 August):8.
      Favorable review of the Williamstown, Mass., Williamstown Theatre production.

56 STASIO, MARILYN. "On the Theatre Scene." Cue 39 (12 December):27.
      Favorable review of Rosencrantz & Guildenstern Are Dead (New York, Classic Stage Company).

57 STUTZIN, LEO. "R & G Revival Loses Depth but Retains High Theatrical Quality." Modesto (Calif.) Bee, 19 April, p. B6.
      Mixed review of the San Francisco, ACT revival.

1970

58 _____. "Successful Shows Add Up to Unexciting Season." Modesto (Calif.) Bee, 12 August, p. C9.
   Includes a brief review of Rosencrantz & Guildenstern Are Dead (San Francisco, ACT revival).

59 SULLIVAN, DAN. "Ruta Carries Tempest Role at the Geary." Los Angeles Times, 6 July, sec. 4, pp. 1, 15.
   Contains a brief review of Rosencrantz & Guildenstern Are Dead (San Francisco, ACT revival).

60 TAYLOR, JOHN RUSSELL. "After Magritte." Plays and Players 17 (May):47.
   Review of the London, Ambiance Lunch-Hour Theatre production. Summarized in 1971.B20.

61 _____. "British Dramatists: The New Arrivals: No. 4: Tom Stoppard: Structure + Intellect." Plays and Players 17 (July):16-18, 78.
   Abridgement of 1971.B20, containing brief analyses and plot summaries of Rosencrantz & Guildenstern Are Dead, After Magritte, and The Real Inspector Hound. Expresses fewer reservations about Stoppard's work than does the later, more complete piece.

62 _____. "Our Changing Theatre, No. 3: Changes in Writing." BBC Radio Four (23 November).
   Transcript of interview in BBC Play Library (Radio). Stoppard discusses the importance of Beckett and Pinter and his early love of Death of a Salesman, insists that while writing he is concerned with technical rather than social or thematic matters, and talks of his respect for plays which blend freedom and discipline ("a free mind working within a disciplined form"). Summarized in 1971.B20.

63 TAYLOR, ROBERT. "Geary Comedy Chilling." Oakland (Calif.) Tribune, 21 April, p. 39.
   Favorable review of Rosencrantz & Guildenstern Are Dead (San Francisco, ACT revival).

64 WADE, DAVID. "Radio." Times (London), 28 November, p. 18.
   Contains a brief review of the edited broadcast of 1970.B62.

65 _____. "'Where Are They Now?' Radio 3." Times (London), 18 December, p. 16.
   Review of the London, BBC Radio, production. Praises Stoppard's craftsmanship but notes that "the incidents . . .

1970

seem . . . not quite resonant--they may arouse private recall, [sic] whether they refer to any more general theme I doubt."

66 WARDLE, IRVING. "Lunch-Time Stoppard." Times (London), 10 April, p. 16.
    Review of After Magritte (London, Ambiance Lunch-Hour Theatre). Claims that whereas "surrealism . . . should never explain itself," Stoppard abandoned "surrealism so as to give [his audience] a good time."

67 _____. "A Link Is Cut." Times (London), 2 July, p. 7.
    Review of Rosencrantz & Guildenstern Are Dead (London, National Theatre) in its third season, with a completely new cast.

68 WASHBURN, MARTIN. "Classics in the Present Tense." Village Voice, 26 November, p. 59.
    Favorable review of Rosencrantz & Guildenstern Are Dead (New York, Classic Stage Company): notes that the play is "more in the continental than the English tradition."

69 WEAVER, GAY. "Rosencrantz Top Rank Every Way." Palo Alto (Calif.) Times, 14 April, p. 15.
    Favorable review of the San Francisco, ACT revival.

70 WILLIAMS, BOB. "On the Air." New York Post, 9 March, p. 63.
    Review of the "failure" of The Engagement (NBC Television).

71 WILLIAMS, JAMES E. "R and G Are Dead Has a Lot of Life." San Rafael (Calif.) Independent Journal, 14 April, p. 18.
    Favorable review of the San Francisco, ACT revival.

72 WILSON, CECIL. "Film: Comedy of a Nobody Is Short and Sweet." Daily Mail (London), 19 August, p. 8.
    Favorable review of The Engagement (London, Memorial Enterprises).

73 WOLFE, MICHAEL. "Walk-On Duo Gives ACT Another Plus." Mill Valley (Calif.) Record, 29 April, p. 2.
    Favorable review of Rosencrantz & Guildenstern Are Dead (San Francisco, ACT revival).

1971

A BOOKS--NONE

Writings about Tom Stoppard

1971

B SHORTER WRITINGS

1 ALLDREDGE, DON. "Rosencrantz and Guildenstern Are Dead." In Survey of Contemporary Literature: Updated Reprints of 1500 Essay-Reviews from Masterplots Annuals: 1954-1969. Edited by Frank N. Magill. Vol. 6. New York: Salem Press, pp. 4002-5.
   Despite the book's subtitle, the essay is a reprint of 1969.B1.

2 ANON. "A Pair of Happy Tragedians." Teacher 88 (19 February): 6.
   Favorable review of Rosencrantz & Guildenstern Are Dead (Cambridge, Cambridge Theatre Company).

3 B., D. F. "Almost-Free Double Bill." Stage and Television Today (London), 16 December, p. 37.
   Review of Dogg's Our Pet (London, Inter-Action Trust).

4 B[ARBER], J[OHN]. "Planks & Tubes Galore for Witty Workman." Daily Telegraph (London), 9 December, p. 14.
   Favorable review of Dogg's Our Pet (London, Inter-Action Trust).

5 BAUMGART, WOLFGANG. "Hamlet's Excellent Good Friends: Beobachtungen zu Shakespeare und Stoppard." In Englische Dichter der Moderne: Ihr Leben und Werk. Edited by Rudolf Sühnel and Dieter Riesner. Berlin: Erich Schmidt, pp. 588-98.
   Analysis (in German) of Rosencrantz & Guildenstern Are Dead as an example of the contemporary impulse to dethrone the classical hero (Hamlet) in favor of less worthy figures.

6 BILLINGTON, MICHAEL. "Stoppard at the Almost Free Theatre." Guardian (London), 9 December, p. 10.
   Favorable review of Dogg's Our Pet (London, Inter-Action Trust).

7 BROICH, ULRICH. "Montage und Collage in Shakespeare-Bearbeitungen der Gegenwart." Poetica 3-4:333-60.
   Analysis (in German); includes a brief examination of Rosencrantz & Guildenstern Are Dead, in which Stoppard uses collage (the employment of a model as a backdrop) as opposed to montage (the remounting of a classic).

8 BULL, JUDITH. "Briefing." Observer (London), 13 June, p. 23.

1971

Brief review of the text of After Magritte: a "very short, very sharp surreal play."

*8a CARROLL, PETER. "They Have Their Entrances and Their Exits: Rosencrantz and Guildenstern Are Dead." Teaching of English 20:50-60.
Listed in MLA International Bibliography.

9 DAWSON, HELEN. "Theatre: Good-Natured Goldsmith." Observer (London), 12 December, p. 24.
Includes a brief favorable review of Dogg's Our Pet (London, Inter-Action Trust).

10 ESSLIN, MARTIN. "Dramatic Ironies: Old Illusions, New Directions." Encounter 31 (July):74-78.
Contains a brief review of the text of After Magritte, Stoppard's "charming extravagance."

11 FUNKE, LEWIS. "One from Tennessee, One from Tom." New York Times, 19 December, pp. 3, 43.
News items, including an announcement of the opening of After Magritte and The Real Inspector Hound (New York, Theatre Four).

12 GORDON, GILES. "Tom Stoppard." In Behind the Scenes: Theater and Film Interviews from "The Transatlantic Review." Edited by Joseph F. McCrindle. New York: Holt, Rinehart & Winston, pp. 77-87.
Reprint of 1968.B51.

13 GROSVENOR-MYER, M. "Cambridge: Rosencrantz." Guardian (London), 18 February, p. 10.
Review of the Cambridge, Cambridge Theatre Company production, which, by stressing the role of the Player, makes the "piece . . . a play about the theatre rather than [an] existential study of the role of the attendant lord in isolation from the main action."

14 GUTHKE, KARL S., ed. "Die Metaphysische Farce im Theater der Gegenwart: Von Les Chaises bis Tiny Alice." In Die Mythologie der entgötterten Welt: Ein literarisches Thema von der Aufklärung bis zur Gegenwart. Göttingen: Vandenhoek & Ruprecht, pp. 331-32.
Brief analysis of Rosencrantz & Guildenstern Are Dead (in German), noting that the vagueness of its references to metaphysical forces recommends it to an age which tries to avoid making direct and unambiguous statements. Revised (in English): 1976.B56.

Writings about Tom Stoppard

1971

15 HOBSON, HAROLD. "Brave New Theatre." Sunday Times (London), 12 December, p. 29.
    Feature article about Ed Berman, director of Dogg's Our Pet (London, Inter-Action Trust); includes brief comments about the play.

16 KILLINGER, JOHN. World in Collapse: The Vision of Absurd Drama. Delta Books. New York: Dell Publishing Co., pp. 156-59.
    Analysis of Rosencrantz & Guildenstern Are Dead: relates the play to contemporary society's "loss of the vertical dimension, of holiness."

17 LEVENSON, JILL. "Views from a Revolving Door: Tom Stoppard's Canon to Date." Queen's Quarterly 78 (Autumn):431-42.
    Analysis of "Albert's Bridge," "If You're Glad I'll Be Frank," Lord Malquist & Mr Moon, The Real Inspector Hound, and Rosencrantz & Guildenstern Are Dead, all of which set out to "examine possible solutions to a problem" (i.e., how is one to "live reasonably in a world that makes no sense?"), but finally reject all the alternatives, leaving "the problem acutely unresolved."
    Claims that Stoppard's characters are similar to Beckett's in that, whereas they are "sympathetic" and "vulnerable," their "significance is generic, not individual," because "their pain and . . . hopes are real, [but] they are not." Abridged in 1975.B117.

18 MARCUS, FRANK. "Theatre: The Essence of Goldsmith." Sunday Telegraph (London), 12 December, p. 14.
    Includes a brief review of Dogg's Our Pet (London, Inter-Action Trust).

19 NAKANISHI, MASAKO. "Tom Stoppard no Sekai-Kyoko to Genjitsu no Mondai" [Tom Stoppard's world: the problem of illusion and reality]. Oberon 13 (December):53-71.
    Analysis of the problem of illusion and reality in Enter a Free Man (where the two are distinct), Rosencrantz & Guildenstern Are Dead (where mask and illusion are the sole reality), The Real Inspector Hound, and After Magritte.

20 TAYLOR, JOHN RUSSELL. "Tom Stoppard." In The Second Wave: British Drama for the Seventies. New York: Hill & Wang, pp. 94-107.
    Biographical information, analyses, and plot summaries of After Magritte, "Another Moon Called Earth," "The Dissolution of Dominic Boot," Enter a Free Man, "If You're Glad I'll Be Frank," "Neutral Ground," The Real Inspector

1971

Hound, Rosencrantz & Guildenstern Are Dead, "A Separate Peace," "Teeth," and "Where Are They Now?" Concludes that Stoppard is concerned with tight, logical structure and that his plays usually exhibit his "metaphysical unease"; nevertheless, he "lacks . . . fundamental seriousness. . . . His ideas remain . . . on the level of fancy rather than imagination."
Chapter contains many opinions found in author's earlier 1967.B124, 1969.B54, and 1970.B60-62; its summary evaluation is abridged in 1975.B97.

21 WARDLE, IRVING. "Stoppard Beginning." Times (London), 15 December, p. 18.
Favorable review of Dogg's Our Pet (London, Inter-Action Trust).

22 WILLIAMS, DAVID H. "Reviews: Tom Stoppard: After Magritte." New Theatre Magazine 11:30-31.
Review of the text of the play; notes that it "plays the same tricks with action and the pictorial side of the theatre that [Stoppard] had previously done with words alone."

1972

A BOOKS--NONE

B SHORTER WRITINGS

1 ALLAN, ELKAN. "The Sunday Times Critical Viewers' Guide to the Week's Television." Sunday Times (London), 2 July, p. 52.
Preview description of "One Pair of Eyes: Tom Stoppard Doesn't Know" (London, BBC Television).

2 ANDERSON, MARJORY. "Weekend: Woman's Hour." BBC Radio Four (15 March).
Interview: Stoppard discusses absence of specific social issues in his plays and problems he had writing Jumpers. Repeated 1 July 1972. Transcript housed, London: BBC Written Archives Centre.

3 ANDERSON, MICHAEL; GUICHARNAUD, JACQUES; MORRISON, KRISTIN; ZIPES, JACK D.; et al., eds. "Tom Stoppard." In A Handbook of Contemporary Drama. London: Pitman Publishing, pp. 428-29.

Writings about Tom Stoppard

1972

Brief plot summaries and analytical comments about The Real Inspector Hound and Rosencrantz & Guildenstern Are Dead (in which Stoppard's mixture of "wit, sentiment, theatrical inventiveness, and apparent profundity" caught the mood of the late 1960s).

4 ANON. "Stoppard, Tom." In Who's Who in the Theatre: A Biographical Record of the Contemporary Stage. Originally compiled by John Parker. 15th ed. London: Pitman Publishing, p. 1448.
   Biographical information, list of plays, Stoppard's home address, agent's name and address.

5 ANON. "Playwright and His Wife Granted Decrees." Times (London), 1 February, p. 3.
   News item reporting Stoppard's divorce from his first wife and his plans to marry Dr. Miriam Moore-Robinson.

6 ANON. "Interview with Tom Stoppard." In The National Theatre: "Jumpers." Production program, 2 February, London, n.p.
   Stoppard discusses the large number of characters named Moon and Boot in his works, their origins in other writers' works and in his own personality, and his dislike of talk about the "existentialism" and "cosmic significance" of Rosencrantz & Guildenstern Are Dead.

7 ANON. "The Saturday Review/Jonathan Cape Detective Story Competition." Times (London), 19 February, p. 6.
   News item announcing Stoppard's participation as a judge of the entries. Also see 1972.B12-13.

8 ANON. "The Times Diary: Rosenberg and Goldenstern." Times (London), 14 March, p. 14.
   Brief news item reporting a letter writer's misspelling of the play's title.

9 ANON. "The Times Diary." Times (London), 1 April, p. 14.
   News item announcing BBC radio's transmission of "Is 'Is' Is?"

10 ANON. "Angels." New York Show Business, 11 May, p. 22.
    News item listing the backers of After Magritte and The Real Inspector Hound (New York, Theatre Four).

11 ANON. "Miscellany: Stage Rights Preserved." Guardian (London), 14 June, p. 13.
    News item quoting Stoppard's claim that "Artist De-

1972

scending a Staircase" is "a radio play that no one will be able to adapt for the stage."

12 ANON. Photograph. Times (London), 15 June, p. 21.
   Stoppard and the other judges of the Saturday Review/Jonathan Cape Detective Story Competition.

13 ANON. Detective story winners. Times (London), 17 June, p. 8.
   News item announcing the names of the winners and judges (including Stoppard) of the Saturday Review/Jonathan Cape Detective Story Competition. (Collection was published by Jonathan Cape in 1972 and by John Day in 1973 as The "Times" of London Anthology of Detective Stories.)

14 ANON. "Stoppard Play Opens European Drama Project." Stage and Television Today (London), 9 November, p. 14.
   News item announcing the transmission of "Artist Descending a Staircase" (London, BBC Radio), written for a consortium of fifteen European broadcasting companies that commissioned it.

15 ANON. "Sky-Blue Life & After Magritte." University of Bristol Baccus, 16 November, p. 5.
   Favorable review of the Bristol New Vic production.

16 ANON. "Londoner's Diary." Evening Standard (London), 24 November, p. 20.
   News item speculating on the size of Stoppard's commission for "Artist Descending a Staircase."

17 ANON. "National Theatre Wins Lion's Share of Awards." Times (London), 12 December, p. 2.
   News item, including a report that Jumpers received the Plays and Players Best Play award as well as a special citation by the magazine's editor as "Most Overrated Play of the Year." See 1973.B2-3.

18 ANON. Review of Jumpers. Times Literary Supplement (London), 29 December, pp. 1569-70.
   Review of the text; claims that "no actor speaking this . . . jargon can talk and move at the same time. . . . Jumpers is textbook stuff which reduces both the actors and the audience to the level of readers."

19 ARTHUR, DOUG. "Rosie and Guildenstern Return." Stanford (Calif.) Daily, 13 January, p. 5.
   Review of the ACT's second revival in San Francisco.

Writings about Tom Stoppard

1972

20 AYER, A. J. "Love among the Logical Positivists." Sunday Times (London), 9 April, p. 16.
    Less a review than a collection of "comments inspired by" Jumpers (London, National Theatre), written by the British philosopher whose logical positivism is one of the play's subjects.
    Agrees with some of the criticisms advanced by the play's protagonist; refutes others; admires Stoppard's parody of philosophical writing; insists that, the play to the contrary, "even logical positivists are capable of love." Translated and abridged in 1973.B12; 1976.B16.

21 BABULA, WILLIAM. "The Play-Life Metaphor in Shakespeare and Stoppard." Modern Drama 15 (December):279-81.
    Brief analytical article noting that, like Hamlet, Stoppard's courtiers in Rosencrantz & Guildenstern Are Dead use the stage as a metaphor for life and think of themselves as actors. But whereas Hamlet has the part of the avenger "thrust upon" him, finds it "hackneyed and debasing," and struggles to be more than a stereotypical ranter, Stoppard's characters find themselves playing roles which are not so much tasteless as "baffling." Also includes some comments about The Real Inspector Hound.

22 BALL, IAN G. "Radio: Stoppard Radio Play." Scotsman (Edinburgh), 20 November, p. 9.
    Favorable review of "Artist Descending a Staircase" (London, BBC Radio).

23 BARBER, JOHN. "Comedy as Erudite as It Is Dotty." Daily Telegraph (London), 3 February, p. 11.
    Review of Jumpers (London, National Theatre), which, unlike Rosencrantz & Guildenstern Are Dead, "lacks the firm underpinning of a sober and powerful myth. . . . The result is inevitably flimsy."

24 BARKER, FELIX. "First Night: Theatre: Jumpers." Evening News (London), 3 February, p. 3.
    Favorable review of the London, National Theatre production.

25 BARNES, CLIVE. "Theater: Two One-Acters by Stoppard." New York Times, 24 April, p. 41.
    Review of After Magritte and The Real Inspector Hound (New York, Theater Four), the latter "rather like Joe Orton without the bite or bitterness, and . . . too flimsy to be especially satisfying." But compare with 1972.B27.

1972

26 _____. "Stage: A London Trio." New York Times, 9 August, p. 24.
  Includes a review of Jumpers (London, National Theatre): proves Stoppard to be "one of the most dazzling wits and surprising minds ever to turn up in the history of British theater."

27 _____. "Theater: A 2d Look at Tom Stoppard Double Bill." New York Times, 16 October, p. 46.
  Second review of After Magritte and The Real Inspector Hound (New York, Theatre Four): unlike 1972.B25, declares them "intellectually stimulating and civilized to just short of a fault."

28 BEAUFORT, JOHN. "Two by Stoppard." Christian Science Monitor, 26 April, p. 4.
  Review of the New York, Theatre Four production of After Magritte ("a ridiculous game of words, enigmas, images and semantics") and The Real Inspector Hound ("the more ingenious" of the two).

29 BEER, PATRICIA. "Radio." Listener 88 (23 November):728.
  Review of "Artist Descending a Staircase" (London, BBC Radio).

30 BILLINGTON, MICHAEL. "Jumpers at the Old Vic." Guardian (London), 3 February, p. 10.
  Review of the London, National Theatre production, which, "under the guise of a madcap farce, [is] . . . deeply moral."

31 BLADEN, BARBARA. "Amusing Losers Revived." San Mateo (Calif.) Times, 13 January, p. 15.
  Favorable review of Rosencrantz & Guildenstern Are Dead (San Francisco, ACT second revival).

32 BOOKSPAN, MARTIN. Review of After Magritte and The Real Inspector Hound. WPIX-TV, Channel 11 (23 April).
  Favorable review of the New York, Theatre Four production. Copy filed in Lincoln Center Theatre Collection, New York Public Library.

33 BOSKIN, LOUISE. "Jumpers." Jewish Voice (Southend-on-Sea, G.B.), 24 March, p. 5.
  Review of the London, National Theatre production.

34 BRIEN, JEREMY. "They'll Pack 'Em in When Word Gets Round." Evening Post (Bristol), 1 November, p. 2.

Writings about Tom Stoppard

1972

Favorable review of <u>After Magritte</u> (Bristol New Vic).

35 BRUKENFELD, DICK. "Theatre: Theatre in the Wry." <u>Village Voice</u>, 27 April, p. 66.
    Review of <u>After Magritte</u> and <u>The Real Inspector Hound</u> (New York, Theatre Four): their "outrageousness . . . a bit mild, a bit genteel, a little too controlled and commercial."

36 BUCKLEY, LEONARD. "'One Pair of Eyes.'" <u>Times</u> (London), 8 July, p. 11.
    Review of the London, BBC Television production, which was "pleasant and even, perhaps, hilarious, if a trifle pretentious at times."

37 CALTA, LOUIS. "Miss Mercouri to Do <u>Lysistrata</u> in Fall: 2 Short Plays by Stoppard." <u>New York Times</u>, 28 March, p. 48.
    News items, one of them announcing the openings of <u>After Magritte</u> and <u>The Real Inspector Hound</u> (New York, Theatre Four).

38 CHAMPLIN, CHARLES. "Antic Magic of London Stage." <u>Los Angeles Times</u>, 2 June, sec. 4, pp. 1, 14.
    Review of <u>Jumpers</u> (London, National Theatre).

39 CLURMAN, HAROLD. "Theatre." <u>Nation</u> 214 (15 May):636-38.
    Reviews, including <u>After Magritte</u> and <u>The Real Inspector Hound</u> (New York, Theatre Four): "undergraduate pranks seasoned by . . . airs of sharp sophistication and British toniness. . . . Such things . . . I shall refrain from designating as silly ass snobbery."

40 CURCIO, CHRIS. "<u>Rosencrantz</u> Revival Wears a Little Thin." <u>Hayward</u> (Calif.) <u>Daily Review</u>, 18 January, p. 11.
    Mixed review of the San Francisco, ACT second revival.

41 CUSHMAN, ROBERT. "The Moon Is on the Other Foot." In <u>The National Theatre: "Jumpers."</u> Production program, 2 February, London, n.p.
    Feature article about Stoppard's habit of naming characters Moon and Boot containing quotations from Stoppard on the subject and brief analytical comments about his plays.

42 DAVIES, MARTIN. "Rocks on the Moon." <u>Evening Echo</u> (Southend-on-Sea, G.B.), 3 February, p. 3.
    Review of <u>Jumpers</u> (London, National Theatre).

43 DAWSON, HELEN. "A Very Public Passing." <u>Observer</u> (London),

1972

    6 February, p. 31.
      Review of *Jumpers* (London, National Theatre).

44 DAY-LEWIS, SEAN. "Television: Extreme Example of 'Don't Know' Man." *Daily Telegraph* (London), 8 July, p. 7.
    Review of "One Pair of Eyes: Tom Stoppard Doesn't Know" (London, BBC Television).

45 _____. "Real Radio of Tom Stoppard." *Daily Telegraph* (London), 15 November, p. 15.
    Review of "Artist Descending a Staircase" (London, BBC Radio): Stoppard is "the best thing that has happened to English drama since . . . Pinter."

46 de JONGH, NICHOLAS. "*Inspector Hound*." *Guardian* (London), 8 November, p. 10.
    Review of *After Magritte* and *The Real Inspector Hound* (London, Dolphin Theatre Company), the latter Stoppard's "sharpest and most important work."

47 DONALD, ANABEL. "Death of Illusion." *Catholic Herald* (London), 18 February, p. 6.
    Review of *Jumpers* (London, National Theatre).

48 [DONALDSON, ANNE.] "Zany Set of Characters in Stoppard's New Play." *Glasgow Herald*, 7 February, p. 2.
    Review of *Jumpers* (London, National Theatre): an "exploration of ideas" through "a series of beautifully contrived theatrical patterns."

49 EICHELBAUM, STANLEY. "A Clever Play Splendidly Revived." *San Francisco Examiner*, 12 January, p. 26.
    Favorable review of *Rosencrantz & Guildenstern Are Dead* (San Francisco, ACT second revival).

50 FERRIS, PAUL. "Radio: Tempting Carrot." *Observer* (London), 19 November, p. 37.
    Mixed review of "Artist Descending a Staircase" (London, BBC Radio); claims Stoppard's commission came to £5000.

51 FIDDICK, PETER. "'One Pair of Eyes': Tom Stoppard on Television." *Guardian* (London), 8 July, p. 8.
    Review of the London, BBC Television production: "45 minutes of . . . unsettling ideas, brilliant paradoxes, and extraordinarily good jokes."

52 FRANKEL, HASKEL. "The New York Stage." *National Observer* 11 (13 May):22.

1972

Review of After Magritte and The Real Inspector Hound (New York, Theatre Four).

53 GOTTFRIED, MARTIN. "The Real Inspector Hound." Women's Wear Daily, 24 April, p. 12.
   Review of the New York, Theatre Four production (with After Magritte). Notes that neither this play nor Rosencrantz & Guildenstern Are Dead "could . . . exist without the pre-existence of another drama" and that in neither does Stoppard give an "indication of a voice or style of his own." Reprinted in 1972.B89.

54 GRAHAM, SIDNEY. "ACT's Rosencrantz Said Superb Theatre." Contra Costa (Calif.) Times (20 January), p. 7C.
   Favorable review of the San Francisco company's second revival.

55 GREEN, VALERIE. "Forget the Avenger, Meet the Dazzler." Evening Gazette (Essex, G.B.), 3 February, p. 5.
   Favorable review of Jumpers (London, National Theatre).

56 GUERNSEY, OTIS L., Jr., ed. "The New York Season." In The Best Plays of 1971-72. The Burns Mantle Yearbook. New York: Dodd, Mead & Co., p. 37.
   Brief analytical comments about After Magritte and The Real Inspector Hound, two "entertaining exercises in the absurd."

57 GUSSOW, MEL. "Stoppard Refutes Himself, Endlessly." New York Times, 26 April, p. 54.
   Interview. Stoppard discusses why he was "an awful critic" during his journalistic career; says that, unlike Beckett, he writes "absolutely traditional straight plays," and defines playwriting as "a respectable way of contradicting yourself."
   Also discusses plays: The Real Inspector Hound is about "the danger of getting what you want"; Jumpers is partially an anti-behaviorist work and partially a reflection of the conflict between his emotions and his rationality concerning God's existence; After Magritte is the result of his desire to "exhibit an absolutely bizarre set of components within an academician context." Also contains some comments about what later became Travesties.

58 H., D. "Stoppard Pleads for a Little Mystery." Evening Post (Bristol), 3 February, p. 7.
   Review of Jumpers (London, National Theatre): despite its virtues, "verbally far too indulgent."

1972

59 HARRIS, LEONARD. "The Real Inspector Hound." WCBS-TV, Channel 2 (23 April).
Review of the New York, Theatre Four production (with After Magritte, which was "probably the better of the two"). Text reprinted: 1972.B89.

60 HAWK. "Shows Abroad: Jumpers." Variety, 23 February, p. 66.
Review of the London, National Theatre production.

61 HAYMAN, RONALD. "Michael Hordern--Playing the Intellectual." Times (London), 22 January, p. 9.
Interview with the British actor who played the leading roles in "A Walk on the Water" (London, Associated Rediffusion Television), Enter a Free Man (London, West End), and Jumpers (London, National Theatre): briefly discusses the plays and Stoppard's skill as "a marvellous word-carpenter." Reprinted in 1973.B44.

62 HEWES, HENRY. "The Theater: The London Scene." Saturday Review 55 (8 April):8-9.
Includes a review of Jumpers (London, National Theatre): although "distinctive" and "unusual," its patches of "wild seriocomic stuff [do not] blend easily with . . . the bulk of the play."

63 _____. "Theater: Summer Solace." Saturday Review 55 (26 August):66.
Review of After Magritte and The Real Inspector Hound (New York, Theatre Four), which do not "pretend to be much more than clever exercises." Abridged in 1975.B97.

64 HILLGATE, JASON. "Farce in a Mental Gymnasium." What's On (11 February):26.
Mixed review of Jumpers (London, National Theatre).

65 HIPP, EDWARD SOTHERN. "New York Stage: Inpector Hound." Newark (N.J.) Evening News, 24 April, p. 23.
Review of the New York, Theatre Four production of After Magritte ("too cutsie-pie") and The Real Inspector Hound (shows that Stoppard "can . . . juggle Luigi Pirandello, Neil Simon and Peter Shaffer and . . . make it come out as Tom Stoppard").

66 HOBSON, HAROLD. "Right on Target." Sunday Times (London), 6 February, p. 29.
Review of Jumpers (London, National Theatre): "Stoppard meets every assertion with its opposite, and the universe is filled with realities that cannot be reconciled with reason."

Writings about Tom Stoppard

1972

67 ____. "Theatre: A Sense of Evil." Sunday Times (London), 12 November, p. 37.
    Review of After Magritte and The Real Inspector Hound (London, Dolphin Theatre Company).

68 HUDDISH, GRANT R. "Recent Theatrical Fare." Our Town (New York), 12 May, p. 14.
    Favorable review of After Magritte and The Real Inspector Hound (New York, Theatre Four).

69 HUDSON-PAGE, MARIAN. "Ruffles and Flourishes." Hillsborough (Calif.) Boutique, 18 January, p. 10.
    Review of Rosencrantz & Guildenstern Are Dead (San Francisco, ACT second revival).

70 HUGHES, CATHARINE. "Four Hit Plays--A London Preview." America 126 (8 April):376-77.
    Includes a favorable review of Jumpers (London, National Theatre).

71 ____. "Theatre: Spring Bonus." America 126 (13 May):515.
    Favorable review of After Magritte and The Real Inspector Hound (New York, Theatre Four).

72 HURREN, KENNETH. "Theatre: The Quick and the Dead." Spectator 228 (12 February):245.
    Review of Jumpers (London, National Theatre): "Stoppard clearly has no patience with the idea that weightiness and wit are incompatible."

73 JACK, TOM. "ACT's Lively Return of R & G Are Dead." Redwood City (Calif.) Tribune, 12 January, p. 8.
    Favorable review of the San Francisco company's second revival.

74 JOHNSTON, CALLUM. "Wooly Jumpers." City Press (London), 10 February, p. 14.
    Review of the "vague" London, National Theatre production.

75 KALEM, T. E. "Spoof Sleuths, Nix Crix." Time 99 (8 May):75.
    Review of the "highly diverting" After Magritte and The Real Inspector Hound (New York, Theatre Four). Reprinted in 1972.B89.

76 ____. "The View from London." Time 100 (18 September):75.
    Includes a favorable review of Jumpers (London, National Theatre), the theme of which is that "a world without ab-

1972

solutes will shortly breed moral anarchy."

77 KEMP, ARNOLD. "Jumpers." Scotsman (Edinburgh), 4 February, p. 6.
    Review of the London, National Theatre production.

78 KERR, WALTER. "Staged without Care or Kindness." New York Times, 7 May, sec. 2, p. 3.
    Review of After Magritte and The Real Inspector Hound (New York, Theatre Four): "a mildly diverting evening of philosophical badminton."

79 KINGSTON, JEREMY. "Theatre." Punch 262 (12 January):58.
    Includes a review of Dogg's Our Pet (London, Inter-Action Trust).

80 _____. "Theatre." Punch 262 (9 February):193-94.
    Mixed review of Jumpers (London, National Theatre).

81 KNICKERBOCKER, PAINE. "It's Still a Very Funny Play." San Francisco Chronicle, 13 January, p. 41.
    Favorable review of Rosencrantz & Guildenstern Are Dead (San Francisco, ACT second revival).

82 KNOX, COLLIE. "Letter from London." New York Morning Telegraph, 10 March, p. 3.
    Includes a mixed review of Jumpers (London, National Theatre).

83 LAMBERT, J. W. Review of Jumpers. Drama: The Quarterly Theatre Review, no. 105 (Summer):15-17.
    Review of the London, National Theatre production. It is "a most imperfect play, . . . but its shortcomings, compared with its shining virtues, are . . . 'as piffle before the wind.' . . . It is long since I have experienced in one evening so many flashes of brilliant comic illumination." Abridged in 1975.B96.

84 LEWIS, PETER. "I Haven't Laughed So Much for Many a Moon!" Daily Mail (London), 3 February, p. 17.
    Favorable review of Jumpers (London, National Theatre).

85 LYONS, LEONARD. "The Lyons Den." New York Post, 20 April, p. 41.
    Brief review of Jumpers (London, National Theatre).

86 M., R. "Double Bill of Pathos and Wit." Western Daily Press (Bristol), 1 November, p. 7.

Writings about Tom Stoppard

1972

Favorable review of <u>After Magritte</u> (Bristol New Vic).

87 MAHON, DEREK. "Theatre: Derek Mahon Writes about Tom Stoppard's New Play." <u>Listener</u> 87 (10 February):191-92.
    Favorable review of <u>Jumpers</u> (London, National Theatre).

88 MARCUS, FRANK. "Theatre: Firework Display." <u>Sunday Telegraph</u> (London), 6 February, p. 18.
    Review of <u>Jumpers</u> (London, National Theatre).

89 MARLOWE, JOAN, and BLAKE, BETTY, eds. "<u>The Real Inspector Hound</u>." <u>New York Theatre Critics' Review</u> 33 (12 June): 263-65.
    Reprints of reviews of the New York, Theatre Four, production: 1972.B53, 59, 75, 108, 137, 138.

90 MAROWITZ, CHARLES. "Theater in London: <u>Alpha Beta</u>, or They Lived Unhappily Ever After." <u>New York Times</u>, 13 February, sec. 2, p. 3.
    Includes a brief mixed review of <u>Jumpers</u> (London, National Theatre).

91 MARRIOTT, R. B. "Michael Hordern and Diana Rigg in Dazzling <u>Jumpers</u>." <u>Stage and Television Today</u> (London), 10 February, p. 13.
    Favorable review of the London, National Theatre production.

92 MATLAW, MYRON. "Stoppard, Tom." In <u>Modern World Drama: An Encyclopedia</u>. New York: E. P. Dutton & Co., p. 723.
    Biographical data and brief critical comments; claims Stoppard has been heavily influenced by Absurdist drama and has shown "little development or originality."

93 MAYERSON, DONALD J. "<u>Hound</u>." <u>New York Villager</u>, 27 July, p. 9.
    Review of the New York, Theatre Four <u>After Magritte</u> (which the reviewer "could have easily done without") and <u>The Real Inspector Hound</u> (a "witty and delightfully provocative" play).

*94 MAYNE, RICHARD. Interview of Tom Stoppard. BBC Radio (10 November).
    Cited in 1974.B122.

95 MORLEY, SHERIDAN. "On the Theatre." <u>Tatler</u> 264 (March):26.
    Mixed review of <u>Jumpers</u> (London, National Theatre). Reprinted in 1975.B83.

1972

96 NATALE, RICHARD. "I'm Always Chasing Peacocks." Women's Wear Daily, 27 April, p. 12.
   Interview; Stoppard discusses After Magritte and The Real Inspector Hound, American and British audiences, and his admiration for Magritte, who "somehow juxtaposed incongruous images within a very formal construction."

97 NATHAN, DAVID. "Between the Lines." Jewish Chronicle (London), 11 February, p. 14.
   Review of Jumpers (London, National Theatre).

98 NIGHTINGALE, BENEDICT. "Theatre: Dons' Delight." New Statesman 83 (11 February):185-86.
   Review of Jumpers (London, National Theatre): "gratuitously difficult" because of Stoppard's "habit of revealing necessary information only very gradually."

99 NORMAN, BARRY. "Tom Stoppard and the Contentment of Insecurity." Times (London), 11 November, p. 11.
   Interview: Stoppard discusses the consortium which commissioned Artist Descending a Staircase, changes in his life brought about by the success of Rosencrantz & Guildenstern Are Dead, his desire to work in several media, and problems he encountered writing Jumpers. Briefly mentions Travesties and a screenplay of Brecht's Galileo.

100 O'CONNOR, GARRY. "After Magritte." Financial Times (London), 9 November, p. 3.
   Review of the London, Dolphin Theatre Company production (billed with The Real Inspector Hound).

101 OLIVER, EDITH. "Off Broadway: At Lady Muldoon's." New Yorker 48 (6 May):61-62.
   Review of After Magritte and The Real Inspector Hound (New York, Theatre Four): two plays about "the English language . . . and the conventions of literature and drama." Abridged in 1975.B96.

102 OPPENHEIMER, GEORGE. "London Has Some Delights." Long Island City (N.Y.) Newsday, 10 September, p. 9.
   Includes a brief review of Jumpers (London, National Theatre), "the most controversial play" in London, which the reviewer "neither liked nor understood."

103 PASQUIER, MARIE-CLAIRE. "Shakespeare ou le lieu commun: à propos de Rosencrantz and Guildenstern Are Dead de Tom Stoppard." Recherches Anglaises et Américaines 5:110-20.
   Analysis (in French) of the relationship between

Writings about Tom Stoppard

1972

Stoppard's play and Hamlet: the former reduces the words of the latter to visual representation, its time is totally inscribed within Hamlet's, and its dialogue and actions determined by it. Nevertheless, "the dramatic presence with full entitlement" is accorded to Stoppard's play, not Shakespeare's, since the fragments of Hamlet merely "intervene like a kind of [cinematographic or recording] trace."

104   PETER, JOHN. "Theatre: Jumping Jumpers." Times Education Supplement (London), 18 February, p. 26.
      Review of the London, National Theatre production: Stoppard very nearly solves "the dilemma of being both an intellectual and a first-rate farceur."

105   POWELL, JANE VAUGHN. "Rosencrantz, Guildenstern Superb Show." Gazette (Berkeley, Calif.), 14 January, p. 9.
      Favorable review of the San Francisco, ACT second revival.

106   RAIDY, WILLIAM A. "Comedy Murders a Critic." New Orleans Times-Picayune, 21 May, sec. 2, p. 12.
      Review of After Magritte and The Real Inspector Hound (New York, Theatre Four) including comments from Stoppard about his intentions in and affection for the former play.

107   ROBERTS, PETER. "Jumpers." Plays and Players 19 (April):34.
      Review of the London, National Theatre production: "we are left with an admiration for the author's ingenuity in manipulating characters in which we do not believe."

108   ROLLIN, BETTY. "The Real Inspector Hound." NBC-TV, Channel 4 (23 April).
      Review of the New York, Theatre Four production (with After Magritte): she "love[s] the kind of plays these are [i.e., "quite dotty"], and . . . wish[es] they were better." Text reprinted in 1972.B89.

109   ROSENWALD, PETER J. "The Theater." Wall Street Journal, 25 September, p. 12.
      Review of Jumpers (London, National Theatre), noting Stoppard's "apprehension at the modern tendency to allow the . . . pyramid of order to crumble without due concern for the consequences or what will rise in its place." Also includes comments from Stoppard, particularly about the visual image which originally inspired him to begin writing the play.

110   _____. "Tom Stoppard." Time Out (3 November):31.

Writings about Tom Stoppard

1972

Analysis, including quotations from Stoppard, whose "concern is with life as an enigma. Unity comes from logical confusion, not by resolution, but by balance." Reprinted in <u>The Dolphin Theatre Company's "After Magritte" and "The Real Inspector Hound</u>," production program, London, 7 November.

111 ROTH, EMALOU. "<u>Rosencrantz and Guildenstern Are Dead</u>." In "Immanent Form: Toward a Dramatic/Theatrical Criticism." Ph.D. dissertation, University of Kansas, pp. 253-75.
Detailed analysis of the play and suggestions for production in a dissertation aiming to establish a theory of criticism which embraces both literary and theatrical values.

112 RUNDALL, JEREMY. "Radio: Inner Vision." <u>Sunday Times</u> (London), 26 November, p. 36.
Review of "Artist Descending a Staircase" (London, BBC Radio), the "real point" of which "is a metaphysical one-- what is the nature of Truth?" However, the play "might have been better treated as a straight whodunnit rather than a philosophical adventure."

113 SAINER, ARTHUR. "Theatre: Man's Fate or Mouse's Fate?" <u>Village Voice</u>, 5 October, p. 63.
Review of <u>Rosencrantz & Guildenstern Are Dead</u> (New York, Classic Stage Company): despite the play's "overly romantic" nature, "all in all it is a fine concoction."

114 SAY, ROSEMARY. "Estimated." <u>Sunday Telegraph</u> (London), 12 November, p. 18.
Brief review of <u>After Magritte</u> and <u>The Real Inspector Hound</u> (London, Dolphin Theatre Company).

115 SCHOLEM, RICHARD J. Review of <u>After Magritte</u> and <u>The Real Inspector Hound</u>. Greater New York Radio Network (24 April).
Finds the New York, Theatre Four production "clever but eventually tiresome." Transcript in Lincoln Center Theatre Collection of the New York Public Library.

116 SEGE. "<u>After Magritte</u> & <u>The Real Inspector Hound</u>." <u>Variety</u>, 10 May, p. 80.
Review of the New York, Theatre Four production of the two "clever and witty playlets"; maintains Stoppard was right to insist they be produced off-Broadway.

117 SHULMAN, MILTON. "At the Old Vic." <u>Evening Standard</u> (London), 3 February, p. 14.

Writings about Tom Stoppard

1972

Review of Jumpers (London, National Theatre).

118 SIMON, JOHN. "A Composer, a Comedienne, a Comic Sparkler." New York 5 (8 May):66.
Review of After Magritte and The Real Inspector Hound (New York, Theatre Four), the latter "a thoroughly ingratiating spoof" constructed with "the jewel-like precision of a maniacal timepiece." Reprinted in 1975.B105.

119 SIMON, RICHARD. "Third Time Around, R & G Starts to Fray." Sacramento Union, 15 January, Weekender section, p. 8.
Review of the San Francisco, ACT second revival which seems "not very much of a play. . . . It continues but it does not develop."

120 S[MITH], L[ISA] G[ORDON]. "Stoppard Double-Bill." Stage and Television Today (London), 16 November, p. 17.
Review of After Magritte and The Real Inspector Hound (London, Dolphin Theatre Company).

121 STEVENS, NEIL. "Jumpers Is Gush, Objectionable and So Tedious." Evening Mail (Slough, G.B.), 2 February, p. 2.
Unfavorable review of the London, National Theatre production.

122 STICKEL, ROBERT. "In San Francisco." After Dark 5 (March): 61-62.
Favorable review of Rosencrantz & Guildenstern Are Dead (San Francisco, ACT second revival).

123 STUTZIN, LEO. "Shakespeare, Anyone?" Modesto (Calif.) Bee, 23 January, p. B11.
Revival of Rosencrantz & Guildenstern Are Dead (San Francisco, ACT second revival).

124 SUSSMAN, SHARRON. "Two Obscure Corpses and the Bard Revisited." Record (Mill Valley, Calif.), 2 February, p. 2.
Review of Rosencrantz & Guildenstern Are Dead (San Francisco, ACT second revival).

125 TALLMER, JERRY. "Tom Stoppard Pops in on the Cast." New York Post, 26 August, p. 15.
Feature article and interview. Describes Stoppard's suggestions to new cast members of The Real Inspector Hound (New York, Theatre Four). Stoppard discusses the visual image which inspired Jumpers, the play's theme, and difficulties he encountered writing it. Also includes his opinions about screenwriting and some thoughts which were

Writings about Tom Stoppard

1972

later incorporated into Travesties.

126 TAYLOR, JOHN V. "Arrows of Desire." Frontier 15 (June):89-93.
Review of Jumpers (London, National Theatre). Notes that Stoppard's protagonist "desperately wants to establish . . . not . . . the existence of a deity [but] the value of a person." Also claims that the play's "best jokes" and its "profoundly tragic insight [both] arise from the device of fragmenting the story and letting the pieces fall into absurd juxtaposition."

127 TAYLOR, ROBERT. "Stage and Screen." Oakland (Calif.) Tribune, 14 January, p. 47.
Review of Rosencrantz & Guildenstern Are Dead (San Francisco, ACT second revival).

128 THIRKELL, ARTHUR. "Theatre." Daily Mirror (London), 3 February, p. 16.
Review of Jumpers (London, National Theatre).

129 TIERNEY, MARGARET. "Marriage Lines." Plays and Players 19 (March):26-27.
Includes an interview with Diana Rigg, the female lead in Jumpers (London, National Theatre), about Stoppard, the play, and the character she portrays.

130 TREWIN, J. C. "New Plays." Lady 175 (17 February):261-62.
Mixed review of Jumpers (London, National Theatre).

131 _____. "Theatre: A Flourish of Farce." Illustrated London News 260 (April):57.
Mixed review of Jumpers (London, National Theatre).

132 WADE, DAVID. "Radio: All One Voice." Times (London), 8 April, p. 8.
Includes a brief favorable review of "Is 'Is' Is?" (London, BBC Radio).

133 _____. "'Artist Descending a Staircase.'" Times (London), 14 November, p. 12.
Review of the London, BBC Radio production: finds the play "almost perfectly adapted to its medium," its unity rooted in the "endless . . . ambiguities [which,] like a stressing wire, bind [it] from end to end."

134 WAHLS, ROBERT. "Footlights: The Stage as Chessboard." New York Sunday News, 24 September, p. 8.

Writings about Tom Stoppard

1972

Interview: covers Stoppard's early life and career, Rosencrantz & Guildenstern Are Dead, and his opinions about writing screenplays and radio plays.

135 WARDLE, IRVING. "Jumpers." Times (London), 3 February, p. 13.
   Review of the London, National Theatre production: "a dazzling, hilarious, and honestly benevolent work, which creates a dramatic structure from a forbidding diversity of materials."

136 _____. "Natural Double." Times (London), 8 November, p. 13.
   Review of After Magritte and The Real Inspector Hound (London, Dolphin Theatre Company), two "brilliant trial runs for" Jumpers. Notes that Stoppard, like some of his characters, seems to "contemplate the human scene from the heights of a suspension bridge."

137 WATT, DOUGLAS. "Stoppard Out to Dazzle in Theatre 4 Twin Bill." New York Daily News, 24 April, p. 48.
   Review of After Magritte and The Real Inspector Hound (New York, Theatre Four). The former "has its funny moments but is somewhat flatly resolved"; the latter is the "better of the two." Reprinted in 1972.B89.

138 WATTS, RICHARD. "Mystery Drama and Critics." New York Post, 24 April, p. 23.
   Review of After Magritte and The Real Inspector Hound (New York, Theatre Four), the former "a piece of nonsense" which the reviewer "didn't understand . . . and was possibly not intended to." Reprinted in 1972.B89. See also 1972.B139.

139 _____. "Theatre Week: Playwright Who Knows Critics." New York Post, 6 May, sec. 2, p. 2.
   Follow-up essay to 1972.B138: corrects an error (attributing the title of After Magritte to the fictional detective Maigret); confesses a fascination with actresses (à la Birdboot in The Real Inspector Hound).

140 _____. "Theater: Tom Stoppard's Enigma." New York Post, 3 August, p. 22.
   Review of Jumpers (London, National Theater): "a bewildering . . . enigma of infuriating deviousness."

141 WEIGHTMAN, JOHN. "A Metaphysical Comedy." Encounter 38 (April):44-46.
   Review of Jumpers (London, National Theatre); concen-

1972

trates upon the play's protagonist and its author, "a Deist [who also] has the makings of a tragic Deist. . . . Lastly, he is a sentimentalist." Abridged in 1975.B117.

142 WHITAKER, THOMAS R. "Notes on Playing the Player." Centennial Review 16 (Winter):1-22.
Analysis of trends in modern drama, devoting one section to the approach to life represented by the Player in Rosencrantz & Guildenstern Are Dead. Also notes that our knowledge of Hamlet allows us to "relax for an evening of flirting with the void [while watching Stoppard's play]. We share bouyantly [sic] in the play's ruthless control of its action. We have become Shakespeare. We have become Death." Slightly revised in 1977.B135.

143 WILLIAMS, JAMES E. "Rosencrantz, Guildenstern Brings New, Fresh Faces." San Rafael (Calif.) Independent Journal, 12 January, p. 19.
Review of the San Francisco, ACT second revival.

144 WOODFORDE, JOHN. "Radio: Life at Fifty." Sunday Telegraph (London), 19 November, p. 19.
Review of "Artist Descending a Staircase" (London, BBC Radio).

145 YOUNG, B. A. "Jumpers." Financial Times (London), 4 February, p. 3.
Review of the London, National Theatre production.

1973

A BOOKS--NONE

B SHORTER WRITINGS

1 A., H. "If I May Make So Bold, It Was Not Very Good." Mercury (Leicester, G.B.), 8 March, p. 8.
Unfavorable review of Jumpers (Leicester, Phoenix Theatre).

2 ANON. "Plays and Players 1972 Awards." Plays and Players 20 (January):20-31.
Brief summaries of the previous season by sixteen London critics; reports that Jumpers won eleven of their votes as Best Play (but also see 1973.B3).

Writings about Tom Stoppard

1973

3   ANON. "Plays and Players Special Awards." Plays and Players 20 (January):32.
    Announces the magazine editor's choice of Jumpers as "Most Overrated Play" of 1972; also announces an award to Michael Hordern, who played the leading role, "For Rising above [His] Material."

4   ANON. "Lord Olivier Wins Best Actor Award." Times (London), 23 January, p. 13.
    News item, including the report that Jumpers won the Evening Standard's Best Play award.

5   ANON. "Playguide: Jumpers." Plays and Players 20 (March): 6.
    Capsule review of the London, National Theatre production, denegrating the play's quality. Reactions against this opinion may be found in 1973.B14 and 1973.B51.

6   ANON. "Enter a Free Man." Booklist 69 (1 March):616.
    Review of the text of the play.

7   ANON. "Re-Birth." Observer (London), 15 April, p. 37.
    Brief news item and photograph reporting Stoppard's intention to direct Garson Kanin's Born Yesterday (London, Greenwich Theatre Company).

8   ANON. "Hamlet in Ten Minutes--By Bus." Sunday Telegraph (London), 3 June, p. 4.
    News item reporting Stoppard's distillation of Hamlet into a ten-minute play for performance on the "Fun Bus," a mobile production unit operating on a double-decker bus as part of Ed Berman's Inter-Action Trust.

9   ANON. "Scary Business." New York Times, 1 July, sec. 2, p. 26.
    News item announcing the opening of Jumpers on Broadway during the coming season.

10 ANON. "Tom Stoppard." In Akademietheater. Production program, 20 October, Vienna, n.p.
    Biographical information (in German), contained in the program for Jumpers (translated Akrobaten).

11 ANON. "Gedanken- und Parterre-Akrobatik." Neue Zürcher Zeitung (Zurich), 16 November, p. 49.
    Review of Jumpers (Vienna, Akademietheater); in German.

12 AYER, A. J. "Auch Logische Positivisten Können Lieben." In

79

1973

Akademietheater. Production program, 20 October, Vienna, n.p.
   Translation (into German) and abridgement of 1972.B20 in the program for Jumpers (translated Akrobaten).

13 B., D. F. "Born Yesterday." Stage and Television Today (London), 26 April, p. 17.
   Review of the London, Greenwich Theatre Company production, directed by Stoppard.

14 BAKER, ANTHONY. "Letters: Up Our Jumpers (1)." Plays and Players 20 (April):10.
   Letter to the editor, pointing out that 1973.B5's characterization of the protagonist of Jumpers as a logical positivist renders its evaluation of the play worthless.

15 BARBER, JOHN. "Rare Modern Classic a Study in Hysteria." Daily Telegraph (London), 23 March, p. 14.
   Review of The House of Bernarda Alba (London, Greenwich Theatre Company).

16 _____. "US Corruption Theme of Skilful Comedy." Daily Telegraph (London), 23 April, p. 5.
   Favorable review of Born Yesterday (London, Greenwich Theatre Company), directed by Stoppard.

17 BARKER, FELIX. "First Night: Women in Torment." Evening News (London), 23 March, p. 2.
   Review of The House of Bernarda Alba (London, Greenwich Theatre Company).

18 _____. "First Night: Born Yesterday." Evening News (London), 21 April, p. 4.
   Review of the London, Greenwich Theatre production, directed by Stoppard.

19 BASTABLE, ADOLPHUS. "Our Theatre in the Seventies." Shavian 4 (Summer):260-62.
   Review of Jumpers (London, National Theatre revival).

20 BERLIN, NORMAND. "Rosencrantz and Guildenstern Are Dead: Theater of Criticism." Modern Drama 16 (December):269-77.
   Analysis. Claims the play's weakness is that it "lacks . . . union of thought and emotion," while its strength is that, because our "critical faculty is not subdued" while watching it, we arrive at insights into Hamlet's character, the nature of Greek and Elizabethan tragedy, and actor-audience relationships. "Stoppard is most successful when

1973

he functions as a critic of drama and when he allows his insights on the theater to lead him to observations on life. He is weakest . . . when he attempts to confront life directly."

21 BIGSBY, C[HRISTOPHER] W[ILLIAM] E[DGAR]. "Tom Stoppard." In Contemporary Dramatists. Edited by James Vinson. Contemporary Writers of the English Language. London: St. James Press, pp. 735-39.
   Plot summaries of and brief analytical comments about "The Dissolution of Dominic Boot," "'M' Is for 'Moon' among Other Things," "If You're Glad I'll Be Frank," "Albert's Bridge," and "A Separate Peace"; more detailed analyses of After Magritte, Enter a Free Man, Jumpers, The Real Inspector Hound, and Rosencrantz & Guildenstern Are Dead; also contains biographical information.
   Identifies major recurring themes (relativity, reluctance to face reality, the inability of language to express convictions and of rationality to account for reality); contrasts him with Beckett (Stoppard emphasizes the relativity of truth rather than its absence and focuses on the "humour and perverse vitality" of men in despair, not their "abandonment"); lists his dramatic virtues (a "mastery of language, a clear sense of style and rhythm," and a visual and verbal wit) and his shortcomings (a willingness to use logic with "more single-mindedness than dramatic effect" and a tendency to displace insight with wit).
   Brought up to date and greatly expanded in 1976.A2.

22 BILLINGTON, MICHAEL. "The Ruthless, Cerebral Logic of Tom Stoppard." Ottawa Citizen, 3 March, p. 40.
   Critical article summarizing plots and recurrent themes of "The Dissolution of Dominic Boot," "Albert's Bridge," Rosencrantz & Guildenstern Are Dead, The Real Inspector Hound, After Magritte, and Jumpers.

23 _____. "Lorca's Alba." Guardian (London), 23 March, p. 12.
   Review of The House of Bernarda Alba (London, Greenwich Theatre Company): Stoppard's "direct, unflowery adaptation . . . convinces you that honour is a meaningful concept" to the characters.

24 _____. "Born Yesterday at Greenwich." Guardian (London), 21 April, p. 10.
   Review of the London, Greenwich Theatre Company production: Stoppard's direction was characterized by "Anglo-Saxon heaviness" instead of a more appropriate "whiplash precision."

1973

25 BLAHA, PAUL. "Crime and Philosophy." Kurier (Vienna), 22 October, p. 27.
   Review (in German) of Jumpers (Vienna, Akademietheater); reports difficulties in following the play's wit and comic nuances. Expands on this problem in 1973.B26.

26 _____. "Ein Stück mit Schlichen." Frankfurter Allgemeine, 26 October, p. 26.
   Review (in German) of Jumpers (Vienna, Akademietheater). Claims that a German audience has trouble appreciating the play's wit and intellectual stimulation because its philosophical assumptions and methods are distinctively English. Stoppard seems deliberately to keep the audience unsure of its bearings in order "to show how poorly we orient ourselves in questions of absolute morality."

27 BRISBANE, KATHARINE. "Delving into Tom Stoppard's Cosmic Logic." Australian (Melbourne), 6 April, p. 10.
   Review of Jumpers (Melbourne Theatre Company): "a magnificent, mind-bending illumination of Anglo-Saxon attitudes."

28 BRUSTEIN, ROBERT. "Plaudits and Brickbats." Observer (London), 25 March, p. 35.
   Review of The House of Bernarda Alba (London, Greenwich Theatre Company): Stoppard's adaptation "crisp, colloquial, but overly jocular."

29 CAVAN, ROMILY. "Scripts." Plays and Players 21 (December): 73.
   Review of the texts of "Artist Descending a Staircase" and "Where Are They Now?"

30 CLURMAN, HAROLD. "Theatre." Nation 217 (13 August):123-24.
   Review of Jumpers (London, National Theatre revival): criticizes the tone of "facile, chirping 'pessimism,' the posture or pose of many in Britain's latest dramatic coterie."

31 COE, RICHARD L. "A Brief, Bubbly Bill." Washington Post, 10 August, sec. 2, pp. 1, 16.
   Favorable review of After Magritte and The Real Inspector Hound (New York, Theatre Four production, playing at Washington's Kennedy Center).

32 COVENEY, MICHAEL. "After Magritte and The Real Inspector Hound." Plays and Players 20 (January):51.
   Review of the London, Dolphin Theatre Company production.

1973

33 _____. "Born Yesterday." Financial Times (London), 24 April, p. 3.
   Review of the London, Greenwich Theatre Company production, directed by Stoppard.

34 CROSSLEY, PETER. "Convey a Sense of Surrealism." Free Press (Winnipeg, Manitoba), 21 March, p. 16.
   Favorable review of Rosencrantz & Guildenstern Are Dead (Winnipeg, Manitoba Theatre Centre).

35 DAVIES, STAN GEBLER. "Reviews: Theatre." Evening Standard (London), 24 April, p. 23.
   Mixed review of Born Yesterday (London, Greenwich Theatre Company), directed by Stoppard.

36 EARLE, ANITA. "House of Bernarda Alba." San Francisco Chronicle, 20 December, p. 41.
   Review of the San Francisco, ACT production: Stoppard's adaptation "vacuums [Lorca's] poetry into prose and sprinkles a few four-letter words over the surface, music into Musak."

37 EDWARDS, SYDNEY. "News of the Arts: Bricklayer Named Stoppard." Evening Standard (London), 13 April, p. 8.
   News item reporting the opening of Born Yesterday (London, Greenwich Theatre Company); includes Stoppard's comments about directing the play, Travesties, his problems with inventing plots, and his hopes to produce his adaptation of Brecht's Galileo at the London Planetarium in the autumn.

38 EICHELBAUM, STANLEY. "Uneven Staging of Lorca's Bernarda Alba." San Francisco Examiner, 19 December, p. 33.
   Review of the San Francisco, ACT production; finds that Stoppard's "erratic" adaptation "does nothing for Lorca's spare poetic prose."

39 GALLOWAY, MYRON. "Centaur Changes Pace with Comic Masterpieces." Montreal Star, 1 February, p. C7.
   Review of After Magritte and The Real Inspector Hound (Montreal, Centaur Theatre), two Absurdist plays of "fiendish ingeniousness."

40 GIFFORD, DENIS. "The Engagement." In The British Film Catalogue: 1895-1970: A Guide to Entertainment Films. Newton Abbot, G.B.: David & Charles, n.p.
   Item No. 14076 supplies production information and a cast list of the film.

1973

41 GLACKLIN, WILLIAM C. "Sewing for Women; Whiplashes for Men." Sacramento (Calif.) Bee (23 December), Leisure section, p. 3.
   Review of The House of Bernarda Alba (San Francisco, ACT); finds the language of Stoppard's adaptation "strong and lifelike."

42 GRIMME, KARL MARIA. "Alte und Junge Burg: Goethe und Tom Stoppard." Furche (Vienna), 27 October, p. 15.
   Includes a review (in German) of Jumpers (Vienna, Akademietheater): "at the end, Stoppard seems to ask, 'Well, wasn't that amusing?' The answer would be, 'In part--in part.'"

43 HAHNL, HANS HEINZ. "Über Gott und das College Schwätzen." Arbeiter Zeitung (Vienna), 23 October, sec. A, p. 2.
   Review of Jumpers (Vienna, Akademietheater). Finds the text witty but gossipy and not as original as it seems; claims the production illustrates the modern tendency to make confusing texts bearable through the use of visual accessories; notes that the audience enjoyed Stoppard's "slightly black humor," social criticism, and Shavian mixture of satire with "a certain anxiety of conscience." In German.

44 HAYMAN, RONALD. "Michael Hordern." In Playback 2. London: Davis-Poynter, pp. 80-96.
   Reprint of 1972.B61.

45 HILL, FRANCES. "Quarter-Laughing Assurance: A Profile of Tom Stoppard." Times Education Supplement (London), 9 February, p. 23.
   Analysis and interview. Notes that Stoppard's plays originate not with views or situations or characters but with "a dramatic idea, often visual and usually ingenious." Stoppard discusses sources of Enter a Free Man and his use of refutation in Jumpers.

46 HOBSON, HAROLD. "Theatre: The Importance of Beaumont." Sunday Times (London), 25 March, p. 29.
   Includes a brief review of The House of Bernarda Alba (London, Greenwich Theatre Company).

47 _____. "Carry on, Doctor." Sunday Times (London), 22 April, p. 38.
   Includes a brief review of Born Yesterday (London, Greenwich Theatre Company), directed by Stoppard.

Writings about Tom Stoppard

1973

48 HUTTON, GEOFFREY. "Fun--But What's It All About?" Age (Melbourne), 23 March, p. 2.
      Mixed review of Jumpers (Melbourne Theatre Company).

49 KAPICA, JACK. "The Inspector Called, and Everyone Laughed." Gazette (Montreal), 1 February, p. 33.
      Review of After Magritte and The Real Inspector Hound (Montreal, Centaur Theatre), the latter the work of a "sardonic craftsman showing off his . . . ability to manipulate an audience."

50 KINGSTON, JEREMY. "Theatre." Punch 264 (25 April):590.
      Includes a brief review of Rosencrantz & Guildenstern Are Dead (London, Young Vic).

51 LAW, J. P. "Letters: Up Our Jumpers (2)." Plays and Players 20 (April):10.
      Letter to the editor reacting against the criticism of Jumpers in 1973.B5.

52 LEECH, MICHAEL. "The Translators: Tom Stoppard." Plays and Players 20 (April):36-38.
      Interview: Stoppard discusses the problems and pleasures of adapting Lorca's The House of Bernarda Alba (London, Greenwich Theatre Company) from a literal translation.

53 LEWSON, CHARLES. "Rosencrantz and Guildenstern Are Dead." Times (London), 10 April, p. 9.
      Review of the London, Young Vic production; finds the play's "emotional power" greater than that of Jumpers.

54 _____. "Born Yesterday." Times (London), 21 April, p. 9.
      Favorable review of the London, Greenwich Theatre Company production, directed by Stoppard.

55 MARCUS, FRANK. "Theatre: Women Alone." Sunday Telegraph (London), 25 March, p. 18.
      Review of The House of Bernarda Alba (London, Greenwich Theatre Company).

56 _____. "Theatre: Comic Types." Sunday Telegraph (London), 22 April, p. 18.
      Review of Born Yesterday (London, Greenwich Theatre Company), directed by Stoppard.

57 MAROWITZ, CHARLES. "Writer in Our Midst." In Confessions of a Counterfeit Critic: A London Theatre Notebook, 1958-1971. London: Eyre Methuen, pp. 123-25.

1973

>Reprint of 1967.B94; appended is a brief introduction describing Marowitz' part in getting Stoppard invited to the colloquium in Berlin in 1964 and his dismissal of the first draft of Rosencrantz & Guildenstern Are Dead.

58 M[ARRIOTT], R. B. "Lorca's Five Sisters." Stage and Television Today (London), 29 March, p. 15.
>Review of The House of Bernarda Alba (London, Greenwich Theatre Company).

59 MAYHEAD, GERALD. "Funny Night of Academic Boredom." Herald (Melbourne), 23 March, p. 14.
>Review of Jumpers (Melbourne Theatre Company): "an over development of a poor Goon Show script."

*60 NORDON, PIERRE. "Le théâtre anglais contemporain: fantaisie et fantastique." Recherches Anglaises et Américaines 6: 71-77.
>Analysis (in French). Minimizes the influence of Osborne upon the revolution in British theatre; emphasizes the importance of the "irrationalism" of other playwrights (including Stoppard, who uses parody and the play-within-the play). (Annotation summarized from Abstracts of English Studies, 1977.)

61 O'CONNOR, GARRY, "The House of Bernarda Alba." Financial Times (London), 26 March, p. 3.
>Review of the London, Greenwich Theatre Company production.

62 PACHE, WALTER. "Pirandellos Urenkel: Formen des Spiels im Spiel bei Max Frisch und Tom Stoppard." Sprachkunst: Beiträge zur Literaturwissenschaft 4:124-41.
>Analysis (in German). Claims that most British critics have erred by placing Rosencrantz & Guildenstern Are Dead on a continuum between Shakespeare and Absurdism, thereby "by-passing the tradition of the play-within-the-play in which the work lives"; that, unlike Brechtian, Absurdist, or documentary works, Stoppard's play and Frisch's Biographie reject the assumption that theatre can "be real in a modified form"; and that, instead, they are examples of the "theatre of resignation" and their authors are "Pirandello's grandchildren" because in these two plays "the possibilities and limits of dramatic illusion . . . become outright thematic."
>Discusses techniques by which Stoppard communicates this theme and experiments with the "paradox" that audiences "forget the fictional nature" of events they are watching

Writings about Tom Stoppard

1973

on stage. Concludes by observing that, unlike more traditionally constructed plays, Stoppard's "finds its final form in its own execution, in the playing with the expectations and reactions of the spectator" and that in his later work, most obviously The Real Inspector Hound, he "attempts . . . to connect with Tieck's romantic irony and to vary the confrontation of artificial plots with their own irreality in a satirical and parodistic manner."

63 PALMER, HOWARD. "A Murder at a Mad Party." Sun (Melbourne), 23 March, p. 23.
    Mixed review of Jumpers (Melbourne Theatre Company), a "wonderful farce."

64 PETER, JOHN. "Plays without People." Sunday Times (London), 7 January, p. 27.
    Includes a brief review of Rosencrantz & Guildenstern Are Dead, performed by Leeds University students at Britain's University Drama Festival.

65 R[AINE], C[RAIG]. "Comedy of Ideas." Times Education Supplement (London), 21 September, p. 60.
    Analysis, with a brief review of Jumpers (London, National Theatre revival). Compares the play's plot to Thurber's "The Macbeth Murder Mystery," in which a reader of detective stories argues that the Macbeths could not have murdered Duncan precisely because all the evidence points to their guilt. Similarly, the Secretary is the culprit in Jumpers because her role is sufficiently peripheral and her guilt would underscore the theme of the misleading nature of logic.

66 RENDLE, ADRIAN. "New Published Plays." Drama: The Quarterly Theatre Review, no. 111 (Winter):87-88.
    Contains a review of the texts of "Artist Descending a Staircase" and "Where Are They Now?" Abridged in 1975.B96.

67 RICHARDS, DAVID. "Two Stoppard Plays: Logical Absurdities." Washington Star, 10 August, p. E3.
    Favorable review of After Magritte and The Real Inspector Hound (New York, Theatre Four production; at Kennedy Center in Washington, D.C.).

68 RILEY, CAROLYN, ed. "Tom Stoppard." In Contemporary Literary Criticism: Excerpts from Criticism of the Works of Today's Novelists, Playwrights, and Other Creative Writers. Vol. 1. Detroit: Gale Research Co., pp. 327-28.
    Consists of abridgements of 1967.B43, 94, 119, 136

Writings about Tom Stoppard

1973

about <u>Rosencrantz & Guildenstern Are Dead</u>; 1968.B33 about <u>The Real Inspector Hound</u>; and 1968.B50, 96 about <u>Lord Malquist & Mr Moon</u>. Similar abridgements of criticism of Stoppard published in volumes 3, 4, 5, and 8 of this series. See 1975.B96, 97, 1976.B87, and 1978.B20.

69 RISMONDO, PIERO. "Philosophischer Zirkus." <u>Presse</u> (Vienna), 22 October, p. 5.
Review of <u>Jumpers</u> (Vienna, Akademietheater), which, like the "modern linguistic capers" of Peter Handke and Thomas Bernhardt, "dissolves bonds between character and language" and "pushes forward until it finds the grotesque is the 'Ultima ratio.'" In German.

70 ROWE, KAYE. "Alternating Performances a Big Hit at MTC." <u>Sun</u> (Brandon, Manitoba), 28 March, p. 3.
Favorable review of <u>Rosencrantz & Guildenstern Are Dead</u> (Winnipeg, Manitoba Theatre Centre).

71 S., P. H. "The Times Diary: Backbreaking." <u>Times</u> (London), 26 March, p. 12.
Columnist complains that uncomfortable seating in the balcony of the Old Vic Theatre had made it difficult to enjoy <u>Jumpers</u> (London, National Theatre).

72 SAY, ROSEMARY. "The Return of R & G." <u>Sunday Telegraph</u> (London), 8 April, p. 18.
Review of the London, Young Vic production.

73 SHULMAN, MILTON. "Look What Adela Did. . . ." <u>Evening Standard</u> (London), 23 March, p. 27.
Review of <u>The House of Bernarda Alba</u> (London, Greenwich Theatre Company).

74 _____. "More about the Odd Couple up at Elsinore." <u>Evening Standard</u> (London), 5 April, p. 27.
Favorable review of <u>Rosencrantz & Guildenstern Are Dead</u> (London, Young Vic).

75 SMITH, GILES. "P. M. Reports." BBC Radio Four (8 June).
Interview with Stoppard concerning his distillation of <u>Hamlet</u> into a ten-minute play for performance on Inter-Action Trust's Fun Arts Bus; claims "there's an awful lot of padding in [<u>Hamlet</u>]. Nine pages is probably its best length." Transcript housed, BBC Written Archives Centre, London.

76 S[MITH], L[ISA] G[ORDON]. "Welcome Young Vic Revival." <u>Stage</u>

1973

and Television Today (London), 12 April, p. 15.
   Review of Rosencrantz & Guildenstern Are Dead (London, Young Vic).

77 STASIO, MARILYN. "Good Grief, Am I Laughing?" Stagebill (August):33, 35, 37.
   Analysis of The Real Inspector Hound in the program of the Washington, D.C., Kennedy Center production (with After Magritte). Discusses its variety of comedy: music hall, satire and parody, idiosyncrasies of language, and the "logical reality of the absurd."

78 TELPNER, GENE. "Fine Acting Marks Comedy." Tribune (Winnipeg, Manitoba), 21 March, p. 24.
   Favorable review of Rosencrantz & Guildenstern Are Dead (Winnipeg, Manitoba Theatre Centre).

79 TINKER, JACK. "This Classy, Sassy Revival of Yesterday." Daily Mail (London), 23 April, p. 19.
   Favorable review of Born Yesterday (London, Greenwich Theatre Company), directed by Stoppard.

80 TREWIN, J. C. "Born Yesterday." Birmingham (G.B.) Post, 27 April, p. 2.
   Favorable review of the London, Greenwich Theatre Company production, directed by Stoppard.

81 _____. "New Plays." Lady (10 May):816.
   Includes a favorable review of Born Yesterday (London, Greenwich Theatre Company), directed by Stoppard.

82 _____. "News from Rumania." Illustrated London News 261 (June):109.
   Includes a favorable review of Born Yesterday (London, Greenwich Theatre Company), directed by Stoppard.

83 W., R. "Stoppard: Pluhar Nackt." Neue Kronenzeitung (Vienna), 20 October, p. 14.
   Brief interview (in German) with Peter Wood, director of Jumpers (Vienna, Akademietheater).

84 WARDLE, IRVING. "The House of Bernarda Alba." Times (London), 23 March, p. 17.
   Review of the London, Greenwich Theatre Company production: although Stoppard "has certainly achieved a more speakable and pithier" script than other translators, the daughters' "switched-on back-chat" is inappropriate.

1973

85 WATTS, JANET. "Tom Stoppard." Guardian (London), 21 March, p. 12.

Interview: Stoppard discusses the commercial failure of Lord Malquist & Mr Moon, the origin of After Magritte, his experience with the Edinburgh production of Rosencrantz & Guildenstern Are Dead, and the theme of Travesties ("committed art is really a kind of bogus enterprise"). Comments briefly upon the importance of consistency and logical structure, the ineffectiveness of theatre as a tool for social change, his concentration upon theatrical rather than intellectual or thematic concerns while writing, his lack of interest in "doing glam things," and the effect of his second marriage upon his work.

86 YOUNG, B. A. "Tom Stoppard Double Bill." Financial Times (London), 2 February, p. 3.

Review of After Magritte and The Real Inspector Hound (London, Dolphin Theatre Company revival).

1974

A BOOKS

1 ELSNER, JUDITH JEAN. "A Production of Tom Stoppard's Rosencrantz and Guildenstern Are Dead." M.A. thesis, California State University-Long Beach, 263 pp.

Director's report of an arena production: 73 pp. analyzing the text and evaluating her production, 190 pp. of appendices (including prompt book, ground plan, and photographs).

Production emphasized the play's comedy and depicted the Player as a tutor whose task it was to help the title characters understand (and thereby overcome their fear of) death.

B SHORTER WRITINGS

1 AMORY, MARK. "The Joke's the Thing." Sunday Times Magazine (London), 9 June, pp. 65, 67-68, 71-72, 74.

Profile; includes quotations by Stoppard and by actor John Wood about the difficulties the plays pose for performers and by A. C. H. Smith, friend and former newspaper editor, about his personality.

Discusses Stoppard's early life and career, his "facetious" attitude as a journalist, his love of jokes, the value of "private and secret" allusions in art, and his

1974

insistence that his plays must make sense on the least demanding level before anything else.
    Discusses the reception of Enter a Free Man in Hamburg, its similarity to Robert Bolt's Flowering Cherry, the source of the character of George Moore in Jumpers, the evolution of Rosencrantz & Guildenstern Are Dead, and the textual complexity of Travesties.

2 ANDERSON, MICHAEL. "Bristol." Plays and Players 21 (July): 52-53.
    Review of Jumpers (Bristol Old Vic).

3 ANDREWS, M. STEPHANIE. "Brecht & Free Man Hit Spot." Portland (Oreg.) Scribe, 30 March, p. 17.
    Includes a favorable review of Enter a Free Man (Portland, Civic Theatre).

4 ANON. "Jumpers Set for Broadway." New York Times, 10 March, p. 57.
    News item summarizing four reviews of the Broadway pro- its Washington, D.C., Kennedy Center tryout to New York.

5 ANON. "Angels." New York Show Business, 4 April, p. 17.
    News item listing the backers of Jumpers (Broadway).

6 ANON. "Jumpers to Land Here April 22." New York Times, 7 April, p. 50.
    News item announcing the date of the Broadway opening and reporting its gross income during its Washington, D.C. tryout.

7 ANON. "Tom Stoppard on the Giants of Zurich." Times (London), 15 April, p. 5.
    News item listing the cast of Travesties (London, Royal Shakespeare Company).

8 ANON. "Broadway Grosses." Variety, 24 April, pp. 59-60.
    News item reporting the potential weekly grosses, break-even point, and investment for Jumpers (Broadway).

9 ANON. "Stoppard's Travesties Due June 10 in London." Variety, 24 April, p. 56.
    News item announcing the London, Royal Shakespeare Company opening of the play.

10 ANON. "Jumpers Gains Mixed N.Y. Reviews." Washington Post, 24 April, sec. B, p. 7.
    News item summarizing four reviews of the Broadway pro-

1974

duction: 1974.B27, 70, 167, and Jack Gaver's UPI Wire-service release.

11 ANON. "B'way Eases as New Shows Falter; Favorable Reviews Fail to Help." Variety, 1 May, p. 56.
    News story; includes a listing of the "mixed" reviews given Jumpers (Broadway).

12 ANON. "Jumpers to Close Saturday." New York Times, 16 May, p. 52.
    Brief news item announcing the impending closing of Jumpers (Broadway). See also 1974.B13.

13 ANON. "Jumpers Extends Its Run." New York Times, 17 May, p. 33.
    Brief news item announcing the indefinite postponement of the closing of Jumpers (Broadway).

14 ANON. Photograph. Sunday Times (London), 2 June, p. 37.
    Members of the cast of Travesties (London, Royal Shakespeare Company).

15 ANON. "Briefing: Dada." Observer (London), 9 June, p. 29.
    Interview, paraphrasing Stoppard's comments about Travesties prior to its London, Royal Shakespeare production.

16 ANON. "B'way Inches Up." Variety, 12 June, p. 50.
    News story; includes an announcement of the closing of Jumpers (Broadway) with an estimated loss of $250,000.

17 ANON. "Lenin and Joyce Are Alive." Newsweek 83 (24 June):77.
    Favorable review of Travesties (London, Royal Shakespeare Company).

18 ANON. "Stoppard, Tom." Current Biography 35 (July):39-42.
    Biographical information, lists of plays and other fiction, plot summaries and brief analysis of Rosencrantz & Guildenstern Are Dead, Lord Malquist & Mr Moon, The Real Inspector Hound, and Jumpers. Reprinted in 1975.B2.

19 ANON. Book Review. Choice 11 (October):1140.
    Review of the text of Jumpers.

20 ANON. "Jumpers: What's the Argument?" San Francisco Sunday Examiner, 15 December, Datebook sec., p. 12.
    Feature article summarizing the play's plot prior to its opening in the San Francisco, ACT production.

Writings about Tom Stoppard

1974

21 ATWOOD, LOIS. "Trinity Square Jumpers Has Liveliness, Momentum." Providence (R.I.) Brown Daily Herald, 20 December, p. 11.
    Mixed review of the Providence company's production: admires the play's "busyness" but is not certain whether a message lies beneath it.

22 BANKER, STEPHEN. "On New Plays: Jumpers." National Public Radio (19 February).
    Interview: Stoppard discusses production problems with Jumpers, the author's function in rehearsals, and his preoccupation with matters of craft and mechanics rather than theme when writing. Audio tape of the five-minute interview is Item No. 74021905; located at the network's Washington, D.C. office. Edited version found in 1974.B23.

23 _____. "Slam, Bam, Thank You, Sam, and Jumpers." National Public Radio (4 March).
    Six-minute interview; shares some material with 1974. B22. Also contains Stoppard's detailed comments about the play's theme ("an insoluble problem, . . . about two . . . philosophies, between which one cannot . . . make a final decision") and its protagonist. Concludes with a protest against the sort of discussion of a play in which one "simply . . . pick[s] all the bones out of it. . . . You can't reduce it to a skeleton because it didn't build from a skeleton." Audio tape is Item No. 7410; located at the network's Washington, D.C. office.

24 BARBER, JOHN. "Stoppard's Variable Literary Frolic." Daily Telegraph (London), 11 June, p. 14.
    Review of Travesties (London, Royal Shakespeare Company): "a lively, . . . sometimes hilarious frolic. . . . But almost all the jokes go on too long."

25 BARNES, CLIVE. "Stage: Stoppard's Jumpers Has U.S. Premiere in Capital." New York Times, 20 February, p. 28.
    Favorable review of the Washington tryout of the Broadway production.

26 _____. "Jumpers." Times (London), 23 February, p. 9.
    Review of the Washington opening of the Broadway production for British readers. "One of the wittiest and most stimulating plays of the past decade or so."

27 _____. "Stage: Stoppard's Murder Play about Philosophy." New York Times, 23 April, p. 36.
    Favorable review of Jumpers (Broadway). Reprinted in

1974

1974.B111. Abridged in 1974.B10.

28 _____. Theater: Two Bright Spots of the London Season." *New York Times*, 9 August, p. 24.
   Includes a review of *Travesties* (London, Royal Shakespeare Company) for American readers: "madly exhilarating."

29 _____. "Stage: Stoppard's *Enter a Free Man*." *New York Times*, 18 December, p. 51.
   Favorable review of the New York, Theatre at St. Clement's production.

30 BEAUFORT, JOHN. "Roundabout's Moving Revival of *Seagull*." *Christian Science Monitor*, 25 January, sec. 2, p. 6.
   Includes a review of *Rosencrantz & Guildenstern Are Dead* (New York, Classic Stage Company revival).

31 _____. "Theater: Tom Stoppard's Provocative *Jumpers* Hits Broadway." *Christian Science Monitor*, 25 April, sec. 2, p. 6.
   Review of the Broadway production of this "complex and demanding play." Reprinted in 1974.B111.

32 _____. "Viewing Things: Theater's Prize-Giving Season." *Christian Science Monitor*, 16 May, p. F10.
   Summary of the Broadway season, including the "brilliantly intricate" *Jumpers*.

33 BELLAMY, PETER. "Kudos Aside, Drury Comedy Is a Bore." *Cleveland Plain Dealer*, 18 March, sec. B, p. 7.
   Review of *Rosencrantz & Guildenstern Are Dead* (Cleveland Playhouse): "a pretentious intellectual bore, filled with pointless conversation."

34 BERGSON, PHILLIP. "Theatre." *Review* (Oxford, G.B.), 15 June, pp. 3, 10.
   Review of *Travesties* (London, Royal Shakespeare Company).

35 BILLINGTON, MICHAEL. "*Travesties*." *Guardian* (London), 11 June, p. 12.
   Review of *Travesties* (London, Royal Shakespeare Company), in which Stoppard's "pastiche" of history, debate, and vaudeville forms "a dense Joycean web [that] radiates sheer intellectual *joie de vivre*."

36 BLADEN, BARBARA. "*Jumpers* Is a Witty and Baffling Charade." *San Mateo* (Calif.) *Times*, 19 December, p. 31.

94

Writings about Tom Stoppard

1974

Mixed review of the San Francisco, ACT production.

37 BOYD, JUDITH. "The Critics: Night of Laughter." Bath & Wilts Evening Chronicle (Bristol), 25 April, p. 5.
    Favorable review of Jumpers (Bristol Old Vic).

38 B[RUKENFELD], D[ICK]. "Theatre: Once in Love with Charley." Village Voice, 30 December, p. 69.
    Includes a review of Enter a Free Man (New York, Theatre at St. Clement's): "stale stuff, indifferently made."

39 CALTA, LOUIS. "News of the Stage: Credit-Card Plan for Jumpers Here." New York Times, 14 April, p. 47.
    News item reporting that tickets to the Broadway production may be charged to credit cards.

40 CLURMAN, HAROLD. "Theatre." Nation 218 (11 May):604.
    Review of Jumpers (Broadway): an "intellectual argument" which contains one good character and "little else." Abridged in 1975.B97. Readers' reactions to this review prompted 1974.B41.

41 _____. "Theatre." Nation 218 (18 May):637-38.
    Amplification of 1974.B40 in response to readers' reactions. Contends that Jumpers (Broadway) is not good theatre because "its point or 'thesis' [which he takes to be George Moore's line, 'Cogito, ergo Deus est'] is not revealed through action: it is only stated." Abridged in 1976.B87.

42 COE, RICHARD L. "Jumpers: Verbal Vaudeville." Washington Post, 19 February, sec. B, pp. 1, 3.
    Review of the Washington, D.C., Kennedy Center tryout of the Broadway production. Praises its "lavishly staged literacy" but notes that "there are still too many gaps for yawning." Elicited a reply: 1974.B102, which in turn prompted 1974.B43.

43 _____. "Jumpers: Further Elaborations on Its Meaning." Washington Post, 24 March, pp. L2, L6.
    Analysis of Jumpers in response to criticisms stated in 1974.B102. Defines it as "a play in humorous perspective about our chaotic present"; admits that it will "outrage those who feel that serious thoughts about the universe must be stated solemnly."

44 COVENEY, MICHAEL. "Travesties." Financial Times (London), 11 June, p. 3.

Writings about Tom Stoppard

1974

Review of the London, Royal Shakespeare Company production: "a brilliant confection. I am less convinced that it is a good play."

45 CRICK, BERNARD. "Travesties." Times Higher Education Supplement (London), 2 August, p. 13.
    Review of the London, Royal Shakespeare Company production: "a masterpiece of serious wit, and a farce so truly intellectual that it comforts one that sheer intelligence can if not redeem, at least sustain one."

46 CUMMING, RICHARD. "A Few Notes on Tom Stoppard." In Trinity Square Repertory Company "Jumpers." Production program, 12 December, Providence, R.I., pp. 4-6, 14.
    Discusses themes and character types common to several of Stoppard's plays, including "Another Moon Called Earth," Enter a Free Man, Jumpers, The Real Inspector Hound, and Rosencrantz & Guildenstern Are Dead.

47 CUSHMAN, ROBERT. "Theatre: Stoppard Run Wilde." Observer (London), 16 June, p. 31.
    Review of Travesties (London, Royal Shakespeare Company). Notes that the intrusion of Lenin's reminiscences into those of Henry Carr "splits the play's fantastic structure."

48 D., D. G. "Review: Travesties." This Week in London, 27 June, p. 14.
    Review of the London, Royal Shakespeare Company production.

49 DOMINITZ, SIDNEY. "Travesties Aptly Titled Burlesque." Los Angeles Times, 20 June, sec. 4, p. 18.
    Review of the London, Royal Shakespeare Company production of Stoppard's "self-lampooning tract on the nature of art and revolution." Says the play "hits a blank spot" when Lenin is onstage.

50 DONNELLY, TOM. "Donnelly's Revue: Jumping for Joy." Washington Post, 17 February, sec. P, pp. 1, 5.
    Interview; Stoppard discusses the theme of Jumpers, his "cross-reference way" of writing, his inability to conduct interviews as a reporter, the influence of psychological themes on modern drama, and some of his favorite modern plays.

51 DRAKE, SYLVIA. "Tom Stoppard--The Entertainer." Los Angeles Times, 12 December, sec. 4, p. 26.

Writings about Tom Stoppard

1974

News article reporting on his lecture in Santa Barbara.

52 ECKERT, THOR, Jr. "Jumpers Bounces to New England." Christian Science Monitor, 17 December, p. 2C.
   Review of the Providence, Trinity Square Repertory production: admires it, but expresses reservations about the "elaborate, often ponderous" text.

53 EDWARDS, SYDNEY, and OWEN, MICHAEL. "Local Boy Makes Good." Evening Standard (London), 13 September, p. 24.
   Interview with André Previn, composer and conductor; discusses his collaboration with Stoppard on what became Every Good Boy Deserves Favour, then scheduled for the 1975 Edinburgh Festival.

54 EICHELBAUM, STANLEY. "Call Me the Thinking Man's Farceur." San Francisco Examiner, 11 December, p. 69.
   Interview; Stoppard discusses the juxtaposition of logic and the bizarre in Jumpers, his fondness for comedy, and his "facetiousness" as a journalist.

55 _____. "The Intellectual High Jinks of Jumpers." San Francisco Examiner, 18 December, p. 46.
   Review of the San Francisco, ACT production: "better realized and more intimate" than the Broadway version.

56 ELLMANN, RICHARD. "The Zealots of Zurich." Times Literary Supplement (London), 12 July, p. 744.
   Review of Travesties (London, Royal Shakespeare Company), written by the biographer of James Joyce and editor of Oscar Wilde, both of whom figure prominently in this "admirable" play. Says Stoppard's techniques resemble vaudeville routines and the methods of Joyce's later novels; their effect is to offer "a continual displacement of perspective as if Argus eyes could make up for the defects of individual vision."

57 ELSOM, JOHN. "Theatre: Pooh-Sticks." Listener 91 (20 June):801.
   Review of Travesties (London, Royal Shakespeare Company): claims that Stoppard's thesis is not clear. Abridged in 1976.B87.

58 EMMET, ALFRED. "April Production--10th Birthday: Rosencrantz and Guildenstern Are Dead by Tom Stoppard." Questopics, no. 91 (April);1-2.
   Feature article announcing the London, Questors Theatre production and recallings its presentation of Guildenstern

1974

and Rosencrantz in 1964.

59 FLETCHER, RICHARD D. "Jumpers--A Maze of Contrasts."
    Christian Science Monitor, 6 March, sec. F, p. 6.
       Review of the Washington, D.C., Kennedy Center tryout
    of the Broadway production.

60 FOOT, DAVID. "Bristol: Jumpers." Guardian (London), 27
    April, p. 8.
       Review of the Bristol Old Vic production. Claims that
    Stoppard, like Shaw, is preoccupied with "words, ideas, and
    the surfeit of ironies that punctuates our human foibles
    . . . although Stoppard's sentences are more gymnastic
    . . . and less turgid."

61 FOOTE, TIMOTHY. "Crime and Panachement." Time 103 (11
    March):103.
       Review of Jumpers (Washington, D.C., Kennedy Center,
    tryout of Broadway production). Says the play's theme is
    "an extraordinary statement: if God does not exist, it
    will shortly be necessary to re-invent him." Reprinted in
    1974.B111. Abridged in 1975.B97.

62 FRAME, COLIN. "Theatre: Travesties." Evening News (London),
    11 June, p. 4.
       Review of the London, Royal Shakespeare Company produc-
    tion. Cannot understand "what on earth Lenin is doing in
    such company"; finds the play "good for plenty of laughs
    but not much more."

63 FRANCE, PETER. "Kaleidoscope." BBC Radio Four (17 April).
       Interview with Stoppard about Travesties and John Wood,
    who played the lead in the London, Royal Shakespeare Com-
    pany production. Transcript housed, London, BBC Written
    Archives Centre. Rebroadcast in abridged form: 1976.B78.

64 GAGNARD, FRANK. "Jumpers Is Trial, Treat." New Orleans Times-
    Picayune, 26 May, sec. 2, pp. 12, 13.
       Mixed review of the Broadway production.

65 _____. "On the Square: Free Man." New Orleans Times-
    Picayune, 19 July, sec. 2, p. 11.
       Review of Enter a Free Man (New Orleans, Tulane Center
    Stage): "a grab bag of styles, ideas and influences."

66 GETLEIN, FRANK. "The Critic at Large: Jumpers Acrobatics."
    Washington Star-News, 24 February, p. C1.
       Favorable review of the Washington, D.C., Kennedy Center

tryout of the Broadway production.

67 GILL, BRENDAN. "The Theatre: Tumbling onto the Truth." New Yorker 50 (6 May):75.
    Favorable review of Jumpers (Broadway). Abridged in 1975.B97.

68 GLACKLIN, WILLIAM C. "Jumpers: There's No Telling Which Way It Will Bounce." Sacramento (Calif.) Bee, 22 December, sec. S, pp. 1, 6.
    Favorable review of the San Francisco, ACT production.

69 GLOVER, WILLIAM. "Jumpers." AP Wireservice. New York Public Library, Lincoln Center Drama Collection.
    Review of the Washington, D.C., Kennedy Center tryout of the Broadway production. Advises readers to enjoy the "clever showmanship" and not to "worry too much about what it means. If anything."

70 _____. "Jumpers." AP Wireservice. New York Public Library, Lincoln Center Drama Collection.
    Review of the Broadway production of Stoppard's "stylish bore." Abridged in 1974.B10.

71 GOTTFRIED, MARTIN. "Theatre: Jumpers." Women's Wear Daily, 24 April, p. 30.
    Review of the Broadway production: the play "reads fascinatingly . . . but on the stage . . . it is as boring as hell." Reprinted in 1974.B111.

72 _____. "Theatre: Stoppard's First Play." New York Post, 18 December, p. 39.
    Review of Enter a Free Man (New York, Theatre at St. Clement's). Enjoys its "love and unpretentiousness"-- qualities which Stoppard "seems to have lost along the way to his later successes."

73 GOW, GORDON. "Feeling Famous." Plays and Players 21 (September):16-20.
    Includes an interview with John Hurt, who played Tzara in Travesties (London, Royal Shakespeare Company); discusses the character and the "fantastic concentration" required of actors in Stoppard's plays.

74 GRIFFIN, WILLIAM. "Stage." Sign 54 (July/August):14.
    Mixed review of Jumpers (Broadway).

75 GUERNSEY, OTIS L., Jr., ed. "The New York Season." In The

1974

Best Plays of 1973-74. The Burns Mantle Yearbook. New York: Dodd, Mead & Co., p. 14.
   Brief analysis of Jumpers, a play with dazzling content but seriously flawed form: it "dares greatly and is great or nothing" when produced.

76   GUNNER, MARJORIE. "On and Off Broadway." Floral Park (N.Y.) Bulletin, 9 May, p. 2.
   Review of Jumpers (Broadway): a "teasingly entertaining play," but "not the most conclusive . . . I've seen in a long time."

77   GUSSOW, MEL. "Jumpers Author Is Verbal Gymnast." New York Times, 23 April, p. 36.
   Interview: Stoppard discusses the play's theme and its stylistic similarity to contemporary philosophical writing, which is "unconsciously hilarious."

78   HARRIS, LEONARD. "Jumpers." WCBS-TV, Channel 2 (23 April).
   Review of the Broadway production. The play does not "move from point to point. It . . . goes round in circles, looking at itself with admiration." Reprinted in 1974.B111.

79   HAYMAN, RONALD. "Peter Wood: A Partnership." Times (London), 8 June, p. 9.
   Interview: the director of six productions of Jumpers, Rosencrantz & Guildenstern Are Dead, and Travesties discusses his work with the plays.

80   _____. "Profile 9: Tom Stoppard." New Review 1 (December): 15-22.
   Analysis and profile: discusses "Artist Descending a Staircase," Jumpers, Lord Malquist & Mr Moon, The Real Inspector Hound, Rosencrantz & Guildenstern Are Dead, and Travesties in detail and Dogg's Our Pet briefly.
   Describes Stoppard's plays as the works "of a man who enjoys arguing with himself and crystallising the contradictions into characters." Traces the development of themes and techniques from 1966 through 1974; attributes the "proliferation of interconnections between his plays" to his habit of "constantly . . . allowing his . . . mind to loop freely backwards and forwards within an evolving structure."
   Characterizes Stoppard as "a collage artist" who selects "the most disparate ingredients he [can] find" in order to tax "his ingenuity . . . to the utmost" when trying to assemble them; notes that he has become better at "accommo-

Writings about Tom Stoppard

1974

dating both halves of a contradiction and then making the sparks fly . . . between them." Also voices a reservation: his interest in parody distracts him from his serious themes, particularly in Jumpers and Travesties.

Also includes many quotations from Stoppard, many of them in answer to questions other interviewers did not ask: the effect of his wide reading upon his writing, the absence of political commitment in his plays, the predominance of his unconscious over his conscious mind and his theatrical over his thematic concerns while writing ("What's wrong with bad art is that the artist knows exactly what he's doing"), his admiration for "The Love Song of J. Alfred Prufrock" and the works of Samuel Beckett. Also discusses the form of Jumpers and the interests which led to Dogg's Our Pet and goes into great detail about his intentions in the much-criticized second act of Travesties.

Quotations expanded and published as an interview in 1977.A1.

81 HEBERT, HUGH. "Domes of Zurich." Guardian (London), 7 June, p. 10.

Feature article describing a visit to a rehearsal of Travesties (London, Royal Shakespeare Company); reports on the director's solution to two ambiguities in the script.

82 HEPPLE, PETER. "Plays: Stoppard's Latest Show-Stopper." Where to Go (4 July):39.

Review of Travesties (London, Royal Shakespeare Company).

83 HILLGATE, JASON. "Theatre: Dazzling Stoppard." What's On In London, 21 June, p. 22.

Review of Travesties (London, Royal Shakespeare Company).

84 HINCHLIFFE, ARNOLD P. British Theatre: 1950-70. Drama and Theatre Studies, edited by Kenneth Richards. Totowa, N.J.: Rowman & Littlefield, pp. 141-42.

Characterizes Rosencrantz & Guildenstern Are Dead as Absurdism done "to little purpose and no more than competently" by a "clever, manipulating rather than exploring" writer. Repeats an error found in 1969.B54, describing After Magritte (instead of "Neutral Ground") as a "cross between John Le Carre [sic] and T. S. Eliot."

85 HOBE. "Shows on Broadway." Variety, 24 April, p. 58.
Review of Jumpers (Broadway).

86 HOBSON, HAROLD. "Theatre: Stoppard in Bloom." Sunday Times (London), 16 June, p. 38.

Writings about Tom Stoppard

1974

Review of Travesties (London, Royal Shakespeare Company): a "miraculous display of verbal fireworks."

87 HOGAN, WILLIAM. "Stoppard's Non-Absurdity." San Francisco Chronicle, 13 December, p. 66.
Interview: Stoppard discusses his early life; the Hamburg, Germany, production of A Walk on the Water (and mentions another in Vienna); and his screenplay of The Romantic Englishwoman.

88 _____. "Jumpers Is a Marvelous, Goofy Put-On." San Francisco Chronicle, 19 December, p. 47.
Favorable review of the San Francisco, ACT production.

89 HOLLAND, JACK. "Holland's Tunnel." Newport Beach (Calif.) Newporter Mesa News, 23 October, p. 6.
Review of After Magritte and The Real Inspector Hound (Costa Mesa, California, South Coast Repertory): the former confusing and the latter "labored and . . . a bit monotonous."

90 HUDSON, ROGER; ITZEN, CATHERINE; and TRUSSLER, SIMON. "Ambushes for the Audience: Towards a High Comedy of Ideas." Theatre Quarterly 4 (May-July):3-17.
Interview. Contains a detailed account of Stoppard's early life and first plays; discusses his preoccupation with matters of craft rather than theme, his moral and ethical beliefs, the absence of an immediate political commitment in his works, and characters named Moon and Boot.
Also discusses his plays' structural characteristics; mentions his sources and intentions in After Magritte, "A Separate Peace," Enter a Free Man, The Gamblers, Jumpers, "'M' Is for 'Moon' among Other Things," and, briefly, "Neutral Ground." Talks in more detail about his problems with and fondness for The Real Inspector Hound, the early version of Rosencrantz & Guildenstern Are Dead, and the theme of Travesties. Published in conjunction with 1974. B135.

91 HUGHES, CATHARINE. "Theatre: More Bundles from Britain." America 130 (18 May):395.
Includes a review of Jumpers (Broadway).

92 _____. "New York." Plays and Players 21 (July):49-50.
Includes a review of Jumpers (Broadway).

93 HURREN, KENNETH. "Review of the Arts: Wilde about Stoppard."

1974

Spectator 232 (22 June):776.
Review of Travesties (London, Royal Shakespeare Company). Finds Stoppard's "skill and wit and irony . . . impudently dazzling" but believes "he is mistaken . . . to resist his parodial impulses in the case of Lenin." Abridged in 1975.B97.

94 JANUSONIS, MICHAEL. "Jumpers in New York. . . . ." Providence (R.I.) Journal-Bulletin Weekend, 21 December, p. 13.
Review of the Providence, Trinity Square Repertory production: finds it superior to the Broadway version. Printed next to 1974.B148.

95 KALEM, T. E. "Ping Pong Philosopher." Time 103 (6 May):85.
Interview and review of Jumpers (Broadway). Stoppard discusses the gulf between "one's emotional response to absolute morality and one's rational sense of the implausibility of there being a God"; also mentions the difficulty he has ending his plays satisfactorily.
Review claims the play assesses "the destinies of 20th century man. . . . Shaw dramatized the sundering of the social fabric. . . . Stoppard is concerned with the moral fabric, the abyss of non-belief." Review (not interview) abridged in 1975.B97.

96 KAUFFMANN, STANLEY. "Stanley Kauffmann on Theater." New Republic 170 (18 May):18, 33.
Review of Jumpers (Broadway). Particularly critical of the play's form ("there is no thematic resonance whatsoever between the scurrying antics in the boudoir and the intellectual meanderings in the study") and its "rhetorically ornate style brandished by a dramatist who has more wish than need to write and who takes the offensive stylistically in order to cow us." Reprinted in 1976.B60. Abridged in 1975.B97.

97 KELLY, KELVIN. "Jumpers Falls Short of Mark." Boston Globe, 28 April, p. 71.
Unfavorable review of the Broadway production.

98 KERR, WALTER. "Jumpers Needs to Settle Down." New York Times, 3 March, sec. 2, pp. 1, 18.
Mixed review of the Washington, D.C., Kennedy Center tryout of the Broadway production.

99 _____. "Three Plays in Search of a Plot." New York Times, 5 May, sec. 2, pp. 1, 3.
Includes an unfavorable review of Jumpers (Broadway).

1974

100 KINGSTON, JEREMY. "Theatre." <u>Punch</u> 266 (19 June):1064.
   Review of <u>Travesties</u> (London, Royal Shakespeare Company): the Lenins "really aren't fitted into the . . . plot," and "when Carr is absent the tension slackens."

101 KRETZMER, HERBERT. "It's a Mind-Boggler--This Play on Words." <u>Daily Express</u> (London), 11 June, p. 12.
   Review of <u>Travesties</u> (London, Royal Shakespeare Company).

102 KRIEGSMAN, ALAN M. "Crosscurrents: <u>Jumpers</u>: After the 'Hoopla.'" <u>Washington Post</u>, 24 February, sec. E, pp. 1, 5, 6.
   Analysis of the play, in response to 1974.B42. Claims that Stoppard's formula is to "assert something, then assert the contrary, and then take the whole thing back. . . . [This] doesn't make a . . . playwright out of a clever wordsmith" because Stoppard never confronts the issues he raises and his plays' ambitions surpass their achievements. Says his best work is <u>The Real Inspector Hound</u>: the large scale and "metaphysical encumbrances" of <u>Jumpers</u> hamstring his talent. For a reply to this analysis, see 1974.B43.

103 KROLL, JACK. "Moonie-Junie." <u>Newsweek</u> 83 (4 March):87.
   Review of <u>Jumpers</u> (Washington, D.C., Kennedy Center tryout of Broadway production) in which Stoppard "attacks the biggest, fattest paradox we have--the breakdown of certainty through the proliferation of knowledge." Reprinted in 1974.B111.

104 LAMBERT, J. W. "Plays in Performance: London." <u>Drama: The Quarterly Theatre Review</u>, no. 114 (Autumn):38-41.
   Includes a review of <u>Travesties</u> (London, Royal Shakespeare Company), which gradually disappointed the reviewer because Joyce and Tzara are not really revolutionaries, while Lenin, who is, is not integrated into the play. Accuses Stoppard of "using that . . . evasive tactic of putting opinions in which he believes . . . into unlikely mouths, so that he cannot be accused of being . . . square." Abridged in 1976.B87.

105 LEECH, MICHAEL T. "Wave of Success for <u>Jumpers</u> Author Tom Stoppard." <u>Christian Science Monitor</u>, 6 March, p. F6.
   Interview: Stoppard compares the London and Broadway productions of <u>Jumpers</u> and discusses John Wood, for whom he wrote the play's leading role, and Michael Hordern, who played it in London.

1974

106 LEVITAN, ALAN. "Variations on the Logic of Absurdity." Boston Phoenix, 9 April, sec. 2, p. 11.
   Review of After Magritte and The Real Inspector Hound (American touring production): the former "tedious" and the latter a "pure delight."

107 LEWIS, ANTHONY. "Art and Politics." New York Times, 17 June, p. 31.
   Analysis of Travesties in a feature article about politics.

108 McLELLAN, DIANA. "Celebrity Bafflement Gives Way to Good Cheer." Washington Star-News, 19 February, sec. C, p. 1.
   News item describing the audience attending the opening of Jumpers (Washington, D.C., Kennedy Center tryout of the Broadway production).

109 MAHON, DEREK. "Tom Stoppard: A Noticeable Absence of Tortoises." Vogue 164 (June):21.
   Brief interview: Stoppard again defines his drama as a "compromise" between "serious propositions and frivolity."

110 MARCUS, FRANK. "Theatre: End Games." Sunday Telegraph (London), 16 June, p. 16.
   Review of Travesties (London, Royal Shakespeare Company). Notes that each character is simultaneously "a figment of Carr's fallible memory, a symbol of an idea, and a living parallel of a creature of Wilde's imagination. It is . . . miraculous that this extraordinary schemer makes sense."

111 MARLOWE, JOAN, and BLAKE, BETTY, eds. "Jumpers." New York Theatre Critics' Review 35 (29 April):298-304.
   Reprintes of 1974.B61, 103, 186, reviews of the Washington, D.C., Kennedy Center tryout; and reprints of 1974. B27, 31, 71, 78, 137, 173, 177, reviews of the Broadway run of the production.

112 MARRIOTT, R. B. "Travesties at the Aldwych." Stage and Television Today (London), 20 June, p. 15.
   Favorable review of the London, Royal Shakespeare Company production.

113 MASTROIANNI, TONY. "Guildenstern Lives on E. 86th St.--Vividly." Cleveland Press, 16 March, p. A8.
   Review of Rosencrantz & Guildenstern Are Dead (Cleveland Playhouse): found it better than the Broadway and national touring productions, largely because the segments

1974

from Hamlet "have the stature they deserve."

114 MAVES, C. E. "ACT Bounces Right Along in Tom Stoppard's Jumpers." Palo Alto (Calif.) Times, 18 December, p. 23.
   Mixed review of the San Francisco company's production.

115 MELLOR, ISHA. "Amateurs." Plays and Players 21 (June):60.
   Includes a review of The Real Inspector Hound (London, City Lit Productions).

116 MOOTZ, WILLIAM. "Stages: A Tribute to the Art." Louisville (Ky.) Courier-Journal, 13 December, p. B10.
   Review of The Real Inspector Hound (Louisville, Actors Theatre of Louisville), a "fiendishly clever comedy . . . superior in every way to the New York production."

117 MORGAN, QUITA. "It Looks So Bizarre from the Stalls." Evening Post (Bristol), 25 April, p. 36.
   Favorable review of Jumpers (Bristol Old Vic).

118 NIGHTINGALE, BENEDICT. "Theatre: From the Zurich Station." New Statesman 87 (14 June):859.
   Review of Travesties (London, Royal Shakespeare Company): applies to Stoppard Samuel Johnson's objection to Shakespeare's "quibbles," for which the playwright "'will always turn aside from his career.' There's so much chasing of ideas that we never get around to evaluating them." Abridged in 1976.B87.

119 NOVICK, JULIUS. "Saved by the Second Act." Village Voice, 2 May, pp. 83-84.
   Review of Jumpers (Broadway): after a "self-indulgent, wayward" first act, the play attains "coherence . . . just in time." Abridged in 1975.B97 and 1975.B117.

120 O'CONNOR, GARRY. "Travesties." Plays and Players 21 (July): 34-35.
   Review of the London, Royal Shakespeare Company production: "the section devoted to the rights and wrongs of Leninism . . . detracts from the comic force of the rest of the evening."

121 OLIVER, EDITH. "The Theatre: Off Broadway." New Yorker 50 (4 March):70.
   Review of Rosencrantz & Guildenstern Are Dead (New York, Classic Stage Company revival). Abridged in 1975.B97.

Writings about Tom Stoppard

1974

122 O'MALLEY, JOHN F. "Tom Stoppard." In "Caryl Churchill, David Mercer, and Tom Stoppard: A Study of Contemporary British Dramatists Who Have Written for Radio, Television, and Stage." Ph.D. dissertation, Florida State University, pp. 120-79.

Evaluates Stoppard's awareness of the characteristics of different media and his ability to write for them. Includes quotations from Peter Wood, John Tydeman, Alan Gibson, and Michael Bakewell (directors of Stoppard's plays) on these subjects; also describes opportunities available to writers of radio drama in the early 1960s, when Stoppard was beginning his career.

Includes brief analyses of After Magritte, "Another Moon Called Earth," "Artist Descending a Staircase," "The Dissolution of Dominic Boot," "If You're Glad I'll Be Frank," Jumpers, "A Paragraph for Mr. Blake," The Real Inspector Hound, Rosencrantz & Guildenstern Are Dead, "A Separate Peace," and "Teeth."

123 OPPENHEIMER, GEORGE. "Bewitched, Bothered, Bewildered." Long Island City (N.Y.) Newsday, 12 May, sec. 2, p. 9.

Review of Jumpers (Broadway), which left the reviewer "completely bewildered . . . and somewhat bored."

124 _____. "London: Quality despite Inflation." Long Island City (N.Y.) Newsday, 18 August, sec. 2, p. 8.

Includes a favorable review of Travesties (London, Royal Shakespeare Company).

125 _____. "Of Mice and Men Still Touching." Long Island City (N.Y.) Newsday, 29 December, sec. 2, p. 7.

Includes a review of Enter a Free Man (New York, Theatre at St. Clement's): finds it unoriginal but humorous, tender, and warm.

126 OWEN, MICHAEL. "News of the Arts: Stoppard's New Electric Notion." Evening Standard (London), 24 May, p. 26.

Interview: Stoppard discusses the trouble he has inventing plots, his habit of procrastinating (particularly with Travesties), and the play's origin in a story told to him by a reporter in Bristol.

127 PAUL. "Shows out of Town: Jumpers." Variety, 20 February, p. 52.

Mixed review of the Washington, D.C., Kennedy Center tryout of the Broadway production.

128 PETER, JOHN. "Theatre: Great Artificer." Times Education

Writings about Tom Stoppard

1974

Supplement (London), 5 July, p. 118.
Review of Travesties (London, Royal Shakespeare Company).

129 PIT. "Shows Abroad." Variety, 19 June, p. 60.
Review of Travesties (London, Royal Shakespeare Company): "a highly personal blend of documentary and fantasy" which "sags . . . when pausing for factual history."

130 QUANTRILL, JAY ALAN. "Academy Play by a Landslide." Washington Post, 22 April, sec. B, p. 7.
Includes a mixed review of Rosencrantz & Guildenstern Are Dead (Washington, American College Theatre Festival, U. S. Naval Academy production).

131 REID, HELEN. "Killing Starts a Murder of the Morals." Western Daily Press (Bristol), 25 April, p. 8.
Favorable review of Jumpers (Bristol Old Vic).

132 RICHARDS, DAVID. "Jumpers: A Zany Brew of Ambition and Tedium." Washington Star-News, 19 February, sec. C, p. 1.
Review of the Washington, D.C., Kennedy Center tryout of the Broadway production: applauds its ambitiousness but regrets its limited achievements.

133 RICHARDSON, JACK. "Theater: Bright Events." Commentary 57 (June):79-80.
Includes a review of Jumpers (Broadway); calls Stoppard "the only writer . . . capable of making the theater a truly formidable and civilized experience again." Abridged in 1975.B97.

134 RIDLEY, CLIFFORD A. "The Expanding Arts: Stoppard's Mad Jumpers Strut Their Stuff." National Observer 13 (9 March):20.
Review of the Washington, D.C., Kennedy Center tryout of the Broadway production.

135 RYAN, RANDOLPH, comp. "Theatre Checklist No. 2: Tom Stoppard." Theatrefacts, no. 2 (May-July):2-9.
Includes a chronology of Stoppard's life and career; plot synopses, analytical comments, staging information, and production and publication data about most of Stoppard's plays and fiction through "Artist Descending a Staircase" (November 1972). Does not mention The Gamblers, "A Paragraph for Mr. Blake," "Is 'Is' Is?" and "One Pair of Eyes." Published in conjuction with 1974.B90.

Writings about Tom Stoppard

1974

136 SAMSON, BLAKE A. "Jumpers Has Elusive Wisdom." San Rafael (Calif.) Independent Journal, 18 December, p. 33.
   Favorable review of the San Francisco, ACT production.

137 SANDERS, KEVIN. "Jumpers." WABC-TV, Channel 7 (22 April).
   Review of the Broadway production. Although "brilliant," the play's "underlying theme . . . [is] totally incoherent." Reprinted in 1974.B111.

138 SAUNDERS, DUDLEY. "Stages Should Be a Delight to All, and a Special Joy to Theater-Lovers." Louisville (Ky.) Times, 13 December, p. B13.
   Includes a favorable review of The Real Inspector Hound (Louisville, Actors Theatre of Louisville).

139 SHEPPARD, EUGENIA. "Inside Fashion: One of the Jumpers." New York Post, 30 May, p. 43.
   Interview with Frederick Brisson, producer of the Broadway production of Jumpers.

140 SHULMAN, MILTON. "Theatre." Evening Standard (London), 11 June, p. 11.
   Mixed review of Travesties (London, Royal Shakespeare Company).

141 SIMON, JOHN. "Theater: Flying Philosophers, Poetic Pederasts." New York 7 (11 March):84.
   Review of Jumpers (Washington, D.C., Kennedy Center tryout of the Broadway production): "a messy work by a witty and intelligent author." Criticizes the absence of "solid character, plot, and structure." Abridged in 1975.B97.

142 _____. "Theater: Ripe, or Merely Ready?" New York 7 (13 May):98.
   Review of Jumpers (Broadway). Observes that "a tart epigram" is not enough: also required is "a sense of underlying character from which the comic retort or aphorism springs." Abridged in 1975.B97.

143 _____. "Theater: London Diary V: Éclat." New York 7 (26 August):67.
   Review of Travesties (London, Royal Shakespeare Company), in which Stoppard's "profound nugacity" and "inveterate trifling" so undermine the play that it is "ultimately about nothing at all." Abridged in 1976.B87.

144 SMITH, A[NTHONY] C. H. "Tom Stoppard." Flourish (10 June):

1974

    n.p.
    Interview: Stoppard discusses the moral and social functions of art, the need artists feel to justify their work, his attempts to perform a "marriage between the play of ideas and farce" in his works. Also mentions his research and attitude toward the protagonist of Jumpers, the theme of Travesties, and his uncertainty while writing The Real Inspector Hound about the identity of the corpse and the resolution of the plot.

145 SMYTH, JEANNETTE, and SHALES, TOM. "Scene: 'Everybody' Was There." Washington Post, 19 February, p. B3.
    Society news item reporting on the audience attending the opening of Jumpers (Washington, D.C., Kennedy Center tryout of the Broadway production).

146 SPAETH, ARTHUR. "Rosencrantz and Friend Play Hamlet Counterpoint." Cleveland Sun Press, 4 April, sec. C, p. 9.
    Favorable review of Rosencrantz & Guildenstern Are Dead (Cleveland Playhouse).

147 STACEY, ROY. "London Theatre Survey." Amateur Stage (July): 25.
    Includes a review of Travesties (London, Royal Shakespeare Company).

148 STARK, JUDY. "Jumpers in London. . . ." Providence (R.I.) Journal-Bulletin Weekend, 21 December, p. 13.
    Review of Jumpers (Providence, R.I., Trinity Square Repertory): finds it better than the London, National Theatre production. Printed next to 1974.B94.

149 STASIO, MARILYN. "Misspent Dreams." Cue 43 (23 December): 31.
    Review of Enter a Free Man (New York, Theatre at St. Clement's): an "interesting, if not terribly prescient look at an important talent in formation."

150 SULLIVAN, DAN. "Stage Review: Inspector Hound in Costa Mesa." Los Angeles Times, 10 October, sec. IV, p. 20.
    Mixed review of the South Coast Repertory production.

151 _____. "Jumpers Keeps ACT Hopping." Los Angeles Times, 19 December, sec. IV, p. 1.
    Favorable review of the San Francisco company's production.

152 SUSSMAN, SHARRON. "ACT's Alba: The Many Firsts that Make It

1974

Work." Mill Valley (Calif.) Record, 30 January, p. 2.
Review of The House of Bernarda Alba (San Francisco, ACT): says that Stoppard's adaptation "capture[s Lorca's] intoxication with language."

153 SWAN, BRADFORD F. "Jumpers Second Production of Trinity Repertory Company." Providence (R.I.) Journal, 13 December, p. A9.
Favorable review of the Providence company's production.

154 TAYLOR, ROBERT. "It's Really about. . . ." Oakland (Calif.) Tribune, 11 December, p. 31.
Interview with Stoppard.

155 _____. "ACT's Jumpers." Oakland (Calif.) Tribune, 19 December, p. 21.
Favorable review of the San Francisco company's production.

156 THIRKELL, ARTHUR. "Theatre: Just Brilliant." Daily Mirror (London), 11 June, p. 18.
Review of Travesties (London, Royal Shakespeare Company).

157 THOMAS, ART. "Hamlet's Friends Are Play House Subjects." Berea (Ohio) Exponent, 2 April, p. 4.
Favorable review of Rosencrantz & Guildenstern Are Dead (Cleveland Playhouse).

158 THOMPSON, HOWARD. "Stage: New Rosencrantz." New York Times, 1 February, p. 15.
Review of the New York, Classic Stage Company production.

159 TINKER, JACK. "The Critics: At Least It's Clever Nonsense." Daily Mail (London), 11 June, p. 3.
Review of Travesties (London, Royal Shakespeare Company): quarrels with the play because, "having selected . . . giants . . . as his stooges, [Stoppard] pretends to make them prophets."

160 TISCHLER, GARY. "It Was No Day for an Interview." Fremont (Calif.) Argus, 20 December, p. 23.
Interview with Stoppard.

161 TORPOR, TOM. "Lunch with a Playwright." New York Post, 10 April, p. 64.
Interview: Stoppard discusses Travesties, Jumpers, and its producer, Roger Stevens.

Writings about Tom Stoppard

1974

162 TREWIN, J. C. "New Plays: *Travesties*." *Lady* (27 June):947.
Review of the London, Royal Shakespeare Company production. Notes that Lenin is not "entirely fitted into [Stoppard's] wild pattern."

163 ———. "Theatre: What Happened in Zurich." *Illustrated London News* 262 (August):67.
Review of *Travesties* (London, Royal Shakespeare Company): preferable to Stoppard's earlier and "perilously self-indulgent" works.

164 WADE, DAVID. "Radio: Prize-Giving." *Times* (London), 27 April, p. 8.
News item reporting Stoppard's service as a judge in a radio drama contest.

165 WAHLS, ROBERT. "Footlights: The Star of a Puzzle." *New York Sunday News*, 5 May, p. 8.
Interview with Brian Bedford, leading actor in *Jumpers* (Broadway).

166 WALKER, JOHN. "London Theater: Stoppard's *Travesties*—Seriously Frivolous." *International Herald Tribune* (Paris), 15 June, p. 6.
Review of the London, Royal Shakespeare Company production. Claims that "the strictly documentary moments are not assimilated into the texture of the play."

167 WALLACH, ALAN. "Stage: Metaphysical Acrobatics." *Long Island City* (N.Y.) *Newsday*, 23 April, p. 8A.
Review of *Jumpers* (Broadway): offers "an abundance of food for thought but . . . never comes fully alive." Abridged in 1974.B10.

168 WARDLE, IRVING. "A Web to Snare Three Giants." *Times* (London), 11 June, p. 7.
Review of *Travesties* (London, Royal Shakespeare Company), which fails to "absorb Lenin" into its structure.

169 ———. "Sense of Exhilaration." *Times* (London), 9 July, p. 7.
Review of *Rosencrantz & Guildenstern Are Dead* (London, Young Vic revival). Notes that Stoppard's strategy leaves his protagonists "nothing . . . to do [when alone]. . . . But every time Stoppard discovers some fresh way out. . . . Fragile at first glance, the play is a cobweb of steel."

170 WASSERMAN, DEBBI. "*Jumpers*: Intellectual In-Joke Becomes

Writings about Tom Stoppard

1974

Wearing." <u>New York Show Business</u>, 25 April, p. 13.
Review of the Broadway production, which becomes so "caught up in its own cleverness [that] the absurdity of the basic situation . . . is lost in verbosity." Abridged in 1975.B97.

171 WATT, DOUGLAS. "Stoppard's <u>Jumpers</u> Makes American Bow." <u>New York Daily News</u>, 21 February, p. 78.
Review of the Washington, D.C., Kennedy Center tryout of the Broadway production: a "swollen piece of theatrical and intellectual chic" which Stoppard "muddied by conceptual thinking of no dramatic value." Continued: 1974.B172.

172 _____. "The Way Stoppard Bounces." <u>New York Sunday News</u>, 3 March, p. 3.
Continuation of 1974.B171. Grants that the play contains "very thoughtful stuff" but insists that "it is not inherently dramatic, and Stoppard hasn't bothered to make it any more so."

173 _____. "<u>Jumpers</u> Plays with Words, Ideas." <u>New York Daily News</u>, 23 April, p. 52.
Review of the Broadway production. Calls the play "a neat trick. . . . But little more when all is said and done." Reprinted in 1974.B111. Summarized in 1974.B174.

174 _____. "Theater: Unfunny Things Happen on Way to the Theater." <u>New York Sunday News</u>, 5 May, p. 3.
Recapitulation of the week's reviews, including 1974.B173.

175 _____. "Watt's Involved with British Plays." <u>New York Sunday News</u>, 4 August, sec. 3, p. 3.
Review of <u>Travesties</u> (London, Royal Shakespeare Company): notes the play's "curious warmth," its "almost affectionate quality," but "Lenin's heavy hand in its middle" is an error.

176 _____. "<u>Enter a Free Man</u> Moving Comedy." <u>New York Daily News</u>, 18 December, p. 86.
Review of the New York, Theatre at St. Clement's production: the play is "witty, and . . . brilliant, too, but it is also moving."

177 WATTS, RICHARD. "Theater: An Enigma from Tom Stoppard." <u>New York Post</u>, 23 April, p. 51.
Review of <u>Jumpers</u> (Broadway), which "first annoyed and

1974

then bored" him. "The London critics who claimed they understood every word of the play must have giant intellects I had never suspected." Reprinted in 1974.B111. Continued in 1974.B178.

178 _____. "Random Notes." New York Post, 30 April, p. 55.
Includes a continuation of 1974.B177, expressing sadness at having been "baffled and bored" by the play. Returns to the subject in 1974.B179.

179 _____. "Theater Week: The Fascination of Tom Stoppard." New York Post, 11 May, p. 2.
Continuation of 1974.B178: Stoppard "was endeavouring to cover too much territory" in Jumpers.

180 _____. "Theater Week." New York Post, 7 September, p. 16.
Review of Travesties (London, Royal Shakespeare Company): "the most fascinating new play I've come across in a long time" but doubts whether it would succeed on Broadway.

181 _____. "Theater Week: A Philosophical Neil Simon." New York Post, 21 December, p. 16.
Includes a favorable review of Enter a Free Man (New York, Theatre at St. Clement's).

182 WEIGHTMAN, JOHN. "Theatre: Art versus Life." Encounter 43 (September):57-59.
Review of Travesties (London, Royal Shakespeare Company); also contains analytical comments about Stoppard's method of transforming "pastiche into a creative statement." Notes that he, unlike other artists, is "not moderate in his cannibalising" of others' styles and conventions; wonders whether the reason is that he "is in love with art and [is] not quite sure that he himself is a true artist." Abridged in 1976.B87.

183 WILLIAMS, GARY JAY. "Theater: Misbegotten Moons." National Review 26 (29 March):377.
Includes a review of Jumpers (Washington, D.C., Kennedy Center tryout of the Broadway production): a "spectacularly barren . . . jumble of vaudeville and philosophy."

184 WILSON, EARL. "It Happened Last Night: More B'way Talent Uncovered." New York Post, 23 April, p. 28.
Brief review of Jumpers (Broadway), concentrating upon its nude scenes.

1975

185 _____. "On Broadway: She Hangs by Her Teeth in the Nude. . . ." New York Post, 11 May, p. 18.
　　　Interview with Joan Byron, who plays the secretary in Jumpers (Broadway).

186 WILSON, EDWIN. "Stoppard's Gem in a Distracting Set." Wall Street Journal, 11 March, p. 14.
　　　Review of Jumpers (Washington, D.C., Kennedy Center tryout of the Broadway production): "one of the most brilliant theatrical charades of our time." Reprinted in 1974.B111.

187 WOOTTEN, DICK. "Bit Players or Stars, These Two Are Both." Cleveland Press, 27 March, p. F7.
　　　Interview with the actors playing Rosencrantz and Guildenstern in the Cleveland Playhouse production: they discuss their difficulty memorizing lines and the play's mixture of serious and comic material.

1975

A　BOOKS--NONE

B　SHORTER WRITINGS

1　AARON, JULES. "Theatre in Review: Jumpers." Educational Theatre Journal 27 (May):267-68.
　　　Review of the San Francisco, ACT production.

2　ANON. "Stoppard, Tom." In Current Biography Yearbook: 1974. Edited by Charles Moritz. New York: The H. W. Wilson Co., pp. 396-99.
　　　Reprint of 1974.B18.

3　ANON. "Plays and Players 1974 Awards." Plays and Players 22 (January):12-23.
　　　Includes brief statements by eighteen of London's theatre critics about the previous season's plays, including Travesties (London, Royal Shakespeare Company).

4　ANON. "Claire Bloom, John Wood Cop London Acting Nods." Variety, 22 January, p. 89.
　　　News item, includes the announcement that Travesties won the London Evening Standard Award for Best Comedy of the past season.

1975

5   ANON. Photograph. Sunday Times (London), 20 April, p. 39.
    A scene from The Romantic Englishwoman (London, DIAL Films); announcement of its entry in the Cannes Film Festival.

6   ANON. "Plays: Revival's Victorious Victim." Where to Go (11 September):45.
    Reviews of the revivals of Rosencrantz & Guildenstern Are Dead (London, Young Vic), "a delight only to the littérateur," and Travesties (London, Royal Shakespeare Company), "the finest example of the work of the cleverest playwright of our time."

7   ANON. "B'way Travesties Knocking on Wood." Variety, 17 September, p. 81.
    News item announcing the transfer of the London, Royal Shakespeare Company production to the Albery Theatre and the play's impending opening on Broadway.

8   ANON. Photograph. Sunday Times (London), 12 October, p. 38.
    A scene from "Three Men in a Boat"; announcement of its transmission on 26 December.

9   ANON. Review of Travesties. Booklist 72 (15 October):273.
    Favorable review of the text.

10 ANON. "Film Guide." Sight and Sound 45 (Winter):66.
    Includes a brief review of The Romantic Englishwoman (London, DIAL Films): Stoppard's screenplay exhibits "a peevish disdain for" the characters and the film's "putative women's lib theme."

11 ANON. "Ex-Registrar Says She Ended Life." Times (London), 19 November, p. 4.
    News item, reporting that Dr. Miriam Stoppard, the playwright's wife, admitted on a late-night television discussion program that she had once allowed a patient to die. Also see 1975.B65.

12 ANON. "The Romantic Englishwoman." Catholic Film Newsletter 40, no. 24 (30 December):114.
    Brief unfavorable review of the film.

13 BARBER, JOHN. "Theatre: Breathtaking Farce of Dazzling Witticisms." Daily Telegraph (London), 30 May, p. 13.
    Review of Travesties (London, Royal Shakespeare Company revival): Stoppard's "jokes and lectures can go on too long."

1975

14 BARKER, FELIX. "First Night: Funny History and a Game of Words." Evening News (London), 30 May, p. 4.
    Favorable review of Travesties (London, Royal Shakespeare Company revival).

15 BARNES, CLIVE. "Stage: Absent Friends." New York Times, 13 September, p. 15.
    Favorable review of Rosencrantz & Guildenstern Are Dead (London, Young Vic revival).

16 _____. "Stoppard Goes Wilde in Travesties." New York Times, 31 October, p. 21.
    Review of the Broadway production: the play surpasses Rosencrantz & Guildenstern Are Dead and Jumpers in terms of "sheer intellectual shimmer." Reprinted in 1975.B81. Essential points summarized in 1975.B17.

17 _____. "Travesties: Ethel Barrymore Theater." Times (London), 1 November, p. 9.
    Review of the Broadway production for British readers: a brief version of 1975.B16.

18 _____. "New York Notebook: Nostalgic Reunions and a Few Home Truths." Times (London), 22 November, p. 10.
    Includes a brief note about the "tremendous [critical] notices" given Travesties (Broadway), but points out that London's and New York's audiences often agree "rather less" than the two cities' critics do.

19 BEAUFORT, JOHN. "Travesties: Dazzling Skyrocket of a Play." Christian Science Monitor, 6 November, p. 22.
    Favorable review of the Broadway production. Reprinted in 1975.B81.

20 BEAUMAN, SALLY. "Footnote in the Spotlight." New York 8 (15 September):56.
    Interview with John Wood, leading actor in Travesties (Broadway); discusses actors' difficulties with Stoppard's characters.

21 BENNETT, JONATHAN. "Philosophy and Mr. Stoppard." Philosophy 50 (January):5-18.
    Analysis by a professor of philosophy: discusses Stoppard's use of the subject in Jumpers (where it is "thin and uninteresting, and . . . serves the play only in a decorative and marginal way") and in Rosencrantz & Guildenstern Are Dead (where it is much more pertinent to the play's concerns). See reply to this article in 1977.B68.

1975

22 BILLINGTON, MICHAEL. "Aldwych: *Travesties*." *Guardian* (London), 30 May, p. 10.
   Favorable review of the London, Royal Shakespeare Company revival.

23 BRUKENFELD, DICK. "*Albert's Bridge*." *Village Voice*, 17 February, p. 78.
   Review of a stage adaptation (New York, Landmark Theatre Production Company): "few scenes . . . gain by being presented in front of us."

24 BUCK, RICHARD M. Review of *Travesties*. *Library Journal* 100 (1 November):2067.
   Review of the text of Stoppard's "marvellously funny political satire."

24a BUFFA, MICHELANGELO. "Lo spettatore critico." *Filmcritica* (September):308-9.
   Review (in Italian) of *The Romantic Englishwoman* (London, DIAL Films).

25 BUTCHER, MARYVONNE. "Cinema." *Tablet* 229 (25 October):1039.
   Favorable review of *The Romantic Englishwoman* (London, DIAL Films).

26 CAEN, HERB. "Friday's Fickle Finger." *San Francisco Chronicle*, 7 February, p. 25.
   Includes a brief favorable review of *Jumpers* (San Francisco, ACT).

27 CAIRD, ROD. "Theatre: Witty Load of Baloney." *Morning Star* (London), 31 May, p. 2.
   Favorable review of *Travesties* (London, Royal Shakespeare Company revival).

28 CANBY, VINCENT. "Obsessed *Romantic Englishwoman*." *New York Times*, 27 November, p. 46.
   Review of the film (London, DIAL Films): notes the "curious reversals," such as the use of mirror images and the theme of truth and reflection, which keep the film "interesting long after you've decided that something is decidedly wrong with it."

29 CLURMAN, HAROLD. "Theatre." *Nation* 221 (16 August):123-24.
   Mixed review of *Travesties* (London, Royal Shakespeare Company revival).

30 _____. "Theatre." *Nation* 221 (22 November):540.

1975

Mixed review of Travesties (Broadway). Abridged in 1978.B20.

31 COLEMAN, JOHN. "Films: Passport Poet." New Statesman 90 (17 October):480-81.
    Review of The Romantic Englishwoman (London, DIAL Films): "more entertaining in the bitten-off scraps of conversation and a few astute instants of domestic observation than in the rather thin and implausible plot."

32 COMBS, RICHARD. "The Country of the Past Revisited: Losey, Galileo and The Romantic Englishwoman." Sight and Sound 44 (Summer):138-43.
    Unfavorable review of the film and interview with its director, Joseph Losey, who says Stoppard "hardly changed the structure" of the author's screenplay draft, "but he largely rewrote the dialogue." Also claims Stoppard had disliked the novel but, "taking something he detested, he brought out all the best things in it."

33 COTTER, JERRY. "Screen." Sign 55 (December 1975-January 1976):31.
    Includes a brief review of The Romantic Englishwoman (London, DIAL Films): "a flimsy attempt to create humor from the menage a trois [sic] situation."

34 CURTISS, THOMAS QUINN. "The Romantic Englishwoman." International Herald Tribune (Paris), 11 June, p. 8.
    Review of the film (London, DIAL Films): it "occasionally threatens to turn to satire but remains indecisive and the result . . . is indistinguishable from a woman's magazine novelette of 1930 vintage."

35 DEAN, JOAN FitzPATRICK. "The Narrator in Contemporary British Drama." Ph.D. dissertation, Purdue University, pp. 169-96.
    Examines "the use of direct address" in plays by Robert Bolt, John Osborne, John Arden, Edward Bond, Peter Shaffer, and Stoppard. Concludes that he is more interested in parodying others' works and playing on an elitist audience's knowledge of drama than in presenting a "cohesive vision."
    Finds his use of narrators is most successful in The Real Inspector Hound, most traditional in Rosencrantz & Guildenstern Are Dead, and nearly uncontrolled in Travesties. Also discusses Jumpers.

36 DETTMER, ROGER. "Padding Hurts A Free Man." Chicago Tribune, 10 March, sec. 4, p. 14.
    Review of Enter a Free Man (Chicago, Summit Forum):

1975

"an anecdote which builds to a sight gag, with a banal denouement."

37 DICKERMAN, STU. "Theatre: Trinity's Jumpers Takes Off." Brown University (Providence, R.I.) Fresh Fruit, 29 January, p. 15.
    Review of the Providence, Trinity Square Repertory production. Finds the play's "serious part . . . considerably less interesting" than its comic moments; criticizes the production for failing to distinguish between them.

38 EDWA. "Review: Jumpers." Los Angeles Variety, 26 September, p. 3.
    Review of the Costa Mesa, South Coast Repertory production, which is "intriguing for the first half hour," but "then becomes thin."

39 EMMET, ALFRED. "Followthrough: Rosencrantz in Embryo." Theatre Quarterly 5 (March-May):95-96.
    Letter to the editors, calling attention to the Questors Theatre's production of a segment of Guildenstern and Rosencrantz in 1964. Also notes similarities between Rosencrantz & Guildenstern Are Dead and Next Time I'll Sing to You, written by James Saunders, who led the British delegation, including Stoppard, to the symposium in Berlin in 1964.

40 FARISH, GILLAN. "Into the Looking-Glass Bowl: An Instant of Grateful Terror." University of Windsor Review 10 (Spring-Summer):14-29.
    Analysis of Jumpers, The Real Inspector Hound, and Rosencrantz & Guildenstern Are Dead; concentrates on Stoppard's language.

41 FEINGOLD, MICHAEL. "The Title Should be Singular." Village Voice, 17 November, p. 119.
    Unfavorable review of Travesties (Broadway).

42 FORNARA, PETER. "Hound: Treat for Word Wits." Portland (Oreg.) Scribe, 21 June-27 June, p. 12.
    Review of The Real Inspector Hound (Portland, Civic Theatre): "the funniest play I've ever encountered."

43 FUNKE, LEWIS. "Tom Stoppard." In Playwrights Talk about Writing: 12 Interviews. Chicago: Dramatic Publishing Co., pp. 217-31.
    Interview (internal evidence suggests conducted in 1968); also contains some biographical data. Stoppard discusses

writing for television (a less "dangerous" medium than the stage), denies that he has "a premeditated intellectual or philosophical motive" while writing, criticizes "social" art for starting "with the message rather than the metaphor," and describes writing as "an act of faith, . . . catching things in mid-flight as they flash by, rather than assembling given components."

Also discusses the images from which "Albert's Bridge" and "If You're Glad I'll Be Frank" grew; his admiration for Beckett (and the lack of influence that feeling has on his own work); his preference for using "emotional, intellectual, and spiritual experience" rather than autobiographical material in his plays; and his conviction (reflected in Rosencrantz & Guildenstern Are Dead) that, far from being an "existential void," there is "something to be comprehended" in life.

44 GALATI, FRANK. "A Loony Farce at New Evanston Theater." Chicago Sunday Sun-Times, 21 September, sec. 3, pp. 1, 5.
Explication of Jumpers, written by the director of the Chicago, Evanston Theatre Company production, prior to its opening.

45 GILL, BRENDAN. "Off Broadway: At the Start." New Yorker 50 (6 January):50.
Review of Enter a Free Man (New York, Theatre at St. Clement's). Abridged in 1976.B87.

46 _____. "The Theatre: Stoppard's Theatre of What If." New Yorker 51 (10 November):135.
Review of Travesties (Broadway): on the basis of the play's treatment of old age, predicts that some of Stoppard's future comedies "will make us cry."

47 GILLETT, JOHN. "The Romantic Englishwoman." Focus on Film, no. 22 (Fall):7-8.
Mixed review of the film.

48 GLOVER, WILLIAM. Review of Travesties. AP Wireservice. New York Public Library, Lincoln Center Drama Collection.
Favorable review of the Broadway production. Abridged in 1975.B49.

49 _____. "Another British Hit on Broadway." San Francisco Examiner, 3 November, p. 34.
Abridged version of 1975.B48.

50 GODDARD, BOB. "Sunny Offerings at Loretto." St. Louis Globe-

1975

      Democrat, 10 February, p. 13A.
         Favorable review of The Real Inspector Hound (St. Louis, Loretto-Hilton Repertory).

51 GOLDSTEIN, LEONARD. "A Note on Tom Stoppard's After Magritte." Zeitschrift für Anglistik und Amerikanistik 23:16-21.
    Analysis: play "constitutes a kind of reply to the Absurdists and Existentialists" in that, while initially seeming to reflect Magritte's style of painting (which "undermines our confidence in reason"), it then supplies reasonable answers to the questions it had raised. Also lists elements and motifs which Stoppard took from Magritte's paintings.

52 GOTTFRIED, MARTIN. "Stoppard's Travesties: Literary Farce in a Universal Madhouse." New York Post, 31 October, p. 26.
    Review of the Broadway production: the play is "not always too literary for the stage. It is sometimes simply smart ass." Reprinted in 1975.B81.

53 _____. "Words, Words, Words." New York Post, 15 November, pp. 14, 40.
    Criticism of Stoppard's habitual "cleverness" and lack of commitment; inspired by Travesties (Broadway).

54 GOW, GORDON. "The Romantic Englishwoman." Films and Filming 22 (December):34.
    Unfavorable review of the film.

55 GUSSOW, MEL. "Playwright, Star Provide a Little Curtain-Raiser." New York Times, 31 October, p. 21.
    Interview, prior to the opening of Travesties (Broadway), largely a dialogue between John Wood (its leading actor) and Stoppard. Discuss the effect of Wood's physique upon the evolution of the play and the character of Henry Carr.

56 HEWES, HENRY. "Theater: Stoppardfoolery." Saturday Review 3 (15 November):36-37.
    Mixed review of Travesties (London, Royal Shakespeare Company revival).

57 HOBSON, HAROLD. "Exhilaration." Sunday Times (London), 1 June, p. 33.
    Includes a brief favorable review of Travesties (London, Royal Shakespeare Company revival).

1975

58 HOLLAND, JACK. "Holland's Tunnel." Newport Beach (Calif.) Newporter Mesa News, 1 October, p. 9.
    Mixed review of Jumpers (Costa Mesa, South Coast Repertory).

59 HOMAN, RICHARD LAWRENCE. "T. S. Eliot as a Dramatic Realist." Ph.D. dissertation, University of Minnesota, pp. 219-24.
    Criticism; describes Rosencrantz & Guildenstern Are Dead as a facile trivialization of "themes, techniques of dialogue, and principles of characterization and action" developed by Eliot in his reaction against the conventionalized "naturalistic realism" of the early 1900s.

60 HOUSTON, PENELOPE. "The Romantic Englishwoman (aa): Plaza 1." Times (London), 17 October, p. 11.
    Review of the film (London, DIAL Films), which bored her either because of its overuse of "gambits" or because of its "excess of cleverness."

61 HUGHES, CATHARINE. "Theatre: Broadway Roundup." America 133 (6 December):408.
    Includes a review of Travesties (Broadway), which was "very funny at times" but "thoroughly tedious" at others.

62 JAMES, CLIVE. "A Letter to Tom Stoppard." New Statesman 89 (9 May):626.
    Appreciative analysis in verse. Notes criticism of Stoppard by "the priests of orthodoxy," who "want the things they know already/Reiterated loud and steady," but who "sell skill short, and then ignore/The way [his] works are so much more/Than clever stunts."
    Particularly appreciates him for refusing to take sides with contesting parties in disputes, instead believing "only in the grief/Their clash must bring." Such men discover that "to use the words [they] feel/Adhere most closely to the Real/Means everything."

63 _____. "Television: Plugging the New Patronage." Observer (London), 27 July, p. 22.
    Mixed review of "The Boundary" (London, BBC Television).

64 _____. "Count Zero Splits the Infinite: Tom Stoppard's Plays." Encounter 45 (November):68-76.
    Analysis by one who, despite his "profound lack of sympathy with the contemporary theatre," finds Stoppard to be a writer he "could admire without reserve." Covers After Magritte, "Albert's Bridge," "Artist Descending a Staircase," Enter a Free Man, "If You're Glad I'll Be Frank,"

1975

        Jumpers, Lord Malquist & Mr Moon, The Real Inspector Hound, Rosencrantz & Guildenstern Are Dead, Travesties, and "Where Are They Now?"
           Describes the plays' "warmth" and emotional engagement, their functions, and their final effects; emphasizes the theme of ambiguity; and finds parallels between Stoppard's and modern physicists' abandonment of fixed points of view.

65 JOHNSTON, LAURIE. "Notes on People: 2 House Members Agree on Marriage Plan." New York Times, 21 November, p. 48.
    News items, including the disclosure by Dr. Miriam Stoppard, the playwright's wife, that she had once allowed a severely brain-damaged patient to die. See also 1975.B11.

66 KAEL, PAULINE. "The Current Cinema: Poses." New Yorker 51 (8 December):165-66.
    Includes a review of The Romantic Englishwoman (London, DIAL Films): "another flaccid essay on infidelity" in the form of a "twist on life imitating art and vice versa; here it's life imitating pulp and vice versa." Stoppard's dialogue does not contain enough "Noel Cowardish bitchnifties."

67 KALEM, T. E. "Dance of Words." Time 106 (10 November):75-76.
    Favorable review of Travesties (Broadway). Reprinted in 1975.B81.

68 KAUFFMANN, STANLEY. "Stanley Kauffmann on Theater." New Republic 173 (22 November):18-19.
    Unfavorable review of Travesties (Broadway).

69 KAVANAGH, JULIE. "The Romantics." Women's Wear Daily, 21 March, pp. 22-23.
    Feature article describing the making of The Romantic Englishwoman (London, DIAL Films): reports that Stoppard was hired to revise the screenplay submitted by the novel's author, Thomas Wiseman.

70 KERR, WALTER. "The Prankish Fevers of Travesties." New York Times, 9 November, sec. 2, pp. 1, 5.
    Review of the Broadway production. Finds the play "a bit lazier" than Rosencrantz & Guildenstern Are Dead and Jumpers, lacking the former's "underlying structural tension" and the latter's "keen intellectual interest."

71 KEYSSAR-FRANKE, HELENE. "The Strategy of Rosencrantz and Guildenstern Are Dead." Educational Theatre Journal 27

(March):85-97.
Close analysis of Stoppard's "grasp on the relationship of every moment of the play to an audience," particularly in the play's early scenes. The juxtaposition of scenes in which the protagonists enact their roles in Hamlet with scenes in which they operate outside those roles creates "a sense of the possibility of freedom and the tension of the improbability of escape"; similarly, Act III is a trap in that it seems to exist outside Hamlet but is actually controlled by it. The play's "underlying assumption . . . [is that] the identity of man is defined by his mortality; the more profoundly one accepts the knowledge of one's finitude, . . . the more fully human one becomes."

72 KINGSTON, JEREMY. "Travesties: Aldwych." Times (London), 30 May, p. 13.
Review of the London, Royal Shakespeare Company revival in which the supporting actors' playing is more appropriate (because less "earnest") than it had been in the premiere production.

73 KISSELL, HOWARD. "Travesties." Women's Wear Daily, 3 November, p. 12.
Review of the Broadway production: "an exhilarating evening of literary burlesque." Reprinted in 1975.B81.

74 KROLL, JACK. "Everyman Bonkers." Newsweek 85 (6 January):64.
Favorable review of Enter a Free Man (New York, Theatre at St. Clement's). Abridged in 1976.B87.

75 _____. "Stars over Zurich." Newsweek 86 (10 November):66.
Review of Travesties (Broadway): "Stoppard's writing . . . seems to be trying to dissolve its super-cleverness in the crucible of a moral power not yet fully formed." Reprinted in 1975.B81.

76 LAMBERT, J. W. "Plays in Performance." Drama: The Quarterly Theatre Review, no 118 (Autumn):47-48.
Includes a review of Travesties (London, Royal Shakespeare Company revival), which, although "full of pleasure and stimulus, [remains] . . . an over-elaborate game in which much pointful argument and insight . . . is . . . nervously disguised by jocular juggling."

77 LAWRENCE, LINDA. "Theatre: Long Laughs, Short Plays." New York Westsider, 1 May, p. 9.
Favorable review of The Real Inspector Hound (New York, Comedy Stage Company).

1975

78 LEONARD, JOHN. "Critic's Notebook: Stoppard's Travesties Stirs New Thoughts of Lenin and Zurich." New York Times, 14 November, p. 25.
   Column of theatre news and gossip; claims that Lenin needed someone to talk to in the play and suggests Sarah Bernhardt.

*79 LEONARD, VIRGINIA E. "Tom Stoppard's Jumpers: The Separation from Reality." Bulletin of the West Virginia Association of College English Teachers 2, no. 1:45-56.
   Listed in Bibliography of English Language and Literature, 1975.

80 LEWSEN, CHARLES. "Stoppard Companion to Hamlet: Rosencrantz and Guildenstern Are Dead." Times (London), 12 August, p. 7.
   Review of the London, Young Vic revival. More "emotional engagement" in this play than in Stoppard's "later, more brilliant pieces."

81 MARLOWE, JOAN, and BLAKE, BETTY, eds. "Travesties." New York Theatre Critics' Review 36 (3 November):166-72.
   Reprints of 1975.B16, 19, 52, 67, 73, 75, 91, 119, 125.

82 MAROWITZ, CHARLES. "Tom Stoppard--The Theater's Intellectual P. T. Barnum." New York Times, 19 October, sec. 2, pp. 1, 5.
   Interview with some analytical comments. Stoppard discusses early influences on his work and discloses that he rewrites passages continuously rather than after finishing a complete draft.

83 MORLEY, SHERIDAN. Review Copies: Plays and Players in London, 1970-74. Totowa, N.J.: Rowman & Littlefield, pp. 109-11.
   Reprint of 1972.B95.

84 _____. "Theatre: Love Me Love My Play." Punch 268 (11 June):1020.
   Favorable review of Travesties (London, Royal Shakespeare Company revival).

85 _____. "Theatre: R & G Are Revived." Punch 269 (20 August):298.
   Review of the London, Young Vic revival of Stoppard's "one-act joke spread across three."

86 MOSK. "The Romantic Englishwoman." Variety, 28 May, p. 19.
   Review of the film (London, DIAL Films): "disappointing

1975

in its over-done mixing of satire, Pirandelloism and uneven scripting."

87 NELSON, DON. "Pardon the Play on Words." New York Daily News, 28 November, p. 118.
    Interview with John Wood, leading actor in Travesties (Broadway); discusses Stoppard's intentions in the much-criticized second act.

88 NOVICK, JULIUS. "A Splendid Assertion of Playfulness." Village Voice, 17 November, p. 119.
    Review of Travesties (Broadway): praises "Stoppard's defiant insistence on making fun of [and] having fun with" Lenin, Tzara, and Joyce.

89 POWELL, DILYS. "Films: Triangular Variations." Sunday Times (London), 19 October, p. 30.
    Includes a review of The Romantic Englishwoman (London, DIAL Films).

90 PRIESTLAND, GERALD. "A London Critic's Personal Winners in the Arts for 1975." Christian Science Monitor, 29 December, p. 27.
    Includes a brief appreciation of Travesties (London, Royal Shakespeare Company revival).

91 PROBST, LEONARD. "Travesties." NBC-TV, Channel 4 (31 October).
    Favorable review of the Broadway production. Reprinted in 1975.B81.

92 R., P. "Aldwych Travesties." Stage and Television Today (London), 5 June, p. 17.
    Favorable review of the London, Royal Shakespeare Company revival.

93 RENAUD, TRISTAN. "Une Anglaise Romantique." Cinéma 75, no. 200 (July):152-54.
    Favorable review (in French) of The Romantic Englishwoman (London, DIAL Films).

94 RICH, ALAN. "Theater: Memorabilia." New York 8 (17 November):102.
    Review of Travesties (Broadway). Suggests Luciano Berio's Sinfonia as a musical parallel to the play's form; praises its "manic virtuosity of language" and "diabolical manipulation of time and notion" [sic]. Abridged in 1978.B20.

Writings about Tom Stoppard

1975

95 RICH, FRANK. "Films That Fail in Opposite Ways." New York Post, 6 December, p. 14.
    Includes an unfavorable review of The Romantic Englishwoman (London, DIAL Films).

96 RILEY, CAROLYN, ed. "Stoppard, Tom." In Contemporary Literary Criticism: Excerpts from Criticism of the Works of Today's Novelists, Poets, Playwrights, and Other Creative Writers. Vol. 3. Detroit: Gale Research Co., p. 470.
    Continuation of 1973.B68. Consists of abridgements of 1967.B117 and 1969.B12 about Rosencrantz & Guildenstern Are Dead; 1972.B101 about After Magritte and The Real Inspector Hound; 1972.B83 about Jumpers; and 1973.B66 about Stoppard's radio plays. Similar abridgements of criticism of Stoppard found in volumes 4, 5, and 8 of this series. See 1975.B97, 1976.B87, and 1978.B20.

97 _____. "Stoppard, Tom." In Contemporary Literary Criticism: Excerpts from Criticism of the Works of Today's Novelists, Poets, Playwrights, and Other Creative Writers. Vol. 4. Detroit: Gale Research Co., pp. 524-28.
    Continuation of 1975.B96. Consists of abridgements of 1971.B20 about Stoppard's corpus in general, 1972.B63 about After Magritte and The Real Inspector Hound, 1974.B121 about Rosencrantz & Guildenstern Are Dead, 1974.B93 about Travesties, and ten items about Jumpers: 1974.B40, 61, 67, 95, 96, 119, 133, 141, 142, 170. Similar abridgements of criticism of Stoppard found in volumes 5 and 8 of this series. See 1976.B87 and 1978.B20.

98 RODWAY, ALLAN. English Comedy: Its Role and Nature from Chaucer to the Present Day. Berkeley: University of California Press, pp. 264-72.
    Discusses Jumpers as a comedy in the Joycean tradition: concludes that, whereas Joyce's "final yea-saying" is "founded . . . upon 'the incertitude of the void'" rather than upon any "optimistic metaphysic," Stoppard goes further by "writing philosophic comedy on incertitude."

99 SANDERS, BOB. "Costa Mesa Repertory: Jumpers Entertaining If Often Incomprehensible." Long Beach (Calif.) Independent Press-Telegram, 26 September, sec. B, p. 5.
    Mixed review of the Costa Mesa, South Coast Repertory production.

100 SARRIS, ANDREW. "Two Hurrahs for Helmut!" Village Voice, 15 December, pp. 145-46.
    Includes a review of The Romantic Englishwoman (London,

DIAL Films); notes a "crippling self-consciousness" in the characters, which he attributes to Stoppard's lack of faith in the plot.

101 SCHILLACI, PETER P. Review of The Romantic Englishwoman. Film Information 6 (December):2, 4.
Mixed review of the film.

102 SCHWARTZMAN, MYRON. "Wilde about Joyce? Da! But My Art Belongs to Dada!" James Joyce Quarterly 13 (Fall):122-23.
Favorable review of Travesties (Broadway).

103 SELF, DAVID. "On the Edge of Reality: Some Thoughts on the Studying of Tom Stoppard." Uses of English 26 (Spring): 195-200.
Biographical data, analytical comments about Stoppard's work, and ideas for teachers of his plays. The latter are particularly important, since the works' highly theatrical qualities would seem to make their inclusion on the British school system's O- and A-level examinations inappropriate.
Suggests "Where Are They Now?" as an introduction to Stoppard's other work, Enter a Free Man as a stimulant to students' essays about personal experiences, and The Real Inspector Hound as an example of effective dramatic construction. Recommends performance of scenes in class for Rosencrantz & Guildenstern Are Dead and Jumpers rather than textual analysis; says Travesties requires knowledge of The Importance of Being Earnest.

104 SHULMAN, MILTON. "Cerebral Slapstick--An Encore." Evening Standard (London), 14 August, p. 5.
Favorable review of Travesties (London, Royal Shakespeare Company revival).

105 SIMON, JOHN. Uneasy Stages: A Chronicle of the New York Theatre, 1963-1973. New York: Random House, p. 397.
Contains a reprint of 1972.B118.

106 _____. "Overblown, But Not Blown Over." New York 8 (8 December):107-10.
Includes a review of The Romantic Englishwoman (London, DIAL Films), in which Stoppard's "glossless dialogue . . . aims mostly for the Pinteresque pause-ridden innuendo."

107 STASIO, MARILYN. "Theatre: Reviews: Deliciously Dense." Cue 44 (15 November):15.
Review of Travesties (Broadway): "a motley mosaic of farce, history, politics, aesthetics, and music-hall nonsense."

Writings about Tom Stoppard

1975

108 _____. "Cue Theatre: Tom Stoppard's Mad Mushrooms." Cue 44 (29 November):15.
   Interview: Stoppard discusses "revolutionary" art and the functions of art and comedy.

*109 STONEMAN, D. Review of Travesties. San Mateo (Calif.) Advocate, 31 December, p. 41.
   Date indicates this item is a review of the Broadway production; item listed in Alternative Press Index, 1975.

110 SULLIVAN, DAN. "Stage Reviews: Two for L.A.'s Off-Broadway Show." Los Angeles Times, 24 September, sec. 4, pp. 1, 18.
   Contains a mixed review of Jumpers (Costa Mesa, South Coast Repertory).

111 TALLMER, JERRY. "John Wood: Space, Time & Travesties." New York Post, 29 November, sec. 2, p. 13.
   Interview with the leading actor in the Broadway production: discusses methods for discovering the proper style in which to perform Stoppard's plays, the technical problems they present, and the complexity of Travesties' form.

112 TAYLOR, CLARKE. "Here, There, and. . . ." After Dark 8 (February):26, 76.
   Includes a review of Enter a Free Man (New York, Theatre at St. Clement's).

113 TAYLOR, LARRY. "Jumpers at Costa Mesa is Funny, Serious Farce." Garden Grove (Calif.) Orange County Evening News, 18 October, p. 110.
   Favorable review of the South Coast Repertory production.

114 TAYLOR, ROBERT. "Dottie--Vulnerable Neurotic Who Brightens Jumpers." Oakland (Calif.) Tribune, 22 January, p. 21.
   Interview with Hope Alexander-Willis, who played the female lead in the San Francisco, ACT production.

115 THRONSON, RON. "On Stage: The Gospel according to St. Stoppard." Orange County Illustrated, October, p. 69.
   Favorable review of Jumpers (Costa Mesa, South Coast Repertory).

116 TINKER, JACK. "Theatre: Dazzling--But What Was It All About?" Daily Mail (London), 30 May, p. 20.
   Review of Travesties (London, Royal Shakespeare Company revival); declares that "Mr. Stoppard has so sugared his pill that most of the customers will leave without ever guessing [that the play] was about anything at all."

Writings about Tom Stoppard

1975

117 TUCKER, MARTIN, and STEIN, RITA, comps. and eds. "Stoppard, Tom." In A Library of Literary Criticism: Modern British Literature. Vol. 4: Supplement. New York: Frederick Ungar Publishing Co., pp. 503-8.
    Consists of abridgements of 1967.B37, 43 about Rosencrantz & Guildenstern Are Dead, 1968.B50 about Lord Malquist & Mr Moon, 1969.B33 about The Real Inspector Hound, 1972.B141 and 1974.B119 about Jumpers, and 1971.B17 about Stoppard's canon in general.

*118 UENO, YOSHIKO. "Ninshiki no geki: Tom Stoppard ni yosete" [About the play: for Tom Stoppard]. Oberon 17:62-75.
    Listed in MLA Bibliography, 1978. In Japanese.

119 WATT, DOUGLAS. "A Dazzling Play and Star." New York Daily News, 31 October, p. 74.
    Favorable review of Travesties (Broadway). Reprinted in 1975.B81.

120 _____. "Smart-Aleck, This Stoppard--But Smart, Funny, Too." New York Sunday News, 16 November, sec. L, p. 3.
    News items about Travesties (Broadway): its box-office receipts, the use of an understudy to play the lead at matinees, and Actors Equity's tacit acceptance of the use of British actors.

121 WATTS, RICHARD. "London Mystery Plays." New York Post, 6 September, pp. 14, 40.
    News items, including the announcement that Travesties will open in New York later in the year.

122 _____. "Travesties Glows as Stoppard's Best." New York Post, 3 November, p. 56.
    Favorable review of the Broadway production.

123 WETZSTEON, ROSS. "Theatre Journal: The Heir to Shaw Comes to Broadway." Village Voice, 6 October, pp. 105-6.
    Review of Travesties (London, Royal Shakespeare Company revival); with analytical comments. Says its protagonist, Henry Carr, seems to have been created simply because he "gives [Stoppard] the greatest scope for his own obsessions. . . . Carr is less a character than a situation." Also finds the play more humane and committed than Stoppard's earlier works, in which he "regarded ideas not as the living, mutable gropings of human minds, . . . but . . . as hard, impersonal artifacts, a kind of coinage of the mind. . . . He never seemed really to believe any of them."

1975

124 ____. "Theatre Journal: Tom Stoppard Eats Steak Tartare with Chocolate Sauce." Village Voice, 10 November, p. 121.
Interview; deals largely with Stoppard's intentions in Travesties. He tried to be "equally just" to Lenin, Tzara, and Joyce, "but not [to give them] equal weight. . . . I find Joyce infinitely the most important."

125 WILSON, EDWIN. "Tom Stoppard's Verbal Fireworks." Wall Street Journal, 3 November, p. 14.
Review of Travesties (Broadway): "the ratio of surface brilliance to profound thought runs too high. Mr. Stoppard is forever in danger of . . . paying more attention to the play on words than to the play." Reprinted in 1975.B81.

126 ZEH, DIETER. "Tom Stoppard: Rosencrantz and Guildenstern Are Dead." In Das zeitgenössische englische Drama: Einführung, Interpretation, Dokumentation. Edited by Klaus-Dieter Fehse and Norbert H. Platz. Frankfort on the Main: Athenäum Fischer Taschenbuch, pp. 229-46.
In German. Includes biographical data and a summary of Stoppard's career; plot summary and brief overview of critical approaches to Rosencrantz & Guildenstern Are Dead (concentrating on German analyses); a discussion of the play's themes (order and chaos, art and reality, humor as a corrective, and "placing" of Hamlet); and a brief bibliography.

127 ZWEIGLER, MARK. "In Chicago." After Dark 8 (May):27.
Includes a brief mixed review of Enter a Free Man (Chicago, Summit Forum Theatre).

1976

A BOOKS

1 BECKWITH, DAVID BRUCE. "Critical Mass: A Director's Approach to Tom Stoppard's The Real Inspector Hound." Senior Thesis, Reed College, 25 pp.
Script analysis and production plan, with brief analytical comments about "Albert's Bridge," Dogg's Our Pet, Enter a Free Man, Jumpers, Lord Malquist & Mr Moon, Rosencrantz & Guildenstern Are Dead, Travesties, and "Where Are They Now?"
Finds Stoppard's characters struggling "to minimize or subdue [the] chaos" caused by "a breakdown of the world-order due to human frailty." His comedy "arises from a lack of consciousness regarding the absurdity of one's

1976

situation"; his works counsel one to become a spectator in order to survive.

2   BIGSBY, C[HRISTOPHER] W[ILLIAM] E[DGAR]. <u>Tom Stoppard</u>. Writers and Their Work Series, edited by Ian Scott-Kilvert. Harlowe, G.B.: Longman Group, 32 pp.

Greatly expanded version of 1973.B21. Surveys themes and stylistic traits of <u>Enter a Free Man</u>, <u>Jumpers</u>, <u>The Real Inspector Hound</u>, <u>Rosencrantz & Guildenstern Are Dead</u>, and <u>Travesties</u>; briefer sections deal with <u>After Magritte</u>, "Albert's Bridge," "If You're Glad I'll Be Frank," and <u>Lord Malquist & Mr Moon</u>.

Largely devoted to exploring the conflict in Stoppard's work between a Wildean vision of life (seeing it as an imitation of art and considering farce "the only valid strategy for artist and individual alike" in an absurd world) and "a more deep-seated humanism which leads him . . . to reveal a compassionate concern for his characters." Says many of his plays' weaknesses stem from his practice of mixing farce (which lives in "an antinomian world of ethical relativity") with comedy (which implies "a world in which values exist").

Also claims that <u>Travesties</u> is flawed by the use of Lenin, "a palpable reality whose particular fictions have assumed an implacable form," in a play which tries to exhibit the insufficiency of any single vision of the world.

3   BRATT, DAVID LEE. "The Ironic Muse of Tom Stoppard." Ph.D. dissertation, University of California (Santa Barbara), 624 pp.

First book-length analysis of all Stoppard's produced plays and published fiction through <u>Travesties</u>. Claims that they spring from an essentially ironic point of view which Stoppard first discovered for himself and then elaborated upon as his career progressed. Examines the influence of this perspective upon his works' themes, characters, and stylistic traits; sees <u>Travesties</u> as the culmination of this development and predicts that future works will strike out in a significantly different direction.

4   CAHN, VICTOR L. "Beyond Absurdity: The Plays of Tom Stoppard." Ph.D. dissertation, New York University, 240 pp.

Analysis of his short stories, <u>After Magritte</u>, "Albert's Bridge," "Artist Descending a Staircase," <u>Enter a Free Man</u>, "If You're Glad I'll Be Frank," <u>Jumpers</u>, <u>Lord Malquist & Mr Moon</u>, <u>The Real Inspector Hound</u>, <u>Rosencrantz & Guildenstern Are Dead</u>, "A Separate Peace," <u>Travesties</u>, and

1976

"Where Are They Now?"
Traces his movement from "semi-realistic beginnings," through an absurdist phase, and into a period in which he "combines both traditions in an original theatrical form" marked by a use of characters who "are aware of absurdity, yet unwilling to resign themselves to it." Published: 1979.A1.

B SHORTER WRITINGS

1 ANON. "Movies." Playboy 23 (March):24, 26.
   Includes a brief review of the "very boring, . . . pretentious and derivative" The Romantic Englishwoman (London, DIAL Films).

2 ANON. "B'way Better; Bubbling $90,096; Travesties Exits, Me Flops Out." Variety, 17 March, p. 96.
   News items, including the announcement of the closing of Travesties (Broadway): reports the length of its run; says "touring plans are uncertain."

3 ANON. "Tom Stoppard: Lebensdaten und Stationen." In Kammerspiele Düsseldorf Jahnstr. 3: Sonderheft. Special edition accompanying production program of Jumpers, 18 March, Düsseldorf, n.p.
   Biographical data and dates of German, Swiss, and Austrian productions of Jumpers and Rosencrantz & Guildenstern Are Dead (in German).

4 ANON. "Fringe Benefits." Sunday Times (London), 23 May, p. 37.
   News item announcing the transfer of Dirty Linen and New-Found-Land (London, Inter-Action Trust) to the West End.

5 ANON. "Business Appointments." Times (London), 28 July, p. 20.
   News items, including the report that Dr. Miriam Stoppard had been promoted to deputy managing director of Syntex Pharmaceuticals.

6 ANON. "London." Variety, 11 August, p. 61.
   News items, including the report that Dirty Linen and New-Found-Land (London, Inter-Action Trust) was chosen Bicentennial Theatre Event by the Theatre Institute of the United States; also announces that Jumpers would re-enter the British National Theatre's repertoire in the fall.

Writings about Tom Stoppard

1976

7   ANON. "Tom Stoppard." In The Guthrie Theater "Rosencrantz and Guildenstern Are Dead." Production program, 18 August, Minneapolis, p. 18.
    Biographical information and brief critical comments about the play.

*8 ANON. No Title in Index. Times Higher Education Supplement (London), 27 August, p. 12.
    Listed in Index to the Times, 1976.

9   ANON. "Stoppard Double-Bill to Play Wash. Tryout." Variety, 8 September, p. 89.
    News item announcing the opening of Dirty Linen and New-Found-Land (Washington, D.C., Kennedy Center tryout of Broadway production).

10 ANON. "Bristol." Stage and Television Today (London), 21 October, p. 19.
    Favorable review of Travesties (Bristol Old Vic).

11 ANON. "Stoppard's Twin Farces to Switch D.C. Theatres." Variety, 10 November, p. 65.
    News item reporting the transfer of Dirty Linen and New-Found-Land from the West End Theatre to the Eisenhower Theatre in Washington.

12 ANON. "London." Variety, 17 November, p. 77.
    News item announcing André Previn's engagement as composer for Every Good Boy Deserves Favour, scheduled for production in July 1977 with the London Symphony at Royal Festival Hall.

13 ANON. "Stoppard's Dirty Linen Scheduled to Open Jan. 11." New York Times, 29 December, p. 22.
    News item announcing the opening of the Broadway production.

14 ANON. "Stoppard Licenses Play to So. Africa." Variety, 29 December, p. 57.
    News item reporting the opening of Dirty Linen and New-Found-Land in Capetown, despite disapproval of Equity.

15 ATKINS, HAROLD. "Theatre: Almost Free: Dirty Linen." Daily Telegraph (London), 13 April, p. 13.
    Favorable review of the London, Inter-Action Trust production.

16 AYER, A. J. "Auch Logische Positivisten Können Lieben." In

Writings about Tom Stoppard

1976

Kammerspiele Düsseldorf Jahnstr. 3: Sonderheft. Special edition accompanying production program of Jumpers, 18 March, Düsseldorf, n.p.
    Abridgement and translation (into German) of 1972.B20.

17 BARNES, CLIVE. "The Stage: David Dukes." New York Times, 5 February, p. 25.
    Review of the understudy's performance as the lead in Travesties (Broadway); also mentions small changes involving Lenin in Act II.

18 _____. "On the London Stage, King Comedy Reigns." New York Times, 26 September, p. 54.
    Includes a brief favorable review of Dirty Linen and New-Found-Land (London, Inter-Action Trust).

19 _____. "Comedies for the Thinking Man." Stagebill 5 (December):7-8, 11, 14.
    Analysis of Travesties and comments about Stoppard's preoccupations in his works; printed in the Washington, Kennedy Center program for the American Ballet Theatre's production of The Sleeping Beauty.
    Discusses Stoppard's fascination with the theme of illusion versus reality: "he is more concerned with fancy than with philosophy."

20 BLACKBURN, TOM. "Brittania Is Alive and Ruling in Fine Drama Guild Production." Trenton (N.J.) Times, 8 December, p. C12.
    Favorable review of Enter a Free Man (Philadelphia Drama Guild).

21 BOYD, JUDITH. "Theatre: Tom Stoppard Back on Home Ground." Bath & Wilts Evening Chronicle (Bristol), 25 September, p. 7.
    News item reporting the opening of Travesties (Bristol Old Vic); includes biographical information (the performance of The Gamblers, Bristol Old Vic Theatre School, University of Bristol Theatre, June 1965, and Stoppard's service as wicket keeper for the Bristol Press XI in the 1950s).

22 _____. "Coincidence." Bath & Wilts Evening Chronicle (Bristol), 30 September, p. 5.
    Favorable review of Travesties (Bristol Old Vic).

23 BRIEN, ALAN. "Theatre: Fencing Matches." Listener 96 (30 September):422.

Writings about Tom Stoppard

1976

Includes a review of Jumpers (London, National Theatre revival): while the impact of the references to moon landings has diminished since 1972, the political situation the play describes now seems "far more prescient and timely."

24 BROWN, GEOFF. "Stoppard Plays." Plays and Players 23 (June): 32-33.
    Review of Dirty Linen and New-Found-Land (London, Inter-Action Trust): "one feels one is watching a splendid machine slowly running down, supplied with insufficient raw material."

25 BUCKLEY, MICHAEL. "The Romantic Englishwoman." Films in Review 27 (January):56.
    Review; criticizes the "pseudo-intellectual oatmeal of a plot."

26 CHAILLET, NED. "The Real Inspector Hound: Young Vic." Times (London), 24 November, p. 13.
    Favorable review of the London company's production; its staging of the radio play, "If You're Glad I'll Be Frank," however, "fails to ignite."

27 COE, JOHN. "The Critics: Wildely Funny Idea Pays Off." Evening Post (Bristol), 30 September, p. 16.
    Favorable review of Travesties (Bristol Old Vic).

28 COE, RICHARD L. "Ed Berman, Tom Stoppard, Dirty Linen and the New-Found-Land" [sic]. Washington Post, 3 October, sec. G, p. 3.
    Interview with Ed Berman, director of the play's London, Inter-Action Trust, and Broadway productions.

29 _____. "Stoppard's Dirty Linen." Washington Post, 8 October, sec. B, pp. 1, 13.
    Favorable review of the Washington, D.C., Kennedy Center tryout of the Broadway production.

30 COLLINS, WILLIAM B. "Stoppard's Enter a Free Man Is the Nicest Surprise of the Season." Philadelphia Inquirer, 3 December, p. 7C.
    Favorable review of the Philadelphia Drama Guild production.

31 _____. "Top of the Week: A Dippy Comedy Saved from Oblivion." Philadelphia Inquirer, 12 December, sec. I, p. 2.
    Brief recapitulation of 1976.B30.

1976

32 CORRY, JOHN. "Broadway." New York Times, 25 June, sec. C, p. 2.
    News items, including the announcement that Doris Cole Abrams would produce Dirty Linen and New-Found-Land in New York in an Off-Broadway theatre. (But see 1976.B33.)

33 _____. "Broadway." New York Times, 8 October, sec. C, p. 2.
    News items, including a report of Actors Equity's refusal to allow Dirty Linen and New-Found-Land to open on Broadway with a cast of British actors.

34 CRAIG, RANDALL. "Plays in Performance: Experimental." Drama: The Quarterly Theatre Review, no. 121 (Summer):77-79.
    Includes a favorable review of Dirty Linen and New-Found-Land (London, Inter-Action Trust).

35 _____. "Plays in Performance: Experimental." Drama: The Quarterly Theatre Review, no. 122 (Autumn):66.
    Includes a review of The Real Inspector Hound (London, Maximus Actors' Arena).

36 _____. "Plays in Performance: Experimental." Drama: The Quarterly Theatre Review, no. 123 (Winter):60.
    Includes a favorable review of "Albert's Bridge," adapted for the stage (Chichester Festival Theatre).

37 CRIST, JUDITH. "The Movies: Kubrick as Novelist." Saturday Review 3 (10 January):64.
    Includes a review of The Romantic Englishwoman (London, DIAL Films): a "pointless fake-feminist pseudo-urbane tale . . . decked . . . out with embarrassing attempts at Cowardish sophistication."

38 CUSHMAN, ROBERT. "Troilus in the Cut." Observer (London), 20 June, p. 26.
    Includes a brief favorable review of Dirty Linen and New-Found-Land (London, Inter-Action Trust).

39 D'ANDREA, PAUL. "'Thou Starre of Poets': Shakespeare as DNA." In Shakespeare: Aspects of Influence. Edited by Gwynne Blakemore Evans. Harvard English Studies, no. 7. Cambridge: Harvard University Press, pp. 163-91.
    Includes an analysis of Stoppard's use of Shakespeare in Rosencrantz & Guildenstern Are Dead. Claims he sets up "a powerful dialectic by setting worlds in contact": one is similar to our own, while the other, "a mighty opposite," is represented by "a massive synecdoche." Compares the two worlds: while "cruelty . . . confers meaning, and is

fatal" in tragedy, Stoppard's courtiers "pay the price [but] take away none of the understanding."

40 de JONGH, NICHOLAS. "Young Vic: Stoppard Plays." Guardian (London), 24 November, p. 10.
Unfavorable review of "If You're Glad I'll Be Frank" (adapted to the stage) and The Real Inspector Hound (London, Young Vic).

41 DRIVER, TOM F. "Travesties: A Review." Christianity and Crisis 36 (16 February):21-23.
Review of the Broadway production. Criticizes the absence of any "obsession that might cause us . . . to laugh at ourselves." Stoppard "doesn't like to write a line that doesn't allude to something somebody else wrote. It's almost as if he can't write an independent line."

42 ELIN, C. K. "And. . . ." New York Soho Weekly News, 1 July, p. 27.
Mixed review of The Real Inspector Hound (New York, TRG Repertory).

43 ELLISON, JANE. "Young Vic." Evening Standard (London), 24 November, p. 16.
Review of "If You're Glad I'll Be Frank" (adapted for the stage) and The Real Inspector Hound (London, Young Vic): the former is unsuited to the stage and the latter is the victim of an excessively deliberate production.

44 ELSOM, JOHN. Post-War British Theatre. London: Routledge & Kegan Paul, pp. 175, 194-95.
Brief analysis of Stoppard as one of Britain's "professional sceptics" who seem "intent upon casting doubt on the assumptions popularly held"; warns that the stance "can become a bad habit."

45 FARBER, STEPHEN. "A Neglected Film about Modern Marriage." New York Times, 18 January, sec. D, p. 13.
Review of The Romantic Englishwoman (London, DIAL Films), which, "like many modern works of art, . . . is about the artist's self-absorption, his coldness and voraciousness." Stoppard's dialogue is "savagely witty."

46 FOOT, DAVID. "Bristol: Travesties." Guardian (London), 5 October, p. 10.
Review of the Bristol Old Vic production; claimed to notice "a degree of intellectual fawning" among those who professed to enjoy it.

1976

47 GARELIK, GLENN. "The Real Inspector Hound." New York Show Business, 10 June, p. 17.
    Favorable review of the New York, TRG Repertory production.

48 GIROUARD, ROBERT L. "The Odds Couple." Mankato (Minn.) Free Press, 20 August, p. 8.
    Favorable review of Rosencrantz & Guildenstern Are Dead (Minneapolis, Guthrie Theatre).

49 GITZEN, JULIAN. "Tom Stoppard: Chaos in Perspective." Southern Humanities Review 10 (Spring):143-52.
    Analysis; covers After Magritte, "Albert's Bridge," Enter a Free Man, Jumpers, Lord Malquist & Mr Moon, The Real Inspector Hound, and Rosencrantz & Guildenstern Are Dead.
    Discusses Stoppard's use of farcical techniques to portray a serious theme ("our society is in imminent danger of going out of control" because of "its own dreadful complexity" and widespread "greedy and unscrupulous conduct"). He exercises upon his works "an artistic control which, in the interest of aesthetic harmony, defies the very chaos which it portrays."

50 GLOVER, WILLIAM. Interview with Stoppard. AP Wireservice. New York Public Library, Lincoln Center Drama Collection.
    Interview; Stoppard claims to have lost interest in trying to marry "the play of ideas with Barnum & Bailey effects"; now prefers to write "a play where someone comes in at the start and turns a light on, and at the end, turns it off." Discusses differences between theatre and other media and his ignorance about metaphors and symbols in his work. Abridged in 1976.B51-2.

51 _____. "Stoppard Leaving 'Circus' for Man and Dog." Cincinnati Enquirer, 11 January, sec. G, p. 5.
    Abridgement of 1976.B50.

52 _____. "Curtain Time." Milwaukee Journal, 21 March, sec. 5, p. 5.
    Greatly abridged version of 1976.B50.

53 GOTTFRIED, MARTIN. "Tom Stoppard: The Blessing and Burden of Brains." In "Dirty Linen & New-Found-Land" and "Travesties." Special edition accompanying Kennedy Center productions, Washington, n.d., n.p.
    Analysis: "Stoppard often hasn't the interest in action that he has in ideas," which vitiates the effective-

ness of some of his plays (e.g., Rosencrantz & Guildenstern Are Dead and Jumpers) in the theatre. Although Travesties achieves more "unity of matter and manner," it is still "more of a mental exercise than a theatrical experience." His best works are Enter a Free Man, which "has heart," and The Real Inspector Hound, which displays "an appealing modesty" in that it "never tries to show off [its author's] intelligence."

54 GUERNSEY, OTIS L., Jr., ed. "The New York Season." The Best Plays of 1975-76. The Burns Mantle Yearbook. New York: Dodd, Mead & Co., p. 12.
   Brief critical remarks about Travesties.

55 GUSSOW, MEL. "Theatre: Tom Stoppard's Sex Scandals of '76." New York Times, 27 June, sec. D, p. 5.
   Favorable review of Dirty Linen and New-Found-Land (London, Inter-Action Trust).

56 GUTHKE, KARL S. "A Stage for the Anti-Hero: Metaphysical Farce in the Modern Theatre." Studies in the Literary Imagination 9 (Spring):119-37.
   Includes a brief analysis of Rosencrantz & Guildenstern Are Dead as a "metaphysical farce." Article is the text of an English lecture based upon the author's German item, 1971.B14.

57 HARRIS, WENDELL V. "Stoppard's After Magritte." Explicator 34 (January):40.
   Brief article identifying Magritte's "L'assassin menacé" as the painting on which After Magritte's opening tableau is modelled.

58 HARVEY, JOHN H. "Character Manipulation Key in Guthrie Play." St. Paul Dispatch, 19 August, p. 41.
   Review of Rosencrantz & Guildenstern Are Dead (Minneapolis, Guthrie Theater): "a serio-comic meditation on death, . . . exuberant and not without self-indulgence."

59 HIGHWATER, JAMAKE. "Places." New York Soho Weekly News, 14 October, p. 12.
   Includes a brief review of Dirty Linen and New-Found-Land (London, Inter-Action Trust): "a charming spoof on government."

60 KAUFFMANN, STANLEY. "Jumpers." In Persons of the Drama: Theater Criticism and Comment. New York: Harper & Row, pp. 239-42.
   Reprint of 1974.B96.

Writings about Tom Stoppard

1976

61 KAUFMAN, STEVE. "Critic's Corner." Minneapolis Skyway News, 25 August, p. 34.
   Favorable review of Rosencrantz & Guildenstern Are Dead (Minneapolis, Guthrie Theater).

62 KERR, WALTER. "Stage View: Why Do Authors Mix Fact and Fantasy?" New York Times, 29 August, pp. 5, 12.
   Essay, including analytical comments about Travesties; discusses the increased use of a mixture of documentary fact and traditional fictional material in novels and drama. Mentions some historical figures (e.g., Tzara) with whom the practice works well and others (e.g., Joyce and Lenin) with whom it does not.

63 KROLL, JACK. "Britain Onstage." Newsweek 87 (22 March):75, 78.
   News article, with quotations from Stoppard and others, about the opening of the new British National Theatre complex.

64 _____. "Knickers Snickers." Newsweek 88 (18 October):103.
   Favorable review of Dirty Linen and New-Found-Land (Washington, D.C., Kennedy Center tryout of Broadway production). Reprinted in 1977.B87.

65 LACK, ALASTAIR. "Beginning New Plays." National Public Radio (20 June).
   Six-minute interview. Stoppard discusses the origins of Jumpers and Dirty Linen and New-Found-Land, describes his attempts to balance the impulse to "structure ahead" against the realization that his best work is done without a plan, and defines the function of art ("a long-term laying down of a matrix of moral sensibility without which no action can be judged in moral terms").
   Audio tape is Item No. 760620; located at the network's Washington, D.C. office; rebroadcast under a different title as 1976.B66.

66 _____. "Writing Plays, Journalism, and Art." National Public Radio (24 July).
   Item No. 760724, but is a rebroadcast of 1976.B65.

67 LEE, CHARLES. Review of Enter a Free Man. WCAU Radio, Philadelphia (6 December).
   Favorable review of the Philadelphia Drama Guild production.

68 LEVIN, BERNARD. "Theatre: How One Man Quenched a French Masterpiece." Sunday Times (London), 28 November, p. 38.

Writings about Tom Stoppard

1976

Includes a review of "If You're Glad I'll Be Frank" (adapted to the stage) and The Real Inspector Hound (London, Young Vic): the former "a dazzling piece of work."

69 LUCAS, JOHN. "Stoppard's Lunch-Party." Observer (London), 25 April, p. 26.
    Favorable review of Dirty Linen and New-Found-Land (London, Inter-Action Trust).

*70 McINTYRE, M. Review of Rosencrantz and Guildenstern Are Dead. Portland (Oreg.) Scribe, 26 February, p. 8.
    City and organization responsible for production not listed. Item listed in Alternative Press Index, 1976.

71 MAZZOCCO, ROBERT. "In Chekhov's Spell." New York Review of Books 22 (22 January):34-38.
    Includes an unfavorable review of Travesties (Broadway).

72 MINTON, LYNN. "Movie Guide for Puzzled Parents." McCalls 103 (February):64.
    Includes a review of The Romantic Englishwoman (London, DIAL Films): "a pretentious, silly clunker."

73 MORRISON, DON. "Rosencrantz Brings Out Very Best in Guthrie Cast." Minneapolis Star, 19 August, sec. C, p. 5.
    Review of the Minneapolis, Guthrie Theatre production of "the most clever and original play of the past decade."

74 MULLINS, EDWIN. "Kaleidoscope." BBC Radio Four (16 April).
    Interview; Stoppard discusses Dirty Linen and New-Found-Land. Transcript housed, London, BBC Written Archives Centre.

75 NELSON, BOB. Review of Enter a Free Man. KYW Radio, Philadelphia (3 December).
    Review of the Philadelphia Drama Guild production: finds more compassion in this play than in Stoppard's other works.

76 NIGHTINGALE, BENEDICT. "Theatre: Indian Summer." New Statesman 91 (16 April):516-17.
    Includes a favorable review of Dirty Linen and New-Found-Land (London, Inter-Action Trust).

77 _____. "The Playwright: Tom Stoppard." Independent Television (20 September).
    Post-production script of twenty-minute television interview: Stoppard discusses his habit of parodying

1976

others' works, his appreciation of tautological jokes, and his personal insecurity. Transcript housed, London, Thames Television Limited.

78 OLIVER, MICHAEL. "Kaleidoscope." BBC Radio Four (20 April).
    Brief excerpts from 1974.B63 rebroadcast.

79 PANTER-DOWNES, MOLLIE. "Letter from London." New Yorker 52 (13 December):118.
    Includes a review of Dirty Linen and New-Found-Land (London, Inter-Action Trust), in which "the usual dazzling Stoppard fireworks seem to fizz rather damply."

80 PAUL. "Show out of Town: Dirty Linen & New-Found-Land." Variety, 13 October, p. 91.
    Favorable review of the Washington, D.C., Kennedy Center tryout of the Broadway production.

81 PETER, JOHN. "Theatre." Sunday Times (London), 18 April, p. 37.
    Review of Dirty Linen and New-Found-Land (London, Inter-Action Trust): "a hilarious diversion" depicting "panic-stricken respectability besieged by panic-stricken sexuality."

82 RATCLIFFE, MICHAEL. "Playing a Very Straight Boat: 'Three Men in a Boat': BBC 2." Times (London), 2 January, p. 5.
    Review of the London, BBC Television production: criticizes Stoppard for "removing a great deal [of Jerome's novel] and too often replacing big bad jokes with more sophisticated, but smaller, jokes of his own."

83 REDMOND, JAMES, and TENNYSON, HALLAM, eds. Introduction to Contemporary One-Act Plays. London: Heinemann Educational Books, pp. x-xi.
    Brief analytical comments about "If You're Glad I'll Be Frank," a farce with "an unexpected depth and poignancy."

84 REID, HELEN. "A Jest from the Master Juggler." Western Daily Press (Bristol), 30 September, p. 5.
    Mixed review of Travesties (Bristol Old Vic).

85 RICH, ALAN. "Theater: Refreshment at the Source." New York 9 (6 September):63.
    Includes a review of Dirty Linen and New-Found-Land (London, Inter-Action Trust): "a whizzing succession of gorgeous sight-and-sound gags horrifyingly on the mark."

1976

86 RICHARDSON, JACK. "Theater: A Dialogue on Travesties or The Impotence of Being Earnest." Commentary 61 (January): 71-74.
    Review of the Broadway production, conducted in dialogue between two old men, Algernon and Jack (John R. Worthseeker). The former declares the play "diverting" at best and notes that "there are depths of dullness that are beyond satire's grasp [e.g., Lenin and the Revolution], and I'm afraid Stoppard sank in the attempt to reach them."

87 RILEY, CAROLYN, and MENDELSON, PHYLLIS CARMEL, eds. "Stoppard, Tom." In Contemporary Literary Criticism: Excerpts from Criticism of the Works of Today's Novelists, Poets, Playwrights, and Other Creative Writers. Vol. 5. Detroit: Gale Research Co., pp. 411-14.
    Continuation of 1975.B97. Consists of abridgements of 1975.B45, 74 about Enter a Free Man; 1974.B41 about Jumpers; and 1974.B57, 104, 118, 143, 182 about Travesties. Similar abridgements of criticism of Stoppard published in volume 8 of this series. See 1978.B20

88 RIPP, JUDITH. Review of The Romantic Englishwoman. Parents' Magazine 51 (January):28.
    Brief mixed review of the film.

89 RODWAY, ALLAN. "Theatre: Stripping Off." London Magazine 16 (August/September):66-73.
    Analysis; argues against "the commonest current view" that Travesties is inferior to Rosencrantz & Guildenstern Are Dead and Jumpers. All share the theme of "the problem of knowledge," which in Travesties becomes "a thematic network [with] some twenty . . . aspects of the problem . . . working in varied permutation." Abridged in 1978.B20.

90 S., R. "Seconds Out." Sunday Telegraph (London), 28 November, p. 16.
    Review of "If You're Glad I'll Be Frank" (adapted to the stage) and The Real Inspector Hound (London, Young Vic): the former is unsuited to the stage, while the production of the latter "fatally slows up into conscious posturing."

91 SALTER, CHARLES H. "Rosencrantz and Guildenstern Are Dead." In Insight IV: Analyses of Modern British and American Drama. Edited by Hermann J. Weiand. Frankfort on the Main: Hirschgraben-Verlag, pp. 143-50.
    Contains biographical data and terse, sometimes inaccurate, plot summaries of major works; detailed plot sum-

1976

mary and analysis of the title play; questions for class discussions and essays; and a brief bibliography.

Analysis includes discussion of similarities between Stoppard's play and Hamlet; briefer sections about existentialist themes and links to Waiting for Godot and Jan Kott's study of Shakespeare.

92 SCHENCK, MARY-LOW TAYLOR. "Action Writing: A Study of Selected Works of Twentieth-Century Drama, Fiction and Film Whose Theme Is the Examination of Their Own Processes." Ph.D. dissertation, Brown University, pp. 58-60, 72-83.

Analysis of Rosencrantz & Guildenstern Are Dead and fourteen other novels, plays, and films whose nature is described in the subtitle. Claims Stoppard's play asks, "What exactly is the reality of any dramatic character?" and the Player expresses his aesthetic theory.

93 SCHIER, ERNEST. "Early Stoppard Play Minor but Agreeable." Philadelphia Evening Bulletin, 3 December, p. 29.

Review of Enter a Free Man (Philadelphia Drama Guild): more a "curiosity" than a "substantial drama."

94 SCHILLACI, PETER. "Current Cinema." Mass Media Newsletter, 12, no. 15 (12 January):6-7.

Includes a review of The Romantic Englishwoman (London, DIAL Films): an "exercise in existential ennui."

95 SEMPLE, ROBERT B., Jr. "How Life Imitates a Stoppard Farce." New York Times, 21 June, p. 45.

Interview and feature article about Dirty Linen and New-Found-Land (London, Inter-Action Trust): discusses its theme, timeliness, and form.

96 SEYMOUR-SMITH, MARTIN. "Stoppard, Tom." In Who's Who in Twentieth Century Literature. New York: Holt, Rinehart & Winston, pp. 354-55.

Brief analytical comments: Stoppard's ideas are "theatrically well developed but intellectually unexplored" in plays which feature "a frothy, infectious, vacuous excitement."

97 SIMON, JOHN. "Theatre Chronicle." Hudson Review 29 (Spring): 79-84.

Includes a review of Travesties (Broadway), with extended comments about the "parasitical" quality of After Magritte, Enter a Free Man, Jumpers, The Real Inspector Hound, and Rosencrantz & Guildenstern Are Dead. Describes Stoppard's "fortes and foibles"; identifies him as one of many contemporary playwrights who resort to "desperate strategies" in order to hold their audiences' attention.

98 STEELE, MIKE. "Stoppard's Play Goes beyond Clever and Becomes Human." Minneapolis Tribune, 20 August, sec. B, p. 5.
   Favorable review of Rosencrantz & Guildenstern Are Dead (Minneapolis, Guthrie Theater).

99 STOOP, N. M. Review of The Romantic Englishwoman. After Dark 9 (January):90.
   Favorable review of the film: Stoppard's screenplay "witty."

100 STRAFFORD, PETER. "Stoppard Play Wins Award as Best on Broadway." Times (London), 20 April, p. 1.
   News item announcing that Travesties won the Tony Award for Best Play of the 1975-76 Broadway season.

101 TAKIFF, JONATHAN. "Free Man Makes Grand Entrance." Philadelphia Daily News, 3 December, p. 34.
   Favorable review of Enter a Free Man (Philadelphia Drama Guild).

102 VAUGHAN, PAUL. "Kaleidoscope." BBC Radio Four (22 September).
   Interview: Stoppard discusses his thoughts and preoccupations while writing. Transcript housed, London, BBC Written Archives Centre.

103 VAUGHAN, PETER. "Old Log Offers First Stoppard Play." Minneapolis Star, 25 October, p. 6.
   Review of Enter a Free Man (Minneapolis, Old Log Theatre): an "uneven" play which "contains glimpses of the wit, wordplay, and concern for human frailty" which characterize Stoppard's later work.

104 VIORST, MILTON. "Report from Washington: A Capital Theater Season." New York Times, 3 October, sec. D, p. 10.
   Contains a report of the coming opening of Dirty Linen and New-Found-Land (Washington, D.C., Kennedy Center).

105 WARDLE, IRVING. "High Farce: Dirty Linen/New-Found-Land: Almost Free." Times (London), 13 April, p. 11.
   Mixed review of the London, Inter-Arts Trust production.

106 _____. "An Essay in Intellectual Impotence: Jumpers." Times

1976

(London), 22 September, p. 15.
Favorable review of the London, National Theatre revival.

107 WATT, DOUGLAS. "London: From <u>Line</u> to <u>Linen</u>." <u>New York Daily News</u>, 28 July, p. 49.
Includes a review of <u>Dirty Linen and New-Found-Land</u> (London, Inter-Arts Trust); doubts whether its British tone and verbal byplay would be comprehensible to American viewers.

108 WATTS, RICHARD. "The Week in Theater: The Frailties of Age Overtake 'The Boss.'" <u>New York Post</u>, 15 March, p. 19.
Claims the use of an understudy in the leading role of <u>Travesties</u> during matinees caused the play's premature closing on Broadway.

109 WEALES, GERALD. "The Stage: <u>Travesties</u>." Commonweal 103 (13 February):114.
Review of the Broadway production. The play "is either [Stoppard's] blackest statement [about 'existential chaos'] to date or his assumption that the surface joke is what counts. I tend toward the second reading." Abridged in 1978.B20.

110 WESTERBECK, COLIN L. "The Screen: Passing Fantasies." <u>Commonweal</u> 103 (16 January):51-52.
Review of <u>The Romantic Englishwoman</u> (London, DIAL Films), which depicts "a world in which people's illusions about each other obstruct our view of their reality."

111 WILSON, EDWIN. "Washington's a Vibrant Theater Town." <u>Wall Street Journal</u>, 13 December, p. 14.
Includes a favorable review of <u>Dirty Linen and New-Found-Land</u> (Washington, D.C., Kennedy Center tryout of Broadway production). Reprinted in 1977.B87.

112 WISZNIOWSKA, MARTA. "Elizabethans on Modern Stage: Shakespeare and Marlowe versus Marowitz and Bond." <u>Studia Anglica Posnaniensia</u>, no. 8:157-66.
Includes a brief discussion of the language in the "once famous" <u>Rosencrantz & Guildenstern Are Dead</u> in an analysis of modern versions of Elizabethan classics.

1977

A BOOKS

1977

1 HAYMAN, RONALD. *Tom Stoppard*. Contemporary Playwrights Series. London: Heinemann; Totowa, N.J.: Rowman & Littlefield. 157 pp.

   Examines nearly all of Stoppard's original published and produced work through *Dirty Linen and New-Found-Land* (1976); omits "A Walk on the Water" and "A Paragraph for Mr. Blake." Includes two interviews conducted prior to and following writing of the book (the former published, in abridged form with analytical comments interspersed, in 1974.B80); detailed biographical data; a chronological list of major radio, television, and stage productions; and a very short bibliography.

   Interviewer asks questions not often raised and elicits unusually complete replies. Each of the twenty-one brief chapters includes a plot summary and some *explication de texte*. Many also trace recurrent character types and pieces of dialogue; included are critical and analytical remarks about the influence of other writers, glimpses his works afford into his life and motives, his themes (particularly the attempt to escape from conformity and convention and the clash between personal standards and political considerations), and the varying success of his attempts to juxtapose serious and comic material.

   Comments about the major plays are similar to favorable judgements found in many other analyses. More original are the chapters about less well-known works and about *Jumpers* and "Artist Descending a Staircase"; also unusual is the explanation of Stoppard's practice of returning in later plays to material first treated in earlier ones: in the initial excitement of exploration, "the idea is . . . over-elaborated"; returning to it later, he makes the point "more economically and casually."

B SHORTER WRITINGS

1 ANON. "Opening This Week." *Variety*, 12 January, p. 106.
   News item announcing the opening of *Dirty Linen and New-Found-Land* (Broadway). Lists incorrect figures for the production's capitalization and opening costs; corrected in 1977.B2.

2 ANON. "Post-Holiday, Cold Chill B'way; *Dirty Linen* OK, *Ipi* N.G." *Variety*, 19 January, p. 87.
   News item reporting two favorable and one unfavorable review of *Dirty Linen and New-Found-Land* (Broadway); corrects financial data reported in 1977.B1.

Writings about Tom Stoppard

1977

3   ANON. "Angels: Dirty Linen Co." New York Show Business, 27 January, p. 29.
    News item naming financial backers of Dirty Linen and New-Found-Land (Broadway); expanded list given in 1977.B5.

4   ANON. "Getting Around. . . ." Los Angeles Enterprise, 4 February, p. 6.
    Includes a favorable review of Travesties (Los Angeles, Center Theatre Group).

5   ANON. "Angels: Dirty Linen Co." New York Show Business, 17 March, p. 31.
    News item completing the list of financial backers reported in 1977.B3.

6   ANON. "Business Diary: Leading Lady." Times (London), 19 April, p. 19.
    News item reporting that Dr. Miriam Stoppard, the playwright's wife, was named managing director of Syntex Pharmaceuticals (manufacturers of birth control pills).

7   ANON. Review of Dirty Linen and New-Found-Land. Choice 14 (May):379-80.
    Review of the text: although "on its own terms . . . very funny and shrewdly penetrating," nevertheless it is "a very light-weight piece" which falls far short of "Stoppard's earlier brilliance."

8   ANON. Photograph. Sunday Times (London), 26 June, p. 37.
    Director Trevor Nunn, composer/conductor André Previn, and Stoppard prior to the opening of Every Good Boy Deserves Favour (London, John Player Centenary Festival).

9   ANON. "Stoppard Fireworks before Noon." Times (London), 6 September, p. 12.
    Review of "Professional Foul" (London, BBC Television): "talkative and witty, sad and funny, elusive and allusive."

*10 ANON. No Title in Index. Times Higher Education Supplement (London), 30 September, p. 5.
    Listed in Index to the Times, 1977.

11 ANON. "Extra Performances to Benefit Charities." Times (London), 21 November, p. 17.
    News item, reporting that proceeds from four extra performances of Dirty Linen and New-Found-Land (London, Inter-Action Trust) would be given to charities. See also 1977.B12.

Writings about Tom Stoppard

1977

12 ANON. "Children's Charity to Benefit from Performance of Play." Times (London), 5 December, p. 4.
    News item, following up 1977.B11, announcing that Make Children Happy would be the first charity to receive the proceeds from an extra performance of Dirty Linen and New-Found-Land (London, Inter-Action Trust).

13 ANON. "New Year Honours." Times (London), 31 December, p. 11.
    Photographs of those honored on the New Year's List, including Stoppard (CBE).

14 ARVIN, STEVE. Review of Travesties. KMPC-Radio, Los Angeles (1 February).
    Review of the Los Angeles, Center Theatre Group production: warns that it is not "for an anti-semantic."

*15 BARBER, JOHN. "Tom Stoppard at a Terminus." Daily Telegraph (London), 4 July, p. 10.
    Listed in British Humanities Index, 1977.

16 BARBOUR, JOHN. Review of Travesties. KNBC-TV, Los Angeles (27 January).
    Review of the Los Angeles, Center Theatre Group production: emphasizes the great amount of concentration and background knowledge expected of the audience.

17 BARNES, CLIVE. "Dirty Linen Sparkles in Wind of Laughter." New York Times, 12 January, sec. C, p. 18.
    Favorable review of the Broadway production. Reprinted in 1977.B87.

18 BEAUFORT, JOHN. "Import from New Playwright; Latest from Tom Stoppard." Christian Science Monitor, 14 January, p. 27.
    Includes a favorable review of Dirty Linen and New-Found-Land (Broadway). Reprinted in 1977.B87.

19 BERKOWITZ, GERALD M. "Theatre in Review: Dirty Linen and New-Found-Land." Educational Theatre Journal 29 (March): 111-12.
    Review of the London, Inter-Action Trust production of Stoppard's "thoroughly controlled . . . satire of foibles public and private."

20 BERKVIST, ROBERT. "New Face: Rags to Breeches." New York Times, 11 March, p. C3.
    Interview with Cecilia Hart, who played Maddie, the secretary, in Dirty Linen and New-Found-Land (Broadway).

Writings about Tom Stoppard

1977

21 BERMAN, DAVE. "<u>Travesties</u>: Something for Everyone." <u>Santa Monica</u> (Calif.) <u>Outlook</u>, 1 February, pp. 19-20.
    Favorable review of the Los Angeles, Center Theatre Group production.

22 BIRNKRANT, SAM. "One on the Aisle." <u>Malibu</u> (Calif.) <u>Times</u>, 11 February, p. 11.
    Includes a favorable review of <u>Travesties</u> (Los Angeles, Center Theatre Group).

23 BLADEN, BARBARA. "Playwright Sees Play as 'Rational.'" <u>San Mateo</u> (Calif.) <u>Times</u>, 29 March, p. 29.
    Interview: Stoppard discusses works in progress and insists his plays' structures are logical and traditional.

24 _____. "<u>Travesties</u> Is ACT's Biggest Hit." <u>San Mateo</u> (Calif.) <u>Times</u>, 31 March, p. 23.
    Review of the San Francisco company's production: finds it better than Broadway's.

25 BRADSHAW, JON. "Tom Stoppard, Nonstop: Word Games with a Hit Playwright." <u>New York</u> 10 (10 January):47-51.
    Interview. Discusses his journalistic and early playwriting career, his way of dealing with interviews ("I now have a repertoire of plausible answers which evade the whole truth"), his intentions in his works ("What interests me is getting a cliché and then betraying it"), tautological jokes, the origins of <u>Dirty Linen and New-Found-Land</u>, and the relationship between "style" and "substance" in his plays.

26 BRATT, DAVID. "Theatre in Review: <u>Rosencrantz & Guildenstern Are Dead</u>." <u>Educational Theatre Journal</u> 29 (May):266-67.
    Review of the Minneapolis, Guthrie Theater production, which combines the best of traditional British "wit and panache" with American "psychological realism and thematic seriousness."

27 BURR, PATRICIA. "<u>Travesties</u> Now at Mark Taper." <u>South Pasadena</u> (Calif.) <u>Review</u>, 23 February, p. 4.
    Favorable review of the Los Angeles, Center Theatre Group production.

28 CASTILLO, OTHON. "Candilejas." <u>Los Angeles La Opinion</u>, 3 February, p. 5.
    Favorable review (in Spanish) of <u>Travesties</u> (Los Angeles, Center Theatre Group).

Writings about Tom Stoppard

1977

29 CHAILLET, NED. "Young Vic: <u>Rosencrantz and Guildenstern Are Dead</u>." <u>Times</u> (London), 3 June, p. 7.
    Review of the London, Young Vic revival, which "amplifies the debts to <u>Waiting for Godot</u>, . . . and makes the banter seem far more trivial than it need be."

30 _____. "Ayckbourn and Stoppard and Plus." <u>Times</u> (London), 4 August, p. 10.
    Includes a review of the stage adaptation of "'M' Is for 'Moon,' among Other Things," (Richmond, Orange Tree Pub), which "does not adjust to the stage very well and looks like a radio play, over-endowed with poignancy."

31 _____. "Dublin's Mini-Festival." <u>Times</u> (London), 13 October, p. 11.
    News item with a brief favorable review of <u>Travesties</u> (Dublin, Abbey Theatre).

32 CHURCH, MICHAEL. "Television: Starting with a Bang." <u>Times</u> (London), 29 September, p. 11.
    Includes a review of "Professional Foul" (London, BBC Television): "a magnificent piece [which] . . . worked perfectly both as realism and as complex dialectic." Discusses its thematic structure; notes that "the yob ethics of football threaded their punning way through far more of the play than just those sections which dealt with the game itself."

33 CLOSE, ROY M. "<u>Jumpers</u> Is Dazzling Play, despite Staging." <u>Minneapolis Star</u>, 5 May, p. 8.
    Mixed review of the Minneapolis, Macalester College production.

34 CLURMAN, HAROLD. "Theatre." <u>Nation</u> 224 (29 January):124-26.
    Includes a review of <u>Dirty Linen and New-Found-Land</u> (Broadway): characterizes Stoppard as "a clever popularizer [of ideas], a deft epigone." Appreciates the play's "lack of intellectual pretension."

35 COLLINS, WILLIAM B. "Stoppard Pulls out Stops; <u>Travesties</u> Is Dazzling." <u>Philadelphia Inquirer</u>, 2 December, sec. E, p. 22.
    Favorable review of the Philadelphia Drama Guild production.

36 COOK, BRUCE. "Tom Stoppard: The Man behind the Plays." <u>Saturday Review</u> 4 (8 January):52-53.
    Profile, with review of <u>Dirty Linen and New-Found-Land</u>

1977

(Washington, D.C., Kennedy Center tryout of Broadway production). Stoppard discusses the play's origins, his early career and domestic life, Jumpers, Travesties, and Ed Berman (director of Dirty Linen and New-Found-Land in London and New York).

37 CROSSLEY, BRIAN M. "An Investigation of Stoppard's 'Hound' and 'Foot.'" Modern Drama 20 (March):77-86.

Analysis of archetypal themes (particularly the Oedipus figure) in The Real Inspector Hound and After Magritte, in which "the main thrust of [Stoppard's] aesthetic attack" is to "turn the [detective] tradition against itself" in order to create "a mock celebration" of the detective/problem-solver, "of all who believe in him, and of the concept of drama which defines itself in terms of the enactment of a riddle and its answer."

38 DAVY, RICHARD. "Chartist Tells of Czech Suppressed Hopes." Times (London), 1 July, pp. 9, 18.

News item, reporting a press conference at which Stoppard and Zdenek Mlynar, an official in Dubcek's administration, presented "a thick new dossier on violations of human rights" in Czechoslovakia.

39 de VOS, JOZEF. "Rosencrantz and Guildenstern Are Dead: Tom Stoppard's 'Artistic Failure.'" Neophilologus 61 (January):152-59.

Analysis. Despite its "brilliant ingenuity," the play "fails to convince . . . completely": because the viewer knows Hamlet while the courtiers do not, he "does not share the characters' experience."

40 DODSWORTH, MARTIN. "The Editorial Miscellany." English 26 (Summer):183-85.

Includes a favorable review of the text of Travesties.

41 DRAKE, SYLVIA. "The Importance of Being Stoppard." Los Angeles Times, 20 January, sec. IV, p. 12.

Interview.

42 DUNN, PETER. "Television." Sunday Times (London), 25 September, p. 37.

Favorable review of "Professional Foul" (London, BBC Television).

43 EASTAUGH, KENNETH. "Weekend Broadcasting." Times (London), 17 September, p. 8.

Preview description of "Professional Foul" (London, BBC

Television) including comments from Stoppard about the play.

44 EDWA. "Legit Reviews: Travesties." Los Angeles Variety, 2 February, p. 6.
Review of the Los Angeles, Center Theatre Group production: finds the script overly literary and self-indulgent, but redeemed by Stoppard's wit and sense of humor.

45 EICHELBAUM, STANLEY. "Stage." San Francisco Sunday Examiner and Chronicle, 20 February, Scene section, p. 8.
Includes a review of Travesties (Los Angeles, Center Theatre Group): "Stoppard's best work to date" receives "a better balanced, crisper production" in Los Angeles than it did in New York.

46 _____. "So Often Produced, He Ranks with Shaw." San Francisco Examiner, 28 March, p. 24.
Interview. Stoppard discusses Travesties, its production in Vienna, Joyce, and works in progress.

47 _____. "The Arts: Stoppard's Uproarious Dazzler." San Francisco Examiner, 30 March, p. 56.
Favorable review of Travesties (San Francisco, ACT).

48 FAIRBANKS, HAROLD. "Travesties." NewsWest (3-17 February), p. 35.
Favorable review of the Los Angeles, Center Theatre Group production.

49 FISHER, JOHN. "Play Entertains and Enlightens." Levittown (Penn.) Bucks County Courier Times, 2 December, p. B20.
Favorable review of Travesties (Philadelphia Drama Guild).

50 FLEMING, EVE. "What Makes Eddie Run." New York Soho Weekly News, 27 January, p. 25.
News item describing Inter-Action Trust, producer of Dirty Linen and New-Found-Land (Broadway), and the involvement of its director, Ed Berman, with the group.

51 GABBARD, LUCINA P. "Stoppard's Jumpers: A Mystery Play." Modern Drama 20 (March):87-95.
Analysis of similarities between Stoppard's play and medieval mysteries: both mix comedy with metaphysics and, in both, characters have dual roles, personal and allegorical.

1977

52 GARWOOD, JUDITH. Review of *Travesties*. KWHY-TV, Los Angeles (1 February).
   Mixed review of the Los Angeles, Center Theatre Group production.

53 GILL, BRENDAN. "The Theatre: Not for Broadway." *New Yorker* 52 (24 January):63.
   Review of *Dirty Linen and New-Found-Land* (Broadway): "a trifle, better suited to summer camp than to Broadway." Abridged in 1978.B20.

54 GLACKIN, WILLIAM C. "Scene." *Sacramento* (Calif.) *Bee*, 16 April, p. A13.
   Includes a favorable review of *Travesties* (San Francisco, ACT).

55 GLOVER, WILLIAM. Review of *Dirty Linen and New-Found-Land*. AP Wireservice. New York Public Library, Lincoln Center Drama Collection.
   Review of the Broadway production of Stoppard's "inane, cheap and . . . tiresome trifles."

56 GOTTFRIED, MARTIN. "Scrubbing *Dirty Linen* Would Help." *New York Post* (12 January), p. 37.
   Review of the Broadway production of Stoppard's "slender and only fitfully amusing burlesque"; he is "less in need of pampering than of discipline." Reprinted in 1977.B87.

57 GRICE, ELIZABETH. "Freedom Fighters." *Sunday Times* (London), 16 October, p. 38.
   Includes a review of *Travesties* (Dublin, Abbey Theatre): "in this theatre and in this city" it was the character of James Joyce who "best regaled the audience."

58 GROSS, LEONARD. "On Stage." *Westways* (March):72.
   Includes a brief review of *Travesties* (Los Angeles, Center Theatre Group) in an assessment of Gordon Davidson's ten years as director at the Mark Taper Forum.

59 GUNNER, MARJORIE. "On and Off Broadway." *Floral Park* (N.Y.) *Bulletin*, 10 February, p. 3.
   Review of *Dirty Linen and New-Found-Land* (Broadway): a "one joke short play."

60 GUSSOW, MEL. "Broadway: John Wood Interrupts His Quest for Reality to Play in *Tartuffe*." *New York Times*, 19 August, sec. C, p. 2.

Interview with the actor; includes comments about Stoppard and <u>Every Good Boy Deserves Favour</u> (London, John Player Centenary Festival), in which Wood played the leading role.

61 HOBE. "<u>Dirty Linen & New-Found-Land</u>." <u>Variety</u>, 19 January, p. 86.
   Mixed review of the Broadway production.

62 HOLDEN, ANTHONY. "Atticus: Tom's SOS." <u>Sunday Times</u> (London), 24 April, p. 32.
   Columnist reports that, in the wake of the "joyous Jubilee announcement from the Palace," Stoppard needed to find a replacement for a slighting reference to Princess Anne's pregnancy in <u>Dirty Linen and New-Found-Land</u>. Further details in 1977.B63.

63 _____. "Atticus: Exit Tom, Enter Edgar." <u>Sunday Times</u> (London), 22 May, p. 32.
   Following 1977.B62, columnist reports that, despite receiving more than two hundred suggestions from readers regarding suitably sensational substitutes for the pregnant Princess Anne, Stoppard had decided to cut the passage in <u>Dirty Linen and New-Found-Land</u>.

64 _____. "Atticus: Supermum." <u>Sunday Times</u> (London), 5 June, p. 32.
   Interview with Dr. Miriam Stoppard regarding her book about baby care.

65 HOLLAND, JACK. "<u>Travesties</u>: Eccentric, Complex, but Exciting." <u>Newport Beach</u> (Calif.) <u>Newporter Mesa News</u>, 17 February, p. 7.
   Mixed review of the Los Angeles, Center Theatre Group production.

66 HOLLIDAY, JON. "<u>Artist Descending a Staircase</u>." <u>Stage and Television Today</u> (London), 23 June, p. 13.
   Review of the Cardiff, Sherman Arena Company adaptation for the stage, which "needs . . . the elaboration and development" possible only when the author and director are working together.

67 HUGHES, CATHARINE. "If It Weren't for the British." <u>America</u> 136 (19 February):149.
   Includes a review of <u>Dirty Linen and New-Found-Land</u> (Broadway): wishes that "Stoppard would dig beneath the surface a bit instead of dashing off whatever comes to his

1977

quick and witty mind."

68 JENSEN, HENNING. "Jonathan Bennett and Mr Stoppard." Philosophy 52 (April):214-17.
   Criticism of Jumpers, which "is not a significantly philosophical play," but not because the protagonist's lecture is "thin and uninteresting," as claimed in 1975.B21. Rather, Stoppard raises real issues (particularly the questions of "what and whom we are to take as credible") and relates them structurally to the play, but "they are neither clearly presented nor well argued." Accordingly, Jumpers "is of little worth as a play."

69 JOHNSON, JIM. "Travesties, Being Earnest in Repertory at Mark Taper." Covina (Calif.) San Gabriel Valley Tribune, 6 February, p. B6.
   Includes a review of the Los Angeles, Center Theatre Group production: "required viewing for those who appreciate modern drama at its most flamboyant and complex."

70 KALEM, T. E. "Unstoppable Stoppard." Time 109 (24 January): 55.
   Review of Dirty Linen and New-Found-Land (Broadway): Stoppard's "most killingly funny play, . . . though . . . also [his] slenderest." Reprinted in 1977.B87.

71 KALSON, ALBERT E. "Theatre in Review: Every Good Boy Deserves Favour." Educational Theatre Journal 29 (December): 562-63.
   Review of the London, John Player Centenary Festival production: a "flawed work of great daring and imagination," which "has about it the committed spirit of the urgent public meeting."

72 KAMHI, BEN. "Stand Wilde--Who's More Earnest?" University of California (Santa Barbara) Daily Nexus, 10 February, p. 5.
   Includes a favorable review of Travesties (Los Angeles, Center Theatre Group).

73 KERENSKY, OLEG. "Tom Stoppard." In The New British Drama: Fourteen Playwrights since Osborne and Pinter. New York: Taplinger Publishing Co., pp. 145-71.
   Brief biographical and production data; largely devoted to plot summaries and analytical comments about Dirty Linen and New-Found-Land, Enter a Free Man, Every Good Boy Deserves Favour, Jumpers, The Real Inspector Hound, Rosencrantz & Guildenstern Are Dead, and Travesties. Remarks by Stoppard about the origin and development of Travesties

1977

and <u>Jumpers</u> (including the earlier "Another Moon Called Earth"), theism, and his fascination with language and logic.

74 _____. "Tom Stoppard: Wizard or Philosopher?" In <u>Every Good Boy Deserves Favour</u>. Production program, 1 July, London, pp. 12-13.
   Analysis. Countering the opinion that Stoppard is "merely a light entertainer," briefly traces themes of human rights and acceptable behavior in <u>Enter a Free Man</u>, <u>Jumpers</u>, <u>Rosencrantz & Guildenstern Are Dead</u>, and <u>Travesties</u>. Claims that all his plays have "broken away from standard theatrical practice" in terms of their form.

75 KERNIS, JAY. "Voices in the Wind." National Public Radio (28 February).
   Interview with John Wood, the actor for whom Stoppard wrote the leading role in <u>Travesties</u>: discusses his contributions to the script, the relationship between his character's two facets, and the importance of technique for an actor in Stoppard's plays. Item No. 770220; audio tape filed in the network's Washington, D.C. offices.

76 KERR, WALTER. "Tom Stoppard Is Too Lazy to Be Really Funny." <u>New York Times</u>, 23 January, sec. D, pp. 3, 17.
   Review of <u>Dirty Linen and New-Found-Land</u> (Broadway): critical of the play's superficiality and of Stoppard's "slovenly" management of his material.

77 KIRKWOOD, JERRIANN. "You'll Be Intrigued by Confusion of <u>Travesties</u>." <u>West Chester</u> (Penn.) <u>Daily Local News</u>, 2 December, p. 30.
   Mixed review of the Philadelphia Drama Guild's production.

78 KISSEL, HOWARD. "<u>Dirty Linen</u>." <u>Women's Wear Daily</u>, 12 January, p. 44.
   Favorable review of the Broadway production. Reprinted in 1977.B87.

79 LAPE, BOB. "<u>Dirty Linen and New-Found-Land</u>." WABC-TV, Channel 7 (11 January).
   Mixed review of the Broadway production. Text printed in 1977.B87.

80 LAST, RICHARD. "Sheer Delight in Stoppard Debut." <u>Daily Telegraph</u> (London), 22 September, p. 15.
   Review of "Professional Foul" (London, BBC Television),

1977

in which Stoppard exhibits a "dazzling virtuostic assurance hardly matched by any recent writer for the medium."

81 LAWSON, CAROL. "Weekender Guide: Saturday: Gala Night in SoHo." New York Times, 12 August, Weekender section, p. C1.
    News item announcing the opening of The Real Inspector Hound (New York, SoHo Repertory).

82 LEONARD, JOHN. "Tom Stoppard Tries on a 'Knickers Farce.'" New York Times, 9 January, sec. 2, pp. 1, 5.
    Interview: Stoppard discusses his intentions in Dirty Linen and New-Found-Land, the play's director, his facility in interviews, Every Good Boy Deserves Favour, and future plans.

83 LEVIN, BERNARD. "Theatre: Stoppard's Political Asylum." Sunday Times (London), 3 July, p. 37.
    Includes a review of Every Good Boy Deserves Favour (London, John Player Centenary Festival): a "profoundly moral work" which "enhance[s] civilisation itself."

84 LUFT, HERBERT G. "As We See It: The Theatre as Hobby Horse." Los Angeles B'nai B'rith Messenger, 11 February, p. 14.
    Includes a favorable review of Travesties (Los Angeles, Center Theatre Group).

85 MACKENZIE, VICKI. "Best Prescription for Coping with a Very Busy Life." Observer (London), 18 September, p. 23.
    Interview with Miriam Stoppard, the playwright's wife and managing director of the British branch of an international pharmaceutical company: discusses dealing with the demands of work, children, and marriage.

86 MARK, CHARLES CHRISTOPHER. Review of Travesties. National Public Radio (13 January).
    Review of the Washington, D.C., Kennedy Center tryout of the Broadway production: compares Stoppard to Shaw. Item No. 770114; audio tape housed in network's Washington, D.C. office.

87 MARLOWE, JOAN, and BLAKE, BETTY, eds. "Dirty Linen and New-Found-Land." New York Theatre Critics' Review 38 (4 January):388-92.
    Reprints of 1977.B17, 18, 56, 70, 78, 79, 102, 130 about the Broadway production; and 1976.B64, 111 about its Washington, D.C., Kennedy Center tryout.

Writings about Tom Stoppard

1977

88 MARRANCA, BONNIE. Review of Dirty Linen and New-Found-Land. Library Journal 102 (1 March):628.
    Review of the text, which has "surface polish" but is "hollow at the core."

89 MAULTSBY, SARA. "The Big Orange: Out and about in Los Angeles." San Diego Reader, 17 February, pp. 16-17.
    Favorable review of Travesties (Los Angeles, Center Theatre Group).

90 MAVES, C. E. "A Playwright on the Side of Rationality." Palo Alto (Calif.) Times, 25 March, p. 16.
    Interview. Stoppard discusses craftsmanship ("there's a correlation between [it] and art--craftsmanship is what crystallizes art"), logic and rationality in his work, Beckett, and works in progress.

91 _____. "A Buoyant Production of Stoppard's Dazzling, [sic] Travesties." Palo Alto (Calif.) Times, 30 March, p. 16.
    Review of the San Francisco, ACT production: finds compassion, gentleness, and poignancy in it in addition to wit and cleverness.

92 MORAN, RITA. "Wit Teamed in Repertory." Ventura (Calif.) County Star-Free Press, 8 February, p. B5.
    Includes a favorable review of Travesties (Los Angeles, Center Theatre Group).

93 MORLEY, SHERIDAN. "The Arts: New Challenge for Non-Stop Trevor Nunn." Times (London), 28 June, p. 8.
    Interview with the director of Every Good Boy Deserves Favour (London, John Player Centenary Festival); discusses it and his association with Rosencrantz & Guildenstern Are Dead "in 1963" [sic; the year was undoubtedly 1965].

94 MOSS, ROSALIND URBACH. "Moral Perception and the Role of Philosophy in Stoppard's Jumpers." Paper read at Conference on Man, Nature, and the Work of Art, 12 May, University of Minnesota. Photocopied.
    Analysis of Stoppard's "competent and comprehensive" use of "dramatic allegory" to "argue moral philosophy . . . out of its ivory tower . . . and into . . . the ordinary lives of us real people." Discusses the influence of logical positivism and G. E. Moore and the pertinence of the play's ambiguities; emphasizes that its protagonist is converted to Wittgenstein's conception of the moral philosopher's task. Available from Wilson Library, University of Minnesota, Minneapolis.

1977

95 MURRAY, WILLIAM. "Theater: I'm Just Wilde about Stoppard." New West Magazine 2 (28 February):SC19.
   Includes a favorable review of Travesties (Los Angeles, Center Theatre Group).

96 NIGHTINGALE, BENEDICT. "Theatre: Catch-77." New Statesman 94 (8 July):62-63.
   Includes a review of Every Good Boy Deserves Favour (London, John Player Centenary Festival): it does not show whether Stoppard's "'Barnum and Baily style' . . . [can] be reconciled with . . . suffering of any substantial kind" because Stoppard concentrates much more on "portraying eccentricity" than on "evoking misery."

97 _____. "Why Do Playwrights Thrive in Britain?" New York Times, 10 July, sec. 2, pp. 1, 8.
   Feature article; includes Stoppard's explanation of why he became a playwright.

98 NOVICK, JULIUS. "Going Plume on Plume." Village Voice, 31 January, pp. 69-70.
   Favorable review of Dirty Linen and New-Found-Land (Broadway), with comments about the purity of Stoppard's wit relative to that of avowedly homosexual playwrights. Abridged in 1978.B20.

99 OPPENHEIMER, GEORGE. "Theater: Dirty Linen Won't Wash." Long Island City (N.Y.) Newsday, 14 January, p. 5.
   Unfavorable review of the Broadway production.

100 PHILBIN, REGIS. Review of Travesties. KABC-TV (7 February).
   Favorable review of the Los Angeles, Center Theatre Group production.

101 POSNER, HOWARD. "Travesties: The Importance of Being Stoppard." University of California (Los Angeles) Daily Bruin, 1 February, pp. 10-11.
   Favorable review of the Los Angeles, Center Theatre Group production.

102 PROBST, LEONARD. "Dirty Linen and New-Found-Land." NBC-TV, Channel 4 (11 January).
   Favorable review of the Broadway production. Reprinted in 1977.B87.

103 PROCTOR, RICHARD. Review of Travesties. KTYD-Radio, Santa Barbara (8 February).
   Favorable review of the Los Angeles, Center Theatre

Group production.

104 REED, REX. "Some Rhythm and Boos." New York Daily News, 14 January, p. 54.
Review of Dirty Linen and New-Found-Land (Broadway): "the most boring play I have ever witnessed."

105 RICH, ALAN. "Dirty Linen Is Pure Silk." New York 10 (24 January):89.
Review of the Broadway production: says its "ability to challenge the intellect . . . raises the level of farce to something approaching sophistication." Abridged in 1978.B20.

106 ROBINSON, DAVID. "In the Picture: Fassbinder after Despair." Sight and Sound 46 (Autumn):216-17.
Interview with Rainer Fassbinder, director of the film, who credits Stoppard with developing a screenplay from Nabokov's novel in a way he had not found for himself.

107 ROBINSON, GABRIELE SCOTT. "Plays without Plot: The Theatre of Tom Stoppard." Educational Theatre Journal 29 (March): 37-48.
Analysis of Jumpers, Lord Malquist & Mr Moon, Rosencrantz & Guildenstern Are Dead, and Travesties; brief mention of "Albert's Bridge," "Artist Descending a Staircase," and Enter a Free Man. Concentrates on his plots' "lack of development and coherence," which produces both farcical effects and "characters who are . . . always subordinate to a conceit." Discusses Stoppard's success with parody, the double-act of his major characters, and the plays' unsatisfactory endings.

108 SCHIER, ERNEST. "Brilliance, Humor Touch Stoppard 'What If?' Play." Philadelphia Evening Bulletin, 2 December, p. 55.
Review of Travesties (Philadelphia Drama Guild): "an undisciplined work that must manage with flash what it lacks in substance."

109 SCHLUETER, JUNE MAYER. "The Theatre of the Double: The Twofold Character in Modern Self-Conscious Drama." Ph.D. dissertation, Columbia University, pp. 135-54.
Analysis of The Real Inspector Hound, one of six plays studied which illustrate the use of a "double character" to depict "the paradox of art--that it is an artificial reality." Says Stoppard creates two plays, one between the critics and the other involving the murder mystery, thus encouraging the audience to compartmentalize the two

1977

worlds, at which he "upset[s] any certainty with respect to those worlds through integrating the plays." Revised and expanded in 1979.B93.

110 SCHNEIDER, ROBERT. "Stoppard's Word Play." <u>Claremont</u> (Calif.) <u>Courier</u>, 5 February, p. 1.
　　Review of <u>Travesties</u> (Los Angeles, Center Theatre Group): "no American playwright would dare demand of his audience what <u>Travesties</u> demands. . . . . If it succeeds . . . it will be a compliment to us all."

111 SCHWARTZ, TONY. "Tony Schwartz." <u>New York Post</u>, 12 January, p. 31.
　　Brief interview following the opening of <u>Dirty Linen and New-Found-Land</u> (Broadway).

112 SHAW-TAYLOR, DESMOND. "Music: Tippett: A Composer for Our Time." <u>Sunday Times</u> (London), 10 July, p. 35.
　　Include a brief review of André Previn's score for <u>Every Good Boy Deserves Favour</u> (London, John Player Centenary Festival): "for the most part a very skilful pastiche of the satirical styles of Shostakovich and Prokofiev."

113 SIMON, JOHN. "On Stage: Fooling Around." <u>New Leader</u> 60 (31 January):23.
　　Review of <u>Dirty Linen and New-Found-Land</u> (Broadway): "among the most unpretentious" of Stoppard's works. Abridged in 1978.B20.

114 _____. "Theater Chronicle." <u>Hudson Review</u> 30 (Summer):259-69.
　　Includes a review of <u>Dirty Linen and New-Found-Land</u> (Broadway): "sophomoric" but "free from all pretentiousness" and "unusually clever," particularly in its "occasionally quite sophisticated verbal structures."

115 STOTHARD, PETER. "<u>Every Good Boy Deserves Favour</u>." <u>Plays and Players</u> 24 (September):33.
　　Review of the London, John Player Centenary Festival production: discusses similarities to <u>Jumpers</u>; the ending is "happier than . . . [those of] Stoppard's fantasy plays."

116 SULLIVAN, DAN. "Stage Review: <u>Travesties</u> at Taper Forum." <u>Los Angeles Times</u>, 31 January, sec. IV, p. 1.
　　Review of the Los Angeles, Center Theatre Group production: claims it is "a joy" but warns that it is also "a show for the overeducated." The production gives the play "a bounce it didn't have in New York. . . . It's not

Writings about Tom Stoppard

1977

so much a head-trip now," and "it's not trying to drown out Stoppard's voice with production values."

117 TAKIFF, JONATHAN. "A Few Will ReJoyce in These <u>Travesties</u>." <u>Philadelphia Daily News</u>, 2 December, p. 32.
   Mixed review of the Philadelphia Drama Guild production.

118 TALCOVE, RICK. "Stoppard's <u>Travesties</u>: A Conceited Play." <u>Van Nuys</u> (Calif.) <u>Valley News</u>, 4 February, "Friday" section, p. 8.
   Review of the Los Angeles, Center Theatre Group production: Stoppard's "brilliance is severely limited by his incredible self-indulgence"; his characters are "mouthpieces rather than humans we can easily identify with."

119 TAYLOR, LARRY. "Two British Plays Turn into a Double Success." <u>Garden Grove</u> (Calif.) <u>Orange County Evening News</u>, 16 February, p. 37.
   Includes a favorable review of <u>Travesties</u> (Los Angeles, Center Theatre Group).

120 TAYLOR, ROBERT. "Tom Stoppard's <u>Travesties</u>: ACT Tops N.Y. with Comedy Smash." <u>Oakland</u> (Calif.) <u>Tribune</u>, 31 March, p. 43.
   Review of the San Francisco company's production, which is superior to the Broadway production in its ability to present a "heart and soul" in addition to the play's more obvious intellectual values.

121 _____. "Tom Stoppard's Plays Are More Than Just 'Clever Nonsense.'" <u>Oakland</u> (Calif.) <u>Tribune</u>, 17 April, p. 2E.
   Includes Stoppard's comments about <u>Travesties</u>, logical structure, and works in progress.

122 TERRY, SARA. "Oldster's Visions Make <u>Travesties</u>." <u>Long Beach</u> (Calif.) <u>Forty-Niner</u>, 1 February, p. 3.
   Favorable review of the Los Angeles, Center Theatre Group production.

123 NO ENTRY

124 TUGEND, TOM. "Stage and Screen." <u>Los Angeles Heritage and Southwest Jewish Press</u>, 11 February, p. 14.
   Favorable review of <u>Travesties</u> (Los Angeles, Center Theatre Group).

125 TYNAN, KENNETH. "Profiles: Withdrawing with Style from the Chaos." <u>New Yorker</u> 53 (19 December):41-111.

1977

Profile, with analytical comments, quotations by Stoppard and by friends about him, and detailed biographical data.
Establishes his early "apolitical" stance (the unproduced "This Way out with Samuel Boot" is "the last Stoppard play with a message that could be described as leftist"); examines "Albert's Bridge," Rosencrantz & Guildenstern Are Dead, The Real Inspector Hound, Jumpers ("his masterpiece"), Travesties (which fails because it exerts no dramatic "pressure" upon its characters and distorts Joyce's political sympathies), and Dirty Linen and New-Found-Land; traces his recent movement from "withdrawal to involvement" in political affairs to his recognition that Czech playwright Václav Havel is his "mirror image," one who has suffered the repression Stoppard avoided by emigration.
Includes Stoppard's comments about Havel; his early career, friends, and family; God's existence; his attitude toward British government and institutions; and his "conventional" artistic attitudes, his plays' plots and characters ("I take a stereotype and betray it, rather than create an original character"), and his refusal to make "my private emotions the quarry for the statue I'm carving."
Also includes accounts of Jumpers' gestation, Stoppard's visits to Oxford and southern California, and Havel's career. Reprinted in 1977.B106. Abridged in 1978.B80.

126 WAHLS, ROBERT. "Footlights: British Sex Symbol." New York Sunday News, 16 January, p. 4.
Interview with Cecilia Hart, who played the secretary, Maddie, in Dirty Linen and New-Found-Land (Broadway).

*127 WALKER, N. Review of Rosencrantz & Guildenstern Are Dead. Boston Gay Community News, 17 December, p. 10.
City and producing organization not named; item listed in Alternative Press Index, 1977.

128 WALSH, CHUCK. Review of Travesties. KFWB-Radio, Los Angeles (31 January).
Favorable review of the Los Angeles, Center Theatre Group production.

129 WARDLE, IRVING. "The Arts: Abundance of Bright Ideas." Times (London), 2 July, p. 7.
Review of Every Good Boy Deserves Favour (London, John Player Centenary Festival), which "supplies the clearest instance so far of Stoppard's capacity to express social indignation and a firm moral viewpoint through the kind of intellectual gymnastics and formal trickery which are often

considered the marks of flippant detachment."

130 WATT, DOUGLAS. "Dirty Linen Is Pure Fun." New York Daily News, 12 January, p. 56.
Favorable review of the Broadway production. Reprinted in 1977.B87.

131 WEALES, GERALD. "The Stage: Message, Farce & Home Movie." Commonweal 104 (18 March):180-81.
Includes a review of Dirty Linen and New-Found-Land (Broadway): "often funny, but . . . insubstantial."

132 WEINER, BERNARD. "A Puzzling, 'Traditional' Stoppard." San Francisco Chronicle, 29 March, p. 40.
Interview: Stoppard discusses Travesties, Joyce ("the finest practitioner of the stream of literature with which I tempermentally [sic] identify with" [sic]), "Professional Foul," and his screenplay of Nabakov's Despair. Claims to be a "traditional writer" of works which are "logical" and "rational" despite their "fragmented look."

133 _____. "High-Speed Wizardry." San Francisco Chronicle, 31 March, p. 55.
Review of Travesties (San Francisco, ACT): admires Stoppard's cleverness but calls him "an egregious show-off . . . [whose] conceits get in the way."

134 WETZSTEON, ROSS. "New York." Plays and Players 24 (June): 37-38.
Includes a brief review of Dirty Linen and New-Found-Land (Broadway), which "aspires to a sublime silliness, [but] founders in cheap titillation."

135 WHITAKER, THOMAS R. Fields of Play in Modern Drama. Princeton: Princeton University Press, pp. 12-17.
Revision of 1972.B142, to illustrate the claim that Rosencrantz & Guildenstern Are Dead is a "more explicit and less demanding form" of the modern theme of "consciousness of consciousness" which is found in Beckett and Genet. Finds Stoppard's play less rich than it might be because its theme ("self-conscious life . . . is . . . an elusive absence signifying nothing") is belied by the "mutuality" occurring during a performance before an audience.

136 WILSON, EDWIN. "The Diversity of Non-Profit Theater." Wall Street Journal, 2 February, p. 16.
Includes comments about a dress rehearsal of Travesties (Los Angeles, Center Theatre Group).

Writings about Tom Stoppard

1977

137 WINE, BILL. "<u>Travesties</u>, Stoppard's Funny Magic Act, Is Clever Cerebral Gamesmanship Play." <u>Cherry Hill</u> (N.J.) <u>Courier-Post</u>, 2 December, p. 12.
   Review of the Philadelphia Drama Guild production: despite its intellectual virtues, the play lacks "momentum or emotional appeal."

138 YOUNG, B. A. "<u>Rosencrantz and Guildenstern</u>." <u>Financial Times</u> (London), 4 June, p. 9.
   Review of the London, Young Vic revival, which is marred by the production's slow pace.

1978

A BOOKS

*1 COOKE, JOHN WILLIAM. "The Optical Allusion: Perception and Form in Stoppard's <u>Travesties</u>." Ph.D. dissertation, American University, 37 pp.
   Analysis of the play in light of the mind's habit of "asserting upon . . . events . . . a unifying structure . . . which makes [them] 'coherent.'" Claims the play is not organized around a thematic statement but rather "reveals the process by which we . . . make order of chaos." (Annotation summarized from <u>Dissertation Abstracts International</u> 39 [September]:1545-A.)

B SHORTER WRITINGS

1 ANON. "Tom Stoppard TV Play 'Best of 1977.'" <u>Daily Telegraph</u> (London), 4 March, p. 10.
   News item, announcing the award given to "Professional Foul" by the Broadcasting Press Guild.

2 ANON. "Further Award for Stoppard Play." <u>Times</u> (London), 6 May, p. 16.
   News item, reporting the Royal Television Society's "Writer's Award" for 1977 had been given to "Professional Foul."

3 ANON. "Stoppard/Previn Piece for Mermaid." <u>Times</u> (London), 30 May, p. 12.
   News item, announcing the coming opening of <u>Every Good Boy Deserves Favour</u> (London, John Player revival).

4 ANON. Award to "Professional Foul." <u>British Theatrelog</u>, no.

Writings about Tom Stoppard

1978

   1 (Summer):21.
   News item, reporting the play had been given the British Academy of Film and Television Arts "TV Writer's Award."

5 ANON. "Good Boy Receives Favour." Sunday Times (London), 18 June, p. 37.
   News item, announcing that Every Good Boy Deserves Favour was to be published with text and score interwoven.

6 ANON. "Tom Stoppard Puts Case for Soviet Jews." Times (London), 12 July, p. 7.
   News story reporting Stoppard's participation at a meeting sponsored by the National Council for Soviet Jewry; says he wrote a part for a boy in Every Good Boy Deserves Favour because (in the reporter's words) "certain truths about human rights have a clarity and simplicity which can best be expressed in the utterances of children."

7 ANON. "New in Paperback." Washington Post, 23 July, p. F2.
   Brief review of the text of "Every Good Boy Deserves Favour" and "Professional Foul."

8 ANON. "Date Set for New Stoppard Play." Times (London), 7 August, p. 14.
   News item, announcing the coming West End opening of Night and Day.

9 ANON. Photograph. Times (London), 26 September, p. 17.
   Stoppard, Diana Rigg, and John Thaw at the opening of rehearsals for Night and Day (London, West End).

10 ANON. Review of "Every Good Boy Deserves Favour" and "Professional Foul." Choice 15 (October):1054.
   Text review; says they are founded on "ironies created by words juxtaposed in word games and intellectual and verbal arabesques of great intricacy."

11 ANON. "New Stoppard Play." Times (London), 17 October, p. 10.
   News item announcing the coming opening of Night and Day (London, West End).

12 ANON. Photograph. Sunday Times (London), 5 November, p. 39.
   Diana Rigg in a scene from Night and Day (London, West End).

13 ARNETT, EARL. "The Critics' Place." Maryland Public Broadcasting Service (20 July).

169

Writings about Tom Stoppard

1978

Favorable review of Rosencrantz & Guildenstern Are Dead (Washington, D.C., Shakespeare & Co.).

14 ASAHINA, ROBERT. "On Screen: Teutonic Tedium" New Leader 61 (23 October):20.
 Review of Despair (London, Marthesheimer): Stoppard's "wretched" writing reduces Nabokov's "complex, civilized ironies to a series of gags."

15 BAKER, BARBARA. "Review: Another Hit at Monmouth." Kennebec (Maine) Journal, 10 July, p. 13.
 Favorable review of Rosencrantz & Guildenstern Are Dead (Monmouth, Theatre at Monmouth).

16 BERGSON, PHILLIP. "The Stars Look Up." Sunday Times (London), 28 May, p. 35.
 Includes a review of Despair (London, Marthesheimer); appreciates Stoppard's "succulent" screenplay.

17 BLUMENFELD, YORICK. "The Dramatic Relationship between Soccer and Freedom." Horizon 21 (April):90-92.
 Feature article with analytical comments about "Professional Foul" (London, BBC Television); includes quotations from Stoppard about the play's evolution and public reception.

18 BRANDON, HENRY. "Stoppard Wins Favour." Sunday Times (London), 3 September, p. 35.
 Brief review of and financial data about Every Good Boy Deserves Favour (Washington, D.C., Kennedy Center), which received a standing ovation on its opening night.

19 BRIEN, ALAN. "Films: A Banquet without the Main Course." Sunday Times (London), 9 July, p. 37.
 Includes a review of Despair (London, Marthesheimer): Stoppard's "jokes prove to be unexpectedly tentative."

20 BRYFONSKI, DEDRIA, and MENDELSON, PHYLLIS CARMEL, eds. "Stoppard, Tom." In Contemporary Literary Criticism: Excerpts from Criticism of the Works of Today's Novelists, Poets, Playwrights, and Other Creative Writers. Vol. 8. Detroit: Gale Research Co., pp. 501-4.
 Continuation of 1976.B87. Consists of abridgements of 1975.B30, 94, 1976.B89, 109 about Travesties; and of 1977.B53, 98, 105, 113 about Dirty Linen and New-Found-Land.

21 BUTCHER, MARYVONNE. "Cinema." Tablet 232 (15 July):682.
 Includes a brief review of Despair (London, Marthesheimer).

1978

22 BUTLER, JOE. "Theater Review: Agatha Christie Spoof Good Fun on Hot Night." Taunton (Mass.) Daily Gazette, 26 July, p. 16.
    Favorable review of The Real Inspector Hound (Providence, R.I., Trinity Square Repertory Company).

*23 CAMROUX, DAVID. "Tom Stoppard: The Last of the Metaphysical Egocentrics." Caliban 15:79-94.
    Analysis. Claims Stoppard's characters exist to display moral lessons, while he continuously examines his purposes and asserts his beliefs: God may exist and life has a purpose, pattern, and order. (Annotation summarized from Abstracts of English Studies, 1978.)

24 CHAILLET, NED. "Every Good Boy Deserves Favour: Mermaid." Times (London), 15 June, p. 15.
    Review of the London, John Player revival: it "works as an entertainment and as a salutary reminder of grim political truths" and claims that "the clumsy lashing out at Lenin that marred . . . Travesties is replaced by . . . rich irony."

25 _____. "Learned Discourse Goes the Way of All Flesh." Times (London), 29 September, p. 9.
    Includes a review of Jumpers (Nottingham, Playhouse); finds the production weak.

26 CLARKE, GERALD. "Theater: Trick and Treat." Time 112 (11 September):59.
    Review of Every Good Boy Deserves Favour (Washington, D.C., Kennedy Center), which "ends where it began, with a brilliant conceit waiting to be developed."

27 CLOSE, ROY. "TRP Production of Complex Travesties Is Well-Paced." Minneapolis Star, 21 March, p. 8.
    Mixed review of the Minneapolis, Theatre in the Round production of the "brilliant, difficult" play.

28 CLUM, JOHN M. "Religion and Five Contemporary Plays: The Quest for God in a Godless World." South Atlantic Quarterly 77 (Autumn):418-32.
    Analysis; traces themes of "the quest for transcendence" and "the conflict between spirituality and sensuality" in Jumpers and plays by Peter Shaffer, Ionesco, and Albee. Unlike the "bizarre parables" of the latter two, Stoppard's plays are "theatrical collages" which suggest that the search for God is equivalent to the search for "reason set against chaos."

1978

29 COLBY, DOUGLAS. "The Game of Coin Tossing: Rosencrantz and Guildenstern Are Dead by Tom Stoppard." In As the Curtain Rises: On Contemporary British Drama, 1966-1976. Rutherford, N.J.: Fairleigh Dickinson University Press, pp. 27-45.
    Analysis of "the opening visual metaphor as the interpretive key to" the play; discusses themes (on- and off-stage action, split characterization, fate, and the relationship between audience and characters) encapsulated therein. Also includes brief analyses of Absurdist themes revealed in opening scenes of After Magritte, "Albert's Bridge," Dirty Linen and New-Found-Land, Enter a Free Man, The Real Inspector Hound, and Travesties.

30 COLEBY, JOHN. "Plays in Print." Drama: The Quarterly Theatre Review, no. 130 (Autumn):78-80.
    Includes a review of the text of The (15 Minute) Hamlet: "highly compressed but not truncated."

31 COLLINS, WILLIAM B. "Stoppard's About-Face: It's Politics This Time." Philadelphia Inquirer, 13 August, p. L1.
    News item announcing the opening of Every Good Boy Deserves Favour (Ambler, Pa.; Temple University Music Festival); also summarizes Stoppard's work with Amnesty International and quotes from Tynan's account (in 1977.B125) of his increasing interest in political issues.

32 COMBS, RICHARD. "Chinese Roulette and Despair." Sight and Sound 47 (Autumn):258-60.
    Includes a review of Despair (London, Marthesheimer): Stoppard's screenplay failed to "find any overall 'holding' metaphor for the novel's shifting levels of fantasy."

33 COVINGTON, GILLIAN. "Letters: Stoppard's Bouncing Joy." Sunday Times (London), 22 January, p. 14.
    Letter to the editor, claiming that, 1978.B80 notwithstanding, Stoppard does write "socially commited" plays, noting his work with Amnesty International, and objecting to Tynan's condescending attitude toward comedy, which makes one "positively bounce with the sheer joy of being alive--which is a lot more than I can say of a play like [Tynan's] Oh Calcutta!"

34 DAVIS, JESSICA MILNER. Farce. The Critical Idiom, no. 39. London: Methuen & Co., pp. 82-84, 86.
    Includes a brief analysis of Dirty Linen and New-Found-Land; claims its implied moral and social comment places it outside the usual bounds of farce.

35 DAY, DORIS M. "One-Act Plays." Drama: The Quarterly Theatre Review, no. 128 (Spring):82.
    Includes a brief review of the text of the stage version of "A Separate Peace": it will make a "good Festival entry" for schools.

*36 DURSO, NICHOLAS ANTHONY. "Play-within-a-Play in Modern Drama." Ph.D. dissertation, University of Notre Dame, 240 pp.
    Analysis of the use of the convention in Rosencrantz & Guildenstern Are Dead and ten other modern plays. (Annotation summarized from Dissertation Abstracts International 38 [January]:4156-A.)

37 EASTMAN, PEGGY. "Two Inconsequential Sparks of Humanity." Bethesda (Md.) Montgomery Journal, 4 August, pp. B2, B4.
    Review of Rosencrantz & Guildenstern Are Dead (Washington, D.C., Shakespeare & Co.): a "difficult and at times tedious vehicle"; claimed Act III was unnecessary.

38 ECKERT, THOR, Jr. "Exclusive Report from Boston." New York Theatre Review 2 (February):34-35.
    Includes a brief review of The Real Inspector Hound and the stage adaptation of "A Separate Peace" (Boston, Next Move Theatre).

39 ERSTEIN, H. A. "Abbott and Costello Meet." Columbia (Md.) Flier, 3 August, p. 54.
    Favorable review of Rosencrantz & Guildenstern Are Dead (Washington, D.C., Shakespeare & Co.).

40 GARDNER, JOHN. On Moral Fiction. New York: Basic Books, pp. 58-59.
    Includes brief analytical comments about Stoppard, who, "even at his best, . . . evades concern" because his plays are based on "obviously contrived" accidents, "have no conclusions," and treat ideas in a manner "more fashionable than earnest."

41 GASKELL, PHILIP. "Example 12: Stoppard, Travesties, 1974." In From Writer to Reader: Studies in Editorial Method. Oxford: Oxford University Press, pp. 245-62.
    Essay using Travesties as an example of the sorts of problems which plays pose for textual bibliographers. Largely devoted to extended examples of differences between the play's "script" (what the author originally intended), its "performance text" (what was actually said), and its "reading text" (the published record); includes Stoppard's explanations of his intentions in various parts of the play.

1978

Notes that, although the performance text of the play's revival (London, Royal Shakespeare Company) was more similar to the premiere performance text (also Royal Shakespeare Company) than to the reading text, future productions will perforce rely upon the reading text.

42 GOLD, MARGARET. "Who Are the Dadas of Travesties?" Modern Drama 21 (March):59-65.
    Analysis of Stoppard's use of others' themes, characters, and techniques in Travesties; the "dadas" include Wilde, Shaw, Joyce, and Lenin.

43 GRANDCHAMP, KATHY. "Theatre: Travesties." Minneapolis Twin Cities Reader, 24 March, p. 17.
    Review of the Minneapolis, Theatre in the Round production, which will test local audiences' maturity.

44 GRAPE, NANCY. "Two Young Actors Light Up Stoppard Play at Monmouth." Lewiston (Maine) Evening Journal, 7 July, p. 3.
    Favorable review of Rosencrantz & Guildenstern Are Dead (Monmouth, Maine; Theatre at Monmouth).

45 GUSSOW, MEL. "Uncommon New Plays by Tom Stoppard and David Rudkin." New York Times, 6 August, sec. 2, pp. 4, 15.
    Includes a review of Every Good Boy Deserves Favour (London, John Player revival): "a hybrid that too readily reveals its individual parentage." While this play "is exceedingly clever, 'Professional Foul' was an act of conscience."

*46 HARVEY, S. Review of Every Good Boy Deserves Favour. Inquiry Magazine 1 (16 October):29.
    Presumably, the Temple University Music Festival production during its tour; item listed in Alternative Press Index, 1978.

*47 HIDALGO, PILAR. La ira la palabria: teatro inglés actual. Madrid: Cupsa, pp. 99-121.
    Listed in Modern Drama 23 (June 1980):144.

48 HUCKERBY, MARTIN. "Arts Diary: KGB to Blame in the End." Times (London), 17 August, p. 12.
    Interview; Stoppard says he is "'baffled that . . . people . . . misunderstand the ending" of Every Good Boy Deserves Favour (in which the KGB officer "deliberately confuses" the political dissident with the lunatic in order to avoid having to admit his "treatment" had failed); "the final anguish is caused by the dissident having to decide

1978

whether to go along with that ploy in order to gain his freedom."

49 JACK, IAN. "Atticus: A Play for Paul." Sunday Times (London), 29 October, p. 32.

Columnist reports that the argument in Night and Day about journalists' unions may have been influenced by Stoppard's talks with his friend and neighbor Paul Johnson, once a socialist and editor of The New Statesman, now a conservative; notes that the play is dedicated to him.

*49a KAHN, COPPÉLIA. "Travesties and the Importance of Being Tom Stoppard." New York Literary Forum 1 (Spring):187-97. Cited in Modern Drama 22 (June 1979):158.

50 K[ALEM], T. E. "Theater: Scoop." Time 112 (27 November): 110.

Review of Night and Day (London, West End): "prevailingly entertaining" despite "odd moments of strain."

51 KROLL, JACK. "Theater: Oh, to Be in England." Newsweek 92 (27 November):65-70.

Includes a review of Night and Day (London, West End): shows Stoppard to be "very much in transition"; he is trying "to blend his explosive high jinks with a morally responsible attitude toward social and political problems," but "the all-too-carefully-crafted combination makes one uneasy."

52 LAHR, JOHN. Prick up Your Ears: The Biography of Joe Orton. New York: Alfred A. Knopf, pp. 259-60.

Quotes from Orton's diary, in which he says that he admired the idea of Rosencrantz & Guildenstern Are Dead, but "it should've been about the futility of students--always talking . . . and never doing anything."

53 LEVIN, BERNARD. "Theatre: The Shining Truth of Tom Stoppard." Sunday Times (London), 18 June, p. 38.

Includes a review of Every Good Boy Deserves Favour (London, John Player revival): "no one who loves the English language and the highest comic art can possibly miss this play. Nor anyone who hates cruelty and loves justice."

54 _____. "Theatre: Tom Stoppard's African Journey." Sunday Times (London), 12 November, p. 37.

Includes a review of Night and Day (London, West End): "a deeply disappointing play." Its "fundamental trouble . . . is that it is raw": themes are awkwardly interwoven,

1978

the dialogue features "some horribly clumsy preaching," and the sub-plot is "jejune." Stoppard "has put his viewpoint before his drama."

55 LUNDEGAARD, BOB. "Theatre in Round Scores with Stoppard's Travesties." Minneapolis Tribune, 18 March, p. 9.
    Favorable review of the Minneapolis company's production.

56 McCOURT, JAMES. "Percival and Other Knights." Film Comment 14 (November):57-60.
    Includes a review of Despair (London, Marthesheimer): Stoppard "deftly simulates" Nabokov's "mordant" style.

57 MORLEY, SHERIDAN. "John Thaw: 'TV Makes You a Star.'" Times (London), 7 November, p. 10.
    Interview with the actor playing Wagner in Night and Day (London, West End); includes some brief comments about Stoppard.

58 NEIL, BOYD. "Green Room: Travesties and Translation." Plays and Players 26 (December):8-9.
    Discusses the play in an essay about the difficulties of translating; includes comments about the Paris, Centre Dramatique de Lausanne production, in which the "unhelpful mise-en-scène . . . turned possible wit into farce."

59 NEWALL, ROBERT H. "Theater Review: Rosencrantz Highly Effective." Bangor (Maine) Daily News, 7 August, p. 18.
    Favorable review of the Monmouth, Theatre at Monmouth production.

60 NIGHTINGALE, BENEDICT. "Theatre: Lab-Rat." New Statesman 95 (23 June):857-58.
    Includes a review of Every Good Boy Deserves Favour (London, John Player revival): "full of indignation and imaginative bravura."

61 _____. "Arts & Entertainment: Debriefing." New Statesman 96 (17 November):671-72.
    Review of Night and Day (London, West End): gives evidence that Stoppard's "theatrical junket, if not exactly over, has evidently entered a new and more earnest phase." However, the play leaves "too little doubt where Stoppard stands on issues that may be more . . . equivocal than he allows," has "sometimes quite inappropriate" discussion and conceptualizing, and fails to elicit "the kind of emotional response an author can only hope to excite if his characters engage their audience somewhere other than the brainbox."

Writings about Tom Stoppard

1978

62 O'CONNOR, JOHN J. "TV: Stoppard's 'Professional Foul' on WNET." New York Times, 26 April, p. C24.
    Review of the "superbly constructed and brilliantly composed" television play, which is "in some ways . . . superior to the playwright's theater works, which often tend to be too clever by half."

*63 OTREMBA, GERALDINE MARIE. "The Importance of Farce for the Study of Modern Absurdist Theatre: Studies of Orton, Stoppard, and Pinter." Ph.D. dissertation, University of North Carolina at Chapel Hill, 150 pp.
    Includes an analysis of Dirty Linen and New-Found-Land, emphasizing the continuity between Theatre of the Absurd and the comic tradition. (Annotation summarized from Dissertation Abstracts International 40 [July 1979]:29-A.)

64 RADCLIFFE, PHILIP. "Tom Stoppard and Andre [sic] Previn." Sunday Times (London), 9 July, p. 38.
    Review of the phonograph record of Every Good Boy Deserves Favour: "very funny and very frightening."

65 RICE, ED. "Theater Review: R & G 'Living' It Up as Befuddled Duo." Portland (Maine) Press Herald, 31 July, p. 13.
    Favorable review of Rosencrantz & Guildenstern Are Dead (Monmouth, Theatre at Monmouth).

66 RINGOLD, FRANCINE LEFFLER. "Theatre." World Literature Today 52 (Winter):111.
    Favorable review of the text of Dirty Linen and New-Found-Land.

67 ROBERTS, PHILIP. "Tom Stoppard: Serious Artist or Siren?" Critical Quarterly 20 (Autumn):84-92.
    Criticism, with analytical comments about After Magritte, Jumpers, The Real Inspector Hound, Rosencrantz & Guildenstern Are Dead, and Travesties. Calls Stoppard "a liberal humanist" (one who believes that "mankind will sort itself out eventually, without anyone prodding it in any particular direction"). Says he resists "any idea of the theatre as an agent of change"; charges that, "if the world is the true Beckettian one as delineated by Stoppard, then there seems little sense even in a gradualist optimism." Nevertheless, his plays "reel away from seriousness" or are weakened by his "insistence upon farce," and he "denigrates" those who write to advance a cause. Response to these claims found in 1980.B24.

1978

68 ROBINSON, DAVID. "Cannes Repeats the Miracle." Times (London), 26 May, p. 11.
  Includes a review of Despair (London, Marthesheimer): Stoppard's dialogue makes Fassbinder's "irony . . . more than usually explicit."

69 SCHIER, ERNEST. "Exclusive Report from Philadelphia." New York Theatre Review 2 (March):36.
  Includes a mixed review of Rosencrantz & Guildenstern Are Dead (Philadelphia Repertory Company).

70 SCHWARZ, ALFRED. From Büchner to Beckett: Dramatic Theory and the Modes of Tragic Drama. Athens, Ohio: Ohio University Press, pp. 326-32.
  Analysis of Rosencrantz & Guildenstern Are Dead. Its "allusion to a monumental tragic act from an essentially comic perspective" illustrates a modern scepticism about the significance of the individual; also traces the influence of the play/life metaphor and notes the mixture of fear and amusement which makes up the audience's reaction. But because the play does not examine "the more radical questions touching on the nature of existence," it remains "an entertaining spin-off from the world of" Waiting for Godot.

71 SHIRLEY, DON. "Rosencrantz and Guildenstern--Alive." Washington Post, 22 July, p. B4.
  Favorable review of the Washington, D.C., Shakespeare & Co. production.

72 SHULMAN, MILTON. "The Politicizing of Tom Stoppard." New York Times, 23 April, sec. 2, pp. 3, 27.
  Interview. Stoppard discusses his "reaction against making heroes for plays who had positive points of view and no qualifications about them. And I became quite good at seeing the other side or, to rephrase that, I became a terrible hedger." Insists that he was nevertheless "morally, if not politically, involved."
  Also discusses Havel's plays and the evolution of "Professional Foul" and Every Good Boy Deserves Favour, which do not represent a "sudden conversion on the road to Damascus."

73 SKOW, JOHN. "Cinema: Doubled Up." Time 112 (6 November): 82, 84.
  Review of Despair (London, Marthesheimer), which Stoppard adapted "effectively, and with suitable reverence."

74 STEIN, ELLIOTT. "Valse Triste." Film Comment 14 (November):

Writings about Tom Stoppard

1978

56, 61-65.
Includes a review of Despair (London, Marthesheimer): the film's concentration upon the rise of Fascism is a poor substitute for the novel's juxtapositioning of plot versus first-person narration.

75 STERRITT, DAVID. "Theater Review: When Pawns and Kings Alternated." Christian Science Monitor, 12 October, p. 18.
Includes a review of Rosencrantz & Guildenstern Are Dead (Madison, New Jersey Shakespeare Festival).

76 STOTHARD, PETER. "Every Good Boy Deserves Favour." Plays and Players 25 (August):23.
Review of the London, John Player revival production. Notes "some curiously dissociated operatic exchanges" and says "the play on ideas seems more polemic and pedestrian second time round."

77 SZYBA, RANDY. "Trinity Theater Review: Wily Whodunit Is Refreshing Fare." Pawtucket (R.I.) Evening Times, 18 July, p. 15.
Favorable review of The Real Inspector Hound (Providence, R.I., Trinity Square Repertory Company).

78 TAYLOR, JOHN RUSSELL. "The Arts: Fassbinder Duo Nobody Should Miss." Times (London), 7 July, p. 11.
Includes a review of Despair (London, Marthesheimer): remarks (cryptically) that Stoppard "is said to be very unhappy about his collaboration with Fassbinder, as maybe he should be."

78a THOMSEN, CHRISTIAN W. "Tom Stoppard, Rosencrantz and Guildenstern Are Dead: Spiel vom Sterben, Spiel vom Tod, Spiel vom Tod im Leben." Maske und Kothurn: Internationale Beiträge zur Theaterwissenschaft 24, no. 3:230-43.
Analysis (in German) of Rosencrantz & Guildenstern Are Dead and a general appreciation of Stoppard as "one of the most important discoveries of the '60's." Surveys other writers' uses of Hamlet and the affinity which Germans feel for it; summarizes influences upon Stoppard's play. Concentrates upon its status as a piece of "metatheatre," which plays with literature, scholarship, and philosophy. Also discusses the sources and types of comedy in it and defines it as an example of "the grotesque."

*79 TOEBOSCH, GUILLAUME. "Les jeunes gens en colore, le théâtre anglais d'après-guerre et Tom Stoppard." Cahiers du Rideau 8:7-16.

1978

In French; listed in Modern Drama 23 (June 1980):145.

80 TYNAN, KENNETH. "The Man in the Moon." Sunday Times (London), 15 January, pp. 33-34.
Abridgement of 1977.B125. Elicited reaction: 1978.B33.

81 WALKER, JOHN. "Top Playwrights." Sunday Times Magazine (London), 26 November, pp. 70-71.
Feature article categorizing contemporary British playwrights: Stoppard is one of the "Top of the Bill."

82 WARDLE, IRVING. "Night and Day: Phoenix." Times (London), 9 November, p. 11.
Review of the London, West End production: its "strength and . . . weakness" both lie in the ideals which Stoppard "still cherishes . . . about journalism"; criticizes characters as "ambulatory attitudes," but appreciates the "strong echoes of vintage Waugh."

83 WASSERMAN, DEBBI. "Rosencrantz and Guildenstern Are Dead." New York Theatre Review 2 (August):53.
Favorable review of the Madison, New Jersey Shakespeare Festival production.

84 WATTERS, TAMIE. "Theater Review: Stoppard Drama Calls for On-Stage Orchestra." Christian Science Monitor, 3 August, p. 19.
Review of Every Good Boy Deserves Favour (London, John Player revival), which, like "Professional Foul," gives evidence of a "strong sense of humanity tempering [Stoppard's] wit."

85 WEBSTER, DANIEL. "Philadelphia." High Fidelity and Musical America 28 (December):MA18.
Favorable review of Every Good Boy Deserves Favour (Ambler, Pa.; Temple University Music Festival).

86 WESTERBECK, COLIN L., Jr. "Screen: Ars Gratia Artis: Fassbinder's Despair." Commonweal 105 (27 October):689-90.
Review of Despair (London, Marthesheimer), in which four "very-polished, self-conscious artists"--Stoppard, Nabokov, Fassbinder, and Dirk Bogarde--"play elaborate aesthetic games."

87 WILLIAMS, DAVID. "Paperbacks: Best of the Month." Punch 275 (15 November):873.
Review of the text of Night and Day: "a tense, thrilling

1979

play" which reveals Stoppard's "unease at the syndicalist state we are swiftly fitting up for ourselves."

88 WILSON, EDWIN. "The Theater: A Funny, Moving, Musical Look at Dissent." Wall Street Journal, 18 July, p. 20.
   Review of the "intensely moving" Every Good Boy Deserves Favour (London, John Player revival).

89 ZIVANOVIC, JUDITH. "Camus' Actor as Tom Stoppard's Player: A Key to Interpreting Rosencrantz and Guildenstern Are Dead." Paper read at Central States Speech Association annual meeting, 13-15 April, Chicago.
   Analysis; adopts Camus' conception of the actor as one who reveals man's mortality and potentiality, applying it to the Player in Stoppard's play: he teaches about death, needs an audience, is aware of life's uncertainty, yet acts on assumptions, unlike the anti-heroic courtiers, who follow orders and fail to act. Reprinted by ERIC, no. ED 155 751.

1979

A BOOKS

1 CAHN, VICTOR L. Beyond Absurdity: The Plays of Tom Stoppard. Rutherford, N.J.: Fairleigh Dickinson University Press, 169 pp.
   Reprint of 1976.A4.

*2 HARLAND, SUSAN SPONZILLIE. "Play, Game, and Playfulness in Tom Stoppard's Plays." Ph.D. dissertation, University of Pittsburgh, 363 pp.
   Analysis, in light of "various psychological theories of play," of After Magritte, "Albert's Bridge," Dirty Linen and New-Found-Land, Enter a Free Man, Every Good Boy Deserves Favour, "If You're Glad I'll Be Frank," Jumpers, "Professional Foul," The Real Inspector Hound, Rosencrantz & Guildenstern Are Dead, "A Separate Peace," and Travesties.
   Claims his early plays use "compulsive games" (which help one "escape the enormity of experience"), while the later ones feature "creative play" (a "playful strategy" for taking effective action).
   (Annotation summarized from Dissertation Abstracts International 41 [July 1980]:261-A.)

*3 ROTHSTEIN, BOBBI (ROBERTA) WYNNE. "Playing the Game: The Work of Tom Stoppard." Ph.D. dissertation, University of

1979

> Rhode Island, 268 pp.
> Analysis; argues that "games are the meaning of . . . Stoppard's canon." Examines his use of games (their players, rules, patterns, and ethics) in Every Good Boy Deserves Favour, Jumpers, "Professional Foul," The Real Inspector Hound, Rosencrantz & Guildenstern Are Dead, and Travesties. (Annotation summarized from Dissertation Abstracts International 40 [November]:2701-A.)

B SHORTER WRITINGS

1 ANON. "Plays and Players 1978 Awards." Plays and Players 26 (January):26-40.
   Summary evaluations by nineteen critics of the past London theatre season; also announces that Diana Rigg had been chosen Best Actress for her work in Night and Day (London, West End).

2 ANON. "New Appeal Is Made to Brezhnev to Let Nureyev's Mother Leave." New York Times, 18 March, p. 36.
   News item: London Daily Telegraph publishes a letter from Stoppard, Previn, Ken Russell, and Yehudi Menuhin asking that the dancer's sick mother be permitted to leave the U.S.S.R. to visit her son in the West.

3 ANON. "Cues." Plays and Players 25 (April):6.
   News item, announcing plans of British-American Repertory Company (BARC) to tour the two countries with Dogg's Hamlet, Cahoot's Macbeth.

4 ANON. "Cinecapsules." Film & Broadcasting Review 44 (15 April):46.
   Includes a brief review of Despair (London, Marthesheimer).

5 ANON. News Item. British Theatrelog, no. 5 (Summer):12.
   Announces that Night and Day had been awarded the Evening Standard's Award for Best Play of the 1978 season.

6 ANON. "Photo Essay: Tom Stoppard's Night and Day." New York Theatre Review 3 (June):27.
   Photographs of scenes from the London, West End production.

7 ANON. "Notes on People." New York Times, 18 July, p. B5.
   Brief interview with the actor playing the son in Every Good Boy Deserves Favour (New York, Metropolitan Opera).

Writings about Tom Stoppard

1979

8 ANON. "Playwrights' Company." British Theatrelog, no. 6 (Autumn):20.
   News item announcing formation of a company in Bristol with the support of Stoppard (£1500), Peter Nichols, and Charles Wood.

9 ANON. "Brunel Honours Tom Stoppard." Times (London), 19 December, p. 14.
   News item reporting that Stoppard had been given an honorary "Doctor of the University" degree.

10 BAILEY, JOHN A. "Jumpers by Tom Stoppard: The Ironist as Theistic Apologist." Michigan Academician 11 (Winter): 237-50.
    Analysis. Concentrates upon Jumpers' characters, themes, and "hybrid" form; also includes brief analytical comments about characters named Moon and Boot and the themes of After Magritte, "If You're Glad I'll Be Frank," Lord Malquist & Mr Moon, The Real Inspector Hound, and Rosencrantz & Guildenstern Are Dead. Claims Jumpers hinges upon McFee's rejection of pragmatism and that, while George is Stoppard's "apologist for God and meaning," he is no Christian and gives no evidence of "moral improvement": the play is a "limited apology."

11 BARBER, JOHN. "Theatre: Tragi-Comical Study of a Philanderer." Daily Telegraph (London), 21 June, p. 15.
    Review of Undiscovered Country (London, National Theatre); praises Stoppard's "spring-heeled" adaptation.

12 _____. "Phoenix: Night and Day." Daily Telegraph (London), 5 July, p. 15.
    Re-review of the London, West End production, following Maggie Smith's assumption of the role created by Diana Rigg.

13 _____. "Theatre: Stoppard's Madness Has Method in It." Daily Telegraph (London), 17 July, p. 13.
    Review of Dogg's Hamlet, Cahoot's Macbeth (London, BARC): "puerile and disturbing in about equal measure."

14 BARNES, CLIVE. "Stoppard's Favour Is a Playgoer's Gift." New York Post, 31 July, p. 34.
    Review of the "brilliant and desperately funny" Every Good Boy Deserves Favour (New York, Metropolitan Opera). Reprinted in 1979.B75.

15 _____. "Beware of Tom Bearing Gifts." New York Post, 4

1979

October, p. 39.
Review of <u>Dogg's Hamlet, Cahoot's Macbeth</u> (New York, BARC): the two plays "do not provide any real statement, but are content to make ultra-chic noises." Reprinted in 1979.B76.

16 _____. "New York Notebook: A Broadway Clogged with Hits." <u>Times</u> (London), 17 November, p. 13.
Includes a brief review of <u>Dogg's Hamlet, Cahoot's Macbeth</u> (New York, BARC): the play was "not quite so well received in New York as in London."

17 _____. "<u>Night & Day</u> Is Dazzling." <u>New York Post</u>, 28 November, pp. 43, 45.
Review of the Broadway production; appreciates the "subject matter" and "unusual reality . . . of the characters." Reprinted in 1979.B77.

18 BEAUFORT, JOHN. "Theater Review: Stoppard Play at the Met: An Experiment That Works." <u>Christian Science Monitor</u>, 3 August, p. 18.
Review of <u>Every Good Boy Deserves Favour</u> (New York, Metropolitan Opera): "a remarkable and stimulating entertainment" which is "always poignantly relevant." Reprinted in 1979.B75.

19 _____. "Tom Stoppard's Blend of Comic Nonsense." <u>Christian Science Monitor</u>, 10 October, p. 18.
Review of <u>Dogg's Hamlet, Cahoot's Macbeth</u> (New York, BARC): "a blend of comic nonsense and astringent political satire." Reprinted in 1979.B76.

20 _____. "Theater Review: Tom Stoppard's Tricky Look at Press Freedom." <u>Christian Science Monitor</u>, 29 November, p. 18.
Review of <u>Night and Day</u> (Broadway); finds the play "witty, sophisticated, [and] provocative," although the character of Ruth is "too inconsistent to be entirely credible." Reprinted in 1979.B77.

21 BERKVIST, ROBERT. "In Cahoots with Tom Stoppard." <u>New York Times</u>, 30 September, sec. 2, pp. 3, 9.
Interview with Ed Berman, director of <u>Dogg's Hamlet, Cahoot's Macbeth</u>, about it, the British-American Repertory Company, and Inter-Action Trust.

22 _____. "This Time, Stoppard Plays It (Almost) Straight." <u>New York Times</u>, 25 November, sec. 2, pp. 1, 5.
Interview with Stoppard. Discusses <u>Night and Day</u>'s

Writings about Tom Stoppard

1979

origin, evolution, and theme ("the aspects of journalism which one might well disapprove of are the price we pay for the part that matters") and his work habits. Also denies that his recent works indicate a deliberate shift in subjects or style and discusses his lack of "any great desire to write plays at all anymore. At the moment, it doesn't seem important."

23 BILLINGTON, MICHAEL. "Exclusive Report from London." New York Theatre Review 3 (January):28-29.
   Includes a brief review of Night and Day (London, West End), in which Stoppard "nails his colours to a . . . mast" and deals with private emotions ("the territory in which he has always been most suspect"); finds it "quite a breakthrough."

24 _____. "Phoenix Theatre: Night and Day." Guardian (London), 5 July, p. 8.
   Re-review of the London, West End production, following Maggie Smith's assumption of the role created by Diana Rigg; notes changes made in the script since the opening of the play.

25 _____. "Collegiate: Dogg's Hamlet, Cahoot's Macbeth." Guardian (London), 17 July, p. 8.
   Review of the London, BARC production: "things sometimes get a bit-over elaborate" in that an "already elaborate" situation is decorated even further as the play continues. "By the end the fun has become diagrammatic rather than, in any sense, spontaneous."

26 BUHR, RICHARD J. "Epistemology and Ethics in Tom Stoppard's 'Professional Foul.'" Comparative Drama 13 (Winter):320-29.
   Analysis of the play as the "culmination and clarification of the epistemological and ethical issues that have always dominated Stoppard's important work." Points out similarities between its world and characters and those of Rosencrantz & Guildenstern Are Dead, Jumpers, and Travesties; claims that the play's protagonist learns he must abandon the security offered by "absolute moral principles" when they "conflict with human rights and emotions"; and relates this decision to a debate in contemporary philosophy.

27 CANBY, VINCENT. "Screen: Nabokov's Despair." New York Times, 16 February, p. C11.
   Review of the film; finds the "script . . . a joy for

185

1979

anyone who likes the English language."

28 CLURMAN, HAROLD. "Theater/Film." Nation 229 (3 November): 442.
Includes a brief review of Dogg's Hamlet, Cahoot's Macbeth (New York, BARC), Stoppard's "latest lark."

29 _____. "Theater." Nation 229 (15 December):636-37.
Includes a review of Night and Day (Broadway), Stoppard's "first example of . . . more or less traditionally plotted drama." Claims that the plot strands "are patched together," the female character is merely decorative, not essential to the play, and the thesis (journalism "brings light") is "not dramatized; it is merely stated."

30 CRUMP, G. B. "The Universe as Murder Mystery: Tom Stoppard's Jumpers." Contemporary Literature 20 (Summer):354-68.
Analysis: "nothing in the play is gratuitous or pointless." Concentrates upon logical positivism, the play's language, and the beliefs of and relationships among the characters. Maintains that "the way Archie, Bones, and George set about solving the murder represent various philosophical approaches to answering [the] larger questions" of who created the world and why.

31 CUNNINGHAM, DENNIS. "Night and Day." WCBS-TV (27 November).
Review of the Broadway production; finds it to be "three incomplete plays." Reprinted in 1979.B77.

32 CURTIS, ANTHONY. "London." Drama: The Quarterly Theatre Review, no. 131 (Winter):47-63.
Includes a review of Night and Day (London, West End); although the play is about "the professional self, and the mutual demands between it and the private self," the asides of the female character are of only "marginal" pertinence.

33 CUYLER, RICHARD R. "Theatre in Review: Hamlet, Rosencrantz and Guildenstern Are Dead." Theatre Journal 31 (December): 550-52.
Includes a review of the Ithaca, Cornell University production of Stoppard's "funny, poignant, spooky play."

34 DANIELD, D. J. "Forward with Stoppard." Theatre News 11, no. 8 (May):20-22.
Brief analyses of "Professional Foul" and Every Good Boy Deserves Favour, which "raise the sights and deepen the tone" of Stoppard's work; also includes an account of the use of mental hospitals to punish political dissidents in

1979

the Soviet Union and of Stoppard's participation in protests against it.

35 DAVIDSON, MARY R. "Historical Homonyms: A New Way of Naming in Tom Stoppard's Jumpers." Modern Drama 22 (September): 305-13.
Analysis: traces the sources of all the characters' names and of many historical and literary references; claims that Stoppard's use of historical names allows him to contrast new and traditional modes of philosophy and "implies that the values in his play are related to values outside it."

36 EGAN, ROBERT. "A Thin Beam of Light: The Purpose of Playing in Rosencrantz and Guildenstern Are Dead." Theatre Journal 31 (March):59-69.
Analysis of the words and actions of the Player, who offsets the play's otherwise "closed, fatalistic perception of existence." Maintains he represents "a way of living" (epitomized by the actor) which allows one to attach "meaning to an existence in which meaning may not be inherent"; contrasts him to the courtiers, who fail to act when given the chance. Also argues that the play is not "a recasting of Waiting for Godot" and discusses the thematic and theatrical importance of the Player's "death" scene.

37 ERICSON, RAYMOND. "Music Notes: Stoppard's Colleague." New York Times, 29 July, sec. 2, p. 19.
Interview with André Previn, composer of the music for Every Good Boy Deserves Favour: he wanted it to be "very Russian in character, . . . but not to the point of parody."

38 FELL, JOHN L. "Reviews: Despair." Film Quarterly 33 (Fall): 59-61.
Review of the film: its "triumph has been to translate Nabokov's largely conversationless world into a glittering mine of snobbish puns and monologues."

39 FLOYD, DAVID. "Russia Lets Boy Join Mother in Britian." Daily Telegraph (London), 26 March, p. 1.
News article reports that a thirteen-year-old Russian boy was being allowed to join his mother, who had been exiled for protesting the abuse of psychiatry in the Soviet Union; notes that his release was due in part to the "Let Misha Go" campaign, chaired by Stoppard. See 1979.B40 for follow-up.

40 _____. "Russians Free Exiled Doctor's Mother and Son." Daily

1979

Telegraph (London), 26 April, p. 1.
News article reporting that the boy and his grandmother (referred to in 1979.B39) had arrived in London; includes comments from Stoppard regarding the effectiveness of public protests in such matters.

41 GILL, BRENDAN. "The Theatre: Frisbees." *New Yorker* 55 (13 August):61.
Review of *Every Good Boy Deserves Favour* (New York, Metropolitan Opera): a "pretty toy" in which Stoppard's "characteristic insouciance [moves] just above the heads of the audience."

42 _____. "The Theatre: Stoppard's Shakespeherian Rag." *New Yorker* 55 (15 October):147.
Review of *Dogg's Hamlet, Cahoot's Macbeth* (New York, BARC): Stoppard's "latest prank," which gives "so much fun, so little food for the imagination." Says the two segments "have the air of having been surprised into marriage by the . . . shotgun known as giving the customers their money's worth."

43 _____. "The Theatre: Trouble in Kambawe." *New Yorker* 55 (10 December):113.
Review of *Night and Day* (Broadway): "a conventionally straightforward melodrama, . . . more garrulous than witty, [which] . . . lacks novelty." The female character is "an essentially genderless puppet, having no connection with her husband, her son, or her ex-lover."

44 GILLIATT, PENELOPE. "The Current Cinema: Lamplights." *New Yorker* 55 (19 March):126.
Includes a review of *Despair* (London, Marthesheimer).

45 GRANT, STEVE. "Night and Day." *Plays and Players* 26 (January):18-19.
Review of the London, West End production of Stoppard's "most perplexing and, in so many respects, least satisfying work, . . . which is still far better . . . than most things London's commercial theatre can offer."

46 GRIEG, SIMON. "Despair." *Films and Filming* 26 (February):34.
Review of the film: "Stoppard does his best," but the result is a "cinematic abortion."

47 GUSSOW, MEL. "Stoppard's Intellectual Cartwheels Now with Music." *New York Times*, 29 July, sec. 2, pp. 1, 22.

1979

Interview. Stoppard discusses his work during the previous eighteen months; the evolution of Every Good Boy Deserves Favour, Night and Day, and Dogg's Hamlet, Cahoot's Macbeth; his characters ("All my people speak the same way, with the same cadences and sentence structure. . . . It limits me in areas in which I'm not interested in expanding."); his love of doing adaptations; his association with Undiscovered Country; and his moral standards ("I'm a conservative. . . . My main objection is to ideology and dogma.").

48 ____. "Theater: Stoppard's Every Good Boy." New York Times, 31 July, p. C8.
Review of the New York, Metropolitan Opera production: an "unusual theatrical and musical event," which was more comical and musical than the London, John Player production had been. Reprinted in 1979.B75.

49 ____. "Stoppard's Dogg's Hamlet Opens." New York Times, 4 October, p. C16.
Review of the New York, BARC production; found Dogg's Hamlet amusing, Cahoot's Macbeth "unfulfilled," and the whole "more a double-jointed exercise than a full . . . spree." Reprinted in 1979.B76.

50 HATCH, ROBERT. "Films." Nation 228 (10 March):284.
Review of Despair (London, Marthesheimer), in which Stoppard provided some "wonderfully witty and mordant lines."

51 HAYMAN, RONALD. British Theatre since 1955: A Reassessment. Oxford: Oxford University Press, pp. 25-27, 41-43.
Brief analytical comments: places Stoppard and Edward Bond at the two poles of attitudes toward past literature (parody and anti-literature), compares Stoppard to Beckett, and discusses his use of his imagination in his radio and stage plays.

52 ____. Theatre and Anti-Theatre: New Movements since Beckett. Oxford: Oxford University Press, pp. 138-46 and passim.
Analyses. Concentrates on Jumpers and Rosencrantz & Guildenstern Are Dead; includes comments about After Magritte, "Albert's Bridge," "Another Moon Called Earth," "Artist Descending a Staircase," Dogg's Our Pet, "If You're Glad I'll Be Frank," Lord Malquist & Mr Moon, The Real Inspector Hound, "A Separate Peace," and Travesties.
Compares Stoppard to Beckett and Pinter; discusses the

1979

   themes of nonconformity, causality and accidents, and multiple perspectives; points out affinities with the Metaphysical poets and Surrealists.

53 HEBERT, HUGH. "A Playwright in Undiscovered Country." Guardian (London), 7 July, p. 10.
   Interview: Stoppard discusses Dogg's Hamlet, Cahoot's Macbeth, Night and Day, "Professional Foul," and Undiscovered Country; the effect of his political activity upon his plays ("I don't want to feel . . . that I now exist to scan the political victims of Eastern Europe, and then reach for my pistol"); and the differences between writing for the theatre and for movies or television.

54 HOBSON, HAROLD. "Hobson's Choice." Drama: The Quarterly Theatre Review, no. 131 (Winter):42-46.
   Includes a review of Night and Day (London, West End): "most exciting and satisfying."

55 _____. "Hobson's Choice." Drama: The Quarterly Theatre Review, no. 134 (Autumn):60-63.
   Includes a review of Undiscovered Country (London, National Theatre): "one of the best things the National has done."

56 HURREN, KENNETH. "Comment." Drama: The Quarterly Theatre Review, no. 132 (Spring):45-48.
   Includes the comment that Rosencrantz & Guildenstern Are Dead and W. S. Gilbert's Rosencrantz and Guildenstern have nothing in common.

57 HURWITT, ROBERT. "Rosencrantz & Guildenstern Are Dead." Berkeley (Calif.) Barb, 15 March, p. 7.
   Review of the "stylistically . . . fascinating, . . . witty, chilling" production by the Actors' Ark Theatre (San Francisco and Berkeley).

58 JANOWITZ, KATHERINE. "Every Good Boy Deserves Favour." New York Theatre Review 3 (August):41.
   Review of the New York, Metropolitan Opera production: the play "suffers from its hybrid nature."

59 KALEM, T. E. "Theater: Katt's Play." Time 114 (15 October):88.
   Unfavorable review of Dogg's Hamlet, Cahoot's Macbeth (New York, BARC). Reprinted in 1979.B76.

60 _____. "Theater: Lady Be Good." Time 114 (10 December):99.

Writings about Tom Stoppard

1979

Review of <u>Night and Day</u> (Broadway): "exhilaratingly Shavian," although there was "too much talk" and most of the characters "began to resemble rhetorical wallpaper." Reprinted in 1979.B77.

61 KENNEDY, ANDREW. "Natural, Mannered, and Parodic Dialogue." In <u>Yearbook of English Studies</u>. Vol. 9, edited by G. K. Hunter and C. J. Rawson, pp. 28-54.
    Theoretical discussion, with analyses, of the "literary subtilization of dramatic dialogue and . . . intensification of theatricality" which has led to "a new mannerist drama and a new pan-parodic theatre." Analyzes <u>Rosencrantz & Guildenstern Are Dead</u> and <u>Travesties</u> as examples of the latter mode: in them, "the serious parody is not hampered by a dominant ideology or style; . . . almost <u>any</u> gesture and language may serve," but at the risk of failing to "find room for anything so grave as a [stylistic or ideological] centre of gravity."

62 KERR, WALTER. "Theater: Stoppard's <u>Night and Day</u>." <u>New York Times</u>, 28 November, p. C21.
    Review of the Broadway production: "the debate . . . is leaked out languorously, in bits and pieces" and is not connected to the action or to the female character's romantic life: "three separate compartments; no connecting doors." Reprinted in 1979.B77.

63 KING, FRANCIS. "Theatre: Over the Top." <u>Sunday Telegraph</u> (London), 24 June, p. 14.
    Includes a review of <u>Undiscovered Country</u> (London, National Theatre): Stoppard's adaptation, like the production, "simultaneously compels admiration and blankets the original."

64 _____. "Two Lords A-Leaping." <u>Sunday Telegraph</u> (London), 21 October, p. 14.
    Includes a review of <u>Rosencrantz & Guildenstern Are Dead</u> (London, Young Vic), which "pulsates with an extraordinary intellectual energy . . . [but] seems longer; more irritatingly jokey; and less profound" than it did in 1967.

65 KISSELL, HOWARD. Review of <u>Every Good Boy Deserves Favour</u>. <u>Women's Wear Daily</u>, 1 August, p. 42.
    Favorable review of the New York, Metropolitan Opera production.

66 _____. "Theater: <u>Night and Day</u>." <u>Women's Wear Daily</u>, 28 November, p. 26.

1979

>Review of the Broadway production, which fell "completely flat--the plot is overly complicated, the characters types, and the tone an odd amalgam of flippancy and stridency." Reprinted in 1979.B77.

67 KLEIN, ALVIN. "Theater in Review: These Thespians Travel." New York Times, 4 November, p. L15.
>Mixed review of The Real Inspector Hound (Nassau County, N.Y., Theater East).

68 KROLL, JACK. "Candy Man." Newsweek 93 (12 March):90.
>Review of Despair (London, Marthesheimer): "too clever for its own good."

69 _____. "Theater: Stoppard at Play." Newsweek 94 (24 September):110.
>Review of Dogg's Hamlet, Cahoot's Macbeth (Washington, D.C., BARC): "the incorrigibly playful Stoppard has never been more serious than in this most playful of his works." Reprinted in 1979.B76.

70 _____. "Theater: Darkest Journalism." Newsweek 94 (10 December):135.
>Review of Night and Day (Broadway): Stoppard "sacrifices many of his best qualities" in an effort to "tap the energy and truth that may still lie in traditional modes." Reprinted in 1979.B77.

71 LAWSON, CAROL. "News of the Theater: Stoppard-Previn Drama to Play at the Met Opera." New York Times, 6 June, sec. 3, p. 22.
>News item, announcing the opening of Every Good Boy Deserves Favour (New York, Metropolitan Opera).

72 LEWIS, FLORA. "Maggie Smith Finds the She on Stage Is Easier to Know Than One at Home." New York Times, 12 September, p. C26.
>Interview with the actress who played the female lead in Night and Day (Broadway).

73 LOCHER, FRANCES CAROL, ed. "Stoppard, Tom." In Contemporary Authors: A Bio-Bibliographical Guide to Current Writers in Fiction, General Nonfiction, Poetry, Journalism, Drama, Motion Pictures, Television and Other Fields. Vols. 81-84. Detroit: Gale Research Co., pp. 543-45.
>Contains biographical data and outline of his career; publication and production data (inaccurate); brief quotations from critics; and a bibliography of one hundred items.

1979

74 LUDLOW, COLIN. "Dogg's Hamlet, Cahoot's Macbeth." Plays and Players 26 (August):28.
Review of the London, BARC production: a "deeply unsatisfying" and "miscalculated" mixture of seriousness and absurdity.

75 MARLOWE, JOAN, and BLAKE, BETTY, eds. "Every Good Boy Deserves Favour." New York Theatre Critics' Review 40 (6 August):195-98.
Consists of reprints of reviews of the New York, Metropolitan Opera production: 1979.B14, 18, 48, 78, 95, 108, 117.

76 _____. "Dogg's Hamlet, Cahoot's Macbeth." New York Theatre Critics' Review 40 (1 October):144-48.
Consists of reprints of reviews of the New York, BARC production--1979.B15, 19, 49, 59, 94, 96, 109--and of the Washington, D.C., BARC production--1979.B69, 118.

77 _____. "Night and Day." New York Theatre Critics' Review 40 (3 December):82-88.
Consists of reprints of reviews of the Broadway production: 1979.B17, 20, 31, 60, 62, 66, 70, 97, 110, 119.

78 MICHENER, CHARLES. "The Odd Couple Soviet Style." Newsweek 94 (13 August):68.
Review of Every Good Boy Deserves Favour (New York, Metropolitan Opera): the "most uneasily ironic thing Stoppard has ever written." Reprinted in 1979.B75.

79 NELSON, BYRON. "Theatre in Review: Night and Day." Theatre Journal 31 (December):544.
Review of the London, West End production: provides evidence that Stoppard "is entering a new phase of dramatic mastery and that he can handle a wide range of themes and moods with astonishing ease."

80 NIGHTINGALE, BENEDICT. "Theatre: Soul Music." New Statesman 97 (29 June):963.
Includes a review of Undiscovered Country (London, National Theatre): Stoppard's adaptation is "as actable as we had expected."

81 _____. "Theatre: Git Away." New Statesman 98 (20 July):104-5.
Includes a review of Dogg's Hamlet, Cahoot's Macbeth (London, BARC): "leaves a sketchier, more fragmented, and finally less eloquent impression than . . . Stoppard's

193

1979

most successful foray into committed hilarity, . . . 'Professional Foul.'"

82 NURSE, KEITH. "Young Vic: Rosencrantz & Guildenstern Are Dead." Daily Telegraph (London), 17 October, p. 15.
    Brief mixed review of the London company's production.

83 O'T[OOLE], L[AURENCE]. "Privacy Evasion." Macleans 92 (7 May):58-59.
    Review of Despair (London, Marthesheimer), which makes "no attempt by words" to understand the characters: the film concentrates on style to the detriment of plot.

84 PEARCE, HOWARD D. "Stage as Mirror: Tom Stoppard's Travesties." MLN 94 (December):1139-58.
    Theory and analysis. First half discusses a phenomenological theory of the "mirror" and "theater-dream" themes: rejects the dichotomy between real and unreal in favor of an "interdependence" between mirror, mirrored object, and viewer.
    Second half analyzes Travesties in light of the foregoing: Carr's "ambivalence toward the successful artist" (Joyce) is the play's "compelling motive"; this "opposition of like principles" is reproduced in the other characters, the major action, and the language; and it leads to a "Joycean doubling [of] multiple, open-ended reflection," with the result that Carr's "ambivalence about Joyce becomes reconciled in [the play, which] demonstrates Joyce's aesthetic."

85 PENNINGTON, RON. "Exclusive Report from Los Angeles." New York Theatre Review 3 (January):36.
    Includes a favorable review of Rosencrantz & Guildenstern Are Dead (Los Angeles, Theatre Exchange).

86 ROCKWELL, JOHN. "Music: Previn Interludes." New York Times, 31 July, p. C8.
    Review of André Previn's music for Every Good Boy Deserves Favour (New York, Metropolitan Opera): a "watered-down version of . . . Prokofiev and Shostakovich, . . . well crafted but bland."

87 ROSENWALD, PETER J. "The Meaning of Nonsense." Horizon 22 (November):38-43.
    Feature article: biographical data and analytical comments about Dogg's Hamlet, Cahoot's Macbeth. Includes incidental remarks about Every Good Boy Deserves Favour and Night and Day and a discussion of the social commitment

evident in Stoppard's recent plays.

88 SALMON, ERIC. "Faith in Tom Stoppard." Queen's Quarterly 86 (Summer):215-32.
   Analysis: includes biographical data and brief comments about "Artist Descending a Staircase"; chiefly devoted to analyses of Jumpers and Travesties (one-third of it in the form of extended quotations from the plays). Claims they are "complementary pieces" which possess a "weight, authority, [and] stature" not present in Stoppard's earlier works and missing, too, from his subsequent ones (because of their preoccupation with immediate social and political matters). Discusses Stoppard's "sense of the way cultural elements feed each other" and argues that it is "seriously misleading and quite untenable" to consider Jumpers an Absurdist play: "it takes account of Absurdism . . . and then, with a wry and tentative optimism, dismisses it."

*89 SALTZMAN, ARTHUR MICHAEL. "Fiction-Making in Contemporary British Drama." Ph.D. dissertation, University of Illinois at Urbana-Champaign, 286 pp.
   Analysis of some plays by Beckett, Pinter, Osborne, and Stoppard: traces "the variety of methods and consequences of [a] wilful alienation from reality" by which one may withdraw "into a seamless imaginative structure." (Annotation summarized from Dissertation Abstracts International 40 [April 1980]:5250-A.)

90 SAY, ROSEMARY. "Show Talk." Sunday Telegraph (London), 21 January, p. 14.
   News items, including the report that Stoppard had been awarded the Shakespeare Prize for 1979 (approximately £6750) by the FVS Foundation in Hamburg.

91 _____. "Show Talk." Sunday Telegraph (London), 8 July, p. 14.
   News items, including the announcement of the opening of Dogg's Hamlet, Cahoot's Macbeth (London, BARC).

92 SCHLESINGER, ARTHUR, Jr. "The Movies: Flics of the Foreign Wrist." Saturday Review 6 (9 June):50.
   Includes a review of Despair (London, Marthesheimer), which has an "elegant script"; Stoppard and Nabokov are both "sensitive to the exquisite and revelatory absurdities of the English language."

93 SCHLUETER, JUNE. "Stoppard's Moon and Boot, Rosencrantz and Guildenstern." In Metafictional Characters in Modern Drama. New York: Columbia University Press, pp. 89-103.

1979

Revision and expansion of 1977.B109: new is an analysis of <u>Rosencrantz & Guildenstern Are Dead</u> which concentrates upon its relationship to <u>Waiting for Godot</u> and the fact that the title characters "have an existence [in <u>Hamlet</u>] which precedes the Stoppard play."

94 SHARP, CHRISTOPHER. "Theater: <u>Dogg's Hamlet, Cahoot's Macbeth</u>." <u>Women's Wear Daily</u>, 5 October, p. 8.
Review of the New York, BARC production: "disjointed, . . . incoherent, . . . [and] smart-ass." Reprinted in 1979.B76.

95 SIEGEL, JOEL. "<u>Every Good Boy Deserves Favour</u>." WABC-TV (30 July).
Incomprehensible "telegraphese" review of the New York, Metropolitan Opera production. Reprinted in 1979.B75.

96 _____. "<u>Dogg's Hamlet, Cahoot's Macbeth</u>." WABC-TC (3 October).
Review of the "hysterical, funny, [and] . . . deadly serious" New York, BARC production. Reprinted in 1979.B76.

97 _____. "<u>Night and Day</u>." WABC-TV (27 November).
Review of the Broadway production; found it boring. Reprinted in 1979.B77.

98 SIMON, JOHN. "Theater: Small Favors." <u>New York</u> 12 (13 August):82-83.
Includes a review of <u>Every Good Boy Deserves Favour</u> (New York, Metropolitan Opera): "perky but undistinguished." Says that "jokes about [Russian dissidents], . . . shared by a cozy playwright and comfortable audience, make for morally cacophonous cachinnation."

99 _____. "Theater: The Past in Our Future." <u>New York</u> 12 (22 October): 97-98.
Includes a review of <u>Dogg's Hamlet, Cahoot's Macbeth</u> (New York, BARC), two "contrivedly interlocking" one-act plays in which Stoppard uses language "for the anesthetizing of our critical faculties."

100 _____. "Theater: Beware of Intersecting Arcs." <u>New York</u> 12 (10 December):154, 156.
Review of <u>Night and Day</u> (Broadway): the play's "stories do not so much intersect as collide. . . . Shouldn't they . . . reinforce one another?" Moreover, "the debate on journalism [was] not illustrated by the story," and the play failed to move him in the "particular way" that great comedy does.

1979

101 STERN, J. P. "Anyone for Tennis, Anyone for Death? The Schnitzler/Stoppard Undiscovered Country." Encounter 53 (October):26-31.
    Review of the London, National Theatre production; devotes considerable space to Stoppard's "brilliant jazzing up of the text" as an example of translation as an act of interpretation and criticism. Claims that "the true grounds of the play's action" is, as in Rosencrantz & Guildenstern Are Dead, "the profound attraction of death."

102 STOOP, N. M. Review of Despair. After Dark 11 (May):85.
    Unfavorable review of the film and its "unaccountably dull" screenplay.

103 TAYLOR, JOHN RUSSELL. "Undiscovered Country." Plays and Players 26 (July):18.
    Review of the London, National Theatre production; notes approvingly that Stoppard "does not seem to obtrude himself noticeably in the text" of his "sensible English version" of the play.

104 _____. "London." Drama: The Quarterly Theatre Review, no. 134 (Autumn):64-73.
    Includes a review of Undiscovered Country (London, National Theatre).

105 TREWIN, J. C. "Night and Day." British Book News, 15 January, p. 120.
    Review of the text: "a direct narrative entirely unlike" Stoppard's other major works. "His touch is less sure than usual" in the story of the rebellion.

106 TYNAN, KENNETH. "Tom Stoppard." In Show People: Profiles in Entertainment. New York: Simon & Schuster, pp. 44-123.
    Reprint of 1977.B125.

107 WASSERMAN, DEBBI. "An American View of London Theatre." New York Theatre Review 3 (June):16-19.
    Includes a review of Night and Day (London, West End), in which "at last, Stoppard has found a balance between poetry, metaphor, intellectual issue, and plot."

108 WATT, DOUGLAS. ". . . Boy Deserves Favour Is Flavorable." New York Daily News, 31 July, p. 23.
    Review of the "trenchant and funny" Every Good Boy Deserves Favour (New York, Metropolitan Opera), "an extraordinary piece of theatre." Reprinted in 1979.B75.

1979

109 _____. "More Verbal Tomfoolery by Stoppard." New York Daily News, 4 October, p. 85.
Review of Dogg's Hamlet, Cahoot's Macbeth (New York, BARC): they are "mere conceits with some verbal and visual fun." Reprinted in 1979.B76.

110 _____. "Style on Broadway: Maggie Smith in New Play." New York Daily News, 28 November, p. 49.
Review of Night and Day (Broadway): "a Shavian discussion superficially treated." Reprinted in 1979.B77.

111 WATTERS, TAMIE. "Theater Review: Stoppard Turning Serious." Christian Science Monitor, 22 March, p. 23.
Review of Night and Day (London, West End): shows evidence "of Stoppard's nervousness at being serious."

112 WATTS, HAROLD H. "Stoppard, Tom." In Great Writers of the English Language: Dramatists. Edited by James Vinson. New York: St. Martin's Press, pp. 554-56.
Includes biographical information; production and publication data; and analytical comments about "Artist Descending a Staircase," Jumpers, The Real Inspector Hound, Rosencrantz & Guildenstern Are Dead, and Travesties. Notes that in Stoppard's plays, "habits of thought and dramatic conventions that are taken seriously in many quarters undergo exaggeration, with results that are disconcerting or delightful according to taste."

113 WELLS, JEFFREY. "Despair." Films in Review 30 (May):309.
Review of the film, "an attempt at refined satire that doesn't quite make it" despite Stoppard's "wonderfully witty" screenplay.

114 WERNER, CRAIG. "Stoppard's Critical Travesty, or, Who Vindicates Whom and Why." Arizona Quarterly 35 (Autumn):228-36.
Analysis. Claims that Travesties is not "a vindication of" Joyce's aesthetic position, inasmuch as that character "wasn't even in [Stoppard's] original plan" for the play. Rather, it "unveils the limitations of the twentieth century's most cherished systems of belief," in that Carr, the play's "central stage presence," is unmoved by all three of the "would-be messiahs," Joyce, Tzara, and Lenin.

*115 WILCHER, ROBERT. "The Museum of Tragedy: Endgame and Rosencrantz and Guildenstern Are Dead." Journal of Beckett Studies 4:43-54.
Listed in Modern Drama 23 (June 1980):145.

116 WILLIAMS, GARY JAY. "Theater in Washington: Stoppard, Chekhov and Clark." Theater 10 (Spring):133-36.
Includes a review of Every Good Boy Deserves Favour (Washington, D.C., Temple University Music Festival): a piece of "sentimental hokum, . . . neither madness nor whimsy, but only the zany and sentimental."

117 WILSON, EDWIN. "The Theater: Even in Summer They're Opening on Broadway." Wall Street Journal, 7 August, p. 20.
Includes a review of Every Good Boy Deserves Favour (New York, Metropolitan Opera): "a witty, moving and absolutely unique theater experience." Reprinted in 1979.B75.

118 _____. "A New Troupe Builds a Trans-Atlantic Bridge." Wall Street Journal, 18 September, p. 24.
Review of Dogg's Hamlet, Cahoot's Macbeth (Washington, D.C., BARC): Stoppard "has chosen the small canvas and madcap fun." Reprinted in 1979.B76.

119 _____. "The Theater: Stoppard Leads a British Show of Strength." Wall Street Journal, 30 November, p. 25.
Review of Night and Day (Broadway), which has "intelligence and . . . wit" and "an unforgettable . . . heroine" but makes no "real connection" among its various plot lines. Reprinted in 1979.B77.

120 ZEIFMAN, HERSH. "Tomfoolery: Stoppard's Theatrical Puns." In Yearbook of English Studies. Vol. 9. Edited by G. K. Hunter and C. J. Rawson, pp. 204-20.
Analysis of the ways in which Stoppard uses puns to reinforce the themes of After Magritte, "Artist Descending a Staircase," Dirty Linen and New-Found-Land, Jumpers, Rosencrantz & Guildenstern Are Dead, and Travesties. Emphasizes their "schizophrenic" nature and their ability to deceive, confuse, and insult.

1980

A BOOKS

*1 FARAONE, CHERYL F. "An Analysis of Tom Stoppard's Plays and Their Productions (1964-1975)." Ph.D. dissertation, Florida State University, 310 pp.
Deals with published and unpublished works; extended analyses of Jumpers, Rosencrantz & Guildenstern Are Dead, and Travesties. Includes production histories; interviews

1980

with actors, directors, and designers; and analyses of unpublished materials in BBC files. Emphasizes Stoppard's willingness to collaborate with actors and the "interrelationship of form and function" in his works. (Annotation summarized from <u>Dissertation Abstracts International</u> 41 [January 1981]:2832-A.)

*2 GREINER, PATRICIA ANN. "The Plays of Tom Stoppard: Recognition, Exploration, and Retreat." Ph.D. dissertation, Ohio State University, 194 pp.
Analysis of <u>After Magritte</u>, "Albert's Bridge," "Artist Descending a Staircase," <u>Enter a Free Man</u>, "If You're Glad I'll Be Frank," <u>Jumpers</u>, <u>Night and Day</u>, <u>The Real Inspector Hound</u>, <u>Rosencrantz & Guildenstern Are Dead</u>, "A Separate Peace," <u>Travesties</u>, and "Where Are They Now?"
Examines the works' relationship to Absurdist drama: finds it to be superficial in Stoppard's short plays; deeper in his best works (<u>Jumpers</u> and <u>Rosencrantz & Guildenstern Are Dead</u>); and reduced in his latest, which concentrate on topical issues but are "less artistically innovative and satisfying."
(Annotation summarized from <u>Dissertation Abstracts International</u> 41 [April 1981]:4393-A.)

B SHORTER WRITINGS

1 ANGELL, ROBERT. "The Current Cinema: Trouble at the Firm." <u>New Yorker</u> 56 (11 February):99-101.
Includes a review of <u>The Human Factor</u> (Los Angeles, Preminger), in which Graham Greene's "elusive" tone of "darkness and despair" has fallen victim to "the more obvious and enticing qualities of plot and place, scene and dialogue and development."

2 ANON. "West End Shows Are Forced to Close." <u>Times</u> (London), 21 June, p. 3.
News items, including the announcement that <u>Dirty Linen and New-Found-Land</u> (London, Inter-Action Trust) was closing after a run of more than four years.

3 ANSEN, DAVID. "Movies: The Wrong End of the Telescope." <u>Newsweek</u> 95 (11 February):82.
Review of <u>The Human Factor</u> (Los Angeles, Preminger); finds Stoppard's "script . . . skillfully super-loyal to the book."

4 BERKOWITZ, GERALD M. "Theatre in Review: <u>Dogg's Hamlet,</u>

Writings about Tom Stoppard

1980

Cahoot's Macbeth." Theatre Journal 32 (March):117-18.
Review of the London, BARC production, which may be "a harbinger of major works to come," for in it Stoppard "harnesses his linguistic ingenuity to his passion for the cause of artistic freedom." Claims its "message" is that "an artist's imagination is itself his greatest weapon against tyranny."

5 BRIEN, ALAN. "Whatever Happened to the Secret Agent?" Sunday Times (London), 3 February, p. 39.
Includes a review of The Human Factor (Los Angeles, Preminger).

6 BROOKS, JEREMY. "News from Everywhere." Sunday Times (London), 11 May, p. 42.
Includes a brief review of Lord Malquist & Mr Moon: "different, funny, and ultimately rather sad."

7 BRUSTEIN, ROBERT. "Robert Brustein on Theater: A Theater for Clever Journalists." New Republic 182 (5 January): 23-24.
Review of Night and Day (Broadway), with critical comments about Stoppard, who "has insinuated himself into the affections of smart people . . . , usurping whatever place might once have been reserved there for genuine artists." Says the play's point "is obscured by an excess of verbal sparks and stylish posturing, distracting us from the author's intention to the author's manner."

8 BUTCHER, MARYVONNE. "Cinema." Tablet 234 (9 February):139.
Includes a review of The Human Factor (Los Angeles, Preminger): Stoppard's "tensile dialogue" caught the "pain, worry, and love" which Greene's novel depicted, but it failed to reflect his "Olympian view" of the subject.

9 CANBY, VINCENT. "Film: Greene Novel, Preminger Style." New York Times, 8 February, p. C8.
Review of The Human Factor (Los Angeles, Preminger), which Stoppard "adapted with extraordinary skill": suggests it "should be studied by anyone interested in the problems of adapting for the screen novels of a more complex order than Jaws."

10 COMBS, RICHARD. "Cuba and The Human Factor." Sight and Sound 49 (Spring):124-25.
Includes a review of the Los Angeles, Preminger film, in which Stoppard's "scrupulously faithful" screenplay preserves the novel's interest in the "fascinating ritual"

1980

of government bureaucracy but loses its "'haunted' quality."

11 CONNOLLY, RAY. "Atticus: Stoppard in Greeneland." Sunday Times (London), 20 January, p. 32.
Interview: Stoppard discusses his screenplay of The Human Factor (Los Angeles, Preminger), his nervousness about displeasing Graham Greene with it, his reasons for disliking work on films, and a meeting with Burt Reynolds; also comments on his recent loss of ambition ("When I started I wrote . . . because I wanted to be a playwright. Now I write . . . because I am a playwright. It's not quite the same thing"). Also briefly mentions revisions he makes after plays open ("I'm quite a good counter puncher. . . . I often do quite a lot of minor tinkering"), with special reference to Night and Day.

12 CORBALLIS, RICHARD. "Extending the Audience: The Structure of Rosencrantz and Guildenstern Are Dead." Ariel: A Review of International English Literature 11 (April):65-79.
Analysis, claiming that the play's "inversion of the Hamlet action is . . . a symptom of" Stoppard's theme: "modern life requires an inversion of the assumptions which . . . underlie Hamlet." Examines ways in which Stoppard compares the world of the courtiers to that of Hamlet; defines the latter's impact upon the former; notes the Player's mediation between the two.

*13 DONAGHE, MICHAEL WAYNE. "Traditions, Conventions, Innovations, Explosions, Inversions: The Comedy of Manners in Contemporary British Drama." Ph.D. dissertation, Purdue University, 212 pp.
Analysis: devotes a chapter to Jumpers, Night and Day, and Travesties, which are comedies of ideas, although their character types and sexual conflicts "derive from the Restoration comedies." (Annotation summarized from Dissertation Abstracts International 41 [February 1981]:3589-A.)

14 DURHAM, WELDON B. "Symbolic Action in Tom Stoppard's Jumpers." Theatre Journal 32 (May):169-79.
Analysis: claims the play is unified when seen as an enactment of Stoppard's "engrossment in" the destructive effects of "rationalism, pragmatism, and individualism" and of his adherence to "the Kantian proposition that playful, 'purposeless purposiveness' can reveal truths inaccessible to rational, purposeful argument." Thus, the coincidences in the play "compel the auditor in the theatre to use the imagination as an alternative to rational ways of knowing," and Dottie is "mysteriously stabilized" in the

Writings about Tom Stoppard

1980

Coda without the intervention of anyone's "purposeful behavior." Also includes a detailed analysis of the scene between George and Dottie in Act I.

15 GUSSOW, MEL. "London to Broadway: How a Culture Shapes a Show." New York Times, 3 February, sec. 2, pp. 1, 35.
    Feature article: discusses four British productions in New York, including Night and Day, as examples of differences between British and American attitudes about theatre and social and personal relationships.

16 HATCH, ROBERT. "Films." Nation 230 (23 February):218-19.
    Includes a mixed review of The Human Factor (Los Angeles, Preminger).

17 HAYMAN, RONALD. "Double Acts." Sunday Times Magazine (London), 2 March, pp. 29-31.
    Feature article, with quotations, about directors and playwrights who often work together, including Stoppard and Peter Wood: Stoppard discusses the nature of rehearsals, the relationship between text and performance, and Wood's contributions to both; Wood discusses Stoppard's additions to the text of Night and Day during rehearsals.

17a HODGSON, GODFREY. "Luring the Truth." Columbia Journalism Review 19 (July/August):58-61.
    Book review of Arnold Wesker's The Journalists with a brief mention of Night and Day (London, West End): the public's interest in it shows that "Stoppard . . . had clearly struck his shovel into a rich vein of ore."

18 HUGHES, CATHARINE. "Theatre: Half Time." America 142 (26 January):64.
    Review of Night and Day (Broadway): supplies evidence that "Stoppard is turning out too many plays, relying on too many tricks and winding up with too much dramatic cleverness."

19 IGOE, W. J. "Theatre: Two Thoughtful Jokes." Month 13 (March):102-4.
    Includes reviews of Night and Day (London, West End) and Undiscovered Country (London, National Theatre), with comparisons of original and new actors in the roles of the former.

20 JACKSON, MARTIN A. "Reviews: Films." USA Today 108 (May): 68-69.
    Includes a review of The Human Factor (Los Angeles,

1980

Preminger): Stoppard's "unnecessarily faithful" adaptation "doesn't meet the needs of a movie script."

21 KAUFFMANN, STANLEY. "Theater: Friends and Lovers." Saturday Review 7 (2 February):30-32.
Includes a review of the "garrulous yet thin" Night and Day (Broadway): "a relatively conventional play" in which Stoppard's "allegedly diamond dialogue now looks the rhinestone it always was."

22 _____. "The Wearing of the Greene." New Republic 182 (16 February):24-25.
Includes a review of The Human Factor (Los Angeles, Preminger): Stoppard's "screenplay hasn't intensified or coalesced the dramatic elements" in the weak novel.

23 LAUDER, ROBERT E. "The Graham Greene That Eludes the Camera." New York Times, 9 March, sec. 2, p. 17.
Includes a brief mention of Stoppard's screenplay for The Human Factor (Los Angeles, Preminger) in an analysis of Graham Greene's novels and the films which have been made of them.

24 LEVY, B[ERNARD] S. "Serious Propositions Compromised by Frivolity." Critical Quarterly 22 (Autumn):79-85.
Evaluation of Stoppard's corpus in response to 1978. B67. Discusses the playwright's conviction that art is of marginal importance, his claim that a play's first goal is to "grip the audience," his uncertainty and lack of commitment, and his admiration for other playwrights (including Edward Bond, Howard Brenton, Athol Fugard, and David Hare). Disputes the claim that Stoppard identifies with the protagonist of Jumpers and the charge that to be a humanist and "aesthetic reactionary" renders one's work "soothing and anodyne."

25 LEWIN, DAVID. "Graham Greene Conjures a Timely Spy Film." New York Times, 3 February, sec. 2, pp. 1, 15.
Interview with Graham Greene, who professed himself "satisfied" with Stoppard's screenplay of The Human Factor (Los Angeles, Preminger).

26 LONDRÉ, FELICIA HARDISON. "Using Comic Devices to Answer the Ultimate Question: Tom Stoppard's Jumpers and Woody Allen's God." Comparative Drama 14 (Winter):346-54.
Analysis of two plays which deal with the confusion and helplessness caused by "uncertainty about God." Notes the use of similar comic devices (including deflation of cli-

Writings about Tom Stoppard

1980

maxes, reversal of expectations, misprisions, allusions, and anachronisms); both use laughter as "a stimulus to thought."

*27 O'NEILL, MICHAEL CHARLES. "The Evolution of Form in Contemporary Drama." Ph.D. dissertation, Purdue University, 263 pp.
   Analysis of the attempts of post-Absurdist playwrights to deal with problems of form in light of the Absurdists' revolts against the traditional varieties. Section on Stoppard includes examinations of Enter a Free Man, Jumpers, Rosencrantz & Guildenstern Are Dead, Travesties, and his early radio plays. His first works "bear witness to his unsuccessful attempts to write in established forms," while his later plays use "eclectic, derivative" ones, made up of "bits and pieces of all that has come before." (Annotation summarized from Dissertation Abstracts International 41 [December 1980]:2600-A.)

27a O'T[OOLE], L[AURENCE]. "Measured in Portions of Port." Macleans 93 (25 February):54.
   Review of The Human Factor (Los Angeles, Preminger): Stoppard's "script . . . captures with deadly accuracy and sour wit the slow sweat of Greene's world."

28 PETERS, PAULINE. "Unstoppable Stoppard." Sunday Times (London), 15 June, p. 36.
   Interview with Dr. Miriam Stoppard, wife of the playwright, in which she discusses their practice of working late at night, her childhood, and her decision to leave her job following what she thought was "a nervous breakdown . . . and hepatitis."

29 PILE, STEPHEN. "Atticus: How I Stumbled on the Monty Python Crowd at Play. . . ." Sunday Times (London), 6 July, p. 32.
   Column includes a description of a cricket match involving Stoppard, John Cleese, Terry Jones, and David Hare for the benefit of the Bristol Playwright Company at Clifton College.

30 POPKIN, HENRY. "Germany 1: Signoret Goes on Trial." Sunday Times (London), 17 February, p. 41.
   News story and review. Reports the performance in Munich of a documentary drama recreating the trial of Václav Havel and five other Czech dissidents; actors included Simone Signoret, Pavel Kohout, and Stoppard (as Havel's defense attorney).

1980

31 RABINOWITZ, PETER J. "'What's Hecuba to Us?' The Audience's Experience of Literary Borrowing." In The Reader in the Text: Essays on Audience and Interpretation. Edited by Susan R. Suleiman and Inge Crosman. Princeton: Princeton University Press, pp. 241-63.
    Theory and analysis: establishes categories of "literary recycling" which are based upon how much the "authorial" and "narrative" audiences know of the work being plundered; analyzes Robbe-Grillet's Les Gommes and Rosencrantz & Guildenstern Are Dead as illustrations.
    Claims that Stoppard uses Hamlet in a way that lets him "infect us with his characters' bewilderment" while simultaneously revealing that they are part of a "larger order": he avoids "driving a wedge between the narrative and authorial audiences" by not contradicting Hamlet and by using the Players' dumbshow to bring the former up to the latter's level of knowledge.

32 RICHARDSON, JACK. "Theater: Three from London." Commentary 69 (March):71-75.
    Review: despite the fact that Night and Day (Broadway) is a "rather sedate and conventional comedy," Stoppard "remains a playwright of surprise and mental agility." Appreciates his "sharp, dramatic arguments," although "not all of [his] subjects mesh neatly" and his conclusion is not "very controversial."

33 ROBINSON, DAVID. "The Arts: Fortunate Timing for the Treacherous Tie." Times (London), 1 February, p. 13.
    Includes a review of The Human Factor (Los Angeles, Preminger); finds Stoppard's screenplay "loyal to the letter" of Greene's novel.

34 ROBINSON, GABRIELLE. "Nothing Left but Parody: Friedrich Dürrenmatt and Tom Stoppard." Theatre Journal 32 (March): 85-94.
    Includes analyses of the parody in Jumpers, Lord Malquist & Mr Moon, The Real Inspector Hound, Rosencrantz & Guildenstern Are Dead, and Travesties. Claims it helps Stoppard develop plots, protects him against succumbing to pathos and sentimentality, and creates a mood which mingles despair (in the face of a world "without certainty, order or moral absolutes") with "unquenchable vitality" (based upon the strategy of "playing a game with life"). Notes that Dürrenmatt uses parody to portray characters who are "monstrous and grotesque distortions," while Stoppard's "are not so much destructive as they are pathetic."

Writings about Tom Stoppard

INCOMPLETE ITEMS

35 S[CHICKEL], R[ICHARD]. "Cinema: Gray Greene." Time 115 (17 March):81.
   Review of The Human Factor (Los Angeles, Preminger): Stoppard's screenplay is "a faithful adaptation" of Greene's "fine novel."

36 SCHLESINGER, ARTHUR, Jr. "The Movies: Defections from Country and Childhood." Saturday Review 7 (29 March):28.
   Includes a review of The Human Factor (Los Angeles, Preminger): Stoppard's screenplay is "an exemplary collaboration of novelist and playwright. What a pleasure it is to hear dialogue at once so economical and rich in implication."

37 TREGLOWN, JEREMY. "Shakespeare's Macbeths: Davenant, Verdi, Stoppard and the Question of Theatrical Text." English 29 (Summer):95-113.
   Review of books about the stage history of Macbeth, with theoretical comments about the relationship between play text and performance. Includes analyses of various adaptations and reworkings of the play as examples of the "critical intuition" that subsequent writers can bring to bear on it: Jumpers, for instance, is "a comically surreal inversion" of Shakespeare's tragedy.

38 WEST, RICHARD. "Fleeing from Life. Cheated?" Times Literary Supplement (London), 1 February, p. 115.
   Review of The Human Factor (Los Angeles, Preminger); concentrates on details which the film got wrong.

Incomplete Items

A BOOKS

  1 BEZENCENET, STEVIE. "The Fall and Fall of Dominic Boot." Undergraduate thesis, Polytechnic of Central London, n.d., n.p.
     Describes the making of The Engagement (London, Memorial Enterprises) from "The Dissolution of Dominic Boot."

 *2 FRIEHLING, KENNETH. Rosencrantz & Guildenstern Are Dead. Modern Drama Series; phonotape. Deland, Florida: Everett/Edwards, 1971. One cassette.
     Listed in Library of Congress National Union Catalog.

  3 GOLDSTEIN, RUTH M., comp. Discussion Guide for "Rosencrantz and Guildenstern Are Dead." New York: Grove Press, Inc.,

Writings about Tom Stoppard

INCOMPLETE ITEMS

    n.d., n.p.
        Contains biographical data, plot summary, questions for discussion, and samples of high school and college essays about the play.

B SHORTER WRITINGS

1 ANON. "Rosencrantz to Be Filmed." Financial Times (London), 20 June 1967, n.p.
    News item reporting that MGM purchased the film rights to the play for about $500,000. Article does not appear in many editions of the paper.

2 ANON. "Die Spielpläne und die Premieren an den Wiener Bundestheatern." Observer (Vienna), 20 October 1967, n.p.
    Includes a review of Rosencrantz & Guildenstern Are Dead (Vienna, Akademietheater); finds it overly long but a good character study. In German.

3 ANON. Interview. London Life (20 January 1968):33.
    Interview with Stoppard: discusses the out-of-town tryouts of Enter a Free Man (London, West End); reports that Rosencrantz & Guildenstern Are Dead brought him about £20,000 in 1967. Author's name and title not able to be traced; magazine defunct.

4 ANON. "California." Scene (February/March 1972), n.p.
    Review of Rosencrantz & Guildenstern Are Dead (San Francisco, ACT second revival).

5 ANON. "Jumpers at SCR: Intellectual Farce Superbly Staged." Costa Mesa (Calif.) Daily Pilot, n.d., n.p.
    Review of the Costa Mesa, South Coast Repertory production (opened 20 September 1975): it will be "either a smashing success or a crashing bore," depending on the number of "intellectual elitists" available to see it.

6 ANON. "Falling off a Trapeze in Jumpers." Chicago Sun-Times, 30 September 1975, n.p.
    Review of Jumpers (Evanston, Ill.; Evanston Theatre Company): "a lively, buoyant . . . exercise," but "you cannot help wishing you could read it instead of seeing it." Also appears in the late editions of the 29 September issue.

*7 BEER, OTTO F. "Warten auf Hamlet: Deutsche Erstaufführung von Rosenkranz und Güldenstern in Wein." Süddeutsche Zeitung (Munich), 20 October 1967, n.p.

Writings about Tom Stoppard

INCOMPLETE ITEMS

Review (in German) of <u>Rosencrantz & Guildenstern Are Dead</u> (Vienna, Akademietheater); cited in 1975.B126.

8 _____. "Alle Lehrer Müssen Turner Sein." Unidentified Newspaper, 31 October 1973, n.p.
Favorable review of <u>Jumpers</u> (Vienna, Akademietheater). In German.

9 CHERNIN, DONNA. "JC Whodunit Is Delightful." <u>Cleveland Plain Dealer</u>, 15 March 1975, n.p.
Favorable review of <u>The Real Inspector Hound</u> (Cleveland, Jewish Community Center).

10 COMPTON, RUSS. "The Prince--From the Back Stairs." <u>San Francisco Progress</u>, 7 May 1969, n.p.
Review of <u>Rosencrantz & Guildenstern Are Dead</u> (San Francisco, ACT).

11 _____. "How Theatre Fared in 1970." <u>San Francisco Progress</u>, 20 January 1971, n.p.
Review of <u>Rosencrantz & Guildenstern Are Dead</u> (San Francisco, ACT revival).

12 CRABILL, CATHLEEN. "<u>Stages</u> Plays Gamut of Emotions." <u>Louisville</u> (Ky.) <u>Journal</u>, 3 January 1975, n.p.
Includes a mixed review of <u>The Real Inspector Hound</u> (Actors Theatre of Louisville).

13 DASSYLVA, MARTIAL. "Theatre: L'inquiétant Vaudeville Anglais." <u>La Presse</u> (Montreal), 2 February 1973, n.p.
Review of <u>After Magritte</u> and <u>The Real Inspector Hound</u> (Montreal, Centaur Theatre): emphasizes the metaphysical dimension beneath the latter's parodic surface. In French.

14 DEAN, DOUGLAS. "ACT's Third <u>Rosencrantz</u> Is Superbly Staged." <u>Los Angeles Advocate</u>, 6 February, 1972, n.p.
Favorable review of the San Francisco company's second revival.

15 EICHHOLZ, ARMIN. "Grosse Dada-Schau für drei Revolutionäre." <u>Merkur</u> (Munich), n.d., n.p.
Review (in German) of <u>Travesties</u> (Munich, Residenztheater); production opened 25 January 1977. Finds it nearly impossible to follow "all the fine points" at the first hearing; yet "one cannot deny the extraordinary success" of the production.

16 FABER, CHARLES. "Earnest Imitation of Wilde by Stoppard."

Writings about Tom Stoppard

INCOMPLETE ITEMS

<blockquote>

Los Angeles Free Press, 4 February 1977, n.p.
   Review of Travesties (Los Angeles, Center Theatre Group): "less a work of art than a literary jigsaw puzzle"; Stoppard's characters "have little charm and no precise definition."

</blockquote>

*17 FERBER, CHRISTIAN. "Labyrinthisches Leben nach Shakespeare: Tom Stoppards Schauspiel Rosenkranz und Güldenstern: Erstaufführung im Schiller-Theater." Die Welt, 4 November 1967, n.p.
   Review of Rosencrantz & Guildenstern Are Dead (Berlin, Schiller-Theater); in German; cited in 1975.B126.

18 FERNANDES, FRANCES C. "Travesties Takes a Leaf from Wilde's Light Comedy." Torrance (Calif.) Tribune, 16 February 1977, n.p.
   Review of the Los Angeles, Center Theatre Group production: "a challenging evening--not . . . recommended after a hard day at the office."

19 FORSCEY, SUZON. "Theater-In-Review: Mystery Night at South Coast." Los Angeles Herald Examiner, n.d., n.p.
   Favorable review of After Magritte and The Real Inspector Hound (Costa Mesa, South Coast Repertory); production opened 5 October 1974.

20 FULLER, RICHARD. "Theatre: The Intellectual Stripper." Philadelphia Drummer, 6 February 1977, n.p.
   Favorable review of Travesties (Philadelphia Drama Guild).

21 GAGNARD, FRANK. "Next-Hound Sprightly Duo." New Orleans Times-Picayune, 9 March 1975, n.p.
   Includes a review of The Real Inspector Hound (New Orleans, Le Petit Théâtre), which "gets a mite literary-precious at times."

*22 GOETSCH, PAUL. "Das englische Drama seit Shaw." In Das Englische Drama. Edited by Josefa Nünning. Darmstadt: n.p., 1973, pp. 487-88.
   Cited in 1978.B78a.

23 GOLDSMITH, LEN. "Keeping Company with the Taper." Downey (Calif.) Southeast News, 4 February 1977, n.p.
   Review of Travesties (Los Angeles, Center Theatre Group): admires the production but says the play demands too much prior knowledge and is too complicated.

Writings about Tom Stoppard

INCOMPLETE ITEMS

24 GRUBER, KLAUS. "Sehr britisch." Heidenheim (W. Germany) Zeitung, 9 November 1973, n.p.
Review of Jumpers (Vienna, Akademietheater): finds the three-hour length too demanding upon an unprepared audience and says many of the play's references are not comprehensible. In German.

*25 HAYES, ANN. "A Note on Travesties." Sycamore, 1 (no year): 5-9.
Cited in MLA International Bibliography.

*26 HILDEBRANDT, DIETER, and SCHWAB-FELISCH, HANS. "Rosenkranz und Güldenstern: Stoppard Stück in Berlin und Bochum." Frankfurter Allgemeine, 6 November 1967, n.p.
Reviews (in German) of Rosencrantz & Guildenstern Are Dead (Berlin, Schiller-Theater; and Bochum, Schauspielhaus); cited in 1975.B126.

27 HYMAN, JACKIE. "Taper Scores 2 Hits." Costa Mesa (Calif.) Daily Pilot, 4 February 1977, n.p.
Review of Travesties (Los Angeles, Center Theatre Group): "a feast for intellectuals."

*28 JACOBI, JOHANNES. "Hamlet am Rande: Rosenkranz und Güldenstern, Schauspiel von Tom Stoppard, Schiller-Theater in Berlin, Schauspielhaus in Bochum." Die Zeit, 10 November 1967, n.p.
Reviews of the two productions of Rosencrantz & Guildenstern Are Dead listed in the title; in German; cited in 1975.B126.

29 KORF, LEE. Review of Travesties. Educational Theatre News 24 (February 1977):n.p.
Mixed review of the Los Angeles, Center Theatre Group production.

*30 KUNZE, MICHAEL. "Geschichtlichkeit von Literatur." In Funkkolleg Literatur. Studienbegleitbrief, no. 9. Weinheim: n.p., 1977, pp. 11-34.
Cited in 1978.B78a.

31 LOSSMANN, HANS. "Schlag nach bei Hamlet." Tagblatt (Wiesbaden), 20 October 1967, n.p.
Review (in German) of Rosencrantz & Guildenstern Are Dead (Vienna, Akademietheater); finds the production long and "leaden." Stoppard, far from being a disciple of Beckett, "is, in fact, . . . making fun of [him] and of a good number of things in the modern theatre."

Writings about Tom Stoppard

INCOMPLETE ITEMS

32 LOVE, WAYNE L. "Ex-Patriots in Zurich Furnish Material for Stoppard's <u>Travesties</u>." <u>Los Angeles Loyolan</u>, 14 February 1977, n.p.
    Review of the Los Angeles, Center Theatre Group production: "quite exhausting, . . . but once acculturated, quite enjoyable."

33 LOYND, RAY. "Joyce, Lenin, Dada!" <u>Los Angeles Herald Examiner</u>, 31 January 1977, n.p.
    Favorable review of <u>Travesties</u> (Los Angeles, Center Theatre Group).

34 McDONOUGH, JACK. "A Dazzling and Profound <u>Rosencrantz and Guildenstern</u>." <u>Night Time</u> (26 January 1972):n.p.
    Favorable review of the San Francisco, ACT second revival.

35 MERRYN, ANTHONY. "Ideas Spoil the Focus." <u>Echo</u> (Liverpool), 12 February 1972, n.p.
    Mixed review of <u>Jumpers</u> (London, National Theatre).

36 MORLEY, SHERIDAN. "Diversions." <u>Nova</u> (December 1971):n.p.
    Interview. Stoppard discusses research as a form of procrastination, his earnings from <u>Rosencrantz & Guildenstern Are Dead</u> (£100,000 from the Broadway production and film rights), and his inability to "take a serious stand in public because I can always see everyone else's point of view." Also says his plays are about "the difference between God's eye view of man and man's eye view of man."
    Clipping housed in British National Theatre Press and Publicity Department, London. Publisher cannot verify article.

37 PENNINGTON, RON. "Stage Review: <u>Travesties</u>." <u>Hollywood Reporter</u>, 1 February 1977, n.p.
    Favorable review of the Los Angeles, Center Theatre Group production.

38 POLLAK, ROBERT. "It Seems to Me." <u>Hyde Park</u> (Ill.) <u>Herald</u>, 7 May 1969, n.p.
    Review of <u>Rosencrantz & Guildenstern Are Dead</u> (American touring production).

39 REGAN, KEITH. Review of <u>Rosencrantz & Guildenstern Are Dead</u>. <u>Theatre News</u> 2 (6 May 1970):n.p.
    Review of the San Francisco, ACT revival.

40 _____. "A Season with ACT." <u>Theatre News</u> 2 (6 September

Writings about Tom Stoppard

INCOMPLETE ITEMS

1970):n.p.
Includes a review of Rosencrantz & Guildenstern Are Dead (San Francisco, ACT revival).

41 _____. Review of Rosencrantz & Guildenstern Are Dead. Theatre News 4 (23 January 1972):n.p.
Review of the San Francisco, ACT second revival.

42 RUIZ, JOSÉ M. RUIZ. "Travesties: Lenin, James Joyce y Tristan Tzara en escena." Letras de Deusto 9 (no year): 137-56.
In Spanish; cited in MLA International Bibliography.

43 RUSSELL, JEFF. "Playhouse Outdoes Itself." Cleveland Scene, 28 March 1974, n.p.
Favorable review of Rosencrantz & Guildenstern Are Dead (Cleveland Playhouse).

44 SALMONY, GEORGE. "Bocksprünge durch den Irrgarten." Abendzeitung (Munich), 27 January 1977, n.p.
Review of Travesties (Munich, Residenztheater): "an irreverent, sharply witty froth mixture with brilliant ideas and a surfeit of talkativeness which does not always ignite." In German.

45 SASSO, LAURENCE J., Jr. "Trinity Offers Summer Jollity with Two One-Acts." Greenville (R.I.) Lincoln Cumberland Observer-News Leader, 20 July 1978, n.p.
Review of the "confusing" but "hilarious" The Real Inspector Hound (Providence, R.I., Trinity Square Repertory Theatre).

46 SELIGSOHN, LEO. "Tom Stoppard." Long Island City (N.Y.) Newsday, 4 November 1975, n.p.
Interview with biographical information: Stoppard discusses his first visit to New York (1960), where he interviewed Lenny Bruce; the evolution of Travesties; and his writing habits.

47 SKINNER, MARGO. "The After-Effects of Gamma Rays on Unsuspecting Audiences." Coast (March 1972):n.p.
Review of Rosencrantz & Guildenstern Are Dead (San Francisco, ACT second revival).

*48 SPIEL, HILDE. "Auf Shakespeares Schultern: Tom Stoppards Rosenkranz und Güldenstern in Wien." Allgemeine (Frankfort), 17 October 1967, n.p.
Review (in German) of Rosencrantz & Guildenstern Are

Writings about Tom Stoppard

INCOMPLETE ITEMS

<blockquote>Dead (Vienna, Akademietheater); cited in 1975.B126.</blockquote>

49 STARK, RANDY. "Stoppard Challenges the Intellect." San Pedro (Calif.) News-Pilot, 4 February 1977, n.p.
    Mixed review of Travesties (Los Angeles, Center Theatre Group).

50 TAYLOR, LARRY. "Real Inspector Hound Is`a Very Funny Satire." Anaheim (Calif.) Independent, 24 October 1974, n.p.
    Favorable review of the Costa Mesa, South Coast Repertory production (with After Magritte).

51 TAYLOR, PAUL. "Concentration Needed for Taper Forum Play." South Gate (Calif.) Press, 5 February 1977, n.p.
    Review of Travesties (Los Angeles, Center Theatre Group): "leaves the audience bewildered, bemused and bothered, but never bored."

52 TAYLOR, ROBERT. "Play Reviews." Hollywood Reporter, 27 April 1970, n.p.
    Review of Rosencrantz & Guildenstern Are Dead (San Francisco, ACT revival).

53 von BECKER, PETER. "Kultur und Revolution auf dem Boulevard." Süddeutsche Zeitung (Munich), n.d., n.p.
    Review of Travesties (Munich, Residenztheater); production opened 25 January 1977. Compares Stoppard to Thomas Bernhardt and Peter Handke. He "always knows too much for a single play." In German.

54 WALKER, JOHN. Review of Travesties. International Herald Tribune (Paris), 18 June 1975, n.p.
    Favorable review of the London, Royal Shakespeare Company revival. Publisher cannot verify.

55 WOOTTEN, DICK. "A Nice Place for Chow Hounds." Cleveland Press, 14 March 1975, n.p.
    Review of the "delightfully literate and loveably absurd" The Real Inspector Hound (Cleveland, Jewish Community Center).

56 ZIEN, LAURIE. "The 'Little Guys' Caught up in Hamlet's Destiny." San Francisco Progress, 19 January 1972, n.p.
    Review of Rosencrantz & Guildenstern Are Dead (San Francisco, ACT second revival).

Index

A., E., 1970.B1
A., H., 1973.B1
Aaron, Jules, 1975.B1
Abendzeitung (Munich), Incomplete. B44
Ability. See Craftsmanship; Skill
Abrams, Doris Cole, 1976.B32
Absurd (-ism, -ity, Theatre of the), 1967.B98, 101; 1968. B49, 95; 1969.B1, 11, 30; 1970.B13, 39; 1971.B1; 1972. B56, 92; 1973.B39, 62, 77; 1974.B84; 1975.B51, 59; 1976. A1, 4; 1978.B29, 63; 1979.A1, B74, 88; 1980.A2, B27; Incomplete.B55. See also Beckett, Samuel; Existential; Ionesco, Eugene
Absurd, The (The Critical Idiom Series), 1969.B30
Acting work (Stoppard's, in untitled documentary)
-review of, 1980.B30
Action, 1967.B77, 110; 1968.B43, 115; 1970.B7; 1971.B22; 1972. B103; 1974.B41, 78, 171-172; 1976,B53, 87; 1977.B37, 125; 1978.B29, 79, 137; 1979.B36, 62, 77, 84, 101, 106; 1980. B12, 14. See also Plot
Actors. See also names of specific actors
-as authors of items and subjects of interviews, 1967.B22, 83, 114, 129; 1972.B61, 129; 1973.B44; 1974.B1, 73, 165, 185, 187; 1975.B20, 55, 72, 87, 111, 114; 1977.B20, 60, 75, 126; 1978.B57; 1979.B7; 1980.A1
-in Stoppard's plays
--comments by others about, 1967. B11; 1972.B18, 21; 1973.B20; 1975.B72, 111, 120; 1976.B17, 33, 108; 1977.B75; 1978.B89; 1979.B1, 12, 24, 36; 1980. B17, 19, 30
--comments by Stoppard about, 1974.B63, 105; 1975.B55; 1979.B17
Actors Equity, 1975.B120; 1976. B14, 33
Adams, Bernard, 1967.B1
Adams, Phoebe, 1968.B1
Adapt (-ation, -ing)
-comments by others about, 1973. B23, 28, 36, 38, 41, 84; 1974. B152; 1978.B56, 73, 78; 1979. B11, 63, 80, 92, 101, 103; 1980.B3, 9-10, 20, 22, 25, 27a, 33, 35-37
-comments by Stoppard about, 1972. B11; 1973.B37, 52, 75; 1979. B47; 1980.B11
Advocate (Los Angeles), Incomplete. B14
Advocate (San Mateo, Calif.) 1975.B109
After Dark, 1972.B122; 1975.B112, 127; 1976.B99; 1979.B102
After Magritte (stage play)
-analyses and criticisms of, 1970. B61; 1971.B19-20; 1972.B56, 94; 1973.B21-22; 1974.B84, 122, 135; 1975.B51, 64; 1976.

Index

A2-4, B49, 57, 97; 1977.A1, B37; 1978.B29, 67; 1979.A1-2, B10, 52, 120; 1980.A2
-comments by Stoppard about, 1970.B3; 1972.B57, 96, 106; 1973.B85; 1974.B90
-news items about, 1971.B11; 1972.B10, 37
-productions, reviews of,
--American touring, 1974.B106
--Bristol, New Vic, 1972.B15, 34, 86
--Costa Mesa, Calif., South Coast Repertory, 1974.B89; Incomplete.B19, 50
--London, Ambiance Lunch-Hour Theatre, 1970.B9, 22, 42-43, 66
--London, Dolphin Theatre Company, 1972.B46, 67, 100, 114, 136; 1973.B32
--London, Dolphin Theatre Company revival, 1973.B86
--Montreal, Centaur Theatre, 1973.B39, 49; Incomplete.B13
--New York, Theatre Four, 1972.B25, 27-28, 32, 35, 39, 52-53, 59, 63, 65, 68, 71, 75, 78, 89, 93, 101, 106, 108, 115-116, 118, 120, 137-139; 1973.B31, 67; 1975.B105
-text, review of, 1971.B8, 10
Age (Melbourne), 1973.B48
Albee, Edward, 1978.B28
"Albert's Bridge" (radio play)
-analyses and criticisms of, 1968.B115; 1969.B54; 1971.B17; 1973.B21-22; 1974.B135; 1975.B64; 1976.A1-4, B49; 1977.A1, B107, 125; 1978.B29; 1979.A1-2, B52, 106; 1980.A2
-comments by Stoppard about, 1970.B3; 1975.B43
-news items about, 1968.B18, 24-26; 1969.B4; 1970.B5
-photographs of, 1968.B24
-productions, reviews of
--Chichester, G.B., Festival Theatre, 1976.B36
--Edinburgh, Oxford Theatre Group, 1969.B8a, 24, 31-32, 49

--London, BBC Radio, 1967.B14, 27, 52, 54, 112, 128, 132, 140; 1968.B111
--London, Lamb & Flag, 1970.B8
--New York, Landmark Theatre Production Company, 1975.B23
--Washington, D.C., St. Albans Repertory Theatre, 1969.B43
-text, reviews of 1969.B5, 20
Albrecht, Ernest, 1967.B2
Alexander-Willis, Hope (actress)
-interview with, 1975.B114
Allan, Elkan, 1972.B1
Alldredge, Don, 1969.B1; 1971.B1
Allegor(-ical, -y), 1966.B4, 26; 1967.B107; 1977.B51, 94. See also Symbol
Allen, Woody, 1980.B26
Allgemeine (Frankfurt, West Germany), 1973.B26; Incomplete. B26, 48
Amateur Stage, 1974.B147
Ambigu(-ity, -ous), 1966.B22; 1971.B14; 1972.B133; 1975.B64; 1976.B56; 1977.B94. See also Obvious; Paradox
America, 1972.B70-71; 1974.B91; 1975.B61; 1977.B67; 1980.B18
America. See Theatre and Society, American
Amnesty International, 1978.B31, 33. See also Dissidents; Human rights
Amory, Mark, 1974.B1
Analys(-is, -es). See Stoppard, Tom, analyses and criticisms of corpus; titles of individual works (listed in Stoppard, Tom, works by)
Anderson, Marjory, 1972.B2
Anderson, Michael, 1972.B3; 1974.B2
Andrews, M. Stephanie, 1974.B3
Angell, Robert, 1980.B1
Angry Theatre, The, 1969.B54
Anguish. See also Despair; Mood
-comments by others about, 1968.B45, 115; 1969.B11; 1973.B43; 1975.B62; 1977.B96
-comments by Stoppard about, 1978.B48

Index

Anne, Princess, 1977.B62-63
"Another Moon Called Earth" (television play). See also Jumpers; Moon (satellite)
-analyses and criticisms of, 1971.B20; 1972.B94; 1974.B46, 122, 135; 1976.A3; 1977.A1; 1979.B52
-comments by Stoppard about, 1967.B91; 1977.B73
-production, reviews of
--London, BBC Television, 1967. B86, 95, 107
Ansen, David, 1980.B3
Anti-hero. See Heroes
AP Wireservice, 1967.B61; 1974. B69-70; 1975.B48; 1976.B50; 1977.B55
Arbeiter Zeitung (Vienna), 1973. B43
Arden, John, 1966.B13
Argu(-e, -ment). See Dialectic
Argus (Fremont, Calif.), 1974. B160
Ariel, 1980.B12
Arizona Quarterly, 1979.B114
Arnett, Earl, 1978.B13
Art (-ist). See also names of specific artists and movements
-comments by others about, 1974. B49, 182; 1975.B51, 66, 126; 1976.A2, B45, 57, 87; 1977. B109; 1979.B84; 1980.B4, 24
-comments by Stoppard about, 1973.B85; 1974.A1, B144; 1975.B43, 108; 1976.B65-66; 1977.B90
Arthur, Doug, 1972.B19
"Artist Descending a Staircase" (radio play)
-analyses and criticisms of, 1972.B94; 1974.B80, 122, 135; 1975.B64; 1976.A3-4; 1977.A1, B107; 1979.A1, B52, 88, 112, 120; 1980.A2
-comments by Stoppard about, 1972.B11, 99
-news items about, 1972.B11, 14, 16
-productions, reviews of

--Cardiff, G.B., Sherman Arena Company, 1977.B66
--London, BBC Radio, 1972.B22, 29, 45, 50, 112, 133, 144
-text, reviews of, 1973.B29, 66; 1975.B96
Arvin, Steve, 1977.B14
Asahina, Robert, 1978.B14
Asbury Park (N.J.) Press, 1967. B40
Asmus, Walter D., 1970.B7
Associated Press. See AP Wireservice
As the Curtain Rises, 1978.B29
As You Like It, 1967.B3
Atkins, Harold, 1976.B15
Atlantic, 1968.B1
Atlas, 1966.B5
Atwood, Lois, 1974.B21
Audience (-s)
-comments by others about, 1967. B96, 138; 1970.B1, 37; 1972. B18; 1973.B20, 26, 43, 49, 62, 71; 1974.B108, 145; 1975.B18, 35, 71, 116; 1976.B46, 97; 1977.B16, 57, 109-110, 116, 135; 1978.B29, 41, 43, 61, 70, 89; 1979.B41, 98; 1980.B14, 24, 31; Incomplete.B5, 18, 23-24, 51
-comments by Stoppard about, 1972.B96; 1974.B1; 1978.B17
Audio tape, items on, 1976.B65-66; 1977.B75, 86; Incomplete. A2
Australian (Melbourne), 1973.B27
Austria. See Theatre and Society, Austrian
Autobiographical fiction. See Personal experience
Automobiles
-comments by Stoppard about, 1967.B48
Ave Maria, 1968.B87
Awards and honors, 1967.B13, 15; 1968.B4, 11-12, 18, 25-26, 111, 122; 1972.B17; 1973.B2-4; 1975.B4; 1976.B6, 100; 1977.B13; 1978.B1-2, 4; 1979. B1, 5, 9, 90
Ayer, A. J. See also Logical

Index

Positivism
- as author of items, 1972.B20; 1973.B12; 1976.B16
- as subject of comments by Stoppard, 1977.B125; 1979.B106

B., D. F., 1970.B8; 1971.B3; 1973.B13
B., P. W., 1970.B9
Babula, William, 1972.B21
Baccus (University of Bristol), 1972.B15
Bailey, John A., 1979.B10
Baker, Anthony, 1973.B14
Baker, Barbara, 1978.B15
Baker, Roger, 1966.B10
Bakewell, Michael (director)
- interview with, 1974.B122
Balance. See Juxtapose
Ball, Ian G., 1967.B27; 1968.B30; 1972.B22
Banker, Stephan, 1974.B22-23
Barber, John, 1971.B4; 1972.B23; 1973.B15-16; 1974.B24; 1975.B13; 1977.B15; 1979.B11-13
Barbour, John, 1977.B16
BARC (British-American Repertory Company), 1979.B3, 21
Barker, Clive, 1969.B6
Barker, Felix, 1966.B11; 1967.B28; 1968.B31-32; 1972.B24; 1973.B17-18; 1975.B14
Barnes, Clive, 1967.B29, 92; 1968.B33; 1970.B10; 1972.B25-27; 1974.B24-29, 111; 1975.B15-18, 81; 1976.B17-19; 1977.B17, 87; 1979.B14-17, 75-77
Barrett, Leslie, 1967.B30
Barron, Karl, 1969.B7
Bastable, Adolphus, 1973.B19
Batdorff, Emerson, 1969.B8
Bates, Merete, 1969.B8a
Bath & Wilts Evening Chronicle (Bristol), 1970.B16; 1974.B37; 1976.B21-22
Baumgart, Wolfgang, 1971.B5
BBC (British Broadcasting Corporation), 1980.A1
BBC Radio, 1972.B94. See also BBC Radio Four; BBC Radio Light Programme; BBC Third Programme
BBC Radio Four, 1970.B62; 1972.B2; 1973.B75; 1974.B63; 1976.B74, 78, 102
BBC Radio Light Programme, 1967.B63
BBC Third Radio Programme, 1967.B35; 1968.B35
Beauchamp, Emerson, 1970.B11
Beaufort, John, 1972.B28; 1974.B30-32, 111; 1975.B19, 81; 1977.B18, 87; 1979.B18-20, 75-77
Beauman, Sally, 1975.B20
Beckett, Samuel. See also Absurd; Endgame; Waiting for Godot
- comments by others about, 1967.B37, 52, 76; 1968.B7, 36, 115; 1969.B12; 1970.B39; 1971.B17; 1973.B21; 1975.B96, 117; 1976.A2; 1977.B135; 1978.B67; 1979.B51-52, 89; Incomplete.B31
- comments by Stoppard about, 1967.B61; 1968.B51; 1969.B38; 1970.B62; 1971.B12, 20; 1972.B57; 1974.B80; 1975.B43; 1977.A1, B90
Beckwith, David Bruce, 1976.A1
Bedford, Brian (actor)
- interview with, 1974.B165
Bee (Modesto, Calif.), 1969.B51; 1970.B57-58; 1972.B123
Bee (Sacramento, Calif.), 1969.B25; 1973.B41; 1974.B68; 1977.B54
Beer, Otto F., Incomplete.B7-8
Beer, Patricia, 1972.B29
Behind the Scenes: Theater and Film Interviews from "The Transatlantic Review," 1971.B12
Bellamy, Peter, 1974.B33
Benedict, Stewart H., 1967.B31
Bennett, Jonathan, 1975.B21
Bergson, Phillip, 1974.B34; 1978.B16
Berio, Luciano, 1975.B94
Berkeley (Calif.) Barb, 1979.B57

218

Index

Berkowitz, Gerald M., 1977.B19; 1980.B4
Berkvist, Robert, 1977.B20; 1979.B21-22
Berlin. See Literarisches Colloquium; Theatre and society, German
Berlin, Normand, 1973.B20
Berliner, Milton, 1970.B12
Berman, Dave, 1977.B21
Berman, Ed (director). See also BARC; Inter-Action Trust
-as subject of comments
--by others, 1971.B15; 1973.B8; 1977.B50
--by Stoppard, 1977.B36, 82
-interviews with, 1976.B28; 1979.B21
Bernhardt, Thomas, 1973.B69; Incomplete.B53
Best Plays of --, The
-1967-68, 1968.B54
-1971-72, 1972.B56
-1973-74, 1974.B75
-1975-76, 1976.B54
Best Sellers, 1968.B43
Beyond Absurdity: The Plays of Tom Stoppard, 1979.A1
Bezencenet, Stevie, Incomplete. A1
Bigsby, Christopher William Edgar, 1973.B21; 1976.A2
Billington, Michael, 1967.B32; 1968.B34; 1971.B6; 1972.B30; 1973.B22-24; 1974.B35; 1975.B22; 1979.B23-25
Biographical data. See Stoppard, Tom, biographical data about; Early life and career
Birmingham (G.B.) Post, 1966.B35; 1973.B80
Birnkrant, Sam, 1977.B22
Bishoff, Don, 1970.B13
Blackburn, Tom, 1976.B20
Bladen, Barbara, 1969.B9; 1970.B14; 1972.B31; 1974.B36; 1977.B23-24
Blaha, Paul, 1967.B33; 1973.B25-26
Blake, Betty, 1967.B92-93; 1972.B89; 1974.B111; 1975.B81;

1977.B87; 1979.B75-77
Blake, Douglas F., 1966.B12
Blevinns, Winnifred, 1969.B10
Blumenfeld, Yorick, 1978.B17
B'nai B'rith Messenger (Los Angeles), 1977.B84
Bogarde, Dirk, 1978.B86
Bolt, Robert. See Flowering Cherry
Bolton, Whitney, 1967.B34
Bond, Edward
-comments by others about, 1979.B51
-comments by Stoppard about, 1980.B24
Bondy, François, 1970.B15
Booklist, 1968.B20; 1973.B6; 1975.B9
Books
-completely devoted to Stoppard, 1970.A1; 1976.A2; 1977.A1; 1979.A1; Incomplete.A3
-devoting chapters or essays to Stoppard, 1970.B7, 39; 1971.B5, 20; 1975.B126; 1976.B39, 91; 1977.B73; 1978.B29, 41; 1979.B61, 93, 106, 120, 1980.B31
-devoting incidental attention to Stoppard, 1968.B54; 1969.B6, 11, 22, 30, 50, 54; 1971.B14, 16; 1972.B56; 1974.B75, 84; 1975.B98; 1976.B44, 54; 1977.B135; 1978.B34, 40, 52, 70; 1979.B51-52; Incomplete.B22
-encyclopedic or reference material about Stoppard, 1968.B109; 1969.B1; 1971.B1; 1972.B3-4, 92; 1973.B21, 40; 1975.B2; 1976.B96; 1979.B73, 112
-interviews with Stoppard, 1971.B12; 1975.B43
-reprinted or abridged reviews, 1968.B84; 1973.B68; 1975.B96-97, 117; 1976.B87; 1978.B20
-undetermined contents, 1978.B47; Incomplete.B30
Books and Bookmen, 1966.B18
Bookspan, Martin, 1972.B32
Boorman, John, 1968.B117-118
Boot (character's name)
-comments by others about, 1972.

Index

B6, 41; 1979.B10
—comments by Stoppard about, 1972.B41; 1974.B90
Bor(-edom, -ing), 1966.B25, 34; 1967.B41, 92; 1968.B39; 1974.B10, 33, 42, 52, 70-71, 89, 100, 106, 111, 123, 177-178; 1975.B21, 60-61; 1976.B1, 86, 94; 1977.B55, 68, 104; 1978.B37, 54; 1979.B77, 97, 102; Incomplete.B5, 31, 51. See also Mood
Born Yesterday (stage play directed by Stoppard)
—comments by Stoppard about, 1973.B37
—news items about, 1973.B7, 37
—photograph of, 1973.B7
—production, reviews of
——London, Greenwich Theatre Company, 1973.B13, 16, 18, 24, 33, 35, 47, 54, 56, 79-82
Borrowing. See Eclectic
Boskin, Louise, 1972.B33
Boston After Dark, 1970.B23, 54
Boston Phoenix, 1974.B106
"Boundary, The" (television play)
—production, review of
——London, BBC Television, 1975.B63
Bowen, John, 1967.B35; 1968.B35
Boyd, Judith, 1970.B16; 1974.B37; 1976.B21-22
Bradbrook, Muriel C., 1969.B11
Bradshaw, Jon, 1977.B25
Brandon, Henry, 1978.B18
Bratt, David L., 1976.A3; 1977.B26
Brecht, Bertolt, 1973.B62. See also Galileo
Brenton, Howard
—comments by Stoppard about, 1980.B24
Brien, Alan, 1967.B36; 1976.B23; 1978.B19; 1980.B5
Brien, Jeremy, 1970.B17; 1972.B34
Brisbane, Katharine, 1973.B27
Brisson, Frederick (producer)
—interview with, 1974.B139

Bristol, 1979.B8. See also Playwrights' Company
Britannica Book of the Year: 1968, 1968.B109
British-American Repertory Company. See BARC
British Book News, 1979.B105
British Broadcasting Corporation. See BBC
British Film Catalogue, The: 1895-1970, 1973.B40
British Theatre: 1950-70, 1974.B84
British Theatrelog, 1978.B4; 1979.B5, 8
British Theatre since 1955: A Reassessment, 1979.B51
Broich, Ulrich, 1971.B7
Brooks, Jeremy, 1980.B6
Brown, Geoff, 1976.B24
Brown Daily Herald (Providence, R.I.), 1974.B21
Bruce, Lenny
—comments by Stoppard about, Incomplete.B46
Brukenfeld, Dick, 1972.B35; 1974.B38; 1975.B23
Brunel University, 1979.B9
Brustein, Robert, 1967.B37; 1968.B36; 1969.B12; 1973.B28; 1980.B7
Bryden, Ronald, 1966.B13; 1967.B38; 1968.B37-38
Bryfonski, Dedria, 1978.B20
Buck, Richard M., 1975.B24
Buckley, Leonard, 1972.B36
Buckley, Michael, 1976.B25
Bucks County Courier Times (Levittown, Pa.), 1977.B49
Buffa, Michelangelo, 1975.B24a
Buhr, Richard J., 1979.B26
Bull, Judith, 1971.B8
Bulletin (Floral Park, N.Y.), 1974.B76; 1977.B59
Bulletin of the West Virginia Association of College English Teachers, 1975.B79
Bunce, Alan N., 1967.B39
Burlesque, 1968.B44; 1969.B1; 1970.B37; 1971.B1; 1974.B49; 1975.B73, 81; 1977.B56, 87.

Index

See also Chiché; Parody;
Satire
Burr, Patricia, 1977.B27
Bush, Miriam, 1967.B40
Butcher, Maryvonne, 1975.B25;
1978.B21; 1980.B8
Butler, Joe, 1978.B22
Byron, Joan (actress)
-interview with, 1974.B185

Caen, Herb, 1975.B26
Cahiers du Rideau, 1978.B79
Cahn, Victor L., 1976.A4;
1979.A1
Caird, Rod, 1975.B27
Caliban, 1978.B23
Callen, Anthony, 1969.B13
Calta, Louis, 1972.B37; 1974.B39
Camroux, David, 1978.B23
Camus, Albert, 1978.B89
Canby, Vincent, 1975.B28; 1979.
B27; 1980.B9
Capitol Journal (Salem, Oreg.),
1970.B25
Capote, Truman
-comments by Stoppard about,
1967.B5
Carr, Henry
-comments by others about, 1974.
B47, 100, 110; 1975.B123
-comments by Stoppard about,
1975.B55
Carroll, Peter, 1971.B8a
Cashin, Fergus, 1968.B39
Cassidy, Claudia, 1968.B40
Castillo, Othon, 1977.B28
Catholic Film Newsletter, 1975.
B12
Catholic Herald (London), 1970.
B33; 1972.B47
Causality, 1969.B37; 1979.B52.
See also Logic
Cavan, Romily, 1973.B29
Cavanaugh, Arthur, 1968.B41
Centennial Review, 1972.B142
Chaillet, Ned, 1976.B26; 1977.
B29-31; 1978.B24-25
Champlin, Charles, 1972.B38
Chaos, 1968.B50; 1973.B68; 1975.
B117, 126; 1976.A1, B49, 109;
1978.A1, B20, 28. See also
Knowledge; Nonsense
Chapman, John, 1967.B41-42, 92
Character (-ization, -s). See
also Boot; Carr, Henry;
Heroes; Joyce, James; Lenin,
Vladimir; Moon (character's
name); Tzara, Tristan
-comments by others about, 1966.
B29; 1967.B83, 111, 114, 116;
1968.B113-114; 1969.B13;
1970.B12, 37; 1971.B17; 1972.
B41, 61, 107, 126, 129, 136,
141; 1973.B44-45, 65, 69;
1974.A1, B40, 46, 73, 80, 104,
110, 141-142, 159; 1975.B10,
20, 55, 59, 71, 97, 100, 117,
123; 1976.A1-4, B87, 92;
1977.A1, B39, 51, 68, 75, 94,
107, 109, 118; 1978.B23, 29,
42, 61, 82; 1979.A1, B10, 17,
20, 26, 29-30, 32, 35-36, 43,
60, 62, 66, 77, 83-84, 114,
119; 1980.B12-13, 24, 31, 34;
Incomplete.B2, 16
-comments by Stoppard about,
1968.B76, 89; 1972.B41; 1974.
B1, 23, 90, 144; 1975.B124;
1977.B125; 1978.B72; 1979.B47,
106
Charities, 1977.B11-12
Chartoff, Bob, 1968.B117-118
Chernin, Donna, Incomplete.B9
Chetwyn, Robert (director)
-interview with, 1968.B82
Chicago Daily News, 1969.B28
Chicago Today, 1969.B21
Children
-comments by Miriam Stoppard
about, 1977.B64, 85
-comments by Tom Stoppard about,
1978.B6
-news items about, 1979.B39-40
Choice, 1968.B28; 1970.B6; 1974.
B19; 1977.B7; 1978.B10
Christianity and Crisis, 1976.B41
Christian Science Monitor, 1966.
B22-23; 1967.B39, 73; 1968.
B77; 1969.B32; 1972.B28;
1974.B30-32, 52, 59, 105;
1975.B19, 90; 1977.B18; 1978.
B75, 84; 1979.B18-20, 111

Index

Chronicle (San Francisco), 1969.B35; 1970.B31; 1972.B81; 1973.B36; 1974.B88; 1975.B26; 1977.B132-133. See also Sunday Examiner and Chronicle (San Francisco)
Church, Michael, 1977.B32
Cinema. See Film
Cinéma 75, 1975.B93
Citizen (Ottawa), 1973.B22
City Press (London), 1972.B74
Clalip, Alice Grace, 1969.B14
Clarke, Gerald, 1978.B26
Classic (-al), 1969.B37; 1970.B39; 1971.B5, 7; 1976.B39, 112. See also Myth; Original
Clayton, Sylvia, 1968.B42
Cleese, John, 1980.B29
Cleveland (Ohio) Press, 1967.B58; 1969.B41; 1974.B113, 187; Incomplete.B55
Clever (-ness), 1966.B36; 1967.B117; 1969.B20, 53-54; 1972.B63, 115-116; 1974.B69, 84, 102, 116, 170; 1975.B6, 53, 60, 62, 75, 81, 96-97; 1976.B73; 1977.B34, 91, 114, 133; 1978.B45, 62; 1979.B68; 1980.B18. See also Wit
Cliché. See also Burlesque; Parody; Satire
-comments by Stoppard about, 1977.B25, 125; 1979.B106
Close, Roy M., 1977.B33; 1978.B27
Clum, John M., 1978.B28
Clurman, Harold, 1967.B43; 1972.B39; 1973.B30; 1974.B40-41; 1975.B29-30; 1977.B34; 1978.B20; 1979.B28-29
Coast, Incomplete.B47
Codron, Michael, 1967.B18
Coe, John, 1976.B27
Coe, Richard L., 1967.B44; 1970.B18; 1973.B31; 1974.B42-43; 1976.B28-29
Cohen, Nathan, 1969.B15-17
Colby, Douglas, 1978.B29
Coleby, John, 1978.B30
Coleman, John, 1975.B31
Collage, 1971.B7; 1974.B80; 1978.B28. See also Eclectic; Juxtapose; Pastiche
Collins, William B., 1976.B30-31; 1977.B35; 1978.B31
Colloquium. See Literarisches Colloquium
Columbia Journalism Review, 1980.B17a
Combs, Richard, 1975.B32; 1978.B32; 1980.B10
Comedy. See also Farce; Humor; Laughter
-comments by others about, 1966.B4; 1967.B57-58, 62, 92; 1968.B39, 52, 80, 97; 1970.B40; 1972.B83; 1973.B25, 77; 1974.A1, B120, 187; 1975.B37, 46, 96, 98; 1976.A1-2, B58; 1977.A1, B51, 125; 1978.B33, 53, 63, 70, 78a, 80; 1979.B19, 48, 75-76; 1980.B13, 26, 37
-comments by Stoppard about, 1967.B5, 67; 1974.B54, 109, 116; 1975.B108
Commentary, 1967.B110; 1974.B133; 1976.B86; 1980.B32
Commonweal, 1967.B116; 1976.B109-110; 1977.B131; 1978.B86
Comparative Drama, 1979.B26; 1980.B26
Compton, Russ, 1969.B18; Incomplete.B10-11
Concept (-ion), 1967.B37, 62, 92, 95, 117, 126; 1968.B36, 41, 85, 121; 1969.B12, 15, 114; 1970.B12, 51; 1973.B45; 1974.B80, 102, 132, 169; 1975.B34, 96, 117; 1978.B52; 1979.B51; 1980.B17a. See also Idea; Intentions
Conclusion. See Resolution
Connolly, Ray, 1980.B11
Consciousness. See Unconscious
Contemporary Authors: A Bio-Bibliographical Guide, 1979.B73
Contemporary Dramatists (Contemporary Writers of the English Language Series), 1973.B21
Contemporary Literary Criticism: Excerpts from Criticism,

Index

1973.B68; 1975.B96-97; 1976.
  B87; 1978.B20
Contemporary Literature, 1979.
  B30
Contemporary Theatre: A Selection of Reviews, 1968.B84
Content, 1968.B7; 1969.B8a;
  1974.B75; 1977.B7, 53, 55-56,
  59, 67, 70, 76, 87-77, 108,
  131; 1978.B20, 30; 1979.B13,
  17, 42, 45, 49, 76-77, 81,
  94, 98, 120; 1980.B21; Incomplete.B53. See also Idea;
  Metaphysical; Political;
  Social; Theme
Contra Costa (Calif.) Times,
  1969.B56; 1972.B54
Convention (-al, -s). See also
  Absurd; Form; Naturalism;
  Play-within-the-play; Style
-comments by others about, 1968.
  B112; 1972.B101; 1974.B182;
  1975.B35, 59, 62, 96; 1976.
  A4, B87; 1977.A1, B16, 37,
  74, 123; 1978.B63; 1979.A1,
  B29, 43, 70, 77, 112; 1980.
  B13, 21, 27, 31-32
-comments by Stoppard about,
  1977.B23, 125, 132; 1979.
  B106
Cook, Bruce, 1977.B36
Cooke, John William, 1978.A1
Cooke, Richard P., 1967.B45, 92
Cooper, R. W., 1967.B46
Corballis, Richard, 1980.B12
Corodimas, Peter, 1968.B43
Corry, John, 1976.B32-33
Cotter, Jerry, 1975.B33
Courier (Claremont, Calif.),
  1977.B110
Courier-Journal (Louisville, Ky.),
  1974.B116
Courier-Post (Cherry Hill, N.J.),
  1977.B137
Coveney, Michael, 1973.B32-33;
  1974.B44
Covington, Gillian, 1978.B33
Coward, Noel, 1975.B66; 1976.B37
Cox, Frank, 1966.B14
Crabill, Cathleen, Incomplete.
  B12

Craft (-smanship). See also
  Skill
-comments by others about, 1967.
  B94; 1968.B38, 45; 1970.B47,
  65; 1973.B49, 57, 68; 1977.
  B80; 1978.B51, 62, 86; 1979.
  B86
-comments by Stoppard about,
  1974.B22, 90; 1977.B90
Craig, Randall, 1976.B34-36
Crick, Bernard, 1974.B45
Cricket, 1976.B21; 1980.B29
Crist, Judith, 1976.B37
Critical Quarterly, 1978.B67;
  1980.B24
Criticism. See Stoppard, Tom,
  analyses and criticisms of
  corpus; titles of individual
  works (listed in Stoppard,
  Tom, works by)
Critics. See Reviewers; names of
  individual reviewers; titles
  of works reviewed (listed in
  Stoppard, Tom, works by)
Crosman, Inge, 1980.B31
Crossley, Brian M., 1977.B37
Crossley, Peter, 1973.B34
Crozier, Mary, 1966.B15
Crump, G. B., 1979.B30
Cue, 1970.B55-56; 1974.B149;
  1975.B107-108
Cumming, Richard, 1974.B46
Cunningham, Dennis, 1979.B31, 77
Curcio, Chris, 1969.B19; 1970.
  B19-20; 1972.B40
Current Biography, 1974.B18
Current Biography Yearbook: 1974,
  1975.B2
Curtis, Anthony, 1979.B32
Curtiss, Thomas Quinn, 1975.B34
Cushman, Robert, 1972.B41; 1974.
  B47; 1976.B38
Cuyler, Richard R., 1979.B33
Czechoslovakia, 1968.B18; 1977.
  B38, 125; 1979.B106; 1980.
  B30. See also Dissidents

D., D. G., 1974.B48
D., T., 1970.B21
Daily Bruin (University of California, Los Angeles), 1977.
  B101

223

Index

Daily Courier (Grants Pass, Oreg.), 1970.B32
Daily Express (London), 1967.B84; 1968.B70; 1974.B101
Daily Gazette (Taunton, Mass.), 1978.B22
Daily Home News (New Brunswick, N.J.), 1967.B2
Daily Local News (West Chester, Pa.), 1977.B77
Daily Mail (London), 1967.B87-88; 1968.B65, 73-74; 1970.B43, 72; 1972.B84; 1973.B79; 1974.B159; 1975.B116
Daily Mirror (London), 1967.B125; 1968.B78, 102-103; 1972.B128; 1974.B156. See also Sunday Mirror (London)
Daily News (Bangor, Maine), 1978.B59
Daily News (New York), 1967.B41, 133; 1972.B137; 1974.B171, 173, 176; 1975.B87, 119; 1976.B107; 1977.B104, 130; 1979.B108-110. See also Sunday News (New York)
Daily News (Philadelphia), 1976.B101; 1977.B117
Daily News (Washington, D.C.), 1970.B12. See also Star-News (Washington, D.C.)
Daily Nexus (University of California, Santa Barbara), 1977.B72
Daily Pilot (Costa Mesa, Calif.), Incomplete.B5, 27
Daily Review (Hayward, Calif.), 1972.B40
Daily Sketch (London), 1968.B39, 86
Daily Star (Toronto, Canada), 1969.B15-17
Daily Telegraph (London), 1966.B16; 1967.B47, 50; 1968.B42, 44, 55, 98; 1970.B50; 1971.B4; 1972.B23, 44-45; 1973.B15-16; 1974.B24; 1975.B13; 1976.B15; 1977.B15, 80; 1978.B1; 1979.B11-13, 39-40, 82. See also Sunday Telegraph (London)

D'Andrea, Paul, 1976.B39
Danield, D. J., 1979.B34
Darlington, W. A., 1966.B16; 1967.B47; 1968.B44
Das englische Drama, Incomplete. B22
Das englische Drama: Von Mittelalter bis zur Gegenwart, 1970.B39
Dassylva, Martial, Incomplete. B13
Das zeitgenössische englische Drama, 1975.B126
Davidson, Mary R., 1979.B35
Davies, Hunter, 1967.B48
Davies, Martin, 1972.B42
Davies, Stan Gebler, 1973.B35
Davis, Anthony, 1965.B2
Davis, Jessica Milner, 1978.B34
Davis, Malcolm McTear, 1967.B49
Davy, Richard, 1977.B38
Dawson, Helen, 1968.B45; 1971.B9; 1972.B43
Day, Doris M., 1978.B35
Day-Lewis, Sean, 1967.B50; 1969.B20; 1972.B44-45
Dean, Douglas, Incomplete.B14
Dean, Joan FitzPatrick, 1975.B35
Death, 1969.B37; 1970.B37; 1972.B142; 1974.A1; 1975.B11, 65, 71; 1976.B39, 58; 1977.B135; 1978.B89; 1979.B36, 101
Death of a Salesman
-comments by Stoppard about, 1970.B62
Debate, 1974.B35; 1975.B62, 76; 1977.B68; 1979.B62, 77, 100. See also Dialectic
de Jongh, Nicholas, 1970.B22; 1972.B46; 1976.B40
Depersonal(-ization, -ize)
-comments by others about, 1970.B37
-comments by Stoppard about, 1967.B78
Designers
-interview with, 1980.A1
Despair, 1970.B37; 1973.B21; 1976.A2; 1980.B1, 34. See also Anguish; Mood
Despair (film with screenplay by

Index

Stoppard)
-comments by Stoppard about, 1977.B132
-reviews of, 1978.B14, 16, 19, 21, 32, 56, 68, 73-74, 78, 86; 1979.B4, 27, 38, 44, 46, 50, 68, 83, 92, 102, 113
Detach (-ed, -ment). See also Mood; Perspective; Tone
-comments by others about, 1968.B115; 1969.B33; 1972.B136; 1975.B117; 1976.A1; 1977.B125, 129; 1978.B79; 1979.B89, 106; 1908.B8
-comments by Stoppard about, Incomplete.B36
Detective story. See also Mystery
-judge of competition, 1972.B7, 12-13
Dettmer, Roger, 1969.B21; 1975.B36
Develop (-ment). See Invention
De Vos, Jozef, 1977.B39
Dexter, John, 1967.B3
Dialectic (-al, -s). See also Debate; Juxtapose
-comments by others about, 1966.B20; 1972.B66; 1974.B80, 102; 1975.B62; 1976.B39; 1977.B32; 1979.B84, 120
-comments by Stoppard about, 1973.B45; 1974.B23; 1978.B72
Dialogue. See also Language
-comments by others about, 1966.B30; 1967.B43, 52, 57-58, 76, 111, 116, 120, 132; 1968.B115; 1970.B7, 11; 1973.B68, 84; 1974.B33; 1975.B31-32, 35, 59, 66, 86, 106; 1976.B45, 107; 1977.A1, B29; 1978.B54, 61, 68, 74, 76; 1979.B38, 50, 61, 77, 110; 1980.B1, 8, 32, 36
-comments by Stoppard about, 1967.B4
Dibb, Frank W., 1966.B17
Dickerman, Stu, 1975.B37
Die Mythologie der entgötterten Welt, 1971.B14
Die Welt, Incomplete.B17

Die Zeit, Incomplete.B28
Dimensions in American Judaism, 1968.B48, 67
Direct (-ing, -ion), by Stoppard
-comments by others about, 1973.B24
-comments by Stoppard about, 1973.B37
Directors (of Stoppard's work). See also names of specific directors
-as authors of items and subjects of interviews, 1967.B89; 1968.B82; 1971.B15; 1973.B83; 1974.B79, 122; 1975.B32, 44; 1976.A1, B28; 1977.B93, 106; 1979.B21; 1980.A1, B17
Dirty Linen and New-Found-Land, (stage play)
-analyses and criticisms of, 1977.A1, B73, 125; 1978.B29, 34, 63; 1979.A2, B106, 120
-comments by others about, 1976.B28; 1977.B20, 62-63, 126
-comments by Stoppard about, 1976.B65-66, 74, 95; 1977.B25, 82
-news items about, 1976.B4, 6, 9, 11, 13-14, 32-33, 104; 1977.B1-3, 5, 11-12, 62-63; 1980.B2
-productions, reviews of
--London, Inter-Action Trust, 1976.B15, 18, 24, 34, 38, 55, 59, 69, 76, 79, 81, 85, 105, 107; 1977.B19
--New York, Broadway, 1976.B29, 64, 80, 111; 1977.B2, 17-18, 34, 36, 53, 55-56, 59, 61, 67, 70, 76, 78-79, 86-87, 98-99, 102, 104-105, 113-114, 130-131, 134; 1978.B20
-text, reviews of, 1977.B7, 88; 1978.B66
Discussion Guide for "Rosencrantz and Guildenstern Are Dead," Incomplete.A3
Dispatch (St. Paul, Minn.), 1976.B58
Dissertations, Ph.D. See also Theses

225

Index

-partially devoted to Stoppard, 1972.B111; 1974.B122; 1975.B35, 59; 1976.B92; 1977.B109; 1978.B36, 63; 1979.B89; 1980.B13, 27
-wholly devoted to Stoppard, 1976.A3-4; 1978.A1; 1979.A2-3; 1980.A1-2
Dissidents. See also Human rights
-comments by others about, 1979.B34, 39-40; 1980.B30
-comments by Stoppard about, 1979.B47, 53
"Dissolution of Dominic Boot, The" (radio play). See also Engagement, The
-analyses and criticisms of, 1971.B20; 1972.B94; 1973.B21-22; 1974.B122, 135; 1976.A2-3; 1977.A1; Incomplete.A1
Divorce, 1972.B5
Documentary. See History
Dodsworth, Martin, 1977.B40
Dogg's Hamlet, Cahoot's Macbeth (stage play). See also Dogg's Our Pet; Dogg's Troupe Hamlet
-analyses and criticisms of, 1979.B87
-comments by others about, 1979.B21
-comments by Stoppard about, 1979.B47, 53
-news items about, 1979.B3, 91
-productions, reviews of
--London, BARC, 1979.B13, 25, 74, 81; 1980.B4
--New York, BARC, 1979.B15-16, 19, 28, 42, 49, 59, 76, 94, 96, 99, 109
--Washington, D.C., BARC, 1979.B69, 76, 118
Dogg's Our Pet (stage play). See also Dogg's Hamlet, Cahoot's Macbeth
-analyses and criticisms of, 1974.B80, 135; 1976.A1, 3; 1977.A1; 1979.B52
-comments by others about, 1971.B15
-comments by Stoppard about, 1974.B80; 1977.A1
-production, reviews of
--London, Inter-Action Trust, 1971.B4, 6, 9, 18; 1972.B79
Dogg's Troupe Hamlet (stage play). See also Dogg's Hamlet, Cahoot's Macbeth
-news item about, 1973.B8
-text, review of, 1979.B30
Domestic (-ity). See Familial
Dominitz, Sidney, 1974.B49
Donaghe, Michael Wayne, 1980.B13
Donald, Anabel, 1972.B47
Donaldson, Anne, 1972.B48
Donnelly, Tom, 1974.B50
Downer, Alan S., 1968.B46
Drake, Sylvia, 1974.B51; 1977.B41
Drama. See Theatre and society
Drama Survey, 1968.B49
Drama: The Quarterly Theatre Review, 1969.B20; 1972.B83; 1973.B66; 1974.B104; 1975.B76; 1976.B34-36; 1978.B30, 35; 1979.B32, 54-56, 104
Drew, Bernard, 1967.B51
Driver, Tom F., 1976.B41
Drummer (Philadelphia), Incomplete.B20
Duchene, Anne, 1967.B52
Duffy, Maureen, 1966.B18
Dunn, Peter, 1977.B42
Durband, Alan, 1969.B22
Durham, Weldon B., 1980.B14
Dürrenmatt, Friedrich, 1980.B34
Durso, Nicholas Anthony, 1978.B36

Earle, Anita, 1973.B36
Early life and career, Stoppard's. See also Short stories; Stoppard, Tom, biographical data about
-comments by others about, 1974.B1; 1977.B125; 1979.B106
-comments by Stoppard about, 1967.B48, 65, 88, 123; 1968.B13; 1972.B134; 1974.B1, 87, 90, 135; 1977.B25, 36, 97, 125; 1979.B106
Eastaugh, Kenneth, 1977.B43

Index

Eastman, Peggy, 1978.B37
Eccentric (-ity), 1968.B107; 1977.B96. See also Original
Echo (Liverpool, G.B.), Incomplete.B35
Eckert, Thor, Jr., 1974.B52; 1978.B38
Eclectic, 1967.B62, 92; 1979.B10; 1980.B27, 31. See also Pastiche; Unoriginal
Educational Theatre Journal, 1968.B75; 1975.B1, 71; 1977.B19, 26, 71, 107. See also Theatre Journal
Educational Theatre News, Incomplete.B29. See also Theatre News
Edwa., 1975.B38; 1977.B44
Edwards, Sydney, 1973.B37; 1974.B53
Egan, Robert, 1979.B36
Eichelbaum, Stanley, 1969.B23; 1972.B49; 1973.B38; 1974.B54-55; 1977.B45-47
Eichholz, Armin, Incomplete.B15
Elin, C. K., 1976.B42
Eliot, T. S., 1969.B54; 1974.B84; 1975.B59. See also "Love Song of J. Alfred Prufrock, The"
Ellison, Jane, 1976.B43
Ellmann, Richard, 1974.B56
Elsner, Judith Jean, 1974.A1
Elsom, John, 1974.B57; 1976.B44
Emmet, Alfred, 1974.B58; 1975.B39
Emotion (-al, -s). See also Feeling; Mood
-comments by others about, 1967.B52, 62, 92, 134; 1968.B97; 1973.B20, 53; 1974.B72, 125; 1975.B64. 80; 1977.B137; 1978.B61; 1979.B23, 26, 75, 117
-comments by Stoppard about, 1975.B43; 1977.B125; 1979.B106
Encounter, 1966.B39; 1967.B137; 1971.B10; 1972.B141; 1974.B182; 1975.B64; 1979.B101
End (-ing). See Resolution

Endgame, 1979.B115
Engagement, The (screenplay by Stoppard). See also "Dissolution of Dominic Boot, The"
-analyses and criticisms of, 1976.A3; 1977.A1; Incomplete.A1
-news item about, 1973.B40
-reviews of
--London, Memorial Enterprises (in cinemas), 1970.B29, 33-34, 36, 44-45, 50, 72
--NBC Television (on television), 1970.B70
Englische Dichter der Moderne, 1971.B5
English, 1977.B40; 1980.B37
English Comedy: Its Role and Nature from Chaucer to the Present Day, 1975.B98
English Studies, 1968.B104
Enquirer (Cincinnati, Ohio), 1976.B51
Enter a Free Man (stage play). See also Home and Dry; Preservation of George Riley, The; Walk on the Water, A
-analyses and criticisms of, 1968.B115; 1969.B54; 1971.B19-20; 1973.B21; 1974.B46, 135; 1975.B64, 103; 1976.A1-4; B49, 53, 97; 1977.A1, B73-74, 107; 1978.B29; 1979.A1-2; 1980.A2, B27
-comments by others about, 1972.B61; 1973.B44
--comments by Stoppard about, 1968.B13, 51, 55; 1971.B12; 1973.B45; 1974.B1, 90; Incomplete.B3
-news items about, 1967.B25; 1968.B3, 8, 14, 53; 1970.B4
-photograph of, 1968.B10
-productions, reviews of
--Chicago, Summit Theatre, 1975.B36, 127
--London, West End, 1968.B31, 37, 39, 59-61, 68, 71, 73, 80-81, 93, 97-99, 103, 105-106, 112, 120
--Minneapolis, Old Log Theatre,

Index

1976.B103
--New Orleans, Tulane Center Stage, 1974.B65
--New York, Theatre at St. Clement's, 1974.B29, 38, 72, 125, 149, 176, 181; 1975. B45, 74, 112; 1976.B87
--Olney, Md., Olney Theatre, 1970.B11-12, 18, 40, 53
--Philadelphia Drama Guild, 1976.B20, 30-31, 67, 75, 93, 101
--Portland, Oreg., Civic Theatre, 1974.B3
-text, reviews of, 1970.B2; 1973.B6
Enterprise (Los Angeles), 1977. B4
Epistemolog(-ical, -y), 1979.B26. See also Knowledge
Equity. See Actors Equity
Ericson, Raymond, 1979.B37
Ernstein, H. A., 1978.B39
Esslin, Martin, 1967.B53; 1968. B47; 1971.B10
Europe (-an). See Theatre and society
Evans, Gwynne Blakemore, 1976. B39
Evening Bulletin (Philadelphia), 1976.B93; 1977.B108
Evening Echo (Southend-on-Sea, G.B.), 1972.B42
Evening Gazette (Essex, G.B.), 1972.B55
Evening Journal (Lewiston, Maine), 1978.B44
Evening Mail (Slough, G.B.), 1972.B121
Evening News (London), 1966.B11; 1967.B28; 1968.B31-32, 53; 1972.B24; 1973.B17-18; 1974. B62; 1975.B14
Evening News (Newark, N.J.), 1967.B69-70; 1972.B65. See also Sunday News (Newark, N.J.)
Evening Post (Bristol), 1970.B17; 1972.B34, 58; 1974.B117; 1976.B27
Evening Standard (London), 1967.

B4, 115; 1968.B11, 99-100; 1972.B16, 117; 1973.B35, 37, 73-74; 1974.B53, 126, 140; 1975.B104; 1976.B43
Evening Star (Washington, D.C.), 1970.B11. See also Star (Washington, D.C.)
Evening Times (Pawtucket, R.I.), 1978.B77
Every Good Boy Deserves Favour (stage play)
-analyses and criticisms of, 1977.B73; 1979.A2-3, B34, 87
-comments by others about, 1974. B53; 1977.B60, 93; 1979.B7, 37
-comments by Stoppard about, 1977.B82; 1978.B48, 72; 1979. B47
-news items about, 1976.B12; 1978.B3, 5, 18, 31
-phonograph record, review of, 1978.B64
-photograph of, 1977.B8
-productions, reviews of
--Ambler, Pa., Temple University Music Festival, 1978.B46, 85. See also reviews of Washington, D.C., production, below
--London, John Player Centenary Festival, 1977.B15[?], 71, 83, 96, 112, 115, 129
--London, John Player Centenary Festival revival, 1978.B24, 45, 53, 60, 76, 84, 88
--New York, Metropolitan Opera, 1979.B14, 18, 41, 48, 58, 65, 71, 75, 78, 86, 95, 98, 108, 117
--Washington, D.C., Temple University Music Festival tour, 1978.B18, 26; 1979.B116. See also reviews of Ambler, Pa., production, above
-text, reviews of, 1978.B7, 10
Everyman, 1967.B59; 1968.B54
Evil, 1968.B48. See also Religion
Evslin, Bernard, 1968.B48
Examiner (San Francisco), 1969. B23; 1970.B41; 1972.B49; 1973.B38; 1974.B54-55; 1975.

Index

B49; 1977.B46-47. See also
Sunday Examiner (San Francisco)
Existential (-ism, -ist). See
  also Absurd; Beckett, Samuel;
  Ionesco, Eugene
-comments by others about, 1967.
  B94; 1969.B13; 1971.B13;
  1973.B57, 68; 1975.B51;
  1976.B91, 94, 109; 1978.B20
-comments by Stoppard about,
  1972.B6; 1975.B43
Experiment (-al), 1969.B17; 1973.
  B62
Explicator, 1976.B57
Exponent (Berea, Ohio), 1974.
  B157

F., R., 1969.B24
Faber, Charles, Incomplete.B16
Fairbanks, Harold, 1977.B48
Famil(-ial, -y). See also
  Children; Marriage
-comments by others about, 1966.
  B26; 1970.B40; 1975.B13;
  1979.B2, 39-40
-comments by Miriam Stoppard
  about, 1980.B28
-comments by Tom Stoppard about,
  1977.B36, 125; 1979.B106
Fanning, Garth, 1969.B25
Fantas(-tic, -y). See also Mood;
  Tone
-comments by others about, 1968.
  B113; 1974.B47, 129; 1978.
  B32
-comments by Stoppard about,
  1974.B54
Faraone, Cheryl F., 1980.A1
Farber, Stephen, 1976.B45
Farce. See also Comedy
-comments by others about, 1967.
  B99; 1968.B87; 1969.B29;
  1972.B30, 104; 1974.B45;
  1975.B107; 1976.A2, B49, 56,
  83; 1977.B105, 107; 1978.B20,
  34, 58, 63, 67; 1980.B24
-comments by Stoppard about,
  1967.B122; 1974.B144
Farce (The Critical Idiom Series),
  1978.B34

Farish, Gillan, 1975.B40
Fassbinder, Rainer Werner (film
  director)
-as subject of comments by others,
  1978.B68, 78, 86
-interview with, 1977.B106
Fate, 1979.B29, 36. See also
  Freedom; Metaphysical
Feature articles. See Profiles
  and feature articles
Feeling (-s), 1969.B54; 1970.B12;
  1974.B175-176; 1976.B53, 83;
  1977.B91; 1979.B41; 1980.B8.
  See also Emotion; Mood
Fehse, Klaus-Dieter, 1975.B126
Feingold, Michael, 1975.B41
Fell, John L., 1979.B38
Ferber, Christian, Incomplete.B17
Fernandes, Frances C., Incomplete.
  B18
Ferris, Paul, 1967.B54; 1972.B50
Fiddick, Peter, 1972.B51
Fields of Play in Modern Drama,
  1977.B135
Fifteen Minute Dogg's Troupe
  Hamlet, The. See Dogg's
  Troupe Hamlet
(15 Minute) Hamlet, The. See
  Dogg's Troupe Hamlet
Filichia, Peter, 1970.B23
Film. See also Media
-scripts. See Adapt; titles of
  individual works (listed in
  Stoppard, Tom, works by)
-comments by Stoppard about,
  1972.B125, 134; 1979.B53;
  1980.B11
Film and Broadcasting Review,
  1979.B4
Film Comment, 1978.B56, 74
Filmcritica, 1975.B24a
Film Information, 1975.B101
Film Quarterly, 1979.B38
Films and Filming, 1975.B54;
  1979.B46
Films in Review, 1976.B25; 1979.
  B113
Financial data. See Stoppard,
  Tom, financial data about;
  titles of individual works
  (listed in Stoppard, Tom,

Index

works by)
Financial Times (London), 1967.
B141; 1968.B120-121; 1970.
B45; 1972.B100, 145; 1973.
B33, 61, 86; 1974.B44; 1977.
B138; Incomplete.B1
Fisher, John, 1977.B49
Flaherty, Pat, 1969.B26
Fleming, Eve, 1977.B50
Fletcher, Richard D., 1974.B59
Flier (Columbia, Md.), 1978.B39
Flourish, 1974.B144
Flowering Cherry
-comments by Stoppard about, 1974.B1
Floyd, David, 1979.B39-40
Focus on Film, 1975.B47
Foot, David, 1974.B60; 1976.B46
Football (soccer), 1977.B32
Foote, Timothy, 1974.B61, 111; 1975.B97
Foreign languages, items in. See French; German; Italian; Japanese; Spanish
Form (-al). See also Convention; Structure; Style
-comments by others about, 1968. B7; 1974.B75, 96; 1975.B97; 1976.A4, B60; 1977.B74, 129; 1979.B10; 1980.A1, B27
-comments by Stoppard about, 1972.B57; 1974.B80; 1976.B95; 1977.A1
Fornara, Peter, 1975.B42
Forscey, Suzon, Incomplete.B19
Forty-Niner (Long Beach, Calif.), 1977.B122
Frame, Colin, 1974.B62
France. See Theatre and society, French
France, Peter, 1974.B63; 1976. B78
Frankel, Haskel, 1972.B52
Freedom. See also Fate; Human rights; Journalism
-comments by others about, 1967. B131; 1968.B84; 1980.B4
-comments by Stoppard about, 1978.B48
Free Press (Los Angeles), Incomplete.B16

Free Press (Mankato, Minn.), 1976.B48
Free Press (Winnipeg, Canada), 1973.B34
Free will. See Freedom
French, items in, 1970.B37; 1972. B103; 1973.B60; 1975.B93; 1978.B79; Incomplete.B13
Fresh Fruit (Brown University, Providence, R.I.), 1975.B37
Frick, N. Alice, 1966.B19
Friehling, Kenneth, Incomplete.A2
Frisch, Max, 1973.B62
From Büchner to Beckett: Dramatic Theory and the Modes of Tragic Drama, 1978.B70
From Writer to Reader: Studies in Editorial Method, 1978.B41
Frontier, 1972.B126
Fry, Christopher, 1967.B95
Fugard, Athol
-comments by Stoppard about, 1980.B24
Fuller, Richard, Incomplete.B20
Fun (-ny), 1966.B25; 1967.B76, 84, 94-95; 1968.B33, 45; 1969.B30; 1970.B13, 66; 1972. B36, 135; 1973.B68; 1974.B24; 1975.B24, 42, 61, 88; 1976. B81; 1977.B7, 9, 70, 87, 131; 1978.B51, 64; 1979.B14, 25, 33, 42, 69, 75-76, 96, 108-109, 118; 1980.B6; Incomplete. B45. See also Comedy; Humor; Joke; Laughter; Mood
Fun Bus. See also Inter-Action Trust
-comments by others about. 1973. B8
-comments by Stoppard about, 1973.B75
Funke, Lewis, 1971.B11; 1975.B43
Funke, Phyllis, 1967.B55
Funkkolleg Literatur, Incomplete. B30
Furche (Vienna), 1973.B42

Gabbard, Lucina P., 1977.B51
Gagnard, Frank, 1974.B64-65; Incomplete.B21
Galati, Frank, 1975.B44
Gale, John, 1967.B56

230

Index

Galileo
-comments by Stoppard about, 1972.B99; 1973.B37
Galloway, Myron, 1973.B39
Gamblers, The (stage play)
-analyses and criticisms of, 1976.A3; 1977.A1
-comments by others about, 1976.B21
-comments by Stoppard about, 1974.B90
Game (-s), 1972.B28; 1975.B76; 1978.B86; 1979.A2-3; 1980.B14, 34. See also Cricket; Football
Game theory. See Game
Gardner, C. O., 1970.B24
Gardner, John, 1978.B40
Garelik, Glenn, 1976.B47
Garwood, Judith, 1977.B52
Gaskell, Philip, 1978.B41
Gaver, Jack, 1967.B57-58
Gay Community News (Boston), 1977.B127
Gazette (Berkeley, Calif.), 1970.B27; 1972.B105
Gazette (Montreal, Canada), 1973.B49
Genet, Jean, 1977.B135
Genres. See Comedy; Grotesque; Melodrama; Tragedy
German, items in, 1964.B2; 1967.B20, 33, 59, 77, 79, 89, 101, 111; 1969.B50; 1970.B15, 39; 1971.B5, 7, 14; 1973.B10-12, 25-26, 42-43, 62, 69, 83; 1975.B126; 1976.B3, 16; 1978.B78a; Incomplete.B2, 7-8, 15, 17, 22, 24, 26, 28, 30-31, 44, 48, 53
Germany. See Theatre and society, German; Berlin; Munich
Gerstinger, Heinz, 1967.B59
Getlein, Frank, 1974.B66
Gianakaris, C. J., 1968.B49
Gibson, Alan (director)
-interview with, 1974.B122
Gifford, Denis, 1973.B40
Gilbert, W. S., 1979.B56
Gill, Brendan, 1974.B67; 1975.B45-46, 97; 1976.B87;
1977.B53; 1978.B20; 1979.B41-43
Gillett, John, 1975.B47
Gilliatt, Penelope, 1979.B44
Girouard, Robert L., 1976.B48
Gitzen, Julian, 1976.B49
Glacklin, William C., 1973.B41; 1974.B68; 1977.B54
Glasgow Herald, 1972.B48
Globe (Boston), 1974.B97
Globe-Democrat (St. Louis, Mo.), 1975.B50
Glover, William, 1967.B60-61; 1970.B25; 1974.B10, 69-70; 1975.B48-49; 1976.B50-52; 1977.B55
God, 1980.B26
Goddard, Bob, 1975.B50
Goetsch, Paul, Incomplete.B22
Gold, Margaret, 1978.B42
Goldman, William, 1969.B27
Goldsmith, Len, Incomplete.B23
Goldstein, Leonard, 1975.B51
Goldstein, Ruth M., Incomplete.A3
Goon Show, 1973.B59
Gordon, David J., 1968.B50
Gordon, Giles, 1968.B51; 1971.B12
Gottfried, Martin, 1967.B62, 92; 1972.B53, 89; 1974.B71-72, 111; 1975.B52-53, 81; 1976.B53; 1977.B56, 87
Gow, Gordon, 1967.B63; 1974.B73; 1975.B54
Graham, Sidney, 1972.B54
Grandchamp, Kathy, 1978.B43
Grant, Louis T., 1968.B52
Grant, Steve, 1979.B45
Grape, Nancy, 1978.B44
Great Britain. See Theatre and society, British
Greater New York Radio Network, 1972.B115
Great Writers of the English Language: Dramatists, 1979.B112
Green, James, 1968.B53
Green, Valerie, 1972.B55
Greene, Graham. See also Human Factor, The
-as subject of comments by others,

Index

1980.B1, 8, 23, 27a, 33, 35
-as subject of comments by Stoppard, 1980.B11
-interview with, 1980.B25
Greiner, Patricia Ann, 1980.A2
Grice, Elizabeth, 1977.B57
Grief. See Anguish
Grieg, Simon, 1979.B46
Griffin, William, 1974.B74
Grimme, Karl Maria, 1973.B42
Gross, Leonard, 1977.B58
Grosvenor-Myer, M., 1971.B13
Grotesque, 1970.B37; 1973.B69; 1978.B78a
Gruber, Klaus, Incomplete.B24
Guardian (London), 1966.B15, 30; 1967.B52, 65, 74, 107-108; 1968.B62-63, 92; 1969.B8a; 1970.B22, 34; 1971.B6; 13; 1972.B11, 30, 46, 51; 1973.B23-24, 85; 1974.B35, 60, 81; 1975.B22; 1976.B40, 46; 1979.B24-25, 53
Guernsey, Otis L., Jr., 1968.B54; 1972.B56; 1974.B75; 1976.B54
Guicharnaud, Jacques, 1972.B3
Guildenstern and Rosencrantz (stage play). See also Questors Theatre; Rosencrantz & Guildenstern Are Dead
-comments by others about, 1974.B58; 1975.B39
-news item about, 1964.B3
-production, review of
--Berlin, 1964.B3
Gunner, Marjorie, 1974.B76; 1977.B59
Gussow, Mel, 1972.B57; 1974.B77; 1975.B55; 1976.B55; 1977.B60; 1978.B45; 1979.B47-49, 75-76; 1980.B15
Guthke, Karl S., 1971.B14; 1976.B56

H., D., 1972.B58
Hahnl, Hanz Heinz, 1973.B43
Halton, Kathleen, 1967.B64
Hamlet. See also Rosencrantz & Guildenstern Are Dead; Shakespeare, William

-comments by others about, 1967.B38, 94; 1968.B48; 1969.B11, 13, 37; 1970.B39; 1972.B21, 103, 142; 1973.B20, 57, 68; 1974.B113; 1975.B71, 126; 1976.B91; 1977.B39, 135; 1978.B70, 78a; 1979.B93; 1980.B12, 31
-comments by Stoppard about, 1967.B122; 1973.B75
Hamlin, Milton, 1970.B26
Handbook of Contemporary Drama, A, 1972.B3
Handke, Peter, 1973.B69; Incomplete.B53
Hare, David
-comments by others about, 1980.B29
-comments by Stoppard about, 1980.B24
Harland, Susan Sponzillie, 1979.A2
Harper, Keith, 1967.B65
Harris, Leonard, 1972.B59, 89; 1974.B78, 111
Harris, Sydney J., 1969.B28
Harris, Wendell V., 1976.B57
Hart, Cecilia (actress)
-interviews with, 1977.B20, 126
Harvey, John H., 1976.B58
Harvey, S., 1978.B46
Hasenclever, Walter, 1964.B3
Hastings, Ronald, 1968.B55
Hatch, Robert, 1979.B50; 1980.B16
Havel, Václav
-comments by others about, 1977.B125; 1979.B106; 1980.B30
-comments by Stoppard about, 1977.B125; 1978.B72; 1979.B106
Hawk, 1972.B60
Hayes, Ann, Incomplete.B25
Hayman, Ronald, 1967.B66; 1972.B61; 1973.B44; 1974.B79-80; 1977.A1; 1979.B51-52; 1980.B17
Hearn, Lawrence, 1970.B27
Hebert, Hugh, 1974.B81; 1979.B53
Hedgepeth, William, 1967.B67
Heidenheim (W. Germany) Zeitung, Incomplete.B24

Index

Hemingway, Ernest
-comments by Stoppard about, 1967.B5
Hepple, Peter, 1974.B82
Herald (Hyde Park, Ill.), Incomplete.B38
Herald (Melbourne, Australia), 1973.B59
Herald (Miami, Fla.), 1969.B52
Herald American (Boston), 1967. B99
Herald Examiner (Los Angeles), 1969.B10; Incomplete.B19, 33
Heritage and Southwest Jewish Press (Los Angeles), 1977. B124
Heroes. See also Character
-comments by others about, 1968. B48; 1971.B5; 1978.B70, 89
-comments by Stoppard about, 1967.B16; 1978.B72
Hewes, Henry, 1967.B68; 1968. B56; 1969.B29; 1970.B28; 1972.B62-63; 1975.B56
Hidalgo, Pilar, 1978.B47
High Fidelity and Musical America, 1978.B85
Highwater, Jamake, 1976.B59
Hildebrandt, Dieter, Incomplete. B26
Hill, Frances, 1973.B45
Hillgate, Jason, 1972.B64; 1974.B83
Hillsborough (Calif.) Boutique, 1969.B47; 1972.B69
Hinchliffe, Arnold, 1969.B30; 1974.B84
Hinxman, Margaret, 1970.B29
Hipp, Edward Sothern, 1967.B69-70; 1972.B65
History, 1974.B35, 47, 129, 166; 1975.B107; 1976.B62; 1979. B35
Hoagland, Joan M., 1968.B57
Hobe, 1967.B71; 1974.B85; 1977. B61
Hobson, Harold, 1966.B20-23; 1967.B72-73; 1968.B58; 1969. B31-32; 1971.B15; 1972.B66-67; 1973.B46-47; 1974.B86; 1975.B57; 1979.B54-55

Hodgson, Godfrey, 1980.B17a
Hogan, William, 1974.B87-88
Holden, Anthony, 1977.B62-64
Holland, Jack, 1974.B89; 1975. B58; 1977.B65
Holland, Mary, 1966.B24; 1968. B59-61
Holliday, Jon, 1977.B66
Hollywood (Calif.) Reporter, Incomplete.B37, 52
Holmstrom, John, 1966.B25
Homan, Richard Lawrence, 1975. B59
Home and Dry, 1968.B55. See also Enter a Free Man
Homonyms, 1979.B35. See also Puns
Homosexuality, 1968.B48, 67; 1977.B98; 1978.B20
Honors. See Awards and honors
Honors List, 1977.B13
Hope-Wallace, Philip, 1967.B74; 1968.B62-63
Hordern, Michael (actor)
-as subject of comments by others, 1968.B31; 1973.B3
-as subject of comments by Stoppard, 1974.B105
-interviews with, 1972.B61; 1973. B44
Horizon, 1978.B17; 1979.B87
House of Bernarda Alba, The (stage play adapted by Stoppard)
-comments by Stoppard about, 1973.B52
-productions, reviews of
--London, Greenwich Theatre Company, 1973.B15, 17, 23, 28, 46, 55, 58, 61, 73, 84
--San Francisco, ACT, 1973.B36, 38, 41; 1974.B152
Houston, Penelope, 1975.B60
Huckerby, Martin, 1978.B48
Huddish, Grant R., 1972.B68
Hudson, Roger, 1974.B90
Hudson-Page, Marian, 1972.B69
Hudson Review, 1967.B117; 1968. B90; 1976.B97; 1977.B114
Hughes, Catharine, 1972.B70-71; 1974.B91-92; 1975.B61;

Index

1977.B67; 1980.B18
Hughes, Pennethorne, 1965.B3
Human (-e, -ism, -ity), 1968.
  B34, 49; 1970.B11; 1972.
  B126; 1975.B123; 1976.A2,
  B75, 103; 1977.B120; 1978.
  B40, 67, 84; 1980.B24. See
  also Detached; Mood
Human Factor, The (film with
  screenplay by Stoppard).
  See also Greene, Graham,
  interview with
-reviews, 1980.B1, 3, 5, 8-10,
  16, 20, 22-23, 27a, 33, 35-
  36, 38
Human rights. See also Dissi-
  dents; Freedom
-comments by others about, 1977.
  B38, 74, 125; 1979.B2, 28,
  39-40, 106
-comments by Stoppard about,
  1978.B6
Humm, 1968.B64
Humor, 1967.B79, 101; 1968.B33;
  1973.B21, 42-43, 68; 1974.
  B43, 125; 1975.B33, 126;
  1976.A2; 1977.B44. See also
  Comedy; Fun; Joke; Laughter
Hunter, G. K., 1979.B61, 120
Hurren, Kenneth, 1972.B72; 1974.
  B93; 1975.B97; 1979.B56
Hurt, John (actor)
-interview with, 1974.B73
Hurwitt, Robert, 1979.B57
Hutton, Geoffrey, 1973.B48
Hybrid. See Eclectic
Hyman, Jackie, Incomplete.B27

Ideas. See also Concept; Intentions; Originality;
  Philosophy; Thought
-comments by others about, 1966.
  B39; 1967.B116, 137; 1968.
  B112; 1971.B20; 1972.B48,
  51; 1974.B60, 65, 104, 110,
  118; 1975.B97, 123; 1976.B53,
  87, 96; 1977.A1, B34; 1978.
  B40, 76; 1980.B13; Incomplete.
  B44
-comments by Stoppard about,
  1974.B144; 1976.B50

Ideolog(-ical, -y). See also
  Ideas; Relativism
-comments by others about, 1979.
  B61, 112, 114
-comments by Stoppard about,
  1979.B47
"If You're Glad I'll Be Frank"
  (radio play)
-analyses and criticisms of,
  1971.B17, 20; 1972.B94;
  1973.B21; 1974.B122, 135;
  1975.B64; 1976.A2-4, B83;
  1977.A1; 1979.A1-2, B10, 52;
  1980.A2
-comments by others about, 1967.
  B52
-comments by Stoppard about,
  1975.B43
-news item about, 1969.B4
-productions, reviews of
--Edinburgh, Oxford Theatre
  Group, 1969.B8a, 24, 31-32,
  49
--London, BBC Radio, 1966.B1, 38
--London, Young Vic, 1976.B26,
  40, 43, 68, 90
-text, reviews of, 1969.B5, 20
Ignorance. See Knowledge
Igoe, W. J., 1980.B19
Illusion, 1968.B49, 113-115;
  1969.B33; 1971.B19; 1973.B62;
  1975.B117; 1976.B19, 110;
  1977.B84, 109. See also
  Real; Unreal
Illustrated London News, 1966.
  B34, 36; 1967.B126; 1968.
  B105, 107; 1972.B131; 1973.
  B82; 1974.B163
Illustrierte Kronenzeitung
  (Vienna), 1967.B89, 101
Imitat(-e, -ion), 1967.B76; 1977.
  B34. See also Original; Un-
  original
Importance. See Significance
Importance of Being Earnest, The,
  1975.B103. See also Wilde,
  Oscar
Independent (Anaheim, Calif.),
  Incomplete.B50
Independent (Livermore, Calif.),
  1970.B52

Index

Independent Journal (San Rafael, Calif.), 1969.B7; 1970.B71; 1972.B143; 1974.B136
Independent Press-Telegram (Long Beach, Calif.), 1975.B99
Independent Television (London), 1976.B77
Influences on Stoppard
-comments by others about, 1967. B48; 1972.B65; 1974.B65; 1975.B39; 1977.A1, B123; 1978.B42
-comments by Stoppard about, 1968.B51; 1971.B12; 1972.B6; 1973.B45; 1974.B1; 1975.B43, 82
"In Parenthesis: 'Is "Is" Is?'" (radio discussion)
-news item about, 1972.B9
-review of, 1972.B132
Inquirer (Philadelphia), 1967. B103; 1976.B30-31; 1977.B35; 1978.B31
Inquiry Magazine, 1978.B46
Insight IV: Analyses of Modern British and American Drama, 1968.B91
Intellect (-ual, -uality)
-comments by others about, 1966. B14, 20; 1967.B52, 68; 1968. B41; 1970.B61; 1972.B26-27, 104; 1973.B26; 1974.B33, 35, 40, 45, 111, 141, 177; 1975. B16, 70, 81, 97; 1976.B25, 46, 53, 96; 1977.B34, 105, 114, 120, 129, 137; 1978. B10, 20; 1979.B64, 77, 107, 119; Incomplete.B5, 27
-comments by Stoppard about, 1968.B89; 1973.B85; 1975. B43; 1977.B90
Intentions. See also Concept; Content; Ideas; Psychology
-comments by others about, 1967. B26, 77, 113; 1975.B35, 87; 1977.B134; 1978.B23, 67; 1979.B34; 1980.B7, 24
-comments by Stoppard about, 1972.B57; 1974.B80, 90; 1975.B124; 1977.A1, B25, 82; 1978.B41

Inter-Action Trust. See also BARC; Berman, Ed
-comments by others about, 1973. B8; 1977.B50; 1979.B21
-comments by Stoppard about, 1973.B75
International Herald Tribune (Paris), 1974.B166; 1975.B34; Incomplete.B54
Interviews. See also Actors; Designers; Directors; Producers; Radio interviews; Television interviews
-comments by Stoppard about, 1977.B25, 82
-with others
--Alexander-Willis, Hope, 1975. B114
--Bakewell, Michael, 1974.B122
--Bedford, Brian, 1974.B165
--Berman, Ed, 1976.B28; 1979.B21
--Brisson, Frederick, 1974.B139
--Byron, Joan, 1974.B185
--Chetwyn, Robert, 1968.B82
--Fassbinder, Rainer Werner, 1977.B106
--Gibson, Alan, 1974.B122
--Greene, Graham, 1980.B25
--Hart, Cecilia, 1977.B20, 126
--Hordern, Michael, 1972.B61; 1973.B44
--Hurt, John, 1974.B73
--Losey, Joseph, 1975.B32
--Meisel, Kurt, 1967.B89
--Murray, Brian, 1967.B22, 83, 114, 129
--Nunn, Trevor, 1977.B93
--Previn, André, 1974.B53; 1979.B37
--Rigg, Diana, 1972.B129
--Smith, Maggie, 1979.B72
--Stoppard, Miriam, 1977.B64, 85; 1980.B28
--Thaw, John, 1978.B57
--Tydeman, John, 1974.B122; 1976.A3
--Williamson, Nicol, 1967.B32
--Wood, John, 1967.B22, 83, 114, 129; 1975.B20, 55, 87, 111; 1977.B60, 75
--Wood, Peter, 1973.B83; 1974.B79,

Index

122; 1980.B17
-with Stoppard, 1965.B2; 1966.
  B28; 1967.B1, 4-5, 16, 35,
  48, 50, 56, 61, 63-65, 67,
  88, 91, 122-123; 1968.B13,
  35, 51, 55, 76; 1970.B3, 62,
  64; 1971.B12; 1972.B2, 6,
  57, 94, 96, 99, 125, 134;
  1973.B37, 45, 52, 75, 85;
  1974.B15, 22-23, 50, 54, 63,
  77, 80, 87, 90, 95, 105,
  109, 126, 144, 154, 160-161;
  1975.B43, 55, 82, 108, 124;
  1976.B50-52, 65-66, 74, 77-
  78, 95, 102; 1977.A1, B23,
  25, 41, 43, 46, 73, 82, 90,
  111, 121, 125, 132; 1978.
  B48, 72; 1979.B22, 47, 53;
  1980.B11, 17; Incomplete.B3,
  36, 46
Invention, 1966.B3, 8, 29, 41;
  1967.B117, 126, 137; 1968.
  B41, 68, 85, 95, 112; 1972.
  B92, 119; 1973.B59; 1974.
  B80, 102, 132; 1975.B38, 96;
  1976.B24, 96; 1977.B59, 66-
  67, 76, 107; 1978.B26; 1979.
  B76, 109; 1980.B1
Ionesco, Eugene, 1978.B28
Ironside, Virginia, 1968.B65
Irony, 1967.B77, 110, 120; 1969.
  B33; 1973.B62; 1974.B60, 93;
  1975.B97, 117; 1976.A2;
  1978.B10, 14, 24, 68; 1979.
  B75, 78. See also Parody;
  Satire
"Is 'Is' Is?" See "In Paren-
  thesis: 'Is "Is" Is?'"
Italian, item in, 1975.B24a
ITV. See Independent Television
  (London)
Itzen, Catherine, 1974.B90

Jack, Ian, 1978.B49
Jack, Tom, 1972.B73
Jackson, Martin A., 1980.B20
Jacobi, Johannes, Incomplete.B26
Jahrbuch der Deutschen
  Shakespeare-Gesellschaft
  West, 1970.B7
James, Clive, 1975.B62-64

James Joyce Quarterly, 1975.B102
Janowitz, Katherine, 1979.B58
Janusonis, Michael, 1974.B94
Japanese, items in, 1971.B19;
  1975.B118
Jensen, Henning, 1977.B68
Jersey Journal (Jersey City, N.J.),
  1967.B31
Jewish Chronicle (London), 1972.
  B97
Jewish Voice (Southend-on-Sea,
  G.B.), 1972.B33
Joel, Yale, 1968.B66
Johnson, Jim, 1977.B69
Johnson, Paul, 1978.B49
Johnson, Samuel, 1974.B118
Johnson, Wayne, 1970.B30
Johnston, Callum, 1972.B74
Johnston, Laurie, 1975.B65
Jok(-es, -ing). See also Comedy;
  Fun; Humor; Laughter
-comments by others about, 1966.
  B3; 1967.B38; 1968.B84; 1970.
  B39; 1972.B39, 51, 126; 1974.
  B24; 1975.B13, 76, 85; 1976.
  B82, 109; 1978.B14, 19-20,
  59; 1979.B64, 98
-comments by Stoppard about,
  1967.B16; 1974.B1; 1976.B77;
  1977.B25
Jones, D. A. N., 1966.B26; 1967.
  B75-76
Jones, Terry, 1980.B29
Journal (Louisville, Ky.), Incom-
  plete.B12
Journal (Milwaukee), 1976.B52
Journal (Providence, R.I.), 1974.
  B153
Journal-Bulletin Weekend (Provi-
  dence, R.I.), 1974.B94, 148
Journalism
-comments by others about, 1978.
  B49, 82; 1979.B22, 29, 100;
  1980.B17a
-comments by Stoppard about,
  1967.B48, 65; 1968.B13; 1972.
  B57; 1974.B1, 50, 54; 1977.
  B25
Journalists, The, 1980.B17a
Journal of Beckett Studies, 1979.
  B115

236

Index

Joyce, James
-comments by others about, 1974.
  B35, 56, 104; 1975.B88, 98;
  1976.B62, 87; 1977.B57, 125;
  1978.B42; 1979.B84, 106,
  114
-comments by Stoppard about,
  1975.B124; 1977.B132
Jumpers (stage play). See also
  "Another Moon Called Earth";
  Moon (satellite)
-analyses and criticisms of,
  1972.B20, 94; 1973.B21-22,
  65; 1974.B18, 43, 46, 75,
  80, 102, 122, 135; 1975.B21,
  35, 40, 44, 64, 79, 98, 103;
  1976.A1-4, B16, 49, 53, 89,
  97; 1977.A1, B51, 68, 73-74,
  94, 107, 125; 1978.B28, 67;
  1979.A1-3, B10, 26, 30, 35,
  52, 88, 106, 112, 120; 1980.
  A1-2, B13-14, 24, 26-27, 34,
  37
-comments by others about, 1972.
  B61, 129, 136; 1973.B44, 53,
  65, 83; 1974.B165; 1975.
  B16, 70, 81, 114; 1977.B115
-comments by Stoppard about,
  1970.B3; 1972.B2, 41, 57,
  99, 109, 125; 1973.B45;
  1974.B1, 22-23, 50, 54, 80,
  90, 144, 161; 1976.B65-66;
  1977.A1, B36, 73, 125
-news items about, 1972.B17;
  1973.B2-4, 9, 71; 1974.B4-
  6, 8, 10-13, 16, 39, 108,
  145; 1976.B3, 6
-productions, reviews of
--Bristol Old Vic, 1974.B2, 37,
  60, 117, 131
--Costa Mesa, Calif., South
  Coast Repertory, 1975.B38,
  58, 99, 110, 113, 115; In-
  complete.B5
--Evanston, Ill., Evanston Theatre Company, Incomplete.B6
--Leicester, G.B., Phoenix Theatre, 1973.B1
--London, National Theatre,
  1972.B20, 23-24, 26, 30,
  33, 38, 42-43, 47-48, 55,
  58, 60, 62, 64, 66, 70, 72,
  74, 76-77, 80, 82-83, 85, 87-
  88, 90-91, 95, 97-98, 102,
  104, 107, 109, 117, 121, 126,
  128, 130-131, 135, 140-141,
  145; 1973.B2-3, 5, 14, 51;
  1975.B83, 117; Incomplete.B35
--London, National Theatre revival, 1973.B19, 30, 65
--London, National Theatre second
  revival, 1976.B23, 106
--Melbourne, Australia, Theatre
  Company, 1973.B27, 48, 59, 63
--Minneapolis, Macalester College,
  1977.B33
--New York, Broadway, 1974.B10-
  11, 25-27, 31-32, 40-42, 59,
  61, 64, 66-67, 69-71, 74, 76,
  78, 85, 91-92, 95-99, 103,
  111, 114, 119, 123, 127, 132-
  134, 137, 141-142, 167, 170-
  174, 177-179, 183-184, 186;
  1975.B97, 117; 1976.B60
--Nottingham, G.B., Playhouse,
  1978.B25
--Providence, R.I., Trinity
  Square Repertory Company,
  1974.B21, 52, 94, 148, 153;
  1975.B37
--San Francisco, ACT, 1974.B36,
  55, 68, 88, 136, 151, 155;
  1975.B1, 26
--Vienna, Akademietheater, 1973.
  B11, 25-26, 42-43, 69; In-
  complete.B8, 24
-text, reviews of, 1972.B18;
  1974.B19
Jürg, Dr., 1967.B77
Juxtapos(-e, -ition). See also
  Surreal
-comments by others about, 1967.
  B110, 132; 1968.B48; 1969.
  B33, 37; 1970.B39; 1972.B126;
  1975.B71, 117; 1977.A1; 1978.
  B10, 74; 1980.B14
-comments by Stoppard about,
  1972.B96; 1974.B54

KABC-TV, 1977.B100
Kael, Pauline, 1975.B66
Kafka, Franz, 1968.B87

Index

Kahn, Coppélia, 1978.B49a
Kahn, Robert I., 1968.B67
Kalem, T. E., 1967.B78; 1972.
  B75-76, 89; 1974.B95; 1975.
  B67, 81, 97; 1977.B70, 87;
  1978.B50; 1979.B59-60, 76
Kalson, Albert E., 1977.B71
Kamhi, Ben, 1977.B72
Kant, Immanuel, 1980.B14
Kapica, Jack, 1973.B49
Kauer, Edmund, 1967.B79
Kauffmann, Stanley, 1974.B96;
  1975.B68, 97; 1976.B60;
  1980.B21-22
Kaufman, Steve, 1976.B61
Kavanagh, Julie, 1975.B69
Kelly, Kelvin, 1974.B97
Kemp, Arnold, 1972.B77
Kennebec (Maine) Journal, 1978.
  B15
Kennedy, Andrew K., 1969.B33;
  1979.B61
Kerensky, Oleg, 1977.B73-74
Kernis, Jay, 1977.B75
Kerr, Walter, 1967.B80, 93;
  1969.B34; 1972.B78; 1974.
  B98-99; 1975.B70; 1976.B62;
  1977.B76; 1979.B62, 77
Keyssar-Franke, Helene, 1975.
  B71
KFWB-Radio, 1977.B128
Killinger, John, 1971.B16
King, Francis, 1979.B63-64
Kingston, Jeremy, 1966.B27;
  1967.B81; 1968.B68-69; 1972.
  B79-80; 1973.B50; 1974.B100;
  1975.B72
Kirkus Service, 1968.B5
Kirkwood, Jerriann, 1977.B77
Kissell, Howard, 1975.B73, 81;
  1977.B78, 87; 1979.B65-66,
  77
Klein, Alvin, 1979.B67
Kleine Volksblatt (Vienna),
  1967.B77
Kleine Volksstimme (Vienna),
  1967.B79
KMPC-Radio, 1977.B14
KNBC-TV, 1977.B16
Knickerbocker, Paine, 1969.B35;
  1970.B31; 1972.B81

Knight, John, 1966.B28
Knowledge, 1974.B103, 111; 1976.
  B89; 1980.B31; Incomplete.
  B23-24. See also Epistem-
  ology
Knox, Collie, 1967.B82; 1972.B82
Kohout, Pavel, 1980.B30
Korf, Lee, Incomplete.B29
Kott, Jan, 1976.B91
Kraft, Daphne, 1967.B83
Kretzmer, Herbert, 1967.B84;
  1968.B70; 1974.B101
Kriegsman, Alan M., 1974.B102
Kroll, Jack, 1967.B85; 1974.B103,
  111; 1975.B74-75, 81; 1976.
  B63-64, 87; 1977.B87; 1978.
  B51; 1979.B68-70, 76-77
KTYD-Radio, 1977.B103
Kuehl, Brooks, 1969.B36
Kunze, Michael, Incomplete.B30
Kurier (Vienna), 1967.B33; 1973.
  B25
KWHY-TV, 1977.B52
KYW-Radio, 1976.B75

Lack, Alastair, 1976.B65-66
Lady, 1967.B127; 1968.B106, 108;
  1972.B130; 1973.B81; 1974.
  B162
Lahr, John, 1978.B52
La ira la palabria: teatro
  ingles actual, 1978.B47
Lambert, J. W., 1966.B29; 1968.
  B71; 1972.B83; 1974.B104;
  1975.B76, 96; 1976.B87
Landmann, David, 1970.B32
Language. See also Dialogue;
  Homonyms; Poetic; Puns
-comments by others about, 1967.
  B42-43, 80, 93, 111, 116-117,
  120, 137-138; 1968.B9, 41,
  43, 115; 1969.B1, 13, 20, 34;
  1970.B37; 1971.B1; 1972.B18,
  28, 58, 61, 103; 1973.B21,
  28, 41, 44, 68-69, 77; 1974.
  B42, 60, 86, 96, 102, 118,
  142-143, 152, 170; 1975.B6,
  40, 52, 62, 81, 94, 97, 117,
  125; 1976.A2, B41, 60, 85,
  87, 103, 112; 1977.A1, B9, 14,
  44, 114; 1978.B10, 14, 16, 20,

53, 82; 1979.B27, 30, 36,
43, 60, 76-77, 83-84, 92,
99, 109; 1980.B4, 7, 21;
Incomplete.B44, 55
-comments by Stoppard about,
1977.B73; 1978.B6; 1979.B47
La Opinion (Los Angeles), 1977.
B28
Lape, Bob, 1977.B79, 87
La Presse (Montreal, Canada),
Incomplete.B13
Larner, Gerald, 1966.B30
Lask, Thomas, 1968.B72
"L'assassin menacé," 1976.B57.
See also Magritte, René
Last, Richard, 1977.B80
Lauder, Robert E., 1980.B23
Laugh (-ing, -ter), 1967.B141;
1968.B49, 84; 1974.B62; 1976.
B41; 1980.B26. See also
Comedy; Fun; Humor; Joke;
Mood
Law, J. P., 1973.B51
Lawrence, Ann, 1967.B86
Lawrence, Linda, 1975.B77
Lawson, Carol, 1977.B81; 1979.B71
Le Carré, John, 1968.B34; 1969.
B54; 1974.B84
Lee, Charles, 1976.B67
Lee, R. H., 1969.B37
Leech, Michael, 1973.B52; 1974.
B105
Lenin, Vladimir
-comments by others about, 1974.
B47, 49, 62, 90, 100, 104,
120, 162, 168, 175; 1975.B78,
88, 97; 1976.A2, B17, 62, 86-
87; 1978.B24, 42; 1979.B114
-comments by Stoppard about,
1975.B124
Leonard, John, 1975.B78; 1977.
B82
Leonard, Virginia E., 1975.B79
Leonard, William, 1969.B38-39
Les Gommes, 1980.B31
Les Langues Modernes, 1970.B37
"Let Misha Go," 1979.B39-40. See
also Dissidents
Letras de Deusto, Incomplete.B42
Levenson, Jill, 1971.B17
Levin, Bernard, 1976.B68; 1977.
B83; 1978.B53-54

Levitan, Alan, 1974.B106
Levy, Bernard S., 1980.B24
Lewin, David, 1980.B25
Lewis, Anthony, 1966.B31; 1974.
B107
Lewis, Flora, 1979.B72
Lewis, Peter, 1967.B87-88; 1968.
B73-74; 1972.B84
Lewson, Charles, 1973.B53-54;
1975.B80
Library Journal, 1967.B121; 1968.
B57; 1975.B24; 1977.B88
Library of Literary Criticism, A:
Modern British Literature,
1975.B117
Life, 1968.B66, 89
"Life, Times: Fragments" (short
story). See also Early life
and career; Short stories
-analyses and criticisms of,
1976.A3-4; 1977.A1; 1979.A1
-comments by Stoppard about,
1967.B5; 1968.B51; 1971.B12
Lincoln Cumberland Observer-News
Leader (Greenville, R.I.),
Incomplete.B45
Listener, 1965.B3; 1966.B37;
1967.B128; 1972.B29, 87;
1974.B57; 1976.B23
Literarisches Colloquium, 1964.
B3-4; 1973.B57; 1975.B39
Locher, Frances Carol, 1979.B73
Lockhart, Freda Bruce, 1970.B33
Logic (-al). See also Causality;
Paradox
-comments by others about, 1967.
B107; 1971.B20; 1972.B110;
1973.B21, 65, 77; 1975.B51,
97; 1976.A2
-comments by Stoppard about,
1973.B85; 1974.B1, 54; 1977.
B23, 73, 90, 121, 132
Logical Positivism, 1972.B20;
1973.B12, 14; 1976.B16; 1977.
B94; 1979.B30; 1980.B14
London Life, 1966.B10; 1967.B139;
Incomplete.B3
London Magazine, 1976.B89
Londré, Felicia Houston, 1980.
B26
Loney, Glenn, 1968.B75

Index

Long Island (N.Y.) Star Journal, 1967.B106
Look, 1967.B67
Lorca, Federico García, 1974. B152. See also House of Bernarda Alba, The
Lord Malquist & Mr Moon (novel)
-analyses and criticisms of, 1971.B17; 1974.B18, 80; 1975.B64; 1976.A1-4, B49; 1977.A1, B107; 1979.A1, B10, 52; 1980.B34
-comments by Stoppard about, 1967.B4, 64-65, 88, 123; 1968.B13; 1970.B3; 1973.B85
-reviews of, 1966.B8, 18, 41; 1968.B1, 5-6, 17, 20, 22, 28, 43, 50, 52, 57, 72, 77, 87, 90, 95-96, 101, 119; 1980.B6
Losey, Joseph (film director)
-interview with, 1975.B32
Lossman, Hans, Incomplete.B31
Louis, Patricia, 1968.B76
Love, Wayne L., Incomplete.B32
"Love Song of J. Alfred Prufrock, The"
-comments by Stoppard about, 1974.B80; 1977.A1. See also Eliot, T. S.
Loynd, Ray, Incomplete.B33
Loyolan (Los Angeles), Incomplete.B32
Lucas, John, 1976.B69
Ludlow, Colin, 1979.B74
Luft, Herbert G., 1977.B84
Lundegaard, Bob, 1978.B55
Lyons, Leonard, 1972.B85

M., A., 1967.B89
M., R., 1972.B86
Macbeth, 1973.B65; 1980.B37. See also Shakespeare, William
McCalls, 1976.B72
McCarten, John, 1967.B90
Maccoun, Wendy, 1969.B40
McCourt, James, 1978.B56
McCrindle, Joseph F., 1971.B12
McDonough, Jack, Incomplete.B34
McIntyre, M., 1976.B70

Mackenzie, Vicki, 1977.B85
Macleans, 1979.B83; 1980.B27a
McLellan, Diana, 1974.B108
MacLoughlin, Shaun, 1967.B91
McNay, Michael, 1970.B34
Maddocks, Melvin, 1968.B77
Magill, Frank N., 1969.B1; 1971. B1
Magritte, René. See also Surreal
-comments by others about, 1975. B51; 1976.B57
-comments by Stoppard about, 1972.B96
Mahar, Ted, 1970.B35
Mahon, Derek, 1972.B87; 1974.B109
Mail Tribune (Medford, Oreg.), 1970.B1
Make Children Happy, 1977.B12
Mallett, Richard, 1970.B36
Malone, Mary, 1968.B78
Mansat, A., 1970.B37
Marcus, Frank, 1968.B79; 1971.B18; 1972.B88; 1973.B55-56; 1974. B110
Mark, Charles Christopher, 1977. B86
Marks, Arnold, 1970.B38
Marlowe, Joan, 1967.B92-93; 1972. B89; 1974.B111; 1975.B81; 1977.B87; 1979.B75-77
Marowitz, Charles, 1967.B94; 1968.B80; 1972.B90; 1973.B57; 1975.B82
Marranca, Bonnie, 1977.B88
Marriage. See also Family
-comments by Miriam Stoppard about, 1977.B85
-comments by Tom Stoppard about, 1973.B85; 1977.B36
Marriott, R. B., 1968.B81-83; 1972.B91; 1973.B58; 1974. B112
Maryland Public Broadcasting Service, 1978.B13
Maske und Kothurn, 1978.B78a
Mass Media Newsletter, 1976.B94
Masterplots: 1968 Annual, 1969. B1
Mastroianni, Tony, 1969.B41; 1974.B113
Matlaw, Myron, 1972.B92

Index

Matter, Sam, 1969.B42
Maultsby, Sara, 1977.B89
Maves, C. E., 1974.B114; 1977. B90-91
Mayerson, Donald J., 1972.B93
Mayhead, Gerald, 1973.B59
Mayne, Richard, 1972.B94
Mazzocco, Robert, 1976.B71
Meaning. See also Nonsense; Theme; Specific themes
-comments by others about, 1967. B59; 1970.B13; 1976.B39; 1979.A3, B10, 36
-comments by Stoppard about, 1968.B76
Media, writing for other. See also Film; Novels; Radio; Television
-comments by others about, 1974. B122
-comments by Stoppard about, 1972.B99; 1976.B50
Mehl, Dieter, 1970.B39
Meisel, Kurt (director)
-interview with, 1967.B89
Mellor, Isha, 1974.B115
Melly, George, 1967.B95
Melodrama, 1979.B43. See also Mystery
Mendelson, Phyllis Carmel, 1976.B87; 1978.B20
Menuhin, Yehudi, 1979.B2
Mercury (Leicester, G.B.), 1973.B1
Mercury-News (San Jose, Calif.), 1969.B26
Merkur (Munich), Incomplete.B15
Merkur: Deutsche Zeitschrift für europäisches Denken, 1970.B15
Merrick, David, 1967.B8-9, 11; 1968.B27
Merryn, Anthony, Incomplete.B35
Metafictional Characters in Modern Drama, 1979.B93
Metaphor (-ical). See also Symbol
-comments by others about, 1970. B7; 1972.B21; 1978.B29, 32, 70; 1979.B107
-comments by Stoppard about, 1975.B43; 1976.B50
Metaphysic(-al, -s). See also Religion
-comments by others about, 1967. B132; 1971.B14, 20; 1972. B112, 126; 1974.B41, 61, 102, 111; 1975.B97; 1976.B56, 87; 1977.B51; 1978.B23, 28; 1979.B10, 30; 1980.B26; Incomplete.B13
-comments by Stoppard about, 1972.B57; 1974.B95; 1975.B43; 1977.B73, 125; 1979.B106
Metaphysical poets, 1979.B52. See also Poetry
Metro-Goldwyn-Mayer, 1968.B117-118
Michener, Charles, 1979.B75, 78
Michigan Academician, 1979.B10
Mick, 1967.B96; 1969.B43; 1970. B40
Miller, Jeanne, 1970.B41
Minton, Lynn, 1976.B72
"'M' Is for 'Moon,' among other Things" (radio play)
-analyses and criticisms, 1973. B21; 1974.B135; 1976.A2-3; 1977.A1
-comments by Stoppard about, 1974.B90
-production, review of,
--Richmond, G.B., Orange Tree Pub, 1977.B30
Missouri English Bulletin, 1969. B48
Mixture. See Pastiche
MLN, 1979.B84
Mlynar, Zdenek, 1977.B38. See also Czechoslovakia; Dissidents
Modern Drama, 1969.B33; 1972.B21; 1973.B20; 1977.B37, 51; 1978.B42; 1979.B35
Modern Language Notes. See MLN
Modern World Drama: An Encyclopedia, 1972.B92
Money. See also Success
-comments by Stoppard about, 1967.B48
Monologue. See Dialogue
Montgomery Journal (Bethesda,

241

Md.), 1978.B37
Month, 1980.B19
Montreal Star, 1967.B109; 1973.B39
Mood, 1968.B96; 1969.B30; 1971.B10; 1972.B3; 1973.B68; 1974.B28, 35; 1976.B37, 96; 1977.B71; 1978.B33, 87-88; 1979.B33, 79; 1980.B6, 10, 34. See also Anguish; Boredom; Fantasy; Feeling; Fun; Humane; Pathos; Pessimism; Poetic; Tone; Romantic
Moon (name of character)
-comments by others about, 1972.B6, 41; 1979.B10
-comments by Stoppard about, 1972.B41; 1974.B90
Moon (satellite)
-comments by others about, 1976.B23
-comments by Stoppard about, 1967.B64
Moore, G. E., 1977.B94
Moore-Robinson, Miriam. See Stoppard, Miriam
Mootz, William, 1974.B116
Moral (-ity, -s). See also Evil; Religion
-comments by others about, 1968.B34, 38, 110; 1969.B33; 1972.B20, 30, 76; 1973.B12, 26; 1974.B95, 97; 1975.B75, 81, 117; 1976.A2, B16, 49; 1977.A1, B32, 74, 83, 94, 129; 1978.B34, 51; 1979.A3, B10, 26, 98; 1980.B34
-comments by Stoppard about, 1968.B89; 1974.B90, 95, 144; 1976.B65-66; 1978.B72; 1979.B47
Moral(-ism, -istic), 1966.B15; 1975.B13; 1978.B23. See also Sermon
Moran, Rita, 1977.B92
Morgan, Geoffrey, 1968.B84
Morgan, Quinta, 1974.B117
Moritz, Charles, 1975.B2
Morley, Sheridan, 1972.B95; 1975.B83-85; 1977.B93; 1978.B57; Incomplete.B36

Morning Star (London), 1967.B86; 1975.B27
Morning Telegraph (New York), 1967.B34, 82; 1972.B82
Morrison, Don, 1976.B73
Morrison, Kristin, 1972.B3
Mortality. See Death
Mosk, 1975.B86
Moss, Rosalind Urbach, 1977.B94
Movies. See Film
Mrozek, Slawomir. See Tango
Mullins, Edwin, 1976.B74
Munich, 1980.B30. See also Theatre and society, German
Murder mystery. See Mystery
Murray, Brian (actor)
-interviews with, 1967.B22, 83, 114, 129
-photograph of, 1968.B66
Murray, William, 1977.B95
Music-hall, 1967.B111; 1973.B77; 1975.B107. See also Revue sketch; Vaudeville
Mystery, 1968.B85; 1972.B112; 1973.B65; 1977.B37; 1979.B30
Myth (-ic), 1966.B38; 1967.B38, 130; 1968.B84; 1969.B13; 1970.B15; 1972.B23; 1977.B37; 1978.B70. See also Classic

Nabokov, Vladimir, 1978.B14, 56, 86; 1979.B38, 92. See also Despair
Nachman, Gerald, 1969.B44
Nadel, Norman, 1967.B97
Nakanishi, Masako, 1971.B19
Narrator. See Dialogue
Natale, Richard, 1972.B76
Nathan, David, 1968.B85; 1972.B97
Nation, 1967.B43; 1972.B39; 1973.B30; 1974.B40-41; 1975.B29-30; 1977.B34; 1979.B28-29, 50; 1980.B16
National Council for Soviet Jewry, 1978.B6. See also Dissidents; U.S.S.R.
National Observer, 1972.B52; 1974.B134
National Public Radio, 1974.B22-23; 1976.B65-66; 1977.B75, 86
National Review, 1967.B98;

242

Index

1974.B183
National Theatre (British)
 -comments by Stoppard about, 1976.B63
Natural(-ism, -istic), 1968.B80; 1975.B59; 1976.A4; 1977.B26, 32; 1979.A1
NBC-TV, 1972.B108; 1975.B91; 1977.B102
Neil, Boyd, 1978.B58
Nelson, Bob, 1976.B75
Nelson, Byron, 1979.B79
Nelson, Don, 1975.B87
Neophilologus, 1977.B39
Neue Kronenzeitung (Vienna), 1973.B83
Neue Zürcher Zeitung (Zurich), 1973.B11
Neurosis. See Psychology
"Neutral Ground" (television play)
 -analyses and criticisms of, 1971.B20; 1974.B135; 1976.A3; 1977.A1
 -comments by others about, 1974.B84
 -comments by Stoppard about, 1974.B90
 -news item about, 1968.B29
 -production, reviews of
 --Manchester, G.B., Granada Television Centre, 1968.B42, 65, 78, 86, 88, 91-92
Newall, Robert H., 1978.B59
New British Drama, The: Fourteen Playwrights since Osborne and Pinter, 1977.B73
New Leader, 1977.B113; 1978.B14
Newporter Mesa News (Newport Beach, Calif.), 1974.B89; 1975.B58; 1977.B65
New Republic, 1967.B37; 1968.B96; 1974.B96; 1975.B68; 1980.B7, 22
New Review, 1974.B80
Newsday (Long Island City, N.Y.), 1967.B100; 1972.B102; 1974.B123-125, 167; 1977.B99; Incomplete.B46
News items, 1964.B3; 1965.B1; 1966.B7, 9; 1967.B3, 8-13, 15, 17-19, 21, 23, 25, 133; 1968.B3-4, 8, 11-12, 14-16, 18-19, 21, 24-27, 29, 53, 109, 117-118, 122; 1969.B3-4, 16; 1970.B4-5; 1971.B11; 1972.B5, 7-11, 13-14, 16-17, 37; 1973.B2-4, 7-9, 37, 71; 1974.B4-13, 16, 39, 51, 81, 108, 145, 164; 1975.B4-5, 7-8, 11, 65, 69, 120-121; 1976.B2-6, 9, 11-14, 21, 32-33, 63, 100, 104; 1977.B1-3, 5-6, 11-12, 31, 38, 43, 50, 62-63, 81; 1978.B1-6, 8, 11, 18, 31; 1979.B1-3, 5, 8-9, 39-40, 90-91; 1980.B2, 29-30; Incomplete.B1. See also Stoppard, Miriam, news items about; Stoppard, Tom, news items about; titles of individual works (listed in Stoppard, Tom, works by)
New Society, 1966.B38
News-Pilot (San Pedro, Calif.), Incomplete.B49
News Register (Fremont, Calif.), 1969.B55
New Statesman, 1966.B26; 1967.B75-76; 1972.B98; 1974.B118; 1975.B31, 62; 1976.B76; 1977.B96; 1978.B60-61; 1979.B80-81
Newsweek, 1967.B16, 85; 1970.B53; 1974.B17, 103; 1975.B74-75; 1976.B63-64; 1978.B51; 1979.B68-70, 78; 1980.B3
NewsWest, 1977.B48
New Theatre Magazine, 1969.B13
New West Magazine, 1977.B95
New Year's List, 1977.B13
New York, 1968.B101; 1970.B51; 1972.B118; 1974.B142-144; 1975.B20, 94, 106; 1976.B85; 1977.B25, 105; 1979.B98-100
New Yorker, 1967.B22, 90; 1968.B13, 17; 1972.B101; 1974.B67, 121; 1975.B45-46, 66; 1976.B79; 1977.B53, 125; 1979.B41-44; 1980.B1
New York Literary Forum, 1978.B49a
New York Review of Books, 1976.B71

Index

New York Theatre Critics' Review, 1967.B92-93; 1972.B89; 1974.B111; 1975.B81; 1977.B87; 1979.B75-77
New York Theatre Review, 1978.B38, 69, 83; 1979.B6, 23, 58, 85, 107
New York Times, 1966.B31; 1967.B8, 26, 29-30, 53, 80, 113-114, 122; 1968.B33, 47, 72, 76, 80, 114, 117-118, 122; 1970.B10; 1971.B11; 1972.B25-27, 37, 57, 78, 90; 1973.B9; 1974.B4, 6, 12-13, 25, 27-29, 39, 77, 98-99, 107, 158; 1975.B15-16, 28, 55, 65, 70, 78, 82; 1976.B13, 17-18, 32-33, 45, 55, 62, 95, 104; 1977.B17, 20, 60, 76, 81-82, 97; 1978.B45, 62, 72; 1979.B2, 7, 21-22, 27, 37, 47-49, 62, 67, 71-72, 86; 1980.B9, 15, 23, 25
New York Times Book Review, 1968.B95
Next Time I'll Sing to You, 1975.B39
Nichols, Christopher, 1967.B98
Nichols, Dorothy, 1969.B45
Nichols, Peter, 1968.B15; 1979.B8
Nickolson, Leonard, 1969.B18
Night and Day (stage play)
-analyses and criticisms of, 1978.B49; 1979.B87; 1980.A2, B13, 15
-comments by others about, 1978.B57; 1979.B72; 1980.B17-17a
-comments by Stoppard about, 1979.B22, 47, 53; 1980.B11, 17
-news items about, 1978.B8, 11; 1979.B1, 5
-photographs of, 1978.B12; 1979.B6
-productions, reviews of
--London, West End, 1978.B50-51, 54, 61, 82; 1979.B1, 12, 23-24, 32, 45, 54, 79, 107, 111; 1980.B19
--New York, Broadway, 1979.B17, 20, 29, 31, 43, 60, 62, 66, 70, 77, 97, 100, 110, 119; 1980.B7, 18, 21, 32
-text, reviews of, 1978.B87; 1979.B105
Nightingale, Benedict, 1972.B98; 1974.B118; 1976.B76-77, 87; 1977.B96-97; 1978.B60-61; 1979.B80-81
Night Time, Incomplete.B34
Nonsense, 1968.B5, 101; 1970.B13; 1972.B89, 138; 1979.B19, 76. See also Chaos; Sense
Nordon, Pierre, 1973.B60
Norman, Barry, 1972.B99
North Central Outlook (Seattle, Wash.), 1970.B26
Norton, Elliot, 1967.B99
Nova, Incomplete.B36
Novels, writing. See also Media, writing for other
-comments by Stoppard about, 1968.B51; 1971.B12
Novick, Julius, 1974.B119; 1975.B88, 97, 117; 1977.B98; 1978.B20
Nunn, Trevor (director)
-interview with, 1977.B93
-photograph of, 1977.B8
Nünning, Josefa, Incomplete.B22
Nureyev, Rudolf, 1979.B2
Nurse, Keith, 1979.B82

Oberon, 1971.B19; 1975.B118
Observer (London), 1966.B13; 1967.B5, 14, 38, 54, 56, 95; 1968.B37-38; 1971.B8-9; 1972.B43, 50; 1973.B7, 28; 1974.B15, 47; 1975.B63; 1976.B38, 69; 1977.B85
Observer (Vienna), Incomplete.B2
Obvious (-ness), 1968.B99; 1978.B61. See also Ambiguity
O'Connor, Garry, 1972.B100; 1973.B61; 1974.B120
O'Connor, John J., 1978.B62
Oedipus, 1977.B37
Oh Calcutta! 1978.B33
Old Vic Theatre, 1973.B71
Oliver, Edith, 1972.B101; 1974.B121; 1975.B97

Index

Oliver, Michael, 1976.B78
O'Malley, John F., 1974.B122
O'Neill, Michael Charles, 1980. B27
"One Pair of Eyes: Tom Stoppard Doesn't Know" (television documentary)
-analyses and criticisms, 1976. A3
-production, reviews of
--London, BBC Television, 1972. B1, 36, 44, 51
On Moral Fiction, 1978.B40
Oppenheimer, George, 1967.B100; 1972.B102; 1974.B123-125; 1977.B99
Opposition. See Dialectic
Optimism. See Pessimism
Orange Country Evening News (Garden Grove, Calif.), 1975.B113; 1977.B119
Orange County Illustrated, 1975.B115
Oregonian (Portland, Oreg.), 1970.B35
Oregon Journal (Portland, Oreg.), 1970.B38
Oregon Shakespearean Festival Teacher's Manual for Tom Stoppard's "Rosencrantz and Guildenstern Are Dead," 1970.A1
Organiz(-ation, -ed). See also Craftsmanship; Form; Structure
-comments by others about, 1966. B3, 26, 30, 36, 39; 1967. B127; 1968.B43, 95, 97; 1969.B6; 1972.B62, 98; 1974. B24; 1975.B103; 1976.B49; 1977.B19, 56, 76, 87; 1978. B51, 54; 1979.B29-31, 42, 77, 81; 1980.B31
-comments by Stoppard about, 1967.B35
Original (-ity). See also Classic; Eccentricity; Eclectic; Imitation; Unoriginal
-comments by others about, 1967. B99-100; 1968.B87; 1972.B62; 1976.A4, B73; 1977.B106; 1979.A1; 1980.B6
-comments by Stoppard about, 1970.B62; 1977.B125; 1979. B106
Orton, Joe, 1972.B25; 1978.B52
Osborne, John, 1973.B60; 1979. B89
O'Toole, Laurence, 1979.B83; 1980.B27a
Otremba, Geraldine Marie, 1978. B63
Ottaway, Robert, 1968.B86
Our Town (New York), 1972.B68
Outlook (Santa Monica, Calif.), 1977.B21
Overmyer, Janet, 1968.B87
Owen, Michael, 1974.B126
Oxford, G.B., 1977.B125; 1979. B106
Oxford Theatre Group, 1966.B7; 1969.B4
Oxford (G.B.) Times, 1966.B17

P., L., 1967.B101
Pache, Walter, 1973.B62
Pacific Sun (Mill Valley, Calif.), 1969.B18
Palmer, Howard, 1973.B63
Palmer, Raymond, 1967.B102-104
Panter-Downes, Mollie, 1967.B105; 1976.B79
Paradox (-ical), 1972.B51; 1973. B62; 1974.B103, 111; 1977. B109. See also Ambiguity; Logic; Uncertainty
"Paragraph for Mr Blake, A" (television play)
-analyses and criticisms of, 1972.B94; 1974.B122; 1976.A3
-comments by Stoppard about, 1965.B2
-news item about, 1965.B1. See also Short stories; "Story, The"
Parents' Magazine, 1976.B88
Parker, John, 1972.B4
Parody. See also Burlesque; Cliché; Irony; Satire
-comments by others about, 1968. B85, 96, 101; 1969.B11, 33; 1970.B7, 24; 1972.B20, 53, 89;

245

1973.B12, 60, 62, 68, 77;
1974.B80, 93, 182; 1975.B35,
88, 97, 117; 1976.B16, 41,
87; 1977.B107; 1979.B37, 51,
61; 1980.B34; Incomplete.B13
—comments by Stoppard about,
1974.B77; 1976.B77
Pasquier, Marie-Claire, 1972.
B103
Pastiche, 1974.B35, 44, 65, 182;
1975.B86, 107; 1976.B87;
1977.B112; 1979.B58, 74;
Incomplete.B16, 44. See
also Collage; Eclectic; Un-
originality
Pathos, 1968.B80; 1980.B34. See
also Mood; Sentiment
Paul, 1974.B127; 1976.B80
Pearce, Howard D., 1979.B84
Pedagogical items, 1969.B48;
1970.A1; 1971.B8a; 1975.B79,
103, 126; 1976.B91; Incom-
plete.A2-3
Pennington, Ron, 1979.B85; In-
complete.B37
Personal experience, use of.
See also Early life and
career; Playwriting
—comments by others about, 1969.
B33; 1975.B103, 117; 1977.
A1
—comments by Stoppard about,
1968.B51; 1971.B12; 1975.
B43; 1977.B125; 1979.B106
Perspective. See also Detach-
ment; Relativism
—comments by others about, 1969.
B17, 37; 1974.B43, 56;
1975.B64; 1976.A2; 1978.B70;
1979.B52, 84
—comments by Stoppard about,
Incomplete.B36
Pessim(-ism, -istic), 1967.B37;
1968.B77; 1970.B37; 1973.
B30; 1978.B67; 1979.B88;
1980.B24. See also Mood;
Tone
Peter, John, 1970.B42; 1972.
B104; 1973.B64; 1974.B128;
1976.B81
Peters, Pauline, 1980.B28

Peterson, Rolfe, 1969.B46
Phenomenology, 1979.B84
Philbin, Regis, 1977.B100
Phillips, John L., 1968.B88
Phillips, Pearson, 1970.B43
Philosophy, 1975.B21; 1977.B68
Philosoph(-ical, -y). See also
Dialectic; Epistemology;
Existential; Humane; Ideas;
Illusion; Intellect; Logic;
Logical Positivism; Meaning;
Metaphysics; Moral; Pessimism;
Phenomenology; Pragmatism;
Relativism; Romantic; and
related topics (Art; Death;
Freedom; Games; Heroes; His-
tory; Myth; Naturalism; Poli-
tics; Psychology; Real;
Society; Surreal)
—comments by others about, 1974.
B183; 1975.B21; 98; 1976.B19;
1977.B68, 94; 1978.B78a;
1979.B26, 30, 35
—comments by Stoppard about,
1974.B77; 1975.B43
Phonograph record. See Every
Good Boy Deserves Favour,
review of phonograph record
Phonotape. See Audio tape
Photographs. See Stoppard, Tom,
photographs of; titles of
individual works (listed in
Stoppard, Tom, works by)
Physics, 1975.B64
Pile, Stephen, 1980.B29
Pinter, Harold
—comments by others about, 1967.
B136; 1972.B45; 1975.B106;
1979.B52, 89
—comments by Stoppard about,
1970.B62; 1971.B20
Pioneer (California State University, Hayward), 1969.B19;
1970.B19-20
Pirandello, Luigi, 1968.B7, 115;
1972.B65; 1973.B62; 1975.B86
Pit, 1974.B129
Pitt News (University of Pitts-
burgh, Pittsburgh, Pa.),
1970.B46
Plain Dealer (Cleveland, Ohio),

Index

1969.B8; 1974.B33; Incomplete.B9
Platz, Norbert H., 1975.B126
Play. See Games; Theatre and society
Playbill Two, 1969.B22
Playboy, 1976.B1
Plays and Players, 1966.B14, 25; 1967.B124; 1968.B4, 36, 45, 60; 1970.B60-61; 1972.B107, 129; 1973.B2-3, 5, 14, 29, 32, 51-52; 1974.B2, 73, 92, 115, 120; 1975.B3; 1976.B24; 1977.B115, 134; 1978.B58, 76; 1979.B1, 3, 45, 74, 103
Play theory. See Games
Play-within-the-play, 1973.B60, 62; 1978.B36
Playwrights' Company, 1979.B8; 1980.B29
Playwrights Talk about Writing: 12 Interviews, 1975.B43
Playwriting. See also Film; Media; Novels; Radio; Television; Work habits
-comments by Stoppard about, 1967.B35; 1968.B35, 89; 1972.B57; 1974.B22, 50, 80, 144; 1975.B43, 82; 1976.B65-66, 102; 1977.A1; 1979.B22, 47, 53; 1980.B11
Plot. See also Action
-comments by others about, 1967.B116, 132; 1969.B13; 1973.B62, 65; 1974.B100, 141; 1975.B31, 97, 100; 1976.B25; 1977.B107; 1978.B54, 74; 1979.B29, 66, 77, 83, 100, 105, 107, 119; 1980.B1, 34
-comments by Stoppard about, 1967.B4; 1973.B37; 1974.B126; 1977.B125; 1979.B106
Plottel, Esther, 1969.B47
Poet(-ic, -ry), 1967.B38, 77, 137; 1969.B8a; 1973.B36, 38; 1979.B107. See also Language; Mood; Tone
Poetica, 1971.B7
Point of view. See Perspective
Polemic (-al), 1968.B87; 1978.B76. See also Moralism; Sermon
Politic(-al, -s). See also Society
-comments by others about, 1966.B26; 1974.B49, 107, 120; 1975.B24, 107; 1976.B23, 59; 1977.A1, B125; 1978.B24, 31, 49, 51, 79; 1979.B19, 34, 76, 88, 106; 1980.A2
-comments by Stoppard about, 1974.B80, 90; 1975.B108; 1977.A1; 1978.B72; 1979.B53
Pollak, Robert, Incomplete.B38
Popkin, Henry, 1980.B30
Posner, Howard, 1977.B101
Post (New York), 1967.B17, 123, 134-135; 1968.B116; 1970.B70; 1972.B85, 125, 138-140; 1974.B72, 139, 161, 177-181, 184-185; 1975.B52-53, 95, 111, 121-122; 1976.B108; 1977.B56, 111; 1979.B14-15, 17
Post (Washington, D.C.), 1967.B44; 1968.B119; 1970.B18; 1973.B31; 1974.B10, 42-43, 50, 102, 130, 145; 1976.B28-29; 1978.B7, 71
Post-War British Theatre, 1976.B44
Powell, Dilys, 1970.B44; 1975.B89
Powell, Jane Vaughn, 1972.B105
Pragmat(-ic, -ism), 1979.B10; 1980.B14. See also Logical Positivism
Preservation of George Riley, The (stage play), 1967.B25; 1968.B55. See also Enter a Free Man
Press (South Gate, Calif.), Incomplete.B51
Presse (Vienna), 1973.B69
Press Herald (Portland, Maine), 1978.B65
Previn, André (composer for Every Good Boy Deserves Favour)
-as subject of comments by others, 1976.B12; 1977.B112; 1979.B2, 86
-interviews with, 1974.B53; 1979.B37
-photograph of, 1977.B8

Index

Prick up Your Ears: The Biography of Joe Orton, 1978.B52
Prideaux, Tom, 1968.B89
Priestland, Gerald, 1975.B90
Pritchard, William H., 1968.B90
Prizes. See Awards and honors
Probst, Leonard, 1975.B81, 91; 1977.B87, 102
Procrastination. See also Work habits
-comments by Stoppard about, 1967.B1, 65, 88; 1974.B126; Incomplete.B36
Proctor, Richard, 1977.B103
Producer, interview with, 1974.B139
"Professional Foul" (television play)
-analyses and criticisms of, 1978.B17; 1979.A2-3, B26, 34
-comments by others about, 1978.B45, 84; 1979.B81
-comments by Stoppard about, 1977.B132; 1978.B17, 72; 1979.B53
-news items about, 1977.B43; 1978.B1-2, 4
-production, reviews of
--London, BBC Television, 1977.B9, 32, 42-43, 80; 1978.B62
-text, reviews of, 1978.B7, 10
Profiles and feature articles, 1967.B64-65, 67, 102-104; 1968.B89; 1969.B38; 1971.B15; 1972.B41, 125; 1973.B45; 1974.B1, 20, 58, 81; 1975.B69; 1976.B95; 1977.B36, 97, 125; 1978.B17, 81, 87; 1980.B15, 17
Profundity. See Meaning; Significance
Progress (San Francisco), Incomplete.B10-11, 56
Prokofiev, Sergei, 1977.B112; 1979.B86
Psycholog(-ical, -y). See also Unconscious
-comments by others about, 1966.B15; 1977.A1, B26; 1979.A2
-comments by Stoppard about, 1967.B16, 64, 67; 1972.B57;
1974.B50
Publishers' Weekly, 1967.B24; 1968.B6
Pubs
-comments by Stoppard about, 1967.B48
Punch, 1966.B27, 41; 1967.B81; 1968.B68-69; 1970.B36; 1972.B79-80; 1973.B50; 1974.B100; 1975.B84-85; 1978.B87
Puns, 1977.B32; 1979.B38, 120. See also Homonyms
Purser, Philip, 1966.B32; 1968.B91

Quality. See Craftsmanship; Significance; Skill
Quantrill, Jay Alan, 1974.B130
Quarterly Journal of Speech, 1968.B46
Queen, 1966.B24; 1967.B66; 1968.B59, 61
Queen's Quarterly, 1971.B17; 1979.B88
Questopics, 1974.B58
Questors Theatre, 1964.B4; 1975.B39
Quinn, James E., 1969.B48

R., P., 1975.B92
Rabinowitz, Peter J., 1980.B31
Radcliffe, Philip, 1978.B64
Radio
-interviews over
--audio tapes of, 1976.B65-66; 1977.B75, 86
--transcripts of, 1967.B35, 63; 1968.B35; 1970.B62; 1973.B75; 1974.B63; 1976.B74, 78, 102
-Stoppard's comments about writing for, 1972.B134. See also Media, writing for other
Radio Times, 1966.B1; 1967.B91
Raidy, William A., 1967.B106; 1972.B106
Raine, Craig, 1973.B65
Ratcliffe, Michael, 1976.B82
Rational (-ism, -ity). See Intellect
Rawson, C. J., 1979.B61, 120
Reader (San Diego, Calif.),

248

Index

1977.B89
Reader in the Text, The: Essays on Audience and Interpretation, 1980.B31
Reading
-comments by Stoppard about, 1974.B80; 1977.A1
Real (-ity), 1968.B96; 1969.B31; 1970.B7; 1971.B19; 1973.B21, 62, 68, 77; 1975.B28, 62, 126; 1976.A2, B19, 92, 110; 1977.B68, 109; 1979.B84, 89. See also Illusion; Unreal
Real Inspector Hound, The (stage play)
-analyses and criticisms of, 1968.B115; 1969.B33; 1970.B61; 1971.B17, 19-20; 1972.B3, 21, 94; 1973.B21-22, 62, 77; 1974.B18, 46, 80, 102, 122, 135; 1975.B35, 40, 64, 103; 1976.A1-4, B49, 53, 97; 1977.A1, B37, 73, 109, 125; 1978.B29, 67; 1979.A1-3, B10, 52, 93, 106, 112; 1980.A2, B34
-comments by others about, 1968.B82
-comments by Stoppard about, 1967.B50; 1968.B55; 1972.B57, 96, 125; 1974.B90, 144
-news items about, 1967.B18, 133; 1968.B16, 19; 1971.B11; 1972.B10, 37; 1977.B81
-productions, reviews of
--American touring company, 1974.B106
--Boston, Emerson College, 1970.B23
--Boston, Next Move Theatre, 1978.B38
--Cleveland, Ohio, Jewish Community Center, Incomplete.B9, 55
--Costa Mesa, Calif., South Coast Repertory, 1974.B89, 150; Incomplete.B19, 50
--London, City Lit Productions, 1974.B115
--London, Dolphin Theatre Company, 1972.B46, 67, 100, 114, 136; 1973.B32
--London, Dolphin Theatre Company revival, 1973.B86
--London, Maximus Actors' Arena, 1976.B35
--London, West End, 1968.B32-33, 38, 44-45, 47, 58, 61, 63, 69-70, 74, 79, 83, 85, 94, 100, 107-108, 113-114, 116, 121; 1969.B33
--London, Young Vic, 1976.B26, 40, 43, 68, 90
--Louisville, Ky., Actors Theatre of Louisville, 1974.B116, 138; Incomplete.B12
--Montreal, Canada, Centaur Theatre, 1973.B39, 49; Incomplete.B13
--Nassau County, New York, Theater East, 1979.B67
--New Orleans, Le Petit Theatre, Incomplete.B21
--New York, Comedy Stage Company, 1975.B77
--New York, Theatre Four, 1972.B25, 27-28, 32, 35, 39, 52-53, 59, 63, 65, 68, 71, 75, 78, 89, 93, 101, 106, 108, 115-116, 118, 120, 137-139; 1973.B31, 67; 1975.B105
--New York, TRG Repertory, 1976.B42, 47
--Portland, Oreg., Civic Theatre, 1975.B42
--Providence, R.I., Trinity Square Repertory Company, 1978.B22, 77; Incomplete.B45
--St. Louis, Mo., Loretto-Hilton Repertory Company, 1975.B50
-text, review of, 1970.B6
Realism. See Naturalism
Recherches Anglaises et Américaines, 1972.B103; 1973.B60
Record (Mill Valley, Calif.), 1970.B73; 1972.B124; 1974.B152
Recording. See Every Good Boy Deserves Favour, review of phonograph record
Redmond, James, 1976.B83
Reed, Rex, 1977.B104

Index

Reflection. See Thought
Regan, Keith, Incomplete.B39-41
Register-Guard (Eugene, Oreg.), 1970.B13
Rehearsal
—comments by others about, 1974.B81; 1977.B75; 1978.B41; 1979.A1; 1980.B17
—comments by Stoppard about, 1974.B22; 1980.B17
Reid, Helen, 1974.B131; 1976.B84
Reid, Walter, 1969.B49
Relativ(-e, -ism, -ist). See also Ideology; Perspective
—comments by others about, 1967.B132; 1968.B111; 1969.B31, 33; 1972.B76; 1973.B21, 26; 1974.B56, 95, 97; 1975.B53, 64, 117, 123; 1976.A2, B44; 1980.B34
—comments by Stoppard about, 1968.B76, 89; 1974.B95; Incomplete.B36
Religion, 1971.B16; 1972.B141; 1975.B117. See also Evil; Metaphysical; Moral
Renaud, Tristan, 1975.B93
Rendle, Adrian, 1973.B66; 1975.B96
Reporter, 1967.B136
Repository (Canton, Ohio), 1967.B104
Resolution
—comments by others about, 1966.B39; 1971.B17; 1972.B89, 110, 137; 1974.B76; 1975.B36, 117; 1977.B107, 115; 1978.B40; 1980.B32
—comments by Stoppard about, 1974.B95, 144; 1978.B48
"Reunion" (short story). See also Early life and career; Short stories
—analyses and criticisms of, 1976.A3-4; 1977.A1; 1979.A1
—comments by Stoppard about, 1967.B5; 1968.B51; 1971.B12
Review (Oxford, G.B.), 1974.B34
Review (South Pasadena, Calif.), 1977.B27

Reviewers
—comments by others about, 1966.B23; 1973.B62; 1974.B111, 117; 1975.B18, 126; 1979.B16
—comments by Stoppard about, 1972.B57
Reviews. See titles of individual works (listed in Stoppard, Tom, works by)
Revue sketch, 1968.B94; 1969.B49. See also Music-hall; Vaudeville
Reynolds, Burt
—comments by Stoppard about, 1980.B11
Reynolds, Stanley, 1967.B107-108; 1968.B92
Rice, Ed, 1978.B65
Rich, 1968.B93-94
Rich, Alan, 1975.B94; 1976.B85; 1977.B105; 1978.B20
Rich, Frank, 1975.B95
Richards, David, 1973.B67; 1974.B132
Richardson, Boyce, 1967.B109
Richardson, Jack, 1967.B110; 1974.B133; 1975.B97; 1976.B86; 1980.B32
Richler, Mordecai, 1968.B95
Ridley, Clifford A., 1974.B134
Riesner, Dieter, 1971.B5
Rigg, Diana (actress)
—as subject of others' comments, 1979.B12, 24
—interview with, 1972.B129
—news item about, 1979.B1
—photograph of, 1978.B9, 12
Riley, Carolyn, 1973.B68; 1975.B96-97; 1976.B87
Ringold, Francine Leffler, 1978.B66
Ripp, Judith, 1976.B88
Rischbieter, Henning, 1967.B111
Rismondo, Piero, 1973.B69
Robbe-Grillet, Alain, 1966.B21; 1980.B31
Roberts, Peter, 1972.B107
Roberts, Philip, 1978.B67
Robinson, David, 1970.B45; 1977.B106; 1978.B68; 1980.B33
Robinson, Gabrielle, 1977.B107;

1980.B34
Rockwell, John, 1979.B86
Rodway, Allan, 1975.B98; 1976.
  B89; 1978.B20
Rogers, F. W., 1970.A1
Rogers, Thomas, 1968.B96
Role-playing, 1971.B13; 1972.
  B21; 1976.A2; 1978.B70
Rollin, Betty, 1972.B89, 108
Romantic (-ism), 1968.B77; 1972.
  B113. See also Mood; Senti-
  mental; Tone
Romantic Englishwoman, The (film
  with screenplay by Stoppard)
-comments by others about, 1975.
  B32
-comments by Stoppard about,
  1974.B87
-news items about, 1975.B5, 69
-photograph of, 1975.B5
-production, reviews of
--London, DIAL Films, 1975.B10,
  12, 24a-25, 28, 31-34, 47,
  54, 60, 66, 86, 89, 93, 95,
  100-101, 106; 1976.B1, 25,
  37, 45, 72, 88, 94, 99, 110
Rosenburg, Arthur, 1970.B46
Rosencrantz and Guildenstern
  (by W. S. Gilbert), 1979.B56
Rosencrantz & Guildenstern Are
  Dead (stage play). See also
  Guildenstern and Rosencrantz
-analyses and criticisms of,
  1966.B23, 39; 1967.B26, 30,
  42, 59, 113; 1968.B48-49,
  54, 67. 115; 1969.B1, 6, 11,
  13, 30, 33, 37, 48. 50, 54;
  1970.A1, B7, 15, 24, 37, 39,
  61; 1971.B1, 5, 7, 8a, 14,
  16-17, 19-20; 1972.B3, 21,
  94, 103, 111, 142; 1973.B20-
  22, 60, 62; 1974.A1, B18, 46,
  80, 84, 122, 135; 1975.B21,
  35, 39-40, 59, 64, 71, 103,
  126; 1976.A1-4, B7, 39, 49,
  53, 56, 89, 91-92, 97, 112;
  1977.A1, B39, 68, 73-74, 107,
  125, 135; 1978.B29, 36, 52,
  67, 70, 78a, 89; 1979.A1-3,
  B10, 26, 36, 52, 56, 61, 93,
  106, 112, 115, 120; 1980.A1-
  2, B12, 27, 31, 34; Incom-
  plete.A2-3

-comments by others about, 1967.
  B22, 83, 89, 114, 132, 187;
  1968.B44, 59-60, 68, 77, 89,
  121; 1972.B53, 89; 1975.B16,
  70, 81; 1977.B93; 1979.B101
-comments by Stoppard about,
  1966.B28; 1967.B16, 35, 50,
  63, 65, 67, 122-123; 1968.
  B35, 51; 1970.B3; 1971.B12;
  1972.B6, 134; 1973.B85; 1974.
  B1, 90; 1975.B43; Incomplete.
  B3, 36
-news items about, 1966.B7, 9;
  1967.B8-9, 11-12, 15, 17, 19,
  21, 23, 133; 1968.B4, 11-12,
  15, 21, 27, 109, 117-118, 122;
  1969.B3, 16; 1972.B8; 1976.
  B3; Incomplete.B1, 3, 36
-photographs of, 1968.B66
-productions, reviews of
--American touring company, 1968.
  B40; 1969.B8, 15, 21, 28, 39,
  41, 53; Incomplete.B38
--Ashland, Oregon Shakespearean
  Festival, 1970.B1, 13, 21, 25-
  26, 28, 30, 32, 35, 38, 52
--Berlin, Schiller-Theater, 1967.
  B111; Incomplete.B17, 26, 28
--Bochum, W. Germany, Schauspiel-
  haus, 1967.B111; Incomplete.
  B26, 28
--Boston, Tufts University, 1970.
  B54
--Bristol, G.B., Old Vic Company,
  1970.B16-17
--Cambridge, G.B., Theatre Com-
  pany, 1971.B2, 13
--Cleveland, Ohio, Playhouse,
  1974.B33, 113, 146, 157; In-
  complete.B43
--Edinburgh, Oxford Theatre Group,
  1966.B6, 12-14, 17, 21-22,
  30-31, 33, 35-36, 38, 40
--Ithaca, N.Y., Cornell Univer-
  sity, 1979.B33
--Leeds, G.B., Leeds University,
  1973.B64
--London, National Theatre, 1967.
  B7, 28, 36, 38, 47, 53, 66,
  72-74, 81-82, 84, 87, 94, 97,
  105, 109, 115, 118, 120, 124-

127, 131, 137, 139, 141; 1968.B84; 1969.B33; 1970.B67
--London, Young Vic, 1973.B50, 53, 72, 74, 76
--London, Young Vic revival, 1974.B169; 1975.B6, 15, 80, 85
--London, Young Vic second revival, 1977.B29, 138
--London, Young Vic third revival, 1979.B64, 82
--Los Angeles, Theatre Exchange, 1979.B85
--Madison, N.J., Shakespeare Festival, 1978.B75, 83
--Miami, Fla., Coconut Grove Playhouse, 1969.B42, 52
--Milan, Italy, Compagnia del Quattro, 1968.B7
--Minneapolis, Guthrie Theatre, 1976.B48, 58, 61, 73, 98; 1977.B26
--Monmouth, Maine, Theatre at Monmouth, 1978.B15, 44, 59, 65
--New York, Broadway, 1967.B2, 21, 29, 31, 34, 37, 39-45, 49, 51, 55, 57-58, 60, 62, 68-71, 78, 80, 85, 90, 92-93, 96, 98-100, 106, 110, 116-117, 119, 134-136, 138; 1968.B36, 41, 46, 48, 56, 64, 75; 1969.B12, 34; 1973.B57
--New York, Classic Stage Company, 1970.B10, 51, 56, 68
--New York, Classic Stage Company revival, 1972.B113
--New York, Classic Stage Company second revival, 1974.B30, 121, 158; 1975.B97
--Paris, 1967.B19, 23
--Philadelphia Repertory Company, 1978.B69
--Pittsburgh, Pa., University of Pittsburgh, 1970.B46
--San Francisco, ACT, 1969.B2, 7, 9-10, 14, 18-19, 23, 25-26, 29, 35-36, 40, 44-47, 51, 55-56; Incomplete.B10
--San Francisco, ACT revival, 1970.B14, 19-20, 27, 31, 41, 48-49, 57-59, 63, 69, 71, 73; Incomplete.B11, 39-40, 52
--San Francisco, ACT second revival, 1972.B19, 31, 40, 49, 54, 69, 73, 81, 105, 119, 122-124, 127, 143; Incomplete.B4, 14, 34, 41, 47, 56
--San Francisco and Berkeley, Calif., Actors' Ark Theatre, 1979.B57
--Toronto, Canada, Royal Alexandria Theatre, 1969.B17
--Vienna, Akademietheater, 1967.B33, 77, 79, 101, 111; Incomplete.B2, 7, 31, 48
--Washington, D.C., Shakespeare & Co., 1978.B13, 37, 39, 71
--Washington, D.C., U.S. Naval Academy, 1974.B130
--Williamstown, Mass., Theatre, 1970.B55
--Winnipeg, Canada, Manitoba Theatre Centre, 1973.B34, 70, 78
--unidentified productions, 1976.B70; 1977.B127
-text, reviews of, 1967.B24, 76, 121; 1968.B23, 104
Rosenwald, Peter J., 1972.B109-110; 1979.B87
Roth, Emmalou, 1972.B111
Rothstein, Bobbi (Roberta) Wynne, 1979.A3
Rowe, Kaye, 1973.B70
Ruiz, José M., Incomplete.B42
Rundall, Jeremy, 1967.B112; 1970.B47; 1972.B112
Runyon, Damon
-comments by Stoppard about, 1967.B5
Russell, Jeff, Incomplete.B43
Russell, Ken, 1979.B2
Ryan, Randolph, 1974.B135

S., C., 1966.B33
S., P. H., 1973.B71
S., R., 1970.B48; 1976.B90
Sainer, Arthur, 1972.B113
Salmon, Eric, 1979.B88
Salmony, George, Incomplete.B44
Salt, Gary, 1970.B49

Index

Salter, Charles H., 1976.B91
Saltzman, Arthur Michael, 1979.
 B89
Samson, Blake A., 1974.B136
Sanders, Bob, 1975.B99
Sanders, Kevin, 1974.B111, 137
San Francisco Bay Guardian,
 1969.B46
San Gabriel Valley Tribune
 (Covina, Calif.), 1977.B69
Santa Barbara, (Calif.), 1974.
 B51; 1977.B125; 1979.B106
Sarris, Andrew, 1975.B100
Sasso, Laurence J., Jr., Incomplete.B45
Satire, 1968.B95, 107; 1973.B43,
 62, 77; 1975.B24, 34, 86;
 1976.B86; 1977.B19, 112;
 1979.B19, 76, 113. See also
 Cliché; Irony; Parody
Saturday Review, 1967.B68; 1968.
 B23, 52, 56; 1969.B29; 1970.
 B28; 1972.B62-63; 1975.B56;
 1976.B37; 1977.B36; 1979.B92;
 1980.B21, 36
Saunders, Dudley, 1974.B138
Saunders, James, 1975.B39
Say, Rosemary, 1968.B97; 1972.
 B114; 1973.B72; 1979.B90-91
Scene, Incomplete.B4
Scene (Cleveland, Ohio), Incomplete.B43
Schenck, Mary-Low Taylor, 1976.
 B92
Schickel, Richard, 1980.B35
Schier, Ernest, 1976.B93; 1977.
 B108; 1979.B69
Schillaci, Peter, 1975.B101;
 1976.B94
Schlesinger, Arthur, Jr., 1979.
 B92; 1980.B36
Schlösser, Anselm, 1969.B50
Schlueter, June Mayer, 1977.B109;
 1979.B93
Schneider, Robert, 1977.B108
Scholem, Richard J., 1972.B115
Schwab-Felisch, Hans, Incomplete.
 B26
Schwartz, Tony, 1977.B111
Schwartzman, Myron, 1975.B102
Schwarz, Alfred, 1978.B70

Scotsman (Edinburgh), 1966.B7,
 40; 1967.B27; 1968.B30; 1969.
 B49; 1972.B22, 77
Scottish Daily Mail (Edinburgh),
 1966.B33
Scott-Kilvert, Ian, 1976.A2
Screenplays. See Adaptation;
 Film
Scribe (Portland, Oreg.), 1974.
 B3; 1975.B42; 1976.B70
Script
-comments by others about, 1974.
 B52, 71, 111; 1977.B75; 1978.
 B41; 1979.B24; 1980.B37
-comments by Stoppard about,
 1978.B41; 1980.B17
Second Wave, The: British Drama
 for the Seventies, 1971.B20
Sege, 1972.B116
Self, David, 1975.B103
Seligsohn, Leo, Incomplete.B46
Semple, Robert B., Jr., 1976.B95
Sense, 1971.B17; 1974.B110, 119,
 123, 137, 178; 1975.B51, 97,
 117; 1976.B39. See also
 Meaning; Nonsense
Sentiment (-al, -alist, -ality),
 1972.B3, 141; 1975.B117;
 1977.B30; 1979.B116; 1980.B34.
 See also Mood; Pathos; Romantic
"Separate Peace, A" (television
 play)
-analyses and criticisms of,
 1971.B20; 1972.B94; 1973.B21;
 1974.B122, 135; 1976.A2-4;
 1977.A1; 1979.A1-2, B52;
 1980.A2
-comments by others about, 1969.
 B22
-comments by Stoppard about,
 1974.B90
-productions, reviews of
--Boston, Next Move Theatre,
 1978.B38
--London, BBC Television, 1966.
 B15, 19, 32
-text, review of, 1978.B35
Serious (-ness),
-comments by others about, 1967.
 B79, 141; 1968.B33, 77, 80,

253

84, 101; 1969.B15; 1970.B40; 1971.B20; 1972.B72; 1973. B68; 1974.B43, 45, 187; 1975.B37, 97; 1976.B49, 58; 1977.A1, B26; 1978.B67; 1979.B69, 74, 76, 96, 111; 1980.B24
-comments by Stoppard about, 1974.B109
Sermon, 1967.B98; 1978.B54. See also Moralism; Polemic
Sex (-ual), 1975.B33, 66; 1976.B81; 1977.B134; 1980.B13. See also Homosexuality
Seymour-Smith, Martin, 1976.B96
Shaffer, Peter, 1972.B65; 1978.B28
Shakespeare, William. See also Hamlet; Macbeth
-as a pseudonym, 1967.B26, 113
-as the subject of comments by others, 1966.B38; 1967.B26, 30, 113, 130; 1973.B62; 1974.B118; 1976.B39; 1980.B37
Shakespeare: Aspects of Influence, 1976.B39
Shakespeare Jahrbuch, 1969.B6, 50
Shakespeare the Craftsman: The Clark Lectures, 1968, 1969.B11
Shales, Tom, 1974.B145
Sharp, Christopher, 1979.B76, 94
Shavian, 1973.B19
Shaw, George Bernard, 1973.B43; 1974.B60, 95; 1975.B97; 1977.B86; 1978.B42; 1979.B60, 77, 110
Shaw-Taylor, Desmond, 1977.B112
Shepard, Richard F., 1967.B114
Sheppard, Eugenia, 1974.B139
Shirley, Don, 1978.B71
Shorter, Eric, 1978.B98; 1970.B50
Short stories. See also Early life and career; titles of short stories ("Life, Times: Fragments"; "Reunion"; "Story, The")
-comments by Stoppard about, 1967.B5; 1968.B61; 1971.B12

Shostakovich, Dmitri, 1977.B112; 1979.B86
Show Business (New York), 1972.B10; 1974.B5, 170; 1976.B47; 1977.B3, 5
Show People: Profiles in Entertainment, 1979.B106
Shulman, Milton, 1967.B115; 1968.B100; 1972.B117; 1973.B73-74; 1974.B140; 1975.B104; 1978.B72
Siegel, Joel, 1979.B75-77, 95-97
Sight and Sound, 1975.B10, 32; 1977.B106; 1978.B32; 1980.B10
Sign, 1968.B41; 1974.B74; 1975.B33
Significance
-comments by others about, 1967.B43, 84, 119; 1968.B47; 1969.B8, 53; 1970.B7, 65; 1972.B3, 46; 1973.B68; 1975.B62, 117; 1977.B68; 1979.B35, 64, 88
-comments by Stoppard about, 1972.B6
Signoret, Simone, 1980.B30
Simenon, Georges, 1972.B138-139
Simmons, Charles, 1968.B101
Simon, John, 1967.B116-117; 1970.B51; 1972.B118; 1974.B141-143; 1975.B97, 105-106; 1976.B87, 97; 1977.B113-114; 1978.B20; 1979.B98-100
Simon, Neil, 1972.B65
Simon, Richard, 1972.B119
Siskiyou (Ashland, Oreg.), 1970.B21
Skill, 1967.B84; 1974.B93; 1975.B62, 97; 1980.B3, 9. See also Craftsmanship
Skinner, Margo, Incomplete.B47
Skow, John, 1978.B73
Skyway News (Minneapolis), 1976.B61
Smeltzer, Vene, 1970.B52
Smith, Anthony C. H., 1974.B144
Smith, Giles, 1973.B75
Smith, Lisa Gordon, 1967.B118; 1972.B120; 1973.B76
Smith, Maggie (actress)
-as subject of comments by others, 1979.B12, 24

Index

-interview with, 1979.B72
Smith, Michael, 1967.B119
Smyth, Jeannette, 1974.B145
Snobbery, 1969.B27; 1972.B39
Soccer. See Football
Soci(-al, -ety). See also
   Politics
-comments by others about, 1968.
   B49-50; 1971.B14, 16; 1972.
   B3; 1973.B43, 68; 1975.B117;
   1976.B49; 1977.B129; 1978.
   B33-34, 51, 53, 80; 1979.B87;
   1980.A2, B15
-comments by Stoppard about,
   1967.B78; 1968.B89; 1970.
   B62; 1972.B2; 1973.B85; 1974.
   B144; 1975.B43; 1977.B125;
   1979.B106
Soho Weekly News (New York),
   1976.B42, 59; 1977.B50
Sokolov, Raymond A., 1970.B53
South Africa. See Theatre and
   society, South African
South Atlantic Quarterly, 1978.
   B28
Southeast News (Downey, Calif.),
   Incomplete.B23
Southern Humanities Review,
   1976.B49
Soyinka, Wole, 1967.B13
Spaeth, Arthur, 1974.B146
Spanish, items in, 1977.B28;
   1978.B47; Incomplete.B42
Spectator, 1967.B120; 1972.B72;
   1974.B93
Speech by Stoppard, 1974.B51
Spiel, Hilde, Incomplete.B48
Spirit. See Mood; Tone
Sports. See Cricket; Football
Sprachkunst, 1973.B62
Spurling, Hilary, 1967.B120
Stacey, Roy, 1974.B147
Stage and Television Today (London), 1966.B12, 19; 1967.
   B118; 1968.B81-83, 88; 1969.
   B24; 1970.B5, 8-9; 1971.B3;
   1972.B14, 91, 120; 1973.B13,
   58, 76; 1974.B112; 1975.B92;
   1976.B10; 1977.B66
Stagebill, 1973.B77; 1976.B19
Stanford (Calif.), Daily, 1970.
   B49; 1972.B19
Star (Minneapolis), 1976.B73,
   103; 1977.B33; 1978.B27
Star (Washington, D.C.), 1973.B67.
   See also Evening Star (Washington, D.C.); Star-News
   (Washington, D.C.); Star Sunday Magazine (Washington, D.C.)
Star-News (Washington, D.C.),
   1974.B66, 108, 132. See also
   Daily News (Washington, D.C.);
   Evening Star (Washington,
   D.C.); Star (Washington, D.C.)
Stark, Judy, 1974.B148
Stark, Larry, 1970.B54
Stark, Randy, Incomplete.B49
Star Sunday Magazine (Washington,
   D.C.), 1968.B24. See also
   Evening Star (Washington,
   D.C.); Star (Washington, D.C.)
Stasio, Marilyn, 1970.B55-56;
   1973.B77; 1974.B149; 1975.
   B107-108
Steele, Mike, 1976.B98
Stein, Elliott, 1978.B74
Stein, Rita, 1975.B117
Stereotype. See Cliché; Convention
Stern, J. P., 1979.B101
Sterritt, David, 1978.B75
Stevens, Neil, 1972.B121
Stevens, Roger
-comments by Stoppard about,
   1974.B161
Stickel, Robert, 1972.B122
Stiles, Patricia, 1967.B121
Stoneman, D., 1975.B109
Stoop, N. M., 1976.B99; 1979.B102
Stoppard, Miriam
-interviews with, 1977.B64, 85;
   1980.B28
-news items about, 1972.B5; 1974.
   B11; 1975.B65; 1976.B5; 1977.
   B6
Stoppard, Tom. See also titles
   of individual works (listed
   in Stoppard, Tom, works by)
-analyses and criticisms of
   corpus, 1968.B115; 1969.B54;
   1970.B61; 1971.B17, 19-20;
   1972.B41, 92, 110; 1973.B21-

255

Index

22, 45; 1974.B46, 80, 135; 1975.B53, 62, 64, 82, 97, 103, 117-118, 123; 1976.A1-4, B19, 49, 53, 89, 97; 1977.A1, B73-74, 107, 125; 1978.B23, 29, 40, 47, 67, 79, 81; 1979.A1-3, B10, 26, 51-52, 87-89, 106, 112, 120; 1980.A1-2, B7, 24, 27, 34; Incomplete.B22, 30
-awards won by. See Awards and honors
-biographical data about, 1964. B1-2, 4; 1967.B4-6, 16, 20, 50, 61, 65, 78, 102-104; 1968.B109; 1969.B22, 38, 48, 54; 1970.A1; 1972.B4, 92; 1973.B10, 21; 1974.B18, 90, 135; 1975.B2, 43, 103, 126; 1976.B3, 7, 21, 91; 1977.A1, B125; 1979.B87-88, 106, 112; Incomplete.A3. See also Awards and honors; Early life and career
-financial data about, 1968. B117-118; 1972.B16, 50; 1979.B8, 90; Incomplete.B1, 3, 36. See also titles of individual works (listed in Stoppard, Tom, works by)
-honors given to. See Awards and honors
-influences upon. See Influences upon Stoppard
-interviews with. See Interviews
-news items about, 1972.B5, 7, 12-13; 1974.B51, 164; 1977. B38; 1978.B6, 31; 1979.B2, 8, 39-40, 90; 1980.B29-30. See also Stoppard, Tom, financial data about; titles of individual works (listed in Stoppard, Tom, works by)
-opinions about. See Stoppard, Tom, analyses and criticisms of corpus; titles of individual works (listed in Stoppard, works by)
-opinions expressed by. See Interviews; specific topics; titles of individual works

(listed in Stoppard, Tom, works by)
-photographs of, 1968.B2; 1972. B12; 1973.B7; 1977.B8, 13; 1978.B9
-prizes won by. See Awards and honors
-speeches. See Speech by Stoppard
-works by. See titles of individual works: Acting in untitled documentary; <u>After Magritte</u>; "Albert's Bridge"; "Another Moon Called Earth"; "Artist Descending a Staircase"; <u>Born Yesterday</u>; "Boundary, The"; <u>Despair</u>; <u>Dirty Linen and New-Found-Land</u>; "Dissolution of Dominic Boot, The"; <u>Dogg's Hamlet, Cahoot's Macbeth</u>; <u>Dogg's Our Pet</u>; <u>Dogg's Troupe Hamlet</u>; <u>Engagement, The</u>; <u>Enter a Free Man</u>; <u>Every Good Boy Deserves Favour</u>; <u>Gamblers, The</u>; <u>Guildenstern and Rosencrantz</u>; <u>House of Bernarda Alba, The</u>; <u>Human Factor, The</u>; "If You're Glad I'll Be Frank"; "In Parenthesis: 'Is "Is" Is?'"; <u>Jumpers</u>; "Life, Times: Fragments"; <u>Lord Malquist & Mr Moon</u>; "'M' Is for 'Moon,' among Other Things"; "Neutral Ground"; <u>Night and Day</u>; "One Pair of Eyes: Tom Stoppard Doesn't Know"; "Paragraph for Mr Blake, A"; "Professional Foul"; <u>Real Inspector Hound, The</u>; "Reunion"; <u>Romantic Englishwoman, The</u>; <u>Rosencrantz & Guildenstern Are Dead</u>; "Separate Peace, A"; "Story, The"; <u>Tango</u>; "Teeth"; "This Way out with Samuel Boot"; "Three Men in a Boat"; <u>Travesties</u>; <u>Undiscovered Country</u>; "Walk on the Water, A"; "Where Are They Now?"
"Story, The" (short story). See also Early life and career; "Paragraph for Mr Blake, A"; short stories

256

Index

-analyses and criticisms of, 1976.A3-4; 1977.A1; 1979.A1
-comments by Stoppard about, 1967.B5; 1968.B51; 1971.B12
Stothard, Peter, 1977.B115; 1978.B76
Strafford, Peter, 1976.B100
Structure. See also Dialectic; Form; Juxtaposition; Music-hall; Organization.
-comments by others about, 1968.B82; 1969.B1; 1970.B11, 39, 61; 1971.B1, 20; 1972.B48, 66, 118, 133, 135; 1973.B62; 1974.B31-32, 47, 78, 80, 111, 141, 162, 166, 168, 175; 1975.B32, 70-71, 94, 97, 105, 111; 1976.B89; 1977.B32, 68; 1978.A1, B20, 23, 37, 58, 62; 1979.B25, 62, 77, 99, 119-120; 1980.B32
-comments by Stoppard about, 1970.B62; 1972.B96; 1973.B85; 1974.B90; 1976.B65-66; 1977.B23, 121
Studia Anglica Posnaniensia, 1976.B112
Studies in the Literary Imagination, 1976.B56
Stutzin, Leo, 1969.B51; 1970.B57-58; 1972.B123
Style. See also Convention; Form; Technique
-comments by others about, 1969.B8a; 1976.A2-3; 1977.B96; 1979.B57, 61, 83; 1980.B7
-comments by Stoppard about, 1976.B50; 1977.B25; 1979.B22
Success. See also Money
-comments by others about, 1968.B89
-comments by Stoppard about, 1967.B61, 88; 1969.B38; 1972.B99
Süddeutsche Zeitung (Munich), Incomplete.B7, 53
Sühnel, Rudolf, 1971.B5
Suleiman, Susan R., 1980.B31
Sullivan, Dan, 1967.B122; 1970.B59; 1974.B150-151; 1975.B110; 1977.B116
Sun (Brandon, Canada), 1973.B70
Sun (London), 1968.B85
Sun (Melbourne, Australia), 1973.B63
Sun (Suffolk, N.J.), 1967.B55
Sunday Examiner (San Francisco), 1974.B20. See also Examiner (San Francisco); Sunday Examiner and Chronicle (San Francisco)
Sunday Examiner and Chronicle (San Francisco), 1977.B45. See also Chronicle (San Francisco); Examiner (San Francisco); Sunday Examiner (San Francisco)
Sunday Mirror (London), 1966.B28. See also Daily Mirror (London)
Sunday News (Newark, N.J.), 1967.B83. See also Evening News (Newark, N.J.)
Sunday News (New York), 1967.B42, 129; 1972.B134; 1974.B165, 172, 174-175; 1975.B120; 1977.B126. See also Daily News (New York)
Sunday Sun-Times (Chicago), 1975.B44. See also Sun Times (Chicago)
Sunday Telegraph (London), 1966.B32; 1967.B36, 140; 1968.B79, 91, 97; 1970.B29; 1971.B18; 1972.B88, 114, 144; 1973.B8, 55-56, 72; 1974.B110; 1976.B90; 1979.B63-64, 90-91. See also Daily Telegraph (London)
Sunday Times (London), 1966.B20-21, 29; 1967.B48, 72, 112; 1968.B58, 71; 1969.B31; 1970.B42, 44, 47; 1971.B15; 1972.B1, 20, 66-67, 112; 1973.B46-47, 64; 1974.B14, 86; 1975.B5, 8, 57, 89; 1976.B4, 68, 81; 1977.B8, 42, 57, 62-64, 83, 112; 1978.B5, 12, 16, 18-19, 33, 49, 53-54, 64, 80; 1980.B5-6, 11, 28-20. See also Sunday Times Magazine (London); Times (London)
Sunday Times Magazine (London),

Index

1974.B1; 1978.B81; 1980.B17.
  See also <u>Sunday Times</u> (London)
<u>Sun Press</u> (Cleveland), 1974.B146
<u>Sun Reporter</u> (Miami Beach, Fla.), 1969.B42
<u>Sun-Times</u> (Chicago), 1967.B60; 1969.B53; Incomplete.B6. See also <u>Sunday Sun-Times</u> (Chicago)
Surreal (-ism, -istic), 1966.B8; 1970.B66; 1971.B8; 1975.B51; 1979.B52; 1980.B37. See also Juxtaposition; Magritte, René
<u>Survey of Contemporary Literature</u>, 1971.B1
Sussman, Sharron, 1972.B124; 1974.B152
Swaebly, Frances, 1969.B52
Swan, Bradford F., 1974.B153
Swift, Janothan, 1970.B37
<u>Sycamore</u>, Incomplete.B25
Symbol (-ic, -ism). See also Allegory; Metaphor
-comments by others about, 1966.B24, 29
-comments by Stoppard about, 1976.B50
Sympathy. See Humane
Syntex Pharmaceuticals, 1976.B5; 1977.B6. See also Stoppard, Miriam
Syse, Glenna, 1969.B53
Szyba, Randy, 1978.B77

<u>Tablet</u>, 1975.B25; 1978.B21; 1980.B8
<u>Tagblatt</u> (Wiesbaden, W. Germany), Incomplete.B31
Takiff, Jonathan, 1976.B101; 1977.B117
Talcove, Rick, 1977.B118
Tallmer, Jerry, 1967.B123; 1972.B125; 1975.B111
<u>Tango</u> (stage play adapted by Stoppard)
-photograph of, 1966.B2
-productions, reviews of
--London, BBC Radio, 1968.B30, 110

--London, Royal Shakespeare Company, 1966.B3-5, 10-11, 16, 20, 24-27, 29, 34, 39
-text, review of, 1968.B9
<u>Tatler</u>, 1972.B95
Taylor, Clarke, 1975.B112
Taylor, John Russell, 1967.B124; 1969.B54; 1970.B60-62; 1971.B20; 1978.B78; 1979.B103-104
Taylor, John V., 1972.B126
Taylor, Larry, 1975.B113; 1977.B119; Incomplete.B50
Taylor, Paul, Incomplete.B51
Taylor, Robert, 1970.B63; 1972.B127; 1974.B154-155; 1975.B114; 1977.B120-121; Incomplete.B52
<u>Teacher</u>, 1971.B2
Teachers, items for. See Pedagogical items
<u>Teaching of English</u>, 1971.B8a
Technique (-s), 1976.B49, 97; 1978.B42; 1980.B26. See also Craftsmanship; Debate; Eclectic; Experiment; Irony; Juxtaposition; Metaphor; Play-within-the-play; Puns
"Teeth" (television play)
-analyses and criticisms of, 1971.B20; 1972.B94; 1974.B122, 135; 1976.A3; 1977.A1
-comments by Stoppard about, 1967.B1
-production, reviews of
--London, BBC Television, 1967.B46, 108
Television. See also Media, writing for other
-comments by Stoppard about writing for, 1975.B43; 1979.B53
-transcript of interview on, 1976.B77
Telpner, Gene, 1973.B78
Tennyson, Hallam, 1976.B83
Terry, Sara, 1977.B122
Text. See Script
Thaw, John (actor)
-interview with, 1978.B57
-photograph of, 1978.B9
<u>Theater</u>, 1979.B116

258

Index

Theater Heute, 1967.B111
Theatre and Anti-Theatre: New Movements since Beckett, 1979.B52
Theatre and society
-American, 1975.B18; 1976.B107; 1977.B26, 110; 1980.B15
-Austrian, comments by Stoppard about, 1977.B46
-British, 1966.B38; 1967.B38, 72, 83, 111, 130; 1968.B84; 1969.B27; 1970.B37, 68; 1972.B26, 39, 45; 1973.B26-27, 30, 60, 62; 1975.B18; 1976.B107; 1977.B26; 1978.B81, 87; 1980.B13, 15
-Continental, 1967.B38; 1968.B84; 1970.B68
-French, 1967.B19, 23, 83; 1970.B15, 37
-German
--comments by others about, 1964.B3-4; 1973.B25-26; 1975.B126
--comments by Stoppard about, 1968.B13; 1974.B1, 87
-medieval, 1977.B51
-modern, 1968.B48; 1970.B68; 1971.B5; 1972.B142; 1973.B43; 1974.B50; 1975.B64; 1977.B135; 1978.B70; 1980.B12; Incomplete.B31
-South African, 1969.B3; 1976.B14
Theatrefacts, 1974.B135
Theatre Journal, 1979.B33, 36, 79; 1980.B4, 14, 34. See also Educational Theatre Journal
Theatre News, 1979.B34; Incomplete.B39-41. See also Educational Theatre News
Theatre of the Absurd. See Absurd
Theatre Quarterly, 1974.B90; 1975.B39
Theatrical (-ity)
-comments by others about, 1967.B45, 62, 68, 92; 1968.B41; 1969.B1; 1970.B51; 1971.B1; 1972.B3; 1975.B103; 1976.B43, 53, 90, 96; 1977.B30; 1978.B28; 1979.A1, B36, 61

-comments by Stoppard about, 1973.B85; 1974.B80; 1977.A1. See also Visual
Them(-atic, -es). See also Meaning; specific themes
-comments by others about, 1968.B60, 87; 1973.B21-22, 62, 65; 1974.B21, 41, 46, 57, 61, 69, 80, 96, 111, 137, 143, 182; 1975.B10, 44, 59, 64, 71, 97, 116, 126; 1976.A2-3, B19, 37, 49, 60, 87, 89, 92; 1977.A1, B26, 32, 37, 74, 125, 135; 1978.A1, B29, 42, 54, 61, 74, 79; 1979.B10, 15, 22, 29, 32, 36, 52, 76, 79, 84, 106, 120; 1980.B4, 12
-comments by Stoppard about, 1967.B91; 1970.B61; 1973.B85; 1974.B22-23, 50, 77, 80, 90, 144; 1975.B43; 1976.B95; 1977.A1, B25
Theoria, 1969.B39; 1970.B24
Theses about Stoppard. See also Dissertations
-Masters, 1974.A1
-undergraduate, 1976.A1; Incomplete.A1
Thirkell, Arthur, 1967.B125; 1968.B102; 1972.B128; 1974.B156
"This Way out with Samuel Boot" (unproduced television play), 1977.B125; 1979.B106
This Week in London, 1974.B48
Thomas, Art, 1974.B157
Thompson, Howard, 1974.B158
Thomsen, Christian W., 1978.B78a
Thorpe, Michael, 1968.B104
Thought, 1966.B30; 1967.B94; 1969.B15, 33; 1970.B7, 37; 1973.B20; 1974.B10, 167, 171-172; 1975.B81, 117, 125; 1980.B26; Incomplete.B51. See also Ideas
"Three Men in a Boat" (television play adapted by Stoppard)
-news items about, 1975.B8
-photograph of, 1975.B8
-production, review of
--London, BBC Television, 1976.B82

259

Index

Thronson, Ron, 1975.B115
Thurber, James, 1973.B65
Tieck, Ludwig, 1973.B62
Tierney, Margaret, 1972.B129
Time, 1967.B78; 1972.B76; 1974. B61, 95; 1975.B67; 1977.B70; 1978.B26, 50, 73; 1979.B59-60; 1980.B35
Time Out, 1972.B110
Times (Hartford, Conn.), 1967. B51
Times (London), 1964.B3; 1966.B1-3, 6, 9; 1967.B3, 9-11, 13, 18-19, 23, 25, 32, 46, 131-132; 1968.B2-3, 7-8, 10, 12, 15-16, 18-19, 22, 25-26, 34, 110-113, 115; 1969.B4; 1970. B3, 65-67; 1972.B5, 7-9, 12-13, 17, 36, 61, 99, 132-133, 135-136; 1973.B4, 53-54, 71, 84; 1974.B7, 26, 79, 164, 168-169; 1975.B11, 17-18, 60, 72, 80; 1976.B5, 26, 82, 100, 105-106; 1977.B6, 9, 11-13, 29-32, 38, 43, 93, 129; 1978.B2-3, 6, 8-9, 11, 24-25, 48, 57, 68, 78, 82; 1979.B9, 16; 1980.B2, 33. See also Sunday Times (London)
Times (Los Angeles), 1970.B59; 1972.B38; 1974.B49, 51, 150-151; 1975.B110; 1977.B41, 116
Times (Louisville, Ky.), 1974. B138
Times (Malibu, Calif.), 1977.B22
Times (Palo Alto, Calif.), 1969. B45; 1970.B69; 1974.B114; 1977.B90-91
Times (San Mateo, Calif.), 1969. B9; 1970.B14; 1972.B31; 1974.B36; 1977.B23-24
Times (Seattle, Wash.), 1970.B30
Times (Trenton, N.J.), 1976.B20
Times Education Supplement (London), 1972.B104; 1973.B45, 65; 1974.B128
Times-Herald (Vallejo, Calif.), 1969.B40
Times Higher Education Supplement (London), 1974.B45; 1976.B8; 1977.B10
Times Literary Supplement (London), 1966.B8; 1968.B9; 1969. B5; 1970.B2; 1972.B18; 1974. B56; 1980.B38
Times-Picayune (New Orleans, La.), 1972.B106; 1974.B64-65; Incomplete.B21
Times-Star (Alameda, Calif.), 1969.B14
Tinker, Jack, 1973.B79; 1974. B159; 1975.B116
Tischler, Gary, 1974.B160
Toebosch, Guillaume, 1978.B79
Tom Stoppard (Contemporary Playwrights Series), 1977.A1
Tom Stoppard (Writers and Their Work Series), 1976.A2
"Tom Stoppard Doesn't Know." See "One Pair of Eyes: Tom Stoppard Doesn't Know"
Tone, 1968.B87, 95; 1972.B25, 35, 39; 1976.B107; 1978.B60; 1979.B34, 66, 76-77, 94; 1980.B21. See also Anguish; Boredom; Fantasy; Feeling; Fun; Humane; Mood; Pathos; Pessimism; Poetic; Romantic
Torpor, Tom, 1974.B161
Tradition (-al). See Convention
Tragedy, 1967.B99; 1969.B37; 1972.B126, 141; 1973.B20; 1975.B117; 1978.B70; 1979. B115. See also Serious
Transatlantic Review, 1968.B51
Transcript (Concord, Calif.), 1969.B36
Travel, 1967.B49
Travesties (stage play)
-analyses and criticisms of, 1974.B80, 107, 182; 1975.B35, 53, 64, 103, 123; 1976.A1-4, B19, 53-54, 62, 89; 1977.A1, B73-74, 107, 125; 1978.A1, B20, 29, 41-42, 49a, 58, 67; 1979.A1-3, B26, 52, 61, 84, 88, 106, 112, 114, 120; 1980. A1-2, B13, 27, 34; Incomplete. B25, 42
-comments by others about,

Index

1974.B73, 81; 1975.B3, 87, 111; 1977.B75; 1978.B24
-comments by Stoppard about, 1972.B57, 99, 125; 1973.B37, 85; 1974.B1, 15, 80, 90, 126, 144, 161; 1975.B55, 124; 1977.A1, B36, 46, 73, 121, 132; 1978.B41; Incomplete.B46
-news items about, 1974.B7, 9, 81; 1975.B4, 7, 120-121; 1976.B2, 21, 100; 1977.B31
-photograph of, 1974.B14
-productions, reviews of
--Bristol Old Vic, 1976.B10, 22, 27, 46, 84
--Dublin, Abbey Theatre, 1977.B31, 57
--London, Royal Shakespeare Company, 1974.B17, 24, 28, 34-35, 44-45, 47-49, 56-57, 62, 82-83, 86, 93, 100-101, 104, 110, 112, 118, 120, 124, 128-129, 140, 143, 147, 156, 159, 162-163, 166, 168, 175, 180, 182; 1975.B3, 97; 1976.B87
--London, Royal Shakespeare Company revival, 1975.B6, 13-14, 22, 27, 29, 56-57, 72, 76, 84, 90, 92, 104, 116, 123; Incomplete.B54
--Los Angeles, Center Theatre Group, 1977.B4, 14, 16, 21-22, 27-28, 44-45, 48, 52, 58, 65, 69, 72, 84, 89, 92, 95, 100-101, 103, 110, 116, 118-119, 122, 124, 128, 136; Incomplete.B16, 18, 23, 27, 29, 32-33, 37, 49, 51
--Minneapolis, Theatre in the Round, 1978.B27, 43, 55
--Munich, Residenztheater, Incomplete.B15, 44, 53
--New York, Broadway, 1975.B16-19, 30, 41, 46, 48-49, 52, 61, 67-68, 70, 73, 75, 81, 88, 91, 94, 102, 107, 109, 119, 122, 125; 1976.B17, 41, 71, 86, 97, 108-109; 1978.B20

--Paris, Centre Dramatique de Lausanne, 1978.B58
--Philadelphia Drama Guild, 1977.B35, 49, 77, 108, 117, 137; Incomplete.B20
--San Francisco, ACT, 1977.B24, 47, 54, 91, 120, 133
-text, reviews of, 1975.B9, 24; 1977.B40
Treglown, Jeremy, 1980.B37
Trewin, J. C., 1966.B34-36; 1967.B126-127; 1968.B105-108; 1972.B130-131; 1973.B80-82; 1974.B162-163; 1979.B105
<u>Tribune</u> (Chicago), 1968.B40; 1969.B38-39; 1975.B36
<u>Tribune</u> (Minneapolis), 1976.B98; 1978.B55
<u>Tribune</u> (Oakland, Calif.), 1969.B44; 1970.B63; 1972.B127; 1974.B154-155; 1975.B114; 1977.B120-121
<u>Tribune</u> (Redwood City, Calif.), 1972.B73
<u>Tribune</u> (Torrance, Calif.), Incomplete.B18
<u>Tribune</u> (Winnipeg, Canada), 1967.B102; 1973.B78
Trilling, Ossia, 1968.B109
Trussler, Simon, 1974.B90
Tucker, Martin, 1975.B117
Tugend, Tom, 1977.B124
Turan, Kenny, 1969.B55
<u>TV Times</u>, 1965.B1-2; 1968.B29
<u>Twin Cities Reader</u> (Minneapolis), 1978.B43
Tydeman, John (director)
-interview with, 1974.B122; 1976.A3
Tynan, Kenneth
-as author of items, 1977.B125; 1978.B80; 1979.B106
-comments by others about, 1978.B33
Tzara, Tristan
-comments by others about, 1974.B73, 104; 1975.B88; 1976.B62, 87; 1979.B114
-comments by Stoppard about, 1975.B124

Index

Ueno, Yoshiko, 1975.B118
Uncertainty, 1969.B37; 1972.B21; 1974.B103, 111; 1975.B98; 1977.B109; 1978.B89; 1980.B24, 26, 31, 34. See also Ambiguity; Knowledge
Unconscious (-ness)
-comments by others about, 1976.A1; 1977.B135
-comments by Stoppard about, 1967.B67; 1974.B80; 1977.A1
Undiscovered Country (stage play adapted by Stoppard)
-comments by Stoppard about, 1979.B47, 53
-production, reviews of
--London, National Theatre, 1979.B11, 55, 63, 80, 101, 103-104; 1980.B19
Unidentified newspaper (German), Incomplete.B8
Union (Sacramento, Calif.), 1969.B2; 1970.B48; 1972.B119
Unions, 1978.B49. See also Actors Equity
United Press International. See UPI Wireservice
University of Windsor Review, 1975.B40
Unoriginal (-ity), 1968.B92; 1972.B53, 89, 92; 1973.B43; 1974.B38, 125; 1976.B1, 41, 97; 1979.B43; 1980.B7, 27. See also Imitation; Originality
Unreal. See Illusion; Reality
UPI Wireservice, 1967.B57
USA Today, 1980.B20
Uses of English, 1975.B103
U.S.S.R., 1979.B2, 34, 39-40. See also Dissidents; Human rights

Valley News (Van Nuys, Calif.), 1977.B118
Variety (Los Angeles), 1975.B38; 1977.B44
Variety (New York), 1966.B4; 1967.B7, 15, 21, 71, 96; 1968.B14, 21, 27, 64, 93-94; 1969.B3, 43; 1970.B4, 40; 1972.B60, 116; 1974.B8-9, 11, 16, 85, 127, 129; 1975.B4, 7, 86; 1976.B2, 6, 9, 11-12, 14, 80; 1977.B1-2, 61
Vaudeville, 1974.B35, 56, 183. See also Music-hall; Revue sketch
Vaughan, Paul, 1976.B102
Vaughan, Peter, 1976.B103
Ventura County Star-Free Press (Ventura, Calif.), 1977.B92
Villager (New York), 1972.B93
Village Voice (New York), 1967.B94, 119; 1970.B68; 1972.B35, 113; 1974.B38, 119; 1975.B23, 41, 88, 100, 123-124; 1977.B98
Vinson, James, 1973.B21
Viorst, Milton, 1976.B104
Visual. See also Theatrical
-comments by others about, 1967.B81; 1971.B22; 1973.B21, 43, 45; 1976.A2, B85; 1978.B29; 1979.B76, 109
-comments by Stoppard about, 1972.B96, 109, 125; 1975.B43
Vogue, 1967.B64, 138; 1974.B109
von Becker, Peter, Incomplete.B53

W., R., 1973.B83
WABC-TV, 1974.B137; 1977.B79; 1979.B95-97
Wade, David, 1966.B37; 1967.B128; 1968.B110-111; 1970.B64-65; 1972.B132-133; 1974.B164
Wahls, Robert, 1967.B129; 1972.B134; 1974.B165; 1977.B126
Waiting for Godot, 1967.B59; 1968.B46; 1969.B13, 37; 1976.B91; 1977.B29; 1978.B70; 1979.B36, 93. See also Beckett, Samuel
Walker, John, 1974.B166; 1978.B81; Incomplete.B54
Walker, N., 1977.B127
"Walk on the Water, A" (stage play adapted for and produced on radio and television). See also Enter a Free Man

262

Index

-analysis and criticism of, 1976.A3
-comments by others about, 1968.B55; 1972.B61; 1973.B44
-comments by Stoppard about, 1974.B87
-production, review of
--London, BBC Radio, 1965.B3
Wallach, Allan, 1974.B10, 167
Wall Street Journal (New York), 1967.B45; 1972.B109; 1974.B186; 1975.B125; 1976.B111; 1977.B136; 1978.B88; 1979.B117-119
Walsh, Chuck, 1977.B128
Wardle, Irving, 1966.B38; 1967.B130-132; 1968.B112-115; 1970.B66-67; 1971.B21; 1972.B135-136; 1973.B84; 1974.B168-169; 1976.B105-106; 1977.B129; 1978.B82
Washburn, Martin, 1970.B68
Wasserman, Debbi, 1974.B170; 1975.B97; 1978.B83; 1979.B107
Watt, Douglas, 1967.B133; 1972.B89, 137; 1974.B111, 171-176; 1975.B81, 119-120; 1976.B107; 1977.B87, 130; 1979.B75-77, 108-110
Watters, Tamie, 1978.B84; 1979.B111
Watts, Harold H., 1979.B112
Watts, Janet, 1973.B85
Watts, Richard, 1967.B92, 134-135; 1968.B116; 1972.B89, 138-140; 1974.B111, 177-181; 1975.B121-122; 1976.B108
Waugh, Evelyn
-comments by Stoppard about, 1972.B6
WCAU-Radio, 1976.B67
WCBS-TV, 1972.B59; 1974.B78; 1979.B31
Weales, Gerald, 1967.B136; 1976.B109; 1977.B131; 1978.B20
Weaver, Gay, 1970.B69
Webster, Daniel, 1978.B85
Weiand, Hermann J., 1976.B91
Weightman, John, 1966.B39; 1967.B137; 1972.B141; 1974.B182; 1975.B117; 1976.B87
Weiler, A. H., 1968.B117-118
Weiner, Bernard, 1977.B132-133
Wells, Jeffrey, 1979.B113
Werner, Craig, 1979.B114
Wesker, Arnold, 1980.B17a
West, Anthony, 1967.B138
West, Richard, 1980.B38
Westerbeck, Colin L., 1976.B110; 1978.B86
Western Daily Press (Bristol), 1972.B86; 1974.B131; 1976.B84
Westsider (New York), 1975.B77
Westways, 1977.B58
Wetzsteon, Ross, 1975.B123-124; 1977.B134
What's On, 1972.B64
What's On in London, 1974.B83
"Where Are They Now?" (radio play)
-analyses and criticisms of, 1971.B20; 1974.B135; 1975.B64, 103; 1976.A1, 3-4; 1977.A1; 1979.A1; 1980.A2
-production, reviews of
--London, BBC Radio, 1970.B47, 65
-text, reviews of, 1973.B29, 66; 1975.B96
Where to Go, 1974.B82; 1975.B6
Whitaker, Thomas R., 1972.B142; 1977.B135
Whitman, Dennis, 1967.B139
Who's Who in the Theatre, 1972.B4
Who's Who in Twentieth Century Literature, 1976.B96
Wilcher, Robert, 1979.B115
Wilde, Oscar, 1968.B82; 1974.B56, 110; 1976.A2; 1978.B42
Williams, Bob, 1970.B70
Williams, David, 1978.B87
Williams, David H., 1971.B22
Williams, Gary Jay, 1974.B183; 1979.B116
Williams, James E., 1970.B71; 1972.B143
Williamson, Nicol (actor)
-interview with, 1967.B32
Wilson, Cecil, 1970.B72
Wilson, Earl, 1974.B184-185

Index

Wilson, Edwin, 1974.B111, 186; 1975.B81, 125; 1976.B111; 1977.B87, 136; 1978.B88; 1979.B75-77, 117-119
Wine, Bill, 1977.B137
Winkler, Irwin, 1968.B117-118
Wiseman, Thomas, 1975.B69. See also Romantic Englishwoman, The
Wiszniowska, Marta, 1976.B112
Wit (-ty), 1966.B31; 1967.B30, 77, 81, 100, 119; 1968.B5, 77, 80; 1969.B1; 1970.B39; 1971.B1; 1972.B3, 26, 72, 93, 116; 1973.B21, 25-26, 43, 68; 1974.B26, 45, 93, 141, 176; 1975.B97; 1976.A2, B45, 99, 103; 1977.B9, 26, 44, 67, 91, 98; 1978.B20, 58, 84; 1979.B20, 43, 50, 57, 75, 77, 113, 117, 119; Incomplete.B44. See also Cleverness
Wittgenstein, Ludwig, 1977.B94
Wolfe, Michael, 1970.B73
Wolff, Geoffrey, 1968.B119
Women, 1975.B10; 1976.B37
Women's Wear Daily, 1967.B62; 1972.B53, 96; 1974.B71; 1975.B69, 73; 1977.B78; 1979.B65-66, 94
Wood, Charles, 1979.B8
Wood, John (actor)
-as subject of comments by Stoppard, 1974.B63, 105; 1975.B55
-interviews with, 1967.B22, 83, 114, 129; 1975.B20, 55, 87, 111; 1977.B60, 75
-photograph of, 1968.B66
Wood, Peter (director)
-as subject of comments by Stoppard, 1980.B17
-interviews with, 1973.B83; 1974.B79, 122; 1980.B17
Woodforde, John, 1967.B140; 1972.B144
Wootten, Dick, 1974.B187; Incomplete.B55
Work habits. See also Playwriting; Procrastination

-comments by Miriam Stoppard about, 1980.B28
-comments by Tom Stoppard about, 1967.B1, 56; 1973.B85; 1975.B82; 1979.B22; Incomplete.B46
World in Collapse: The Vision of Absurd Drama, 1971.B16
World Journal Tribune (New York), 1967.B97
World Literature Today, 1978.B66
WPIX-TV, 1972.B32
Wright, Allen, 1966.B40

Yale Review, 1968.B50
Yale Theater. See Theater
Yearbook of English Studies, 1979.B61, 120
Yeomans, Jeannine, 1969.B56
Young, B. A., 1966.B41; 1967.B141; 1968.B120-121; 1972.B145; 1973.B86; 1977.B138

Zeh, Dieter, 1975.B126
Zeifman, Hersh, 1979.B120
Zeitschrift für Anglistik und Amerikanistik, 1975.B51
Zien, Laurie, Incomplete.B56
Zipes, Jack D., 1972.B3
Zivanovic, Judith, 1978.B89
Zolotow, Sam, 1968.B122
Zweigler, Mark, 1975.B127